AIA

S T U D Y   T E X T

PAPER 6
INFORMATION PROCESSING

> **In this 2020 edition**
> - A **user-friendly format** for easy navigation
> - **Exam-centred topic coverage**, directly linked to AIA's syllabus
> - **Exam focus points** showing you what the examiner will want you to do
> - Regular **fast forward** summaries emphasising the key points in each chapter
> - **Questions** and **quick quizzes** to test your understanding
> - **Exam question bank** containing exam standard questions with answers
> - **2 Mock exams** containing the November 2017 and May 2018 papers
> - **A full index**

FOR EXAMS IN 2020

First edition April 2011
Ninth edition January 2020

ISBN 9781 5097 8721 0
(previous ISBN 9781 5097 2504 5)

eISBN 9781 5097 2893 0
(previous eISBN 9781 5097 2571 7)

British Library Cataloguing-in-Publication Data
A catalogue record for this book
is available from the British Library

Published by

BPP Learning Media Ltd
BPP House, Aldine Place
London W12 8AA

www.bpp.com/learningmedia

Printed in the United Kingdom

Your learning materials, published by BPP Learning Media Ltd, are printed on paper obtained from traceable sustainable sources.

All rights reserved. No part of this publication may be reproduced, stored in a retrieval system or transmitted in any form or by any means, electronic, mechanical, photocopying, recording or otherwise, without the prior written permission of BPP Learning Media.

The contents of this book are intended as a guide and not professional advice. Although every effort has been made to ensure that the contents of this book are correct at the time of going to press, BPP Learning Media makes no warranty that the information in this book is accurate or complete and accept no liability for any loss or damage suffered by any person acting or refraining from acting as a result of the material in this book.

We are grateful to the Association of International Accountants for permission to reproduce past examination questions. The suggested solutions in the exam answer bank have been prepared by BPP Learning Media Ltd.

©
BPP Learning Media Ltd
2020

A note about copyright

Dear Customer

What does the little © mean and why does it matter?

Your market-leading BPP books, course materials and e-learning materials do not write and update themselves. People write them: on their own behalf or as employees of an organisation that invests in this activity. Copyright law protects their livelihoods. It does so by creating rights over the use of the content.

Breach of copyright is a form of theft – as well as being a criminal offence in some jurisdictions, it is potentially a serious breach of professional ethics.

With current technology, things might seem a bit hazy but, basically, without the express permission of BPP Learning Media:

- Photocopying our materials is a breach of copyright

- Scanning, ripcasting or conversion of our digital materials into different file formats, uploading them to facebook or emailing them to your friends is a breach of copyright

You can, of course, sell your books, in the form in which you have bought them – once you have finished with them. (Is this fair to your fellow students? We update for a reason.) But the e-products are sold on a single user license basis: we do not supply 'unlock' codes to people who have bought them second hand.

And what about outside the UK? BPP Learning Media strives to make our materials available at prices students can afford by local printing arrangements, pricing policies and partnerships which are clearly listed on our website. A tiny minority ignore this and indulge in criminal activity by illegally photocopying our material or supporting organisations that do. If they act illegally and unethically in one area, can you really trust them?

Contents

Page

Introduction

The introduction pages contain lots of valuable advice and information. They include tips on studying for and passing the exam, also the content of the syllabus and what has been examined.

How the BPP Learning Media Study Text can help you pass – Help yourself study for your AIA exams – Syllabus – Command words and learning outcomes – The exam paper

PART A - Data Collection and Analysis

1	Basic mathematical techniques	3
2	Statistical sources	49
3	Presentation of data	67
4a	Summary statistics - averages	97
4b	Summary statistics - dispersion	111
5	Applying probability to decision making	127
6	Measuring the relationship between two variables	171
7	Time series analysis	187
8	Index numbers	207

PART B - Business Information Technology

9	Overview of information systems	229
10	Computer hardware and software	247
11	Managing data and information	267
12	Telecommunications and networks	287
13	Electronic commerce	299

Answers to end of chapter questions	307
Exam question bank	323
Exam answer bank	335
Mock exam 1	351
Mock exam 2	369
Formulae	387
Index	393

How the BPP Learning Media Study Text can help you pass

> It provides you with the knowledge and understanding, skills and application techniques that you need to be successful in your exams

This Study Text has been targeted at the **Information Processing** syllabus.

- It is **comprehensive**. It covers the syllabus content. No more, no less.
- It is written at the **right level**. Each chapter is written with AIA's syllabus in mind.
- It is aimed at the **exam**. We have taken account of recent exams, guidance the examiner has given and the assessment methodology.

> It allows you to study in the way that best suits your learning style and the time you have available, by following your personal Study Plan (see page vii)

You may be studying at home on your own or you may be attending a course. You may like to read every word, or you may prefer to do a fast read through and learn through doing practise questions the rest of the time. However you study, you will find the BPP Learning Media Study Text meets your needs in designing and following your personal Study Plan.

Help yourself study for your AIA exams

Exams for professional bodies such as AIA are very different from those you have taken at college or university. You will be under **greater time pressure before** the exam – as you may be combining your study with work. Here are some hints and tips.

The right approach

1 **Develop the right attitude**

Believe in yourself	Yes, there is a lot to learn. But thousands have succeeded before and you can too.
Remember why you're doing it	You are studying for a good reason: to advance your career.

2 **Focus on the exam**

Read through the Syllabus	This tells you what you are expected to know and is supplemented by **Exam focus points** in the text.
Study the Exam paper section	Past papers are likely to be good guides to what you should expect in the exam.

3 **The right method**

See the whole picture	Keeping in mind how all the detail you need to know fits into the whole picture will help you understand it better. • The **Introduction** of each chapter puts the material in context. • The **Syllabus content** and **Exam focus points** show you what you need to **grasp**.
Use your own words	To absorb the information (and to practise your written communication skills), you need to **put it into your own words**. • **Take notes**. • Answer the **questions** in each chapter. • Draw **mindmaps**. • Try **'teaching' a subject** to a colleague or friend.
Give yourself cues to jog your memory	The Study Text uses **bold** to **highlight key points**. • Try **colour coding** with a highlighter pen. • Write **key points** on cards.

4 **The right recap**

Review, review, review	Regularly reviewing a topic in summary form can **fix it in your memory**. The Study Text helps you review in many ways. • **Chapter roundups** summarise the 'Fast forward' key points in each chapter. Use them to recap each study session. • The **Quick quiz** actively tests your grasp of the essentials. • Go through the **Examples** in each chapter a second or third time.

Developing your personal Study Plan

BPP recommends that you follow a study plan. Planning and sticking to the plan are key elements of learning successfully.

There are five steps you should work through.

Step 1 **How do you learn?**

What types of intelligence do you display when learning? You might be advised to brush up on certain study skills before launching into this Study Text, but refer to the 'tackling your studies' section below which will help.

Step 2 **What do you prefer to do first?**

If you prefer to get to grips with a theory before seeing how it is applied, we suggest you concentrate first on the explanations we give in each chapter before looking at the examples and case studies. If you prefer to see first how things work in practice, read through the detail in each chapter, and concentrate on the examples and case studies, before supplementing your understanding by reading the detail.

Step 3 **How much time do you have?**

Work out the time you have available per week, given the following:

- The standard you have set yourself
- The other exam(s) you are sitting
- Practical matters such as work, travel, exercise, sleep and social life

Note your time available in box A.   A [   ] Hours

Step 4 **Allocate your time**

- Take the time you have available per week for this Study Text shown in box A, multiply it by the number of weeks available and insert the result in box B.   B [   ]

- Divide the figure in box B by the number of chapters in this text and insert the result in box C.   C [   ]

Remember that this is only a rough guide. Some of the chapters in this book are longer and more complicated than others, and you will find some subjects easier to understand than others.

Step 5 **Implement**

Set about studying each chapter in the time shown in box C, following the key study steps in the order suggested by your particular learning style.

This is your personal **Study Plan**. You should try to combine it with the study sequence outlined below. You may want to modify the sequence to adapt it to your **personal style**.

Tackling your studies

The best way to approach this Study Text is to tackle the chapters in order. Taking into account your individual learning style, you could follow this sequence for each chapter.

Key study steps	Activity
Step 1 Topic list	This topic list helps you navigate each chapter; each numbered topic is a numbered section in the chapter.
Step 2 Introduction	This sets your objectives for study by giving you the big picture in terms of the context of the chapter. The content is referenced to the syllabus, and Exam guidance shows how the topic is likely to be examined. The Introduction tells you **why** the topics covered in the chapter need to be studied.
Step 3 Fast forward	Fast forward boxes give you a quick summary of the content of each of the main chapter sections. They are listed together in the roundup at the end of each chapter to help you review each chapter quickly.
Step 4 Explanations	Proceed methodically through each chapter, particularly focusing on areas highlighted as significant in the chapter introduction, or areas that are frequently examined.
Step 5 Key terms and Exam focus points	• Key terms can often earn you **easy marks** if you state them clearly and correctly in an exam answer. They are highlighted in the index at the back of this text. • Exam focus points state how the topic has been or may be examined, difficulties that can occur in questions about the topic, and examiner feedback on common weaknesses in answers.
Step 6 Note taking	Take brief notes, if you wish. Don't copy out too much. Remember that being able to record something yourself is a sign of being able to understand it. Your notes can be in whatever format you find most helpful; lists, diagrams, mindmaps.
Step 7 Examples	Work through the examples very carefully as they illustrate key knowledge and techniques.
Step 8 Case studies	Study each one, and try to add flesh to them from your own experience. They are designed to show how the topics you are studying come alive in the real world.
Step 9 Questions	Attempt each one, as they will illustrate how well you have understood what you have read.
Step 10 Answers	Check yours against ours, and make sure you understand any discrepancies.
Step 11 Chapter roundup	Review it carefully, to make sure you have grasped the significance of all the important points in the chapter.
Step 12 Quick quiz	Use the Quick quiz to check how much you have remembered of the topics covered and to practise questions in a variety of formats.
Step 13 Question practice	Attempt the Question suggested at the very end of the chapter. These are all AIA past exam questions, so provide an excellent indication of the type and standard of question that you can expect in your real exam. Some of these questions cover more than one subject area, which is a common feature of exam questions.

AIA Achieve

AIA provides an interactive course of study AIA Achieve, which offers students the tools, resources and learning environment to study for the exams. The study tools include a course of study e-book, marked practice questions, marked mock exam paper and feedback and technical advice via an e-Tutor. Contact the Study Support team at: Achieve@aiaworldwide.com.

Moving on...

When you are ready to start revising, you should still refer back to this Study Text:

- As a source of **reference** (you should find the index particularly helpful for this)
- As a way to **review** (the Fast forwards, Exam focus points, Chapter roundups and Quick quizzes help you here)

Syllabus

Aims

To examine the candidate's knowledge and understanding of:

- statistical sources and techniques
- the concepts and methods of business information technology, and its application to practical business situations

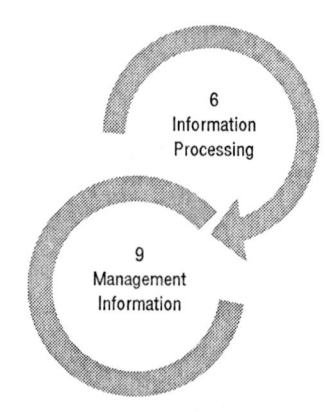

FIG. 6   INTER-RELATIONSHIP OF UNITS

Descriptors

After successfully completing this paper candidates should be able to:

- identify, select and explain appropriate statistical techniques used in the collection, summarisation and presentation of data
- identify, select and explain appropriate statistical techniques used in the basic modelling of situations involving probability, correlation, regression and time series forecasting
- describe and explain the role of information technology and methodology used in the processing of business data

Structure of the Paper

A three hour 15 minute paper consisting of two sections:

Section A Data Collection and Analysis

- this section scores 60% of the overall marks for the paper.
- four compulsory questions must be attempted.
- all questions carry equal marks (15%).
- where appropriate the allocation of marks to individual parts of a question is stated.
- the emphasis is mainly on computational aspects although candidates may be required to discuss assumptions made and to interpret results and conclusions and may also be required to draw graphs or diagrams.
- relevant statistical tables and formulae are printed on the question paper.

Section B – Business Information Processing

- this section scores 40% of the overall marks for the paper.
- four compulsory questions must be attempted.
- all questions carry equal marks (10%).
- where appropriate the allocation of marks to individual parts of a question is stated.
- all questions require answers in either essay or report format.

Syllabus

Section A – Data Collection and Analysis

6.1 Statistical Sources

Topic Weighting 5%

- data classification methods and the differences between primary and secondary data
- methods of primary data collection
- practical aspects of designing questionnaires and survey methods
- sampling methods and techniques
- the range of sources of secondary data

6.2 Presentation of Data

Topic Weighting 5%

- preparation of frequency distributions, in grouped and ungrouped form, from raw data
- presentation of data in a variety of types of charts, tables, diagrams and graphs
- the merits of the different types of presentation and the interpretation of data presented in different formats

6.3 Summary Statistics

Topic Weighting 10%

- averages: arithmetic mean, mode and median, for sets of data in various formats
- measures of dispersion such as range, inter-quartile range, variance and standard deviation for sets of data in various formats
- the relevance of different summary statistics in describing data in different situations
- the relationship between the summary measures and the shape of distributions and the difference between symmetrical and skewed distributions

6.4 Applying Probability to Decision Making

Topic Weighting 10%

- basic Laws of Probability
- decision trees and Venn diagrams
- conditional probability
- discrete and continuous probability distributions and their use in solving problems
- binomial, Poisson and Normal distributions

6.5 Measuring the Relationship Between Two Variables

Topic Weighting 10%

- scatter diagrams
- simple linear regression, correlation, product moment and rank correlation coefficients
- best-fit linear regression equations
- graphical presentation
- business forecasting

6.6 Time Series Analysis

Topic Weighting 10%

- time series models, time series graph plots
- additive and multiplicative models
- the estimation of trend and seasonal values and their use to produce forecasts

6.7 Index Numbers

Topic Weighting 10%

- simple index numbers and chain based index numbers
- Laspeyre's and Paasche's index numbers for expenditure, price and volume and their interpretation
- the index of retail prices in business

Section B – Business Information Technology

6.8 Overview of Information Systems

Topic Weighting 5%

- the capabilities of computer-based information systems in business
- the different types of systems including data processing systems, control information systems and planning information systems
- the basic stages involved in the systems development life cycle

6.9 Computer Hardware

Topic Weighting 5%

- the differences between mainframe systems, minicomputers and personal computers in terms of their hardware and capabilities
- the technology and purpose of the Central Processing Unit and computer memory
- the advantages and disadvantages of the different input and output technologies

6.10 Computer Software

Topic Weighting 10%

- the purpose of computer systems software and operating systems and of their use in business
- the purpose and use of common applications software such as spreadsheets, word processing, databases, graphics, multimedia, communications and accounting software

6.11 Managing Data and Information

Topic Weighting 5%

- the main methods of data storage and file access and their respective merits
- database management systems and data warehousing

6.12 Telecommunications and Networks

Topic Weighting 5%

- telecommunications systems, local area networks and wide area networks
- telecommunications applications such as electronic mail, electronic data interchange and electronic funds transfer

6.13 Electronic Commerce

Topic Weighting 10%

- the internet and the World Wide Web in e-commerce
- extranets and global information systems
- business-to-consumer and business-to-business applications of e-commerce

Relationship to Overall Syllabus

The use of quantitative techniques and the application of information technology in general are seen as important aspects of information processing within business decision making. Accountants, in their various roles in practice and in business, are key users of the technology and of many quantitative techniques and, therefore, it is important that they have a good grounding in these areas. Paper 6 Information Processing is designed to ensure that candidates have practical knowledge of the basic statistical techniques used in the collection and analysis of data and of the methods and technology involved in the processing of the data. As well as helping accountants in their own field it is intended that the material will assist them in understanding and communicating with specialists in other areas of their work.

Ethics

Candidates are advised that the standards outlined in The Code of Ethics for Professional Accountants issued by the International Ethics Standards Board for Accountants (IESBA Code) are implicit in, and examinable throughout, the AIA syllabus. The Code can be accessed via the AIA website at www.aiaworldwide.com.

Recommended Reading – Data Collection and Analysis

AIA Magazine International Accountant
ISSN: 1465 – 5144

AIA Text Book
Paper 6 Information Processing
Publisher: BPP Learning Media
ISBN: 9781 5097 8721 0

The e-Book is available at: exams@aiaworldwide.com
Contact our publisher BPP for information on purchasing a hard copy of the text book at:
http://www/bpp.com/learning-media-listing/lmlist/6293

You can purchase any of the books listed below quickly and easily through the publisher's website or link stated below.

Statistics for Economics, Accounting & Business Studies (7th Edition)
Authors: Barrow, M
Publisher: Pearson Education Limited
ISBN: 9781292118703
Website: http://www.pearsoned.co.uk/bookshop/detail.asp?WT.oss=9781292118703&WT.oss_r=1&item=100000000623410

Quantitative Methods for Business Decisions (7th Edition)
Authors: Curwin, J, Slater, R and Eadson, D
Publisher: Cengage Learning
ISBN: 9781408060193
Website: https://www.cengage.co.uk/search/?keyword=9781408060193

Quantitative Approaches in Business Studies (8th Edition)
Author: Morris, C
Publisher: Pearson Education Limited
ISBN: 9780273738633
Website: http://catalogue.pearsoned.co.uk/educator/product/Quantitative-Approaches-in-Business-Studies/9780273738633.page

Recommended Reading – Business Information Technology

AIA Journal – International Accountant
ISSN: 1465 – 5144

AIA Text Book
Paper 6 Information Processing
Publisher: BPP Learning Media
ISBN: 9781 5097 8721 0

The e-Book is available at: exams@aiaworldwide.com
Contact our publisher BPP for information on purchasing a hard copy of the text book at:
https://www.bpp.com/learning-media-listing/lmlist/6293

You can purchase any of the books listed below quickly and easily through the publisher's website or link below.

Fundamentals of Business Information Systems (2nd Edition)
Authors: Chesney, T, Reynolds, G and Stair, R.M
Publisher: Cengage Learning
ISBN: 9781408064269
Website: https://www.cengage.co.uk/search/?keyword=9781408064269

Electronic Commerce 2012 (7th Edition)
Authors: Turban, E, King, D
Publisher: Pearson Education Limited
ISBN: 9780273761341
Website: http://www.pearsoned.co.uk/bookshop/detail.asp?item=100000000404894

INTRODUCTION

Command words and learning outcomes

The following list contains active command words and generic learning outcomes appropriate for use at each stage of the AIA qualification. Reference to the learning outcomes and use of the command words is essential to understanding how the assessment is applied in AIA exams.

Foundation Level Command Words

WORD	DEFINITION
ADVISE	To inform as necessary
CALCULATE	Work out a value mathematically
DEFINE	To state and or explain clearly
EXPLAIN	To make clear giving reasons for
EXPRESS	To present thoughts and ideas
DESCRIBE	To give an account of in words or formula including key features
IDENTIFY	Recognise and select
PLAN	Present a method or argument for doing or achieving a task
PREPARE	To make or get ready for use
SELECT	To choose in preference to another
STATE	Express fully and clearly the details/facts
TABULATE	Arrange in a table

The exam paper

Analysis of past papers

The analysis below shows the topics which have been examined in sittings of the current syllabus from November 2008.

May 2018

Section A

1. Probabilities, normal distribution
2. Display of data, central tendency, measure of dispersion, types of data and data collection
3. Graphical display, coefficients, seasonal indices, forecasting
4. Relationships between variables using correlation analysis

Section B

5. General computer software, hardware, specialist accounting and financial management software
6. Database characteristics, security and controls, advantages and disadvantages of database systems
7. Management information systems (MIS), role and limitations of MIS
8. Considerations in setting up an e-business

November 2017

Section A

1. Probabilities, binomial and normal distribution
2. Display of data, data collection, sampling, and central tendency
3. Time series, coefficients, and seasonal indices
4. Graphical display of data, correlation coefficient, relationship between variables

Section B

5. Personal computers (PC's), mainframe computers, integrated and specialist computer software
6. Database implementation
7. Implementation of a new computer system
8. Advantages of voice messaging, computer telephony, computer bulletin boards, and use of email

May 2017

Section A

1. Probabilities, normal distribution
2. Sampling, display of data, frequency distribution, median
3. Index numbers, Laspeyre index
4. Display of data, correlation coefficient

Section B

5. Information systems, system components
6. Database systems
7. Types of computer
8. E-commerce

INTRODUCTION

November 2016

Section A

1. Probabilities
2. Display of data, data collection, sampling
3. Display of data, time series
4. Display of data, correlation coefficient, regression

Section B

5. Types of system
6. The relational database model
7. Expert systems
8. Electronic mail

May 2016

Section A

1. Display of data, probabilities, binomial distribution
2. Display of data, sampling, data sources
3. Time series models, seasonal indices, forecasts
4. Correlation coefficients

Section B

5. OMR, OCR. EFTPOS, smart cards
6. Databases
7. Management information systems
8. Telecommunication systems

November 2015

Section A

1. Data sources, sampling, Laspeyre index and Paasche index
2. Display of data, mean mode and medians, standard deviation, normal distribution
3. Time-series models, seasonal indices, forecasts
4. Display of data, correlation coefficient

Section B

5. Computer software and hardware
6. The role of information, internal and external sources of data and information
7. Project management of systems
8. Legal and ethical implications of web applications

May 2015

Section A

1. Data sources, sampling, graphical display, mean, mode and medians
2. Display of data, correlation coefficient, regression model
3. Time-series models, forecasts, Paasche index
4. Expected value, probability

Section B

5	Computer software and hardware
6	Database management systems
7	Systems development life cycle
8	B2C applications of e-commerce and e-business

November 2014

Section A

1	Sampling, mean mode and medians, inter-quartile range
2	Display of data, correlation coefficient
3	Time-series models, indices
4	Tree diagram, probabilities

Section B

5	Application software, integrated accounting software
6	Database management systems
7	LANS, WANS, electronic data interchange, electronic funds transfer
8	Management information systems, decision support systems

May 2014

Section A

1	Data collection and graphical display
2	Display of data, mean mode and medians, range and standard deviations
3	Binomial distribution, Laspeyre and Paasche indices
4	Time series analysis

Section B

5	Databases, benefits of email and electronic funds transfer
6	E-commerce and small and medium-sized enterprises
7	Hardware, software and communications technology
8	Computer-based information system, function of a CPU

November 2013

Section A

1	Time series, moving averages and seasonal indices
2	Data display – bar chart, mode, median and mean, Spearman's rank correlation
3	Binomial and normal distributions
4	Sampling

Section B

5	Transaction processing systems in a manufacturing company
6	OMR, OCR and smart cards
7	Databases
8	Electronic data interchange and electronic funds transfer; extranets

May 2013

Section A

1 Sampling techniques
2 Probability tree
3 Mean, median and modal, standard deviation; frequency distribution
4 Indices

Section B

5 Project management
6 Operating systems
7 Databases
8 Internet use in commerce

November 2012

Section A

1 Primary and secondary data
2 Statistical distribution
3 Mean, median and modal, standard deviation, frequency distribution
4 Time series

Section B

5 IS and IT, MIS
6 Computer capability, CPU and memory
7 Database use and design
8 LAN and WAN

May 2012

Section A

1 Mean, median and modal, standard deviation, frequency distribution
2 Probability
3 Correlation and regression analysis
4 Indices

Section B

5 E-commerce
6 Development life-cycle
7 Applications software
8 Database management

November 2011

Section A

1 Mean, median and modal, standard deviation; frequency distribution
2 Time series
3 Correlation and regression analysis
4 Primary and secondary data

Section B

5 Computer hardware
6 LAN, WAN, email, EDI, funds transfer
7 Computer hardware and software, spreadsheet packages
8 Database management system

May 2011

Section A

1 Mean, median and modal, standard deviation, frequency distribution
2 Indices, sales forecast
3 Time series
4 Probability

Section B

5 Internet
6 Computer hardware and software, communications technology, networking technology
7 Computerised systems
8 Data organisation, database management

November 2010

Section A

1 Mean, median and modal, standard deviation, frequency distribution
2 Indices
3 Probability
4 Correlation and regression analysis

Section B

5 Computer hardware
6 Application software
7 LAN, WAN, email, EDI, funds transfer
8 E-commerce

May 2010

Section A

1 Mean, median and modal, standard deviation, frequency distribution
2 Indices, sales forecast
3 Probability
4 Correlation analysis

Section B

5 E-commerce
6 Computer hardware and software, database and spreadsheet packages
7 Development life-cycle
8 Database management

INTRODUCTION

November 2009

Section A

1. Dispersion and frequency graph
2. Decision making, probability
3. Price indices
4. Correlation and regression analysis

Section B

5. Benefits of computerised systems
6. File organisation
7. Printers and scanners
8. E-commerce

May 2009

Section A

1. Questionnaires and data analysis
2. Binomial distribution and probability
3. Correlation analysis
4. Time series

Section B

5. Development life cycle
6. Operating system, hardware
7. E-commerce
8. Database, LAN

November 2008

Section A

1. Data collection and analysis
2. Correlation analysis
3. Probability
4. Price indices

Section B

5. Keyboards and printers
6. Filling and storage
7. Word processing and spreadsheets
8. E-commerce

Data collection and analysis

Basic mathematical techniques

Topic list	Syllabus reference
1 Integers, fractions and decimals	–
2 Using a scientific calculator	–
3 Order of operations	–
4 Percentages and ratios	–
5 Roots and powers	–
6 Errors	–
7 Formulae and equations	–
8 Manipulating inequalities	–
9 Linear equations	–
10 Linear equations and graphs	–
11 Simultaneous equations	–
12 Non-linear equations	–

Introduction

This Study Text is divided into two parts:

SECTION A: Data collection and analysis
SECTION B: Business information technology

Many students do not have a mathematical background and so this chapter is intended to cover the basic mathematics skills that you will need for Section A of the syllabus and then beyond in your further studies.

Even if you have done mathematics in the past don't ignore this chapter. Skim through it to make sure that you are aware of all the concepts and techniques covered. Since it provides the foundation for much of what is to follow, it is an **extremely important chapter**.

PART A   DATA COLLECTION AND ANALYSIS

1 Integers, fractions and decimals

Exam focus point

Throughout Section A of this Text you will, at times, need to use a calculator. Our suggestion is to make sure you use one calculator throughout your studies and, if appropriate, at work. You will not then find yourself in the real exam working with an unfamiliar calculator. If you want to take the concept of prudence to the extreme then buy two identical calculators and you then have an identical spare for the real exam.

FAST FORWARD

- An **integer** is a whole number and can be either positive or negatives.
- **Fractions** and **decimals** are ways of showing parts of a whole.

1.1 Integers

Examples of integers are …, −5, −4, −3, −2, −1, 0, 1, 2, 3, 4, 5, …

Examples of fractions are 1/2, 1/4, 19/35, 10/377 …

Examples of decimals are 0.1, 0.25, 0.3135, …

1.2 Negative numbers

FAST FORWARD

The **negative number rules** are as follows:

$-p + q = q - p$

$q - (-p) = q + p$

$-p \times -q = pq$ and $\dfrac{-p}{-q} = \dfrac{p}{q}$

$-p \times q = -pq$ and $\dfrac{-p}{q} = -\dfrac{p}{q}$

1.2.1 Adding and subtracting negative numbers

When a negative number (−p) is **added** to another number (q), the net effect is to **subtract** p from q.

(a) $10 + (-6) = 10 - 6 = 4$ (b) $-10 + (-6) = -10 - 6 = -16$

When a negative number (−p) is **subtracted** from another number (q), the net effect is to **add** p to q.

(a) $12 - (-8) = 12 + 8 = 20$ (b) $-12 - (-8) = -12 + 8 = -4$

1.2.2 Multiplying and dividing negative numbers

When a negative number is **multiplied** or **divided** by another negative number, the result is a **positive** number.

(a) $-8 \times (-4) = +32$ (b) $\dfrac{-18}{-3} = +6$

If there is only **one negative number** in a multiplication or division, the result is **negative**.

(a) $-8 \times 4 = -32$ (b) $3 \times (-2) = -6$ (c) $\dfrac{12}{-4} = -3$ (d) $\dfrac{-20}{5} = -4$

1: BASIC MATHEMATICAL TECHNIQUES

 Question *Negative numbers*

Work out the following.

(a) $(72 - 8) - (-2 + 1)$

(b) $\dfrac{88 + 8}{12} + \dfrac{(29 - 11)}{-2}$

(c) $8(2 - 5) - (4 - (-8))$

(d) $\dfrac{-36}{9 - 3} - \dfrac{84}{3 - 10} - \dfrac{-81}{3}$

Answer

(a) $64 - (-1) = 64 + 1 = 65$

(b) $8 + (-9) = -1$

(c) $-24 - (12) = -36$

(d) $-6 - (-12) - (-27) = -6 + 12 + 27 = 33$

1.3 Fractions

A fraction has a numerator (the number on the top line) and a denominator (the number on the bottom line).

Formula to learn

$$\text{FRACTION} = \dfrac{\text{NUMERATOR}}{\text{DENOMINATOR}}$$

For example, the fraction 1/2 has a numerator equal to 1 and a denominator of 2.

1.4 Reciprocals

The reciprocal of a number is 1 divided by that number for example. For example, the reciprocal of 2 is 1 divided by 2 = 1/2. The reciprocal of 3 is 1 divided by 3 = 1/3.

1.5 Decimals

A fraction can be turned into a decimal by dividing the numerator by the denominator. For example, the fraction 1/2 equates to 0.5, and the fraction 1/4 equates to 0.25. When turning decimals into fractions, you need to remember that places after the decimal point stand for tenths, hundredths, thousandths and so on.

1.5.1 Decimal places

Sometimes a decimal number has too many figures in it for practical use. For example, consider the fraction 6/9 which when turned into a decimal = 0.666666 recurring. This problem can be overcome by **rounding** the decimal number to a specific number of **decimal places** by discarding figures using the following rule.

If the first figure to be discarded is greater than or equal to five then add one to the previous figure. Otherwise the previous figure is unchanged.

1.5.2 Example: Decimal places

(a) 49.28723 correct to four decimal places is 49.2872

Discarding a 3 causes nothing to be added to the 2.

(b) 49.28723 correct to three decimal places is 49.287

Discarding a 2 causes nothing to be added to the 7.

(c) 49.28723 correct to two decimal places is 49.29

Discarding the 7 causes 1 to be added to the 8.

(d) 49.28723 correct to one decimal place is 49.3

Discarding the 8 causes 1 to be added to the 2.

1.6 Significant figures

Another method for giving an approximated answer is to round off using **significant** figures. Significant means important and the closer a digit is to the beginning of a number, the more significant it is.

For example, if we want to express 95,431 to 3 significant figures, '31' will be discarded, leaving 95,400 (3 sf).

Zeros have specific rules. All zeros **between** non-zeros are significant. For example, 20,606 has 5 significant figures. Leading zeros in a decimal are **not** significant. For example, 0.025 has 2 significant figures.

Question   Significant figures and decimal places

(a) Round off the number 37,649 to one significant figure

(b) Round off the number 0.073184 to one significant figure

(c) Round off the number 0.0073184 to four decimal places

(d) Work out the answer to 974 × 586 on a calculator and round off the answer to three significant figures

(e) Work out the answer to 23 ÷ 946 on a calculator and round off the answer to three decimal places

Answer

(a) 40,000

(b) 0.07

(c) 0.0073

(d) 974 × 586 = 570,764
          = 571,000 (3 sf)

(e) 23 ÷ 946 = 0.02431289641
          = 0.024 (3 dp)

1.7 Extra symbols

We will come across several other mathematical signs in this book but there are five which you should learn **now**.

(a) > means 'greater than'. So 46 > 29 is true, but 40 > 86 is false.
(b) ≥ means 'is greater than or equal to'. So 4 ≥ 3 and 4 ≥ 4.
(c) < means 'is less than'. So 29 < 46 is true, but 86 < 40 is false.
(d) ≤ means 'is less than or equal to'. So 7 ≤ 8 and 7 ≤ 7.
(e) ≠ means 'is not equal to'. So we could write 100.004 ≠ 100.

2 Using a scientific calculator

FAST FORWARD Scientific calculators can make calculations quicker and easier.

2.1 The need for a scientific calculator

For this exam and for your future AIA studies you will need to have an up to date scientific calculator. They are not expensive and if you spend time now getting to know what it can do for you, you will have a much better chance of succeeding in your studies. You should be aware of what your calculator can do for you and that you should not take a new calculator into an exam without knowing how to use it.

The calculator can make calculations quicker and easier but it is very important that you show all your workings to numerical calculations. The marker will not award you marks where your final answer is wrong if they can't see your workings and how you arrived at your answer.

2.2 A typical scientific calculator

The illustration below shows a typical scientific calculator that is widely available. It has a natural textbook display which allows you to input and display fractions, square roots and other numeric expressions as they appear in your textbook and assessment. Your calculator may be slightly different and it is essential that you read its instruction leaflet and practise using it.

PART A   DATA COLLECTION AND ANALYSIS

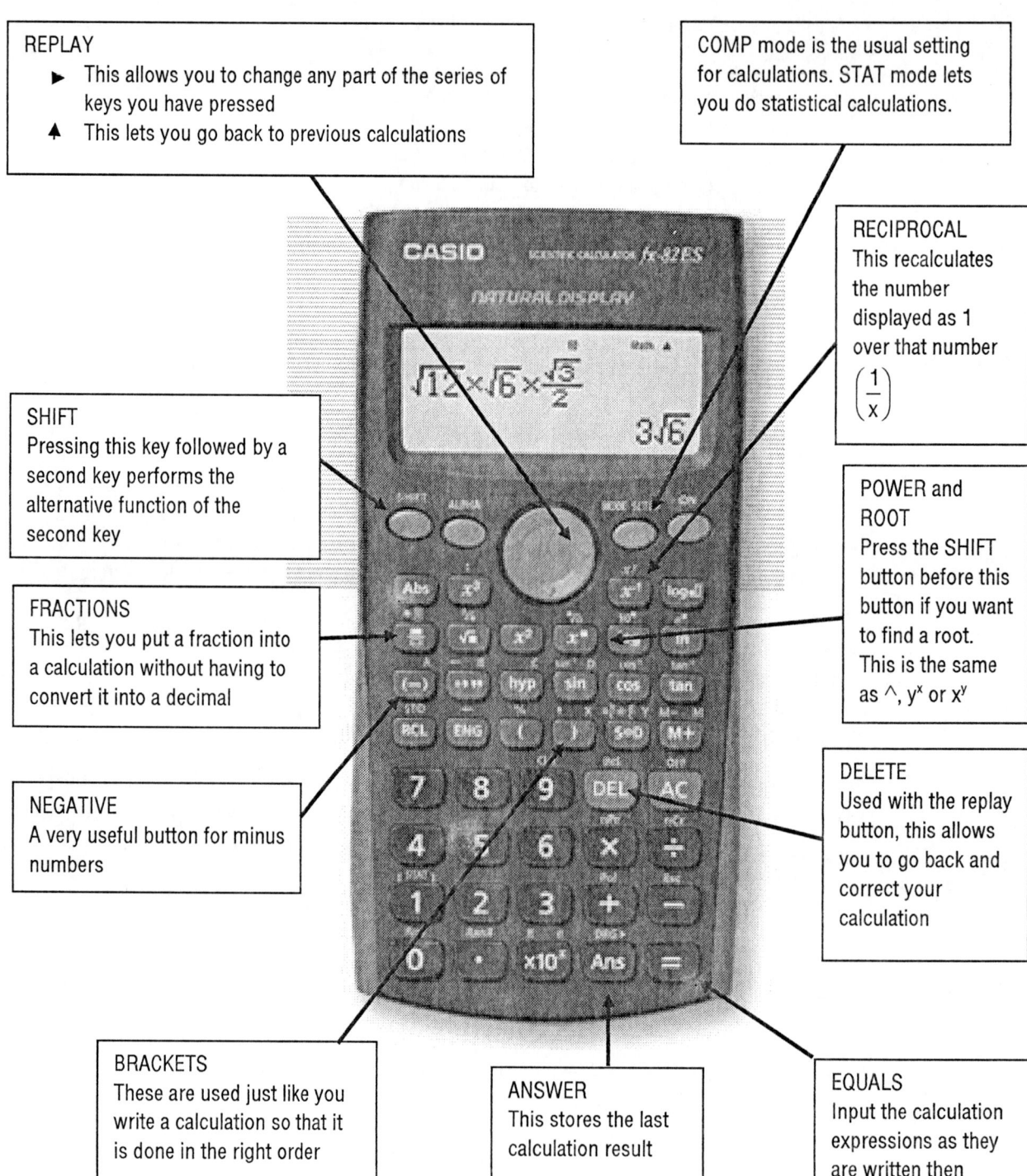

REPLAY
► This allows you to change any part of the series of keys you have pressed
▲ This lets you go back to previous calculations

COMP mode is the usual setting for calculations. STAT mode lets you do statistical calculations.

RECIPROCAL
This recalculates the number displayed as 1 over that number $\left(\frac{1}{x}\right)$

SHIFT
Pressing this key followed by a second key performs the alternative function of the second key

POWER and ROOT
Press the SHIFT button before this button if you want to find a root. This is the same as ^, y^x or x^y

FRACTIONS
This lets you put a fraction into a calculation without having to convert it into a decimal

DELETE
Used with the replay button, this allows you to go back and correct your calculation

NEGATIVE
A very useful button for minus numbers

BRACKETS
These are used just like you write a calculation so that it is done in the right order

ANSWER
This stores the last calculation result

EQUALS
Input the calculation expressions as they are written then press = to execute it

8

1: BASIC MATHEMATICAL TECHNIQUES

 Question — Using a scientific calculator

(a) Put the following calculation into your calculator exactly as it is written

$3 + 6 \times 5 =$

What does this tell you about how your calculator carries out the order of operation?

(b) Calculate the following using the brackets buttons on your calculator

$(3 + 5) \times 2$

What happens if you don't use brackets?

(c) Use the fraction button to calculate the following:

$\frac{1}{2} + \frac{1}{4} + \frac{1}{8}$

(d) What is $6^{2.75}$?

(e) What is $\sqrt[7]{78{,}125}$?

(f) What is $1/0.2 \times (3 - (1 + 0.7)^5)$?

(g) What is $\dfrac{2.25^4 + 0.025^{-3}}{2.653}$?

Answer

(a) 33

This tells you that the calculator carries out mathematical operations in the correct order (see section 3 below).

(b) 16

If brackets are not used the answer is 13. The calculator has done the multiplication before the addition.

(c) $\frac{7}{8}$

(d) 138.0117105

(e) 5

(f) −55.99285

(g) 24,133.29397

PART A DATA COLLECTION AND ANALYSIS

3 Order of operations

3.1 Brackets

FAST FORWARD

Brackets indicate a priority or an order in which calculations should be made.

Brackets are commonly used to indicate which parts of a mathematical expression should be grouped together, and calculated before other parts. The rule for using brackets is as follows:

(a) Do things in brackets before doing things outside them:

(b) Subject to rule (a), do things in this order.

  (1) Powers and roots
  (2) Multiplications and divisions, working from left to right
  (3) Additions and subtractions, working from left to right

3.1.1 Brackets – clarity

Brackets are used for the sake of clarity.

(a) $3 + 6 \times 8 = 51$. This is the same as writing $3 + (6 \times 8) = 51$.
(b) $(3 + 6) \times 8 = 72$. The brackets indicate that we wish to multiply the sum of 3 and 6 by 8.
(c) $12 - 4 \div 2 = 10$. This is the same as writing $12 - (4 \div 2) = 10$ or $12 - (4/2) = 10$.
(d) $(12 - 4) \div 2 = 4$. The brackets tell us to do the subtraction first.

A figure outside a bracket may be multiplied by two or more figures inside a bracket, linked by addition or subtraction signs. Here is an example:

$$5(6 + 8) = 5 \times (6 + 8) = (5 \times 6) + (5 \times 8) = 70$$

This is the same as $5(14) = 5 \times 14 = 70$

The multiplication sign after the 5 can be omitted, as shown here ($5(6 + 8)$), but there is no harm in putting it in ($5 \times (6 + 8)$) if you want to.

Similarly:

$5(8 - 6) = 5(2) = 10$; or
$(5 \times 8) - (5 \times 6) = 10$

3.1.2 Brackets – multiplication

When two sets of figures linked by addition or subtraction signs within brackets are multiplied together, each figure in one bracket is multiplied in turn by every figure in the second bracket. Thus:

$(8 + 4)(7 + 2) = (12)(9) = 108$; or
$(8 \times 7) + (8 \times 2) + (4 \times 7) + (4 \times 2) = 56 + 16 + 28 + 8 = 108$

3.1.3 Brackets on a calculator

A modern scientific calculator will let you do calculations with brackets in the same way they are written. Try doing the examples above using the brackets buttons.

1: BASIC MATHEMATICAL TECHNIQUES

Question — Four decimal places

Work out all answers to four decimal places, using a calculator.

(a) $(43 + 26.705) \times 9.3$

(b) $(844.2 \div 26) - 2.45$

(c) $\dfrac{45.6 - 13.92 + 823.1}{14.3 \times 112.5}$

(d) $\dfrac{303.3 + 7.06 \times 42.11}{1.03 \times 111.03}$

(e) $\dfrac{7.6 \times 1{,}010}{10.1 \times 76{,}000}$

(f) $(43.756 + 26.321) \div 171.036$

(g) $(43.756 + 26.321) \times 171.036$

(h) $171.45 + (-221.36) + 143.22$

(i) $66 - (-43.57) + (-212.36)$

(j) $\dfrac{10.1 \times 76{,}000}{7.6 \times 1{,}010}$

(k) $\dfrac{21.032 + (-31.476)}{3.27 \times 41.201}$

(l) $\dfrac{-33.33 - (-41.37)}{11.21 + (-24.32)}$

(m) $\dfrac{-10.75 \times (-15.44)}{-14.25 \times 17.15} + \left(\dfrac{16.23}{8.4 + 3.002}\right)$

(n) $\dfrac{-7.366 \times 921.3}{10{,}493 - 2{,}422.8} - \left(\dfrac{8.4 + 3.002}{16.23}\right)$

Answer

(a) 648.2565

(b) 30.0192

(c) 0.5313

(d) 5.2518

(e) 0.01

(f) 0.4097

(g) 11,985.6898

(h) 93.31

(i) –102.79

(j) 100 (Note that this question is the reciprocal of part (e), and so the answer is the reciprocal of the answer to part (e).)

(k) –0.0775

(l) –0.6133

(m) 0.7443

(n) –1.5434

4 Percentages and ratios

4.1 Percentages

FAST FORWARD

Percentages are used to indicate the **relative size** or **proportion** of items, rather than their **absolute** size.

If one office employs ten accountants, six PAs (Personal Assistants) and four supervisors, the **absolute** values of staff numbers and the **percentage** of the total work force in each type would be as follows.

	Accountants	PAs	Supervisors	Total
Absolute numbers	10	6	4	20
Percentages	50%	30%	20%	100%

The idea of percentages is that the whole of something can be thought of as 100%. The whole of a cake, for example, is 100%. If you share it out equally with a friend, you will get half each, or 100%/2 = 50% each.

FAST FORWARD To turn a percentage into a fraction or decimal you **divide by 100%**. To turn a fraction or decimal back into a percentage you **multiply by 100%**.

4.1.1 Percentages, fractions and decimals

Consider the following:

(a) $0.16 = 0.16 \times 100\% = 16\%$

(b) $\dfrac{4}{5} = 4/5 \times 100\% = \dfrac{400}{5\%} = 80\%$

(c) $40\% = \dfrac{40}{100\%} = \dfrac{2}{5} = 0.4$

4.2 Situations involving percentages

4.2.1 Find X% of Y

Suppose we want to find 40% of $64

40% of $64 = $\dfrac{40}{100} \times \$64 = 0.4 \times \$64 = \$25.60$.

4.2.2 Express X as a percentage of Y

Suppose we want to know what $16 is as a percentage of $64

$16 as a percentage of $64 = $16/64 \times 100\% = 1/4 \times 100\% = 25\%$

In other words, put the $16 as a fraction of the $64, and then multiply by 100%.

4.2.3 Find the original value of X, given that after a percentage increase of Y% it is equal to X_1

Fred Bloggs' salary is now $60,000 per annum after an annual increase of 20%. Suppose we wanted to know his annual salary before the increase.

	%
Fred Bloggs' salary **before** increase (original)	100
Salary increase	20
Fred Bloggs' salary after increase (final)	120

We know that Fred's salary after the increase (final) also equals $60,000.

Therefore 120% = $60,000.

We need to find his salary **before** the increase (original), ie 100%.

We can do this as follows:

Step 1 **Calculate 1%**

If 120% = $60,000

1% = $\dfrac{£60,000}{120}$

1% = $500

Step 2 Calculate 100% (original)

If 1% = $500

100% = $500 × 100

100% = $50,000

Therefore, Fred Bloggs' annual salary before the increase was $50,000.

4.2.4 Find the final value of A, given that after a percentage increase/decrease of B% it is equal to A_1

If sales receipts in Year 1 are $500,000 and there was a percentage decrease of 10% in Year 2, what are the sales receipts in Year 2?

Adopt the step by step approach used in paragraph 4.2.3 as follows:

	%
Sales receipts – Year 1 (original)	100
Percentage decrease	10
Sales receipts – Year 2 (final)	90

This question is slightly different to that in paragraph 4.2.3 because we have the original value (100%) and not the final value as in paragraph 4.2.3.

We know that sales receipts in Year 1 (original) also equal $500,000.

We need to find the sales receipts in Year 2 (final). We can do this as follows:

Step 1 Calculate 1%

If 100% = $500,000

1% = $5,000

Step 2 Calculate 90% (original)

If 1% = $5,000

90% = $5,000 × 90

90% = $450,000

Therefore, sales receipts in Year 2 are $450,000.

4.2.5 Summary

You might think that the calculations involved in paragraphs 4.2.3 and 4.2.4 above are long-winded but it is vitally important that you understand how to perform these types of calculation. As you become more confident with calculating percentages you may not need to go through all of the steps that we have shown. The key to answering these types of question correctly is to be very clear about which values represent the **original** amount (100%) and which values represent the **final** amount (100 + X%).

	Increase %	Decrease %
Original Value	100	100
Increase/(decrease)	X	–X
Final value	100 + X	100 – X

4.3 Percentage changes

A **percentage increase** or **reduction** is calculated as (change ÷ original) × 100%.

You might also be required to calculate the value of the **percentage change**, ie in paragraph 4.2.3 you may have been required to calculate the percentage increase in Fred Bloggs' salary, or in paragraph 4.2.4 you may have been required to calculate the percentage decrease of sales receipts in Year 2 (as compared with Year 1).

The formula required for calculating the **percentage change** is as follows.

Formula to learn

$$\text{Percentage change} = \frac{\text{'Change'}}{\text{Original value}} \times 100\%$$

Note that it is the **original value** that the change is compared with and not the final value when calculating the percentage change.

Question — Percentage reduction

A television has been reduced from $490.99 to $340.99. What is the percentage reduction in price to three decimal places?

A   30.550   B   30.551   C   43.990   D   43.989

Answer

Difference in price = $(490.99 − 340.99) = $150.00

$$\text{Percentage reduction} = \frac{\text{change}}{\text{original price}} \times 100\% = \frac{150}{490.99} \times 100\% = 30.551\%$$

The correct answer is B.

4.3.1 Discounts

A business may offer a discount on a price to encourage sales. The calculation of discounts requires an ability to manipulate percentages. For example, a travel agent is offering a 17% discount on the brochure price of a particular holiday to the US. The brochure price of the holiday is $795. What price is being offered by the travel agent?

Solution

$$\text{Discount} = 17\% \text{ of } \$795 = \frac{17}{100} \times \$795 = \$135.15$$

Price offered = $(795 − 135.15) = $659.85

= ∴ 17% = 17 × 1% = 17 × $7.95 = $135.15

Alternatively, price offered = $795 × (100 − 17)% = $795 × 83% = $795 × 0.83 = $659.85

4.3.2 Quicker percentage change calculations

If something is increased by 10%, we can calculate the increased value by multiplying by (1 + 10%) = 1 + 0.1 = 1.1. We are multiplying the number by itself plus 10% expressed as a decimal.

For example, a 15% increase to $1,000 = $1,000 × 1.15
= $1,150

In the same way, a 10% decrease can be calculated by multiplying a number by (1 – 10%) = 1 – 0.1 = 0.9. With practice, this method will speed up your percentage calculations and will be very useful in your future studies.

Question — Percentage price change

Three years ago a retailer sold action man toys for $17.50 each. At the end of the first year he increased the price by 6% and at the end of the second year by a further 5%. At the end of the third year the selling price was $20.06. The percentage price change in Year 3 was:

A   –3%   B   +3%   C   –6%   D   +9%

Answer

Selling price at end of Year 1 = $17.50 × 1.06 = $18.55
Selling price at end of Year 2 = $18.55 × 1.05 = $19.48
Change in selling price in Year 3 = $(20.06 – 19.48) = $0.58

∴ Percentage change in Year 3 was $\frac{£0.58}{£19.48} \times 100\%$ = 2.97%, say 3%

The correct answer is B.

4.4 Profits

You may be required in your assessment to calculate profit, selling price or cost of sale of an item or number of items from certain information. To do this you need to remember the following crucial formula.

	%
Cost of sales	100
Plus Profit	25
Equals Sales	125

Profit may be expressed either as a percentage of **cost of sales** (such as 25% (25/100) mark-up) or as a percentage of **sales** (such as 20% (25/125) **margin**).

4.4.1 Profit margins

If profit is expressed as a percentage of sales (**margin**) the following formula is also useful.

	%
Selling price	100
Profit	20
Cost of sales	80

It is best to think of the selling price as 100% if profit is expressed as a **margin** (percentage of sales). On the other hand, if profit is expressed as a percentage of cost of sales (**mark-up**) it is best to think of the cost of sales as being 100%. The following examples should help to clarify this point.

4.4.2 Example: Margin

Delilah's Dresses sells a dress at a 10% margin. The dress cost the shop $100. Calculate the profit made by Delilah's Dresses.

Solution

The margin is 10% (ie 10/100)

∴ Let selling price = 100%

∴ Profit = 10%

∴ Cost = 90% = $100

∴ 1% = $\left(\dfrac{\$100}{90}\right)$

∴ 10% = profit = $\$\dfrac{100}{90} \times 10 = \$11.11$

4.4.3 Example: mark-up

Trevor's Trousers sells a pair of trousers for $80 at a 15% mark-up.

Required

Calculate the profit made by Trevor's Trousers.

Solution

The markup is 15%.

∴ Let cost of sales = 100%

∴ Profit = 15%

∴ Selling price = 115% = $80

∴ 1% = $\left(\dfrac{\$80}{115}\right)$

∴ 15% = profit = $\left(\dfrac{\$80}{115}\right) \times 15 = \$10.43$

Question   Profits

A skirt which cost the retailer $75 is sold at a profit of 25% on the selling price. The profit is therefore:

A $18.75 B $20.00 C $25.00 D $30.00

Answer

Let selling price = 100%

Profit = 25% of selling price

∴ Cost = 75% of selling price

Cost = $75 = 75%

∴ 1% = $\dfrac{\$75}{75}$

∴ 25% = profit = $\dfrac{\$75}{75} \times 25 = \$25$

The correct answer is C.

4.5 Proportions

FAST FORWARD
A **proportion** means writing a percentage as a proportion of 1 (that is, as a decimal). 100% can be thought of as the whole, or 1. 50% is half of that, or 0.5.

4.5.1 Example: Proportions

Suppose there are 14 women in an audience of 70. What proportion of the audience are men?

Number of men = 70 − 14 = 56

Proportion of men = $\frac{56}{70} = \frac{8}{10}$ = 80% = 0.8

- The **fraction** of the audience made up of men is 8/10 or 4/5
- The **percentage** of the audience made up of men is 80%
- The **proportion** of the audience made up of men is 0.8

Question — Proportions

There are 30 students in a class room, 17 of whom have blonde hair. What proportion of the students (to four decimal places) do not have blonde hair (delete as appropriate).

0.5667	0.5666
0.4334	0.4333

Answer

~~0.5667~~	~~0.5666~~
~~0.4334~~	0.4333

$\frac{(30-17)}{30} \times 100\% = 43.33\% = 0.4333$

4.6 Ratios

FAST FORWARD
Ratios show relative shares of a whole.

Suppose Tom has $12 and Dick has $8. The **ratio** of Tom's cash to Dick's cash is 12:8. This can be cancelled down, just like a fraction, to 3:2. Study the following examples carefully.

4.6.1 Example: Ratios

Suppose Tom and Dick wish to share $20 out in the ratio 3:2. How much will each receive?

Solution

Because 3 + 2 = 5, we must divide the whole up into 5 equal parts, then give Tom 3 parts and Dick 2 parts.

$20 ÷ 5 = $4 (so each part is $4)

Tom's share = 3 × $4 = $12

Dick's share = 2 × $4 = $8

Check: $12 + $8 = $20 (adding up the two shares in the answer gets us back to the $20 in the question)

This method of calculating ratios as amounts works no matter how many ratios are involved.

4.6.2 Example: Ratios again

A, B, C and D wish to share $600 in the ratio 6:1:2:3. How much will each receive?

Solution

Number of parts = 6 + 1 + 2 + 3 = 12

Value of each part = $600 ÷ 12 = $50

A: 6 × $50 = $300
B: 1 × $50 = $50
C: 2 × $50 = $100
D: 3 × $50 = $150

Check: $300 + $50 + $100 + $150 = $600

Question   Ratios

Tom, Dick and Harry wish to share out $800. Calculate how much each would receive if the ratio used was:

(a) 3 : 2 : 5
(b) 5 : 3 : 2
(c) 3 : 1 : 1

Answer

(a) Total parts = 10

Each part is worth $800 ÷ 10 = $80

Tom gets 3 × $80 = $240
Dick gets 2 × $80 = $160
Harry gets 5 × $80 = $400

(b) Same parts as (a) but in a different order.

Tom gets $400
Dick gets $240
Harry gets $160

(c) Total parts = 5

Each part is worth $800 ÷ 5 = $160

Therefore Tom gets $480

Dick and Harry each get $160

5 Roots and powers

FAST FORWARD

The **nth root** of a number is a value which, when multiplied by itself (n − 1) times, equals the original number. **Powers** work the other way round.

Key terms

The **square root** of a number is a value which, when multiplied by itself, equals the original number.
$\sqrt{9} = 3$, since $3 \times 3 = 9$

The **cube root** of a number is the value which, when multiplied by itself twice, equals the original number.
$\sqrt[3]{64} = 4$, since $4 \times 4 \times 4 = 64$

5.1 Powers

A **power** is the result when equal numbers are multiplied together.

The 6th power of $2 = 2^6 = 2 \times 2 \times 2 \times 2 \times 2 \times 2 = 64$.

Similarly, $3^4 = 3 \times 3 \times 3 \times 3 = 81$.

Familiarise yourself with the power button on your calculator. ($x^\blacksquare$, $\wedge$, x^y or y^x). Most calculators will also have separate buttons to square (x^2) and cube a number (x^3).

5.2 Roots

A **root** is the reverse of a power. When 5 is squared, the answer is 25. That is $5^2 = 25$. The reverse of this process is called finding the square root. $\sqrt[2]{25} = \sqrt{25} = 5$. Most calculators have a square root button $\sqrt{}$ or $\sqrt[\blacksquare]{}$. Higher roots eg $\sqrt[5]{7,776}$ can be found by using 'shift' before the power ($x^\blacksquare$, $\wedge$, x^y, y^x) button. On a modern scientific calculator, press 5 shift $x^\blacksquare$ 7,776 = to obtain the answer = 6.

5.3 Rules for powers

Use your calculator to enter each of the following examples to practise this very important topic.

5.3.1 Powers – Rule 1

When a number with a power is multiplied by the **same** number with the same or a different power, the result is that number to the power of the **sum** of the powers.

(a) $5^2 \times 5 = 5^2 \times 5^1 = 5^{(2+1)} = 5^3 = 125$
(b) $4^3 \times 4^3 = 4^{(3+3)} = 4^6 = 4,096$

5.3.2 Powers – Rule 2

Similarly, when a number with a power is divided by the **same** number with the same or a different power, the result is that number to the power of the first index **minus** the second power.

(a) $6^4 \div 6^3 = 6^{(4-3)} = 6^1 = 6$
(b) $7^8 \div 7^6 = 7^{(8-6)} = 7^2 = 49$

PART A   DATA COLLECTION AND ANALYSIS

5.3.3 Powers – Rule 3

When a number x with a power is raised to the power y, the result is the number raised to the power xy.

The powers are simply multiplied together.

(a) $(2^2)^3 = 2^{2 \times 3} = 2^6 = 64$
(b) $(5^3)^3 = 5^{3 \times 3} = 5^9 = 1,953,125$

5.3.4 Powers – Rule 4

Any figure to the power of one always equals itself: $2^1 = 2$, $3^1 = 3$, $4^1 = 4$ and so on.

5.3.5 Powers – Rule 5

Any figure to the power of **zero** always equals **one**. $1^0 = 1$, $2^0 = 1$, $3^0 = 1$, $4^0 = 1$ and so on.

5.3.6 Powers – Rule 6

One to any power always equals one. $1^2 = 1$, $1^3 = 1$, $1^4 = 1$ and so on.

5.3.7 Powers – Rule 7

A power can be a **fraction**, as in $16^{\frac{1}{2}}$. What $16^{\frac{1}{2}}$ means is the square root of 16 $\left(\sqrt{16} \text{ or } 4\right)$ If we multiply $16^{\frac{1}{2}}$ by $16^{\frac{1}{2}}$ we get $16^{(\frac{1}{2}+\frac{1}{2})}$ which equals 16^1 and thus 16.

Similarly, $216^{\frac{1}{3}}$ is the cube root of 216 (which is 6) because $216^{\frac{1}{3}} \times 216^{\frac{1}{3}} \times 216^{\frac{1}{3}} = 216^{(\frac{1}{3}+\frac{1}{3}+\frac{1}{3})} = 216^1 = 216$.

5.3.8 Powers – Rule 8

An power can be a **negative** value. The negative sign represents a **reciprocal**. Thus 2^{-1} is the reciprocal of, or one over, 2^1.

$2^{-1} = \dfrac{1}{2^1} = \dfrac{1}{2}$

Likewise $2^{-2} = \dfrac{1}{2^2} = \dfrac{1}{4}$

$2^{-3} = \dfrac{1}{2^3} = \dfrac{1}{8}$

$5^{-6} = \dfrac{1}{5^6} = \dfrac{1}{15,625}$

5.4 Example: Powers

When we multiply or divide by a number with a negative power, the rules previously stated still apply.

(a) $9^2 \times 9^{-2} = 9^{(2+(-2))} = 9^0 = 1$ (That is, $9^2 \times \dfrac{1}{9^2} = 1$)

(b) $4^5 \div 4^{-2} = 4^{(5-(-2))} = 4^7 = 16,384$

(c) $3^8 \times 3^{-5} = 3^{(8-5)} = 3^3 = 27$

(d) $3^{-5} \div 3^{-2} = 3^{-5-(-2)} = 3^{-3} = \dfrac{1}{3^3} = \dfrac{1}{27}$. (This could be re-expressed as $\dfrac{1}{3^5} \div \dfrac{1}{3^2} = \dfrac{1}{3^5} \times 3^2 = \dfrac{1}{3^3}$.)

1: BASIC MATHEMATICAL TECHNIQUES

A fraction might have a power applied to it. In this situation, the main point to remember is that the power must be applied to both the top and the bottom of the fraction.

(a) $\left(2\dfrac{1}{3}\right)^3 = \left(\dfrac{7}{3}\right)^3 = \dfrac{7^3}{3^3} = \dfrac{343}{27}$

(b) $\left(5\dfrac{2}{5}\right)^{-4} = \left(\dfrac{27}{5}\right)^{-4} = \dfrac{1}{\left(\dfrac{27}{5}\right)^4} = \dfrac{1}{\dfrac{27^4}{5^4}} = \dfrac{5^4}{27^4} = \dfrac{625}{531{,}441}$

FAST FORWARD

The **main rules** to apply when dealing with powers and roots are as follows:

- $2^x \times 2^y = 2^{x+y}$
- $2^x \div 2^y = 2^{x-y}$
- $(2^x)^y = 2^{x \times y} = 2^{xy}$
- $x^0 = 1$
- $x^1 = x$
- $1^x = 1$
- $2^{-x} = \dfrac{1}{2^x}$
- $\left(1\dfrac{1}{2}\right)^x = \left(\dfrac{3}{2}\right)^x = \dfrac{3_x}{2_x}$

Question — Powers

Work out the following, using your calculator as necessary.

(a) $(18.6)^{2.6}$

(b) $(18.6)^{-2.6}$

(c) $\sqrt[2.6]{18.6}$

(d) $(14.2)^4 \times (14.2)^{\frac{1}{4}}$

(e) $(14.2)^4 + (14.2)^{\frac{1}{4}}$

Answer

(a) $(18.6)^{2.6} = 1{,}998.6358$

(b) $(18.6)^{-2.6} = \left(\dfrac{1}{18.6}\right)^{2.6} = 0.0005$

(c) $\sqrt[2.6]{18.6} = 3.078$

(d) $(14.2)^4 \times (14.2)^{\frac{1}{4}} = (14.2)^{4.25} = 78{,}926.976$

(e) $(14.2)^4 + (14.2)^{\frac{1}{4}} = 40{,}658.6896 + 1.9412 = 40{,}660.6308$

6 Errors

If calculations are made using values that have been rounded, then the results of such calculations will be **approximate**. The maximum possible error can be calculated.

6.1 Errors from rounding

If calculations are made using values that have been rounded then the results of such calculations will only be **approximate**. However, provided that we are aware of the maximum errors that can occur, we can still draw conclusions from the results of the calculations.

Suppose that the population of a country is stated as 40m. It is quite likely that this figure has been rounded to the nearest million. We could therefore say that the country's population is 40m ± 500,000 where 40m is the **estimate** of the population and 500,000 is the **maximum absolute error**.

When two or more rounded or approximate numbers are added or subtracted the **maximum absolute error** in the result equals the sum of the individual maximum absolute errors. In general terms an estimate with a maximum absolute error can be expressed as a ± b.

6.2 Example: Errors

A chemical producer plans to sell 50,000 litres (to the nearest 1,000 litres) of a particular chemical at a price of $10 (to the nearest dollar) per litre.

The cost of materials used to produce the chemicals is expected to be $100,000 but depending on wastage levels this is subject to an error of ± 5%. Labour costs are estimated to be $300,000 ± 10%, depending on overtime working and pay negotiations.

Required

Calculate the maximum absolute error for revenue and costs of production.

Solution

	Estimate	Maximum absolute error
Quantity sold	50,000 litres	500 litres*
Price	$10	$0.50**
Materials	$100,000	$5,000
Labour	$300,000	$30,000

* This is because 41,500 litres would be rounded up to 42,000 litres but 41,499 litres would be rounded down to 41,000 litres.

** This is because $9.50 would be rounded up to $10 but $9.49 would be rounded down to $9.00.

(a) **Revenue** = quantity sold × price
= (50,000 ± 1%) × ($10 ± 5%)
= (50,000 × $10) ± (1% + 5%)
= $500,000 ± 6%
= $500,000 ± $30,000

∴ Approximate maximum absolute error = $30,000

1: BASIC MATHEMATICAL TECHNIQUES

(b) Costs of production = material + labour
   = ($100,000 ± $5,000) + ($300,000 ± $30,000)
   = ($100,000 + $300,000) ± ($5,000 + $30,000)
   = $400,000 ± $35,000
   = $400,000 ± 8.75 %

∴ Maximum absolute error = $35,000

Question — Maximum errors

The costs for component C are estimated to be as follows for the coming year.

Direct materials $5.00 ± 5%
Direct labour $3.00 ± 6%
Direct overheads $1.70 ± 7%

Required

(a) Calculate the maximum expected cost per unit.
(b) At a production level of 100,000 units, calculate the maximum absolute error in the total cost to the nearest $.

Answer

(a) Maximum expected costs:

Direct materials	5.00 + 5% =	5.25
Direct labour	3.00 + 6% =	3.18
Direct overheads	1.70 + 7% =	1.82
Maximum expected cost per unit		10.25

(b) Expected cost per unit = $(5.00 + 3.00 + 1.70) = $9.70

Maximum absolute error per unit = $(10.25 – 9.70) = $0.55

Maximum absolute error for 100,000 units = 100,000 × $0.55 = $55,000

7 Formulae and equations

7.1 Formulae

So far all our problems have been formulated entirely in terms of specific numbers. However, we also need to be able to use letters to represent numbers in formulae and equations.

> **FAST FORWARD**
>
> A formula enables us to calculate the value of one variable from the value(s) of one or more other variables.

7.1.1 Use of variables

The use of variables enables us to state general truths about mathematics and you will come across many formulae in your AIA studies.

For example:

- $x = x$
- $x^2 = x \times x$
- If $y = 0.5 \times x$, then $x = 2 \times y$

These will be true **whatever** values x and y have.

For example, let y = 0.5 × x

- If y = 3, x = 2 × y = 6
- If y = 7, x = 2 × y = 14
- If y = 1, x = 2 × y = 2, and so on for any other choice of a value for y.

We can use **variables** to build up useful **formulae**, we can then put in values for the variables, and get out a value for something we are interested in. It is usual when writing formulae to leave out multiplication signs between letters. Thus p × u – c can be written as pu – c. We will also write (for example) 2x instead of 2 × x.

7.1.2 Example: Variables

For a business, profit = revenue – costs. Since revenue = selling price × units sold, we can say that:

profit = (selling price × units sold) – costs.

'(Selling price × units sold) – costs' is a formula for profit.

Notice the use of brackets to help with the order of operations.

We can then use single letters to make the formula quicker to write.

Let p = profit
    s = selling price
    u = units sold
    c = cost

Then p = (s × u) – c.

If we are then told that in a particular month, s = $5, u = 30 and c = $118, we can find out the month's profit.

Profit = p = (s × u) – c = ($5 × 30) – $118
       = $150 – $118 = $32

7.1.3 Example: A more complicated formula

In your later AIA studies in Management Accounting 2, you will come across the learning curve formula, $Y = aX^b$ which shows how unit labour times tend to decrease at a constant rate as production increases.

Y = cumulative average time taken per unit

a = time taken for the first unit

X = total number of units

b = index of learning

What is the average time taken per unit if the time taken for the first unit is 10 minutes, the total number of units is 8 and the index of learning is – 0.32?

Solution

$Y = aX^b$

a = 10 minutes

X = 8

b = – 0.32

$Y = 10 \times 8^{-0.32} = 5.14$

On your calculator, press 10 × 8 X■ (–) 0.32 =

7.2 Equations

In the above example, su – c was a formula for profit. If we write p = su – c, we have written an **equation**. It says that one thing (profit, p) is **equal** to another (su – c).

7.2.1 'Solving the equation'

Sometimes, we are given an equation with numbers filled in for all but one of the variables. The problem is then to find the number which should be filled in for the last variable. This is called **solving the equation**.

(a) Returning to p = su – c, we could be told that for a particular month s = $4, u = 60 and c = $208. We would then have the **equation** p = ($4 × 60) – $208. We can solve this easily by working out ($4 × 60) – $208 = $240 – $208 = $32. Thus p = $32.

(b) On the other hand, we might have been told that in a month when profits were $172, 50 units were sold and the selling price was $7. The thing we have not been told is the month's costs, c. We can work out c by writing out the equation:

$172 = ($7 × 50) – c

$172 = $350 – c

(c) We need c to be such that when it is taken away from $350 we have $172 left. With a bit of trial and error, we can get to c = $178.

7.2.2 The rule for solving equations

FAST FORWARD

The **general rule for solving equations** is that you must always do the same thing to both sides of the equal sign so the 'scales' stay balanced.

(a) To solve an equation, we need to get it into the following form.

Unknown variable = something with just numbers in it, which we can work out.

We therefore want to get the unknown variable on one side of the = sign, and everything else on the other side.

(b) **The rule is that you must always do the same thing to both sides of the equal sign so the 'scales' stay balanced. The two sides are equal, and they will stay equal so long as you treat them in the same way.**

$172 + c = $350

Take $172 from both sides: $172 + c –$172 = $350 – $172

c = $350 – $172

c = $178

PART A   DATA COLLECTION AND ANALYSIS

7.2.3 Example: Solving the equation

For example, you can do any of the following: add 37 to both sides; subtract 3x from both sides; multiply both sides by –4.329; divide both sides by (x + 2); take the reciprocal of both sides; square both sides; take the cube root of both sides.

We can do any of these things to an equation either before or after filling in numbers for the variables for which we have values.

(a) If
$172 = $350 – c   (as in Paragraph 7.2.1) we can then get
$172 + c = $350   (add c to each side)
c = $350 – $172   (subtract $172 from each side)
c = $178   (work out the right hand side)

(b)
450 = 3x + 72   (initial equation: x unknown)
450 – 72 = 3x   (subtract 72 from each side)
$\frac{450 - 72}{3} = x$ (divide each side by 3)
126 = x   (work out the left hand side)

(c)
3y + 2 = 5y – 7   (initial equation: y unknown)
3y + 9 = 5y   (add 7 to each side)
9 = 2y   (subtract 3y from each side)
4.5 = y   (divide each side by 2)

(d)
$\frac{\sqrt{3x^2 + x}}{2\sqrt{x}} = 7$ (initial equation: x unknown)

$\frac{3x^2 + x}{4x} = 49$ (square each side)

$\frac{(3x + 1)}{4} = 49$ (cancel x in the numerator and the denominator of the left hand side: this does not affect the value of the left hand side, so we do not need to change the right hand side)

3x + 1 = 196   (multiply each side by 4)
3x = 195   (subtract 1 from each side)
x = 65   (divide each side by 3)

(e) Our example in Paragraph 7.2 was p = su – c. We could change this, so as to give a formula for s.
s = su – c
p + c = su   (add c to each side)
$\frac{p + c}{u} = s$ (divide each side by u)
$s = \frac{p + c}{u}$ (swap the sides for ease of reading)

Given values for p, c and u we can now find s. We have rearranged the equation to give s in terms of p, c and u.

(f) Given that $y = \sqrt{3x + 7}$, we can get an equation giving x in terms of y.
$y = \sqrt{3x + 7}$
$y^2 = 3x + 7$ (square each side)
$y^2 - 7 = 3x$ (subtract 7 from each side)
$x = \frac{y^2 - 7}{3}$ (divide each side by 3, and swap the sides for ease of reading)

7.2.4 Solving the equation and brackets

In equations, you may come across expressions like $3(x + 4y - 2)$ (that is, $3 \times (x + 4y - 2)$). These can be re-written in separate bits without the brackets, simply by multiplying the number outside the brackets by each item inside them. Thus $3(x + 4y - 2) = 3x + 12y - 6$.

Question — Solving the equation (1)

(a) If $47x + 256 = 52x$, then $x =$ ☐

(b) If $4\sqrt{x} + 32 = 40.6718$, then $x =$ ☐

(c) If $\dfrac{1}{3x+4} = \dfrac{5}{2.7x-2}$, then $x =$ ☐

Answer

(a) $\boxed{x = 51.2}$

$$
\begin{aligned}
47x + 256 &= 52x \\
256 &= 5x \quad &&\text{(subtract } 47x \text{ from each side)} \\
51.2 &= x \quad &&\text{(divide each side by 5)}
\end{aligned}
$$

(b) $\boxed{x = 4.7}$

$$
\begin{aligned}
4\sqrt{x} + 32 &= 40.6718 \\
4\sqrt{x} &= 8.6718 \quad &&\text{(subtract 32 from each side)} \\
\sqrt{x} &= 2.16795 \quad &&\text{(divide each side by 4)} \\
x &= 4.7 \quad &&\text{(square each side)}
\end{aligned}
$$

(c) $\boxed{x = -1.789}$

$$
\begin{aligned}
\frac{1}{3x+4} &= \frac{5}{2.7x-2} \\
3x + 4 &= \frac{2.7x-2}{5} \quad &&\text{(take the reciprocal of each side)} \\
15x + 20 &= 2.7x - 2 \quad &&\text{(multiply each side by 5)} \\
12.3x &= -22 \quad &&\text{(subtract 20 and subtract } 2.7x \text{ from each side)} \\
x &= -1.789 \quad &&\text{(divide each side by 12.3)}
\end{aligned}
$$

Question — Solving the equation (2)

(a) Rearrange $x = (3y - 20)^2$ to get an expression for y in terms of x.
(b) Rearrange $2(y - 4) - 4(x^2 + 3) = 0$ to get an expression for x in terms of y.

PART A DATA COLLECTION AND ANALYSIS

Answer

(a) $\quad x = (3y - 20)^2$

$\quad\quad \sqrt{x} = 3y - 20 \quad$ (take the square root of each side)

$\quad\quad 20 + \sqrt{x} = 3y \quad$ (add 20 to each side)

$\quad\quad y = \dfrac{20 + \sqrt{x}}{3} \quad$ (divide each side by 3, and swap the sides for ease of reading)

(b) $\quad 2(y - 4) - 4(x^2 + 3) = 0$

$\quad\quad 2(y - 4) = 4(x^2 + 3) \quad$ (add $4(x^2 + 3)$ to each side)

$\quad\quad 0.5(y - 4) = x^2 + 3 \quad$ (divide each side by 4)

$\quad\quad 0.5(y - 4) - 3 = x^2 \quad$ (subtract 3 from each side)

$\quad\quad x = \sqrt{0.5(y - 4) - 3} \quad$ (take the square root of each side, and swap the sides for ease of reading)

$\quad\quad x = \sqrt{0.5y - 5}$

8 Manipulating inequalities

FAST FORWARD

An inequality is a statement that shows the relationship between two (or more) expressions with one of the following signs: >, ≥, <, ≤. We can solve inequalities in the same way that we can solve equations.

8.1 Inequality symbols

Equations are called inequalities when the '=' sign is replaced by one of the following:

(a) > means 'greater than'
(b) ≥ means 'is greater than or equal to'
(c) < means 'is less than'
(d) ≤ means 'is less than or equal to'+

8.2 Using inequalities

Inequalities are used in a short-term decision making technique called linear programming which you will come across in your managerial studies. It involves using inequalities to represent situations where resources are limited.

8.2.1 Example: Using inequalities 1

If a product needs 3 kg of material and 700 kg is available, express this as an inequality

Solution

If the number of units of the product = X

$3X \leq 700$

8.2.2 Example: Using inequalities 2

Product Z needs 3 minutes of machining time and product Y needs 2 minutes of machining time. There are 10 hours of machining time available. Express this as an inequality.

Solution

10 hours of machining time = 600 minutes

The total machining time must be less than or equal to 600 minutes.

$3Z + 2Y \leq 600$

where Z = no of units of product Z
Y = no of units of product Y

8.3 Solving inequalities

We can solve inequalities in the same way we can solve equations. For example, the inequality $7x - 2 > 0$ can be solved by getting x on its own, but the answer will be a range of values rather than a specific number.

$7x - 2 > 0$
$\quad 7x > 2 \quad$ (add 2 to both sides)
$\quad x > \frac{2}{7} \quad$ (divide both sides by 7)

8.4 Rules for manipulating inequalities

(i) Adding or subtracting the same quantity from both sides of an inequality leaves the inequality symbol unchanged

(ii) Multiplying or dividing both sides by a **positive** number leaves the inequality symbol unchanged

(iii) Multiplying or dividing both sides by a **negative** number **reverses** the inequality so < changes to >

8.5 Example: Solving inequalities

Find the range of values of x satisfying $x - 5 < 2x + 7$

$x - 5 < 2x + 7$
$\quad x < 2x + 12 \quad$ (add 5 to both sides)
$\quad -x < 12 \quad$ (subtract 2x from both sides)
$\quad x > -12 \quad$ (multiply both sides by -1 and so reverse the inequality)

Question — Solving inequalities

Solve the following inequalities

(a) $2x > 11$
(b) $x + 3 > 15$
(c) $-3x < 7$
(d) $7x + 11 > 2x + 5$
(e) $2(x + 3) < x + 1$

PART A DATA COLLECTION AND ANALYSIS

Answer

(a) $2x > 11$
   $x > \dfrac{11}{2}$ (divide both sides by 2)
   $x > 5.5$

(b) $x + 3 > 15$
   $x > 12$ (subtract 3 from both sides)

(c) $-3x < 7$
   $-x < \dfrac{7}{3}$ (divide both sides by 3)
   $x > -\dfrac{7}{3}$ (multiply both sides by -1 and so reverse the inequality)

(d) $7x + 11 > 2x + 5$
   $5x > -6$ (subtract 2x and 11 from both sides)
   $x > -\dfrac{6}{5}$ (divide both sides by 5)

(e) $2(x + 3) < x + 1$
   $2x + 6 < x + 1$ (multiply out the brackets)
   $x < -5$ (subtract x and 6 from both sides)

9 Linear equations

FAST FORWARD

A **linear equation** has the general form $y = a + bx$

where y is the **dependent variable**, depending for its value on the value of x
       x is the **independent variable** whose value helps to determine the corresponding value of y
       a is a **constant**, that is, a fixed amount
       b is also a **constant**, being the **coefficient** of x (that is, the number by which the value of x should be multiplied to derive the value of y)

9.1 Example: Establishing basic linear equations

(a) Let us establish some basic linear equations. Suppose that it takes Joe Bloggs 15 minutes to walk one mile. How long does it take Joe to walk two miles? Obviously it takes him 30 minutes. How did you calculate the time? You probably thought that if the distance is doubled then the time must be doubled. How do you explain (in words) the relationships between the distance walked and the time taken? One explanation would be that every mile walked takes 15 minutes. Now let us try to explain the relationship with an equation.

(b) First you must decide which is the **dependent variable** and which is the **independent variable**. In other words, does the time taken depend on the number of miles walked or does the number of miles walked depend on the time it takes to walk a mile? Obviously the time depends on the distance. We can therefore let y be the dependent variable (time taken in minutes) and x be the independent variable (distance walked in miles).

(c) We now need to determine the **constants a** and **b**. There is no fixed amount so a = 0. To ascertain b, we need to establish the number of times by which the value of x should be multiplied to derive the value of y. Obviously y = 15x where y is in minutes. If y were in hours then y = x/4.

9.2 Example: Deriving a linear equation

A salesman's weekly wage is made up of a basic weekly wage of $100 and commission of $5 for every item he sells. Derive an equation which describes this scenario.

Solution

x = number of items sold and y = weekly wage

a = $100 (fixed weekly wage paid however many items he sells) and b = $5 (variable element of wage, depends on how many items he sells)

∴ y = 5x + 100

Note. The letters used in an equation do not have to be x and y. It may be sensible to use other letters, for example we could use p and q if we are describing the relationship between the price of an item and the quantity demanded.

10 Linear equations and graphs

Exam focus point

The examiner is especially keen on you showing your graphing skills. In nearly every exam there is at least one part of a question that invites you to draw a graph.

FAST FORWARD

The **graph of a linear equation is a straight line**. The intercept of the line on the y axis is a in:

y = a + bx

where a = the intercept of the line on the y axis
b = the slope of the line

One of the clearest ways of presenting the relationship between two variables is by plotting a **linear equation** as a **straight line** on a graph.

10.1 The rules for drawing graphs

A graph has a **horizontal axis**, the **x axis** and a **vertical axis**, the **y axis**. The x axis is used to represent the **independent variable** and the y axis is used to represent the **dependent variable**. If calendar time is one variable, it is always treated as the independent variable. When time is represented on the x axis of a graph, we have the graph of a **time series**.

(a) If the data to be plotted are derived from calculations, rather than given in the question, make sure that there is a neat table in your workings.

(b) The scales on each axis should be selected so as to use as much of the graph paper as possible. Do not cramp a graph into one corner.

(c) In some cases it is best not to start a scale at zero so as to avoid having a large area of wasted paper. This is perfectly acceptable as long as the scale adopted is clearly shown on the axis. One way of avoiding confusion is to break the axis concerned, as shown below:

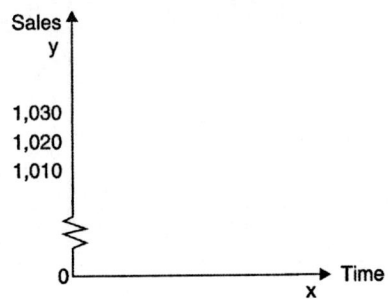

PART A   DATA COLLECTION AND ANALYSIS

(d) The scales on the x axis and the y axis should be marked. For example, if the y axis relates to amounts of money, the axis should be marked at every $1, or $100 or $1,000 interval or at whatever other interval is appropriate. The axes must be marked with values to give the reader an idea of how big the values on the graph are.

(e) A graph should not be overcrowded with too many lines. Graphs should always give a clear, neat impression.

(f) A graph must always be given a **title**, and where appropriate, a reference should be made to the **source** of data.

10.2 Example: Drawing graphs

Plot the graph for $y = 4x + 5$.

Consider the range of values from $x = 0$ to $x = 10$.

Solution

The first step is to draw up a table for the equation. Although the problem mentions $x = 0$ to $x = 10$, it is not necessary to calculate values of y for $x = 1, 2, 3$ etc. A graph of a linear equation can actually be drawn from just two (x, y) values but it is always best to calculate a number of values in case you make an arithmetical error. We have calculated five values, but three would be enough in your exam.

x	y
0	5
2	13
4	21
6	29
8	37
10	45

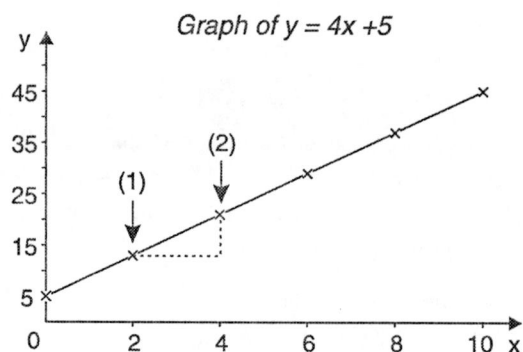

Graph of y = 4x +5

10.3 The intercept and the gradient

The graph of a linear equation is determined by two things:

- The gradient (or slope) of the straight line
- The point at which the straight line crosses the y axis

Key terms

- The **intercept** is the point at which a straight line crosses the y-axis.
- The **gradient** of the graph of a linear equation is $\frac{\text{change in y}}{\text{change in x}} = (y_2 - y_1)/(x_2 - x_1)$ where (x_1, y_1) and (x_2, y_2) are two points on the straight line.

10.3.1 The intercept

The intercept of y = 4x + 5 is where y = 5. It is no coincidence that the intercept is the same as the constant represented by a in the general form of the equation y = a + bx. a is the value y takes when x = 0, in other words a constant.

10.3.2 The gradient

If we take two points on the line (see graph in 10.2):

(1)   x = 2, y = 13
(2)   x = 4, y = 21

The gradient of $y = 4x + 5 = \dfrac{\text{change in y}}{\text{change in x}} = \dfrac{(21-13)}{(4-2)} = \dfrac{8}{2} = 4$

Notice that the gradient is also given by the number multiplied by x in the equation (b in the general form of the equation).

Question — Gradient

If y = 10 – x, the gradient = ☐

Answer

The gradient = −1

If y = 10 – x, then a = 10 and b = −1 (−1 × x = −x).

Therefore gradient = −1

10.3.3 Positive and negative gradients

Note that the gradient of y = 4x + 5 is positive whereas the gradient of y = 10 − x is negative.

- A positive gradient slopes upwards from left to right
- A negative gradient slopes downwards from left to right
- The greater the value of the gradient, the steeper the slope

Question — Intercept and gradient

What is the intercept and gradient of the graph of 4y = 16x − 12?

	Intercept	Gradient
A	−3	+4
B	−4	+3
C	+3	−4
D	+4	−3

Answer

4y = 16x − 12

Equation must be in the form y = a + bx

PART A DATA COLLECTION AND ANALYSIS

y = 4x – 3 (divide both sides by 4)

y = –3 + 4x (rearrange the RHS)

Intercept = a = –3

Gradient = b = 4

Therefore the correct answer is A.

If you selected option D, you have obviously confused the intercept and the gradient. Remember that with an equation in the form y = a + bx, a = intercept (ie where the line of the graph crosses the y axis) and b = the slope or gradient of the line.

Question — Linear graphs

A company manufactures a product. The total fixed costs are $75 and the variable cost per unit is $5.

Required

(a) Find an expression for total costs (c) in terms of q, the quantity produced.
(b) Use your answer to (a) to determine the total costs if 100 units are produced.
(c) Prepare a graph of the expression for total costs.
(d) Use your graph to determine the total cost if 75 units are produced.

Answer

(a) Let C = total costs
       C = total variable costs + total fixed costs
       C = 5q + 75

(b) If q = 100, C = (5 × 100) + 75 = $575

(c) If q = 0,   C = $75
    If q = 100, C = $575

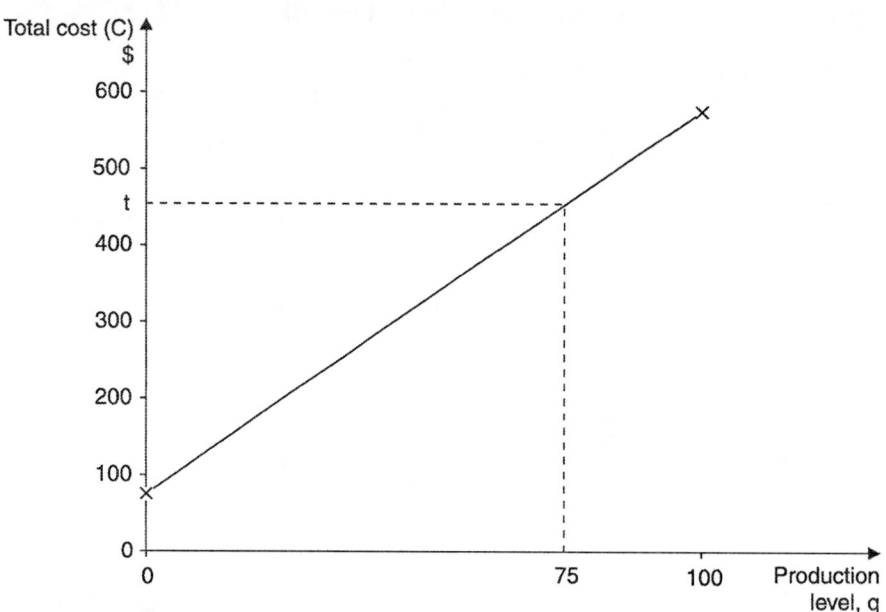

(d) From graph above, if q = 75, C = $450

11 Simultaneous equations

FAST FORWARD

Simultaneous equations are two or more equations which are satisfied by the same variable values. They can be solved graphically or algebraically.

11.1 Example: Simultaneous equations

The following two linear equations both involve the unknown values x and y. There are as many equations as there are unknowns and so we can find the values of x and y.

$y = 3x + 16$
$2y = x + 72$

11.1.1 Solution: Graphical approach

One way of finding a solution is by a **graph**. If both equations are satisfied together, the values of x and y must be those where the straight line graphs of the two equations **intersect**.

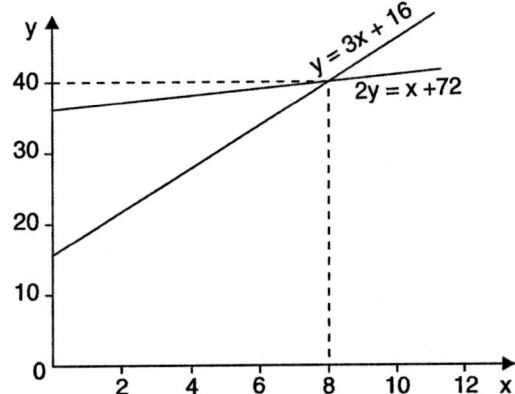

Since both equations are satisfied, the values of x and y must lie on both the lines. Since this happens only once, at the intersection of the lines, the value of x must be 8, and of y 40.

11.1.2 Solution: Algebraic approach

A more common method of solving simultaneous equations is by **algebra**.

(a) Returning to the original equations, we have:

$y = 3x + 16$ (1)
$2y = x + 72$ (2)

(b) Rearranging these, we have:

$y - 3x = 16$ (3)
$2y - x = 72$ (4)

(c) If we now multiply equation (4) by 3, so that the coefficient for x becomes the same as in equation (3) we get:

$6y - 3x = 216$ (5)
$y - 3x = 16$ (3)

(d) Subtracting (3) from (5) we get:

$5y = 200$
$y = 40$

(e) Substituting 40 for y in any equation, we can derive a value for x. Thus substituting in equation (4) we get:

$2(40) - x = 72$
$80 - 72 = x$
$8 = x$

(f) The solution is y = 40, x = 8.

Question — Simultaneous equations

Solve the following simultaneous equations using algebra.

$5x + 2y = 34$

$x + 3y = 25$

Answer

$5x + 2y = 34$		(1)
$x + 3y = 25$		(2)

Multiply (2) × 5:

$5x + 15y = 125$ (3)

Subtract (1) from (3):

$13y = 91$
$y = 7$

Substitute into (2):

$x + 21 = 25$
$x = 25 - 21$
$x = 4$

The solution is x = 4, y = 7.

12 Non-linear equations

So far we have looked at equations in which the highest power of the unknown variable(s) is one (that is, the equation contains x, y but not x^2, y^3 and so on). We are now going to turn our attention to **non-linear equations**.

> **FAST FORWARD**
>
> In **non-linear equations**, one variable varies with the nth power of another, where n > 1. The graph of a non-linear equation is **not** a straight line.

12.1 Examples: Non-linear equations

(a) $y = x^2$; $y = 3x^3 + 2$; $2y = 5x^4 - 6$; $y = -x^{12} + 3$

(b) It is common for a non-linear equation to include a number of terms, all to different powers. Here are some examples:

$y = x^2 + 6x + 10$ $y = -12x^9 + 3x^6 + 6x^3 + 3x^2 - 1$

$2y = 3x^3 - 4x^2 - 8x + 10$ $3y = 22x^8 + 7x^7 + 3x^4 - 12$

12.2 Graphing non-linear equations

The graph of a **linear equation**, as we saw earlier, is a **straight line**. The graph of a **non-linear equation**, on the other hand, **is not a straight line**. Let us consider an example.

12.2.1 Example: Graphing non-linear equations

Graph the equation $y = -2x^3 + x^2 - 2x + 10$.

Solution

The graph of this equation can be plotted in the same way as the graph of a linear equation is plotted. Take a selection of values of x, calculate the corresponding values of y, plot the pairs of values and join the points together. The joining must be done using as smooth a curve as possible.

x	-3	-2	-1	0	1	2	3
$-2x$	6	4	2	0	-2	-4	-6
x^2	9	4	1	0	1	4	9
$-2x^3$	54	16	2	0	-2	-16	-54
10	10	10	10	10	10	10	10
y	79	34	15	10	7	-6	-41

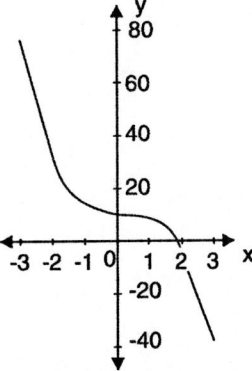

12.3 Quadratic equations

FAST FORWARD

Quadratic equations are a type of **non-linear equation** in which one variable varies with the square (or second power) of the other variable. They can be expressed in the form
$y = ax^2 + bx + c$.

A **quadratic equation** may include both a term involving the square and also a term involving the **first power** of a variable. Here are some examples.

$y = x^2$ $y = x^2 + 6x + 10$ $2y = 3x^2 - 4x - 8$ $y = 5x^2 + 7$

In the equation $y = 3x^2 + 2x - 6$, a = 3, b = 2, c = -6.

12.3.1 Graphing a quadratic equation

The graph of a quadratic equation can be plotted using the same method as that illustrated in Paragraph 11.2.1.

12.3.2 Example: Graphing a quadratic equation

Graph the equation $y = -2x^2 + x - 3$

Solution

x	−3	−2	−1	0	1	2	3
−2x²	−18	−8	−2	0	−2	−8	−18
−3	−3	−3	−3	−3	−3	−3	−3
y	−24	−13	−6	−3	−4	−9	−18

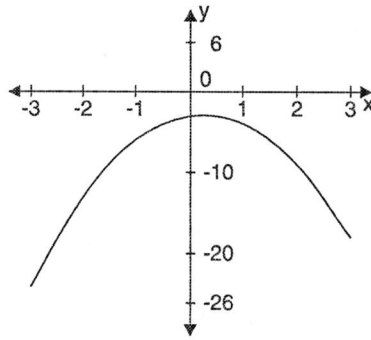

12.3.3 Parabolas

> **FAST FORWARD**
>
> The graphs of quadratic equations are **parabolas**, the sign of 'a' in the general form of the quadratic equation ($y = ax^2 + bx + c$) determining the way up the curve appears.

(a) The constant term 'c' determines the value of y at the point where the curve crosses the y axis (the intercept). In the graph above, c = −3 and the curve crosses the y axis at y = −3.

(b) The sign of 'a' determines the way up the curve appears.

- If 'a' is positive, the curve is shaped like a ditch
- If 'a' is negative, as in Paragraph 6.3.2, the curve is shaped like a bell

A ditch-shaped curve is said to have a **minimum point** whereas a bell-shaped curve is said to have a **maximum point**.

(c) The graph enables us to find the values of x when y = 0 (if there are any). In other words the graph allows us to solve the quadratic equation $0 = ax^2 + bx + c$. For the curve in Paragraph 6.3.2 we see that there are no such values (that is, $0 = -2x^2 + x - 3$ cannot be solved).

12.4 Solving quadratic equations

The graphical method is not, in practice, the most efficient way to determine the solution of a quadratic equation. Many quadratic equations have two values of x (called **'solutions for x'** or **'roots of the equation'**) which satisfy the equation for any particular value of y.

> **FAST FORWARD**
>
> Quadratic equations can be solved by the formula:
>
> $$x = \frac{-b \pm \sqrt{(b^2 - 4ac)}}{2a}$$ when $ax^2 + bx + c = 0$

12.4.1 Example: Quadratic equations

Solve $x^2 + x - 2 = 0$.

Solution

For the equation $x^2 + x - 2 = 0$

$a = 1$
$b = 1$
$c = -2$

We can insert these values into the quadratic equation formula.

$$x = \frac{-b \pm \sqrt{(b^2 - 4ac)}}{2a}$$

$$x = \frac{-1 \pm \sqrt{(1^2 - (4 \times 1 \times (-2)))}}{2 \times 1} = \frac{-1 \pm \sqrt{(1+8)}}{2} = \frac{-1 \pm 3}{2}$$

$\therefore \quad x = \frac{-4}{2}$ or $\frac{2}{2}$ ie $x = -2$ or $x = 1$

12.5 Quadratic equations with a single value for x

Sometimes, $b^2 - 4ac = 0$, and so there is only one solution to the quadratic equation. Let us solve $x^2 + 2x + 1 = 0$ using the formula above where $a = 1$, $b = 2$ and $c = 1$.

$$x = \frac{-2 \pm \sqrt{(2^2 - (4 \times 1 \times 1))}}{2} = \frac{-2 \pm 0}{2} = -1$$

This quadratic equation can only be solved by one value of x.

Question — Non-linear graphs

A company manufactures a product, the total cost function for the product being given by $C = 25q - q^2$, where q is the quantity produced and C is in $.

Required

(a) Calculate the total costs if 15 units are produced.
(b) Draw a graph of the total cost function and use it to calculate the total cost if 23 units are produced.

Answer

(a) $C = 25q - q^2$

If $q = 15$, $C = (25 \times 15) - 15^2 = 375 - 225 = \$150$

(b)

q	C
0	0
5.0	100.00
10.0	150.00
12.5	156.25
15.0	150.00
20.0	100.00
25.0	0

PART A DATA COLLECTION AND ANALYSIS

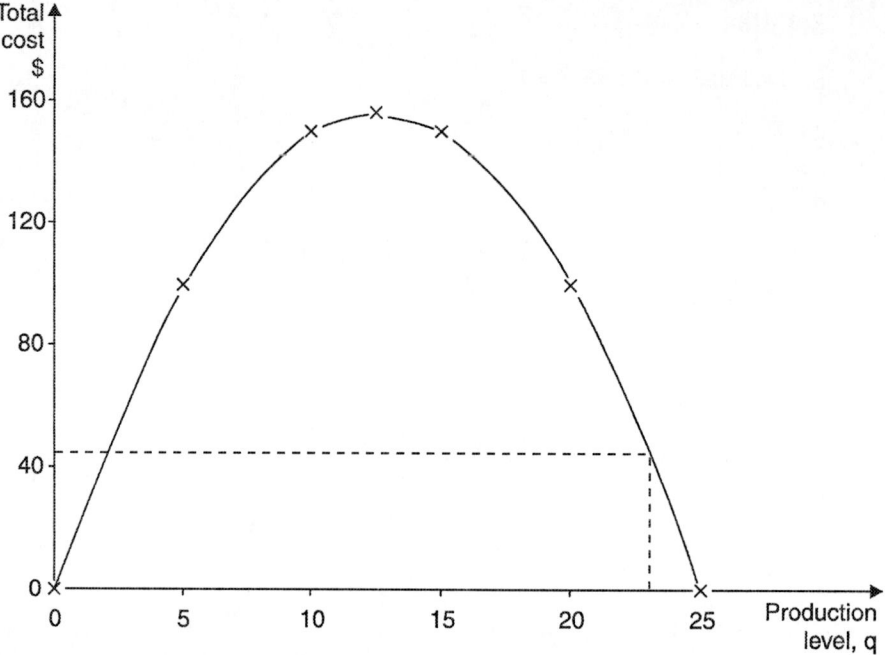

From the graph, if 23 units are produced the total cost is approximately $45.

Chapter Roundup

- An **integer** is a whole number and can be either positive or negative.
- **Fractions** and **decimals** are ways of showing parts of a whole.
- The **negative number rules** are as follows:

  $-p + q = q - p$
  $q - (-p) = q + p$
  $-p \times -q = pq$ and $\dfrac{-p}{-q} = \dfrac{p}{q}$
  $-p \times q = -pq$ and $\dfrac{-p}{q} = -\dfrac{p}{q}$

- Scientific calculators can make calculations quicker and easier.
- **Brackets** indicate a priority or an order in which calculations should be made.
- **Percentages** are used to indicate the **relative size** or **proportion** of items, rather than their **absolute** size.
- To turn a percentage into a fraction or decimal you **divide by 100%**. To turn a fraction or decimal back into a percentage you **multiply by 100%**.
- A **percentage increase** or **reduction** is calculated as (change ÷ original value) × 100%.
- A **proportion** means writing a percentage as a proportion of 1 (that is, as a decimal). 100% can be thought of as the whole, or 1. 50% is half of that, or 0.5.
- **Ratios** show relative shares of a whole.
- The **nth root** of a number is a value which, when multiplied by itself (n–1) times, equals the original number. **Powers** work the other way round.
- The **main rules** to apply when dealing with powers and roots are as follows:

  - $2^x \times 2^y = 2^{x+y}$
  - $2^x \div 2^y = 2^{x-y}$
  - $(2^x)^y = 2^{x \times y} = 2^{xy}$
  - $x^0 = 1$
  - $x^1 = x$
  - $1^x = 1$
  - $2^{-x} = \dfrac{1}{2^x}$
  - $\left(1\dfrac{1}{2}\right)^x = \left(\dfrac{3}{2}\right)^x = \dfrac{3^x}{2^x}$

- If calculations are made using values that have been rounded, then the results of such calculations will be **approximate**. The maximum possible error can be calculated.
- A formula enables us to calculate the value of one variable from the value(s) of one or more other variables.
- The **general rule for solving equations** is that you must always do the same thing to both sides of the equal sign so the scales stay balanced.
- An inequality is a statement that shows the relationship between two (or more) expressions with one of the following signs: >, ≥, <, ≤. We can solve inequalities in the same way that we can solve equations.

PART A DATA COLLECTION AND ANALYSIS

- A **linear equation** has the general form **y = a + bx**, where

  y   is the **dependent variable**, depending for its value on the value of x

  x   is the **independent variable** whose value helps to determine the corresponding value of y

  a   is a **constant**, that is, a fixed amount

  b   is also a **constant**, being the **coefficient** of x (that is, the number by which the value of x should be multiplied to derive the value of y)

- The **graph of a linear equation is a straight** line, where y = a + bx. The intercept of the line on the y axis = a and the slope of the line = b.

- **Simultaneous equations** are two or more equations which are satisfied by the same variable values. They can be solved graphically or algebraically.

- In **non-linear equations**, one variable varies with the nth power of another, where n > 1. The graph of a non-linear equation is **not** a straight line.

- **Quadratic equations** are a type of **non-linear equation** in which one variable varies with the square (or second power) of the other variable. They can be expressed in the form $y = ax^2 + bx + c$.

- The graphs of quadratic equations are **parabolas**, the sign of 'a' in the general form of the quadratic equation ($y = ax^2 + bx + c$) determining the way up the curve appears.

- **Quadratic equations** can be solved by the formula

  $$x = \frac{-b \pm \sqrt{(b^2 - 4ac)}}{2a} \text{ when } ax^2 + bx + c = 0$$

Quick Quiz

1. $3\frac{3}{4}$ is an:

   (a) Integer
   (b) Fraction
   (c) Decimal

2. 1004.002955 to nine significant figures is ☐

3. The product of a negative number and a negative number is

   Positive ☐

   Negative ☐

4. What is the value of $\dfrac{22.034 \times (-26.4)}{-13.051 - 2.06} + \left(\dfrac{33.5 \times (-2)}{66}\right)$

   To 2 decimal places? ☐

5. Sales for a business two years ago were $30 million. Last year sales were 8% higher than the year before and this year, sales were 6% higher than last year. What are this year's sales? (correct to 3 significant figures) ☐

6. 3^{-1} can also be written as

   (a) 3^{-1}
   (b) 3^{1}
   (c) $\dfrac{1}{3}$
   (d) -1^{3}

7. The cost of materials for a component is $20.00 to the nearest $1. What is the maximum absolute error in the cost?

   ☐ c

8. The expression $\dfrac{(X^3)^2}{X^5}$ equals.

   (a) X
   (b) 1
   (c) 0
   (d) X^2

9. An employee does not pay tax on the first $4,000 of earnings and then 25% tax on the rest of earnings. If he wants to have $20,000 net of tax earnings, what gross earnings (to the nearest $) does he need?

   $ ☐

10. A linear equation has the general form y = a + bx where

    y ⎤   ⎡ independent variable
    x ⎥   ?   ⎢ constant (fixed amount)
    b ⎥   ⎢ constant (coefficient of x)
    a ⎦   ⎣ dependent variable

PART A DATA COLLECTION AND ANALYSIS

11 The horizontal axis on a graph is known as the y axis.

　　True ☐
　　False ☐

　　　　　　　　　　　　　　　　　　　　　　　　　　　　　　True　False

12 (a) A positive gradient slopes upwards from right to left　☐　☐
　　(b) A negative gradient slopes downwards from left to right　☐　☐
　　(c) The greater the value of the gradient, the steeper the slope　☐　☐

13 Find the co-ordinates of the intersection point of the two lines $y = 6x - 7$ and $y = -3x - 4$

　　(x, y) = (☐ , ☐)

14 Consider the equation $y = -4x^2 + 3x - 2$

　　(a) The graph of the equation is shaped like a **ditch/bell**
　　(b) The graph of the equation has a **minimum/maximum** point
　　(c) The point at which the curve crosses the y axis is ……………..

15 A formula used in financial mathematics is $s = x(1+r)^n$

　　Rearrange the formula to make r the subject.

　　Which of the following is correct?

　　(a) $r = \dfrac{s}{x} + 1$

　　(b) $r = n\sqrt{\dfrac{x}{s}} - 1$

　　(c) $r = \sqrt[n]{\dfrac{s}{x}} - 1$

　　(d) $r = \dfrac{s-1}{x^n}$

16 If $x = 300$, $r = 0.06$ and $n = 5$, using the formula $s = x(1+r)^n$, what is the value of s? (to 2 decimal places)

　　☐

17 If $1{,}200 = 4x^2 + 20x$, then the two values of x that satisfy this equation are:

　　☐　☐

18 Solve this inequality

　　$3(x + 2) < x + 4$

　　(a) $x < -2$
　　(b) $x < -1$
　　(c) $x < 2$
　　(d) $x > -1$

Answers to Quick Quiz

1. (b) Fraction

2. 1004.00296

3. Positive

4. 37.48

5. 34.3

Sales 2 years ago	=	$30m
Sales 1 year ago	=	$30m + 8%
	=	$30m × 1.08
	=	$32.4m
Sales this year	=	$32.4 + 6%
	=	$32.4 × 1/06
	=	34.344
	=	34.3 (3 sf)

6. (c) = $\frac{1}{3}$

7. 50c

8. (a) $\frac{(X^2)^3}{X^5} = \frac{X^6}{X^5} = X$

9. $ ☐25,333☐

Taxable part of earnings	=	20,000 – 4,000
	=	$16,000
Taxable earnings	=	$\frac{16,000}{(1-0.25)}$
	=	$21,333
Gross earnings	=	$21,333 + $4,000
	=	$25,333

10. y = dependent variable
    x = independent variable
    b = constant (coefficient of x)
    a = constant (fixed amount)

11. False

12. (a) False
    (b) True
    (c) True

13. y = 6x – 7   (1)
    y = –3x – 4   (2)

    Multiply (2) by 2

    2y = –6x – 8   (3)

    Add (1) + (3)

    3y = –15
    y = –5

PART A DATA COLLECTION AND ANALYSIS

Substitute into (2)

$-5 = -3x - 4$

$-1 = -3x$

$1 = 3x$

$x = 1/3$

The co-ordinates of the intersection point are therefore (1/3, −5)

14 (a) bell
   (b) maximum point
   (c) −2

15 (c) $\dfrac{S}{x} = (1 + r)^n$

$\sqrt[n]{\dfrac{S}{x}} = 1 + r$

$r = \sqrt[n]{\dfrac{S}{x}} - 1$

16 401.47

$S = x(1 + r)^n$

$= 300 \times (1 + 0.06)^5$

$= 401.47$

17 $1{,}200 = 4x^2 + 20x$

$4x^2 + 20x - 1{,}200 = 0$

$x = \dfrac{-b \pm \sqrt{b^2 - 4ac}}{2a}$

$a = 4, b = 20, c = -1{,}200$

$x = \dfrac{-20 \pm \sqrt{20^2 - (4 \times 4 \times -1{,}200)}}{2 \times 4}$

$= \dfrac{-20 \pm \sqrt{19{,}600}}{8}$

$= \dfrac{-20 \pm 140}{8}$

$= 15 \text{ or } -20$

18 (b) $3(x + 2) < x + 4$

$3x + 6 < x + 4$

$2x + 6 < 4$

$2x < -2$

$x < -1$

End of Chapter Question

There is no end of chapter question for this first introductory chapter as it is not directly examined. Even if you have studied this level of maths before, ensure that you are happy with the contents of this chapter before moving on.

PART A DATA COLLECTION AND ANALYSIS

Statistical sources

Topic list	Syllabus reference
1 Data and information	6.1
2 Characteristics of good information	–
3 Data types	6.1
4 Sampling	6.1

Introduction

The words 'quantitative methods' often strike terror into the hearts of students. They conjure up images of complicated mathematical formulae, scientific analysis of reams of computer output and the drawing of strange graphs and diagrams. Such images are wrong. Quantitative methods simply involves:

- **Collecting data**
- **Presenting the data in a useful form**
- **Inspecting the data**

A study of the subject will demonstrate that quantitative methods is nothing to be afraid of and that a knowledge of it is extremely advantageous in your working environment.

We will start our study of quantitative methods by looking at **data collection**. In Chapter 3 we will consider how to **present data** once they have been collected.

PART A   DATA COLLECTION AND ANALYSIS

Exam focus point

The contents of this chapter were examined a couple of times as parts of questions. These are reproduced as the Chapter Question at the end of the Chapter. They are an example of 'learn and churn' questions. Our advice is to learn, churn and pass!

1 Data and information

Data are the raw materials for data processing. **Information** is data that has been processed.

1.1 Examples of data

- The number of tourists who visit Hong Kong each year
- The sales turnovers of all restaurants in Moscow
- The number of people (with black hair) who pass their driving test each year

Information is sometimes referred to as processed data. The terms 'information' and 'data' are often used interchangeably. Let us consider the following situation in which data is **collected** and then **processed** in order to produce meaningful information.

1.2 Example: Data and information

Many companies providing a product or service like to research consumer opinion, and employ market research organisations to do so. A typical market research survey employs a number of researchers who request a sample of the public to answer questions relating to the product. Several hundred questionnaires may be completed. The questionnaires are input to a system. Once every questionnaire has been input, a number of processing operations are performed on the data. A report which summarises the results and discusses their significance is sent to the company that commissioned the survey.

Individually, a completed questionnaire would not tell the company very much, only the views of one consumer. In this case, the individual questionnaires are **data**. Once they have been processed, and analysed, the resulting report is **information**. The company will use it to inform its decisions regarding the product. If the report revealed that consumers disliked the product, the company would scrap or alter it.

The **quality of source data** affects the value of information. Information is worthless if the source data is flawed. If the researchers filled in questionnaires themselves, inventing the answers, then the conclusions drawn from the processed data would be wrong, and poor decisions would be made.

This therefore makes the issue of **questionnaire and survey design** highly important. If data is to be successfully captured using questionnaires and surveys then it important that they are carefully designed.

There are a number of **practical considerations** which researchers need to consider when designing questionnaires and surveys:

- It is important that the purpose of the questionnaire/ survey is stated at the beginning. In some cases it may be necessary to offer an incentive for an individual to agree to take part.

- Following the completion of the questionnaire/survey the respondent should be thanked and assured of their anonymity.

- In order to entice individuals to take part in completing the questionnaire/survey it is important that it is given a meaningful title, be sufficiently short as possible and be attractively presented.

- The questions used should be presented in a logical sequence, and should ideally be relatively simple, not misleading, not too technical and not too personal.

Questions used in questionnaires and surveys typically fall into one of three types:

Dichotomous questions – these questions only allow the respondent to choose from two possible answers, eg Male/Female, Yes/No, Agree/Disagree.

Multiple choice questions – these provide the respondent with the choice of a number of options, eg Excellent/Good/OK/Poor/Very poor.

Open-ended questions – where respondents can respond as they feel appropriate, eg when any additional comments are requested.

In order to generate meaningful results, questions used should not be biased. This issue can be addressed in part if respondents are permitted to provide additional comments to support any responses provided.

1.3 Quantitative and qualitative data

> **FAST FORWARD**
>
> **Quantitative data** are data that can be measured. A **'variable'** is something which can be measured.
>
> **Qualitative data** cannot be measured, but have **attributes** (an attribute is something an object either has or does not have).

Examples of quantitative data include the following.

- The temperature on each day of January in Singapore. This can be **measured** in degrees Fahrenheit or Celsius.
- The time it takes you to swim 50 lengths. This can be **measured** in hours and minutes.

An example of **qualitative data** is whether someone is male or female. Whether you are male or female is an **attribute** because the sex of a person cannot be measured.

1.4 Quantitative and qualitative information

Just as data may be quantitative or qualitative, so too may information.

Key terms

> - **Quantitative information** is information which is capable of being expressed in numbers.
> - **Qualitative information** is information which may not be expressed very easily in terms of numbers. Information of this nature is more likely to reflect the quality of something.

An example of **quantitative information** is 'The Chairman of the company has announced that the revenue for the year is **$4 million**.' You can see how this information is easily expressed in numerical terms.

An example of **qualitative information** is 'The standard of the books produced was **very high**.' This information cannot easily be expressed in terms of numbers, as the standard of something is usually described as being very high, quite low, or average and so on.

2 Characteristics of good information

> **FAST FORWARD**
>
> The main characteristics of good information are as follows:
> - It should be **relevant** for its purpose.
> - It should be **complete** for its purpose.
> - It should be sufficiently **accurate** for its purpose.
> - It should be **clear** to the user.
> - The user should have **confidence** in it.
> - It should be **communicated** to the right person.

> - It should not be excessive – its **volume** should be manageable.
> - It should be **timely** – in other words communicated at the most appropriate time.
> - It should be communicated by an appropriate **channel** of communication.
> - It should be provided at a **cost** which is less than the value of its benefits.

Let us look at these characteristics in more detail.

(a) **Relevance**. Information must be relevant to the purpose for which a manager wants to use it. In practice, far too many reports fail to 'keep to the point' and contain purposeless, irritating paragraphs which only serve to vex the managers reading them.

(b) **Completeness**. An information user should have all the information needed to do a job properly. An incomplete picture of the situation could result in bad decisions.

(c) **Accuracy**. Information should obviously be accurate because using incorrect information could have serious and damaging consequences. However, information should only be accurate enough for its purpose and there is no need to go into unnecessary detail for pointless accuracy.

(d) **Clarity**. Information must be clear to the user. If the user does not understand it properly it cannot be used properly. Lack of clarity is one of the causes of a breakdown in communication. It is therefore important to choose the most appropriate presentation medium or channel of communication.

(e) **Confidence**. Information must be trusted by the managers who are expected to use it. However not all information is certain. Some information has to be certain, especially operating information, for example, related to a production process. Strategic information, especially relating to the environment, is uncertain. However, if the assumptions underlying it are clearly stated, this might enhance the confidence with which the information is perceived.

(f) **Communication**. Within any organisation, individuals are given the authority to do certain tasks, and they must be given the information they need to do them. An office manager might be made responsible for controlling expenditures in his office, and given a budget expenditure limit for the year. As the year progresses, he might try to keep expenditure in check but unless he is told throughout the year what is his current total expenditure to date, he will find it difficult to judge whether he is keeping within budget or not.

(g) **Volume**. There are physical and mental limitations to what a person can read, absorb and understand properly before taking action. An enormous mountain of information, even if it is all relevant, cannot be handled. Reports to management must therefore be **clear** and **concise** and in many systems, control action works basically on the 'exception' principle.

(h) **Timing**. Information which is not available until after a decision is made will be useful only for comparisons and longer-term control, and may serve no purpose even then. Information prepared too frequently can also be a problem. If, for example, a decision is taken at a monthly meeting about a certain aspect of a company's operations, information to make the decision is only required once a month, so weekly reports would be a time-consuming waste of effort.

(i) **Channel of communication**. There are occasions when using one particular method of communication will be better than others. For example, job vacancies should be announced in a medium where they will be brought to the attention of the people most likely to be interested. The channel of communication might be the company's website, a dedicated jobs website, a professional magazine, or a job centre. Some internal communication may be better sent by email. Some information is best communicated informally by telephone or word of mouth, whereas other information ought to be formally communicated in writing or figures.

(j) **Cost**. Information should have some value, otherwise it would not be worth the cost of collecting and filing it. The benefits obtainable from the information must exceed the costs of acquiring it.

3 Data types

3.1 Classifying data

We have already seen how data can be classified as being **quantitative** (can be measured (variables)) or **qualitative** (cannot be measured, has an **attribute**). We shall now consider the ways in which data may be further classified as follows:

- Primary and secondary data
- Discrete and continuous data

3.2 Primary and secondary data

> **FAST FORWARD**
>
> Data may be **primary** (collected specifically for the purpose of a survey) or **secondary** (collected for some other purpose).

3.2.1 Primary data

Primary data are data collected especially for the purpose of whatever survey is being conducted. Raw data are primary data which have not been processed at all, and which are still just a list of numbers.

The main sources of primary data are personal investigation, teams of investigators, interviews, questionnaires and online and telephone surveys.

It is reliable as you know where the data has come from and are aware of any inadequacies or limitations. However, it can take time to collect and is expensive.

3.2.2 Secondary data

Secondary data are data which have already been collected elsewhere, for some other purpose, but which can be used or adapted for the survey being conducted. For example from government, banks, newspapers, the internet.

Secondary data sources may be satisfactory in certain situations, or they may be the only convenient means of obtaining an item of data. It is essential to ensure secondary data used is accurate and reliable.

3.3 Primary external sources of information

An organisation's data is full of invoices, correspondence, emails, letters, advertisements and so on, received from customers and suppliers, in both paper and electronic format. These documents provide data from an **external primary source**. A primary source of data is, as the term implies, **as close as you can get to the origin of an item of data**: the eyewitness to an event, the place in question, the document under scrutiny.

The **advantage** of using a primary source of data is that the **user** of the information **knows where it came from, the circumstances under which it was collected, and any limitations or inadequacies in it.**

3.4 Secondary external sources of information

> **FAST FORWARD**
>
> The main **secondary external data sources** are Governments, banks, newspapers, trade journals, information bureaux, consultancies, libraries and information services. Many of the sources can be accessed through their websites.

Secondary external sources of data are stores of data collected by outside organisations. The data is collected for general rather than specific purposes and so there are a number of possible **limitations**.

PART A DATA COLLECTION AND ANALYSIS

(a) The user will be unaware of any limitations which might be present.
(b) The data may not be suitable for the purpose it is being used for.
(c) The data may be out of date.

Secondary data sources may be satisfactory in certain situations, or they may be the only convenient means of obtaining an item of data. It is essential that the secondary external source used is **accurate** and **reliable**.

Despite the limitations of secondary external data sources, they can be valuable in some situations. Most of the data will be available on the internet, either in the public domain or through a paid service. This allows data to be sourced very quickly. There are four main secondary external data **sources**.

(a) Governments
(b) Banks
(c) Newspapers
(d) Trade journals

3.5 Governments

Official statistics are supplied by many Governments. In the UK, official statistics are supplied by the Office for National Statistics and are available via the government website www.gov.uk, and include the following:

Title	Detail
Annual Abstract of Statistics	This is a general reference book for the United Kingdom which includes data on climate, population, social services, justice and crime, education, defence, manufacturing and agricultural production.
Financial Statistics	A monthly compilation of financial data. It includes statistics on Government income, expenditure and borrowing, financial institutions, companies, the overseas sector, the money supply, exchange rates, interest rates and share prices.
The United Kingdom National Accounts (The Blue Book)	A source of data on the gross national product, the gross national income and the gross national expenditure. It gives a clear indication of how the nation makes and spends its money.
The United Kingdom Balance of Payments (The Pink Book)	This annual publication gives data on the inflows and outflows of private capital in the United Kingdom.

Monthly statistics are also published by many Government departments. For example, the Department for Work and Pensions in Britain publishes details of employment, unemployment, unfilled job vacancies and other statistics.

The Department for Business, Energy and Industrial Strategy (BEIS) in the UK publishes data on production, prices and trade which can also be accessed through www.gov.uk.

Population data is published by many Governments around the world, and includes population numbers, births, deaths, marriages and so on. In the UK the Government carries out a full census of the whole population every ten years.

3.6 Banks and financial institutions

Regular reports on the money supply, government borrowing and other data are issued by central banks such as the European Central Bank, the Federal Reserve, and the Bank of England. The International Monetary Fund publishes reports on the world economic outlook and reports on the borrowing and financial transactions of various countries.

3.7 Financial newspapers

Financial newspapers contain detailed business data and information. Financial newspapers include the *Financial Times*, the *Wall Street Journal*, the Singapore *Business Times* and the *Nikkei Asian Review*. Such newspapers provide data on foreign exchange rates, interest rates, gilts and other inventory prices.

3.8 Trade journals

Most industries are served by one or more trade journals. Journals contain data on new developments in the industry, articles about competitors' products, details of industry costs and prices and so on.

3.9 Other sources

(a) **Advice or information bureaux.** Provide information in the form of advice, information leaflets or fact sheets.

(b) **Consultancies.** These include general market research organisations such as Ipsos, MORI and Gallup. There are also specialist market research companies which provide data on specific industries.

(c) **Specific reference works.** Different businesses will have different reference works or so called 'bibles' which are always used as a point of reference.

(d) **Libraries and information services.** Most countries have free public library systems. Educational institutes and business organisations may also provide library services which are available to their members.

(e) Other **electronic sources** such as local and national radio and TV, and other websites on the internet. The internet is of central importance as a data source. Many of the sources described in this section can be also accessed through their website on the internet. Companies like Thomson Reuters offer access to a range of predominantly business related information.

3.10 Discrete and continuous data

Quantitative data may be further classified as being **discrete** or **continuous.**

> **FAST FORWARD**
>
> **Discrete** data/variables can only take on a countable number of values. **Continuous** data/variables can take on any value.

(a) **Discrete data** are the number of goals scored by Arsenal against Chelsea in the FA Cup Final: Arsenal could score 0, 1, 2, 3 or even 4 goals (**discrete variables** = 0, 1, 2, 3, 4), but they cannot score $1\frac{1}{2}$ or $2\frac{1}{2}$ goals.

(b) **Continuous data** include the heights of all the members of your family, as these can take on any value: 1.542m, 1.639m and 1.492m for example. **Continuous variables** = 1.542, 1.639, 1.492.

PART A DATA COLLECTION AND ANALYSIS

The following diagram should help you to remember the ways in which data may be classified.

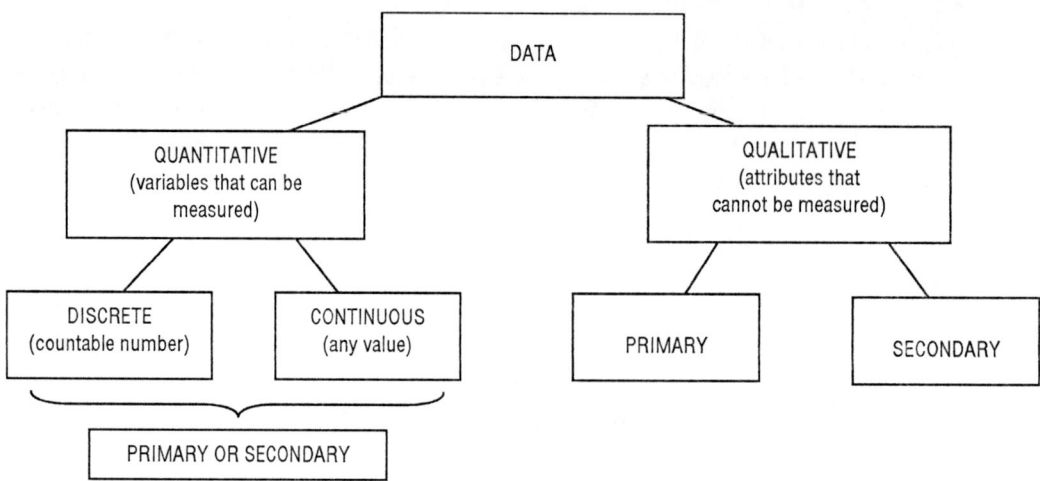

  Question Quantitative and qualitative data

Look through the following list of surveys and decide whether each is collecting qualitative data or quantitative data. If you think the data is quantitative, indicate whether it is discrete or continuous.

(a) A survey of accountancy textbooks, to determine how many diagrams they contain.

(b) A survey of greetings cards on a convenience store's shelf, to determine whether or not each has a price sticker on it.

(c) A survey of the results in a cost accounting assessment, to determine what percentage of marks the students obtained.

(d) A survey of heights of telegraph poles in Papua New Guinea, to find out if there is any variation across the country.

(e) A survey of swimmers to find out how long they take to swim a kilometre.

Answer

(a) The number of diagrams in an accountancy text book is an example of **quantitative** data, because it can be measured. Because the number of diagrams can only be counted in whole number steps, the resulting data is **discrete.** You cannot for example have $42\frac{1}{2}$ diagrams, but you can have 42 or 43 diagrams.

(b) Whether or not a greetings card has a price sticker on it is not something that can be measured. This is therefore an example of **qualitative** data, as a greetings card either has a price sticker on it, or it does not have a price sticker on it.

(c) The results of a cost accounting assessment can be measured, and are therefore an example of **quantitative** data. The assessment results can only take on whole number values between 0% and 100%, and the data are therefore **discrete**. (It may be possible to score $62\frac{1}{2}$%, or $64\frac{1}{2}$%, but it is not possible to score 62.41%, so the variable is not continuous.)

(d) The heights of telegraph poles is an example of **quantitative** data as they can be measured. Since the telegraph poles may take on any height, the data is said to be **continuous.**

(e) The time taken to swim a kilometre may be measured and is therefore **quantitative** data. Because the time recorded can take on any value, in theory, the data is said to be **continuous.**

4 Sampling

4.1 Samples and populations

FAST FORWARD — Data are often collected from a **sample** rather than from a population. If the whole population is examined, the survey is called a **census**.

In many situations, it will not be practical to carry out a survey which considers every item of the **population.** For example, if a poll is taken to try to predict the results of an election, it would not be possible to ask all eligible voters how they are going to vote. To ask the whole population would take far too long and cost too much money.

In such situations where it is not possible to survey the whole population, a **sample** is selected. The results obtained from the sample are used to estimate the results of the whole population.

In situations where the whole population is examined, the survey is called a **census** but this has a number of disadvantages.

(a) The high cost of a census may exceed the value of the results obtained.
(b) It might be out of date by the time you complete it.

The **advantages of a sample** are:

(a) It can be shown mathematically that once a certain sample size has been reached, very little accuracy is gained by examining more items. The **larger the size** of the sample, however, the **more accurate** the results.

(b) It is possible to **ask more questions** with a sample.

4.2 Sampling methods

One of the most important requirements of sample data is that they should be **complete**. That is, the data should **cover all areas** of the population to be examined. If this requirement is not met, then the sample will be **biased**.

4.2.1 Random sampling

If a sample is selected using random sampling, it will be **free from bias** (since every item will have an equal chance of being selected). Once the sample has been selected, valid inferences about the population being sampled can be made.

If random sampling is used then it is necessary to construct a **sampling frame,** which is a numbered list of all items in a population.

Once a numbered list of all items in the population has been made, it is easy to select a random sample, simply by generating a list of random numbers.

For instance, if you wanted to select a random sample of children from a school, it would be useful to have a list of names:

0   J Adams
1   R Brown
2   S Brown
...

Now the numbers 0, 1, 2 and so on can be used to select the random sample. It is normal to start the numbering at 0, so that when 0 appears in a list of random numbers it can be used.

PART A   DATA COLLECTION AND ANALYSIS

Sometimes it is not possible to draw up a sampling frame. For example, if you wanted to take a random sample of Americans, it would take too long to list all Americans.

4.2.2 Stratified random sampling

A variation on the random sampling method is **stratified random sampling**. This is a method of sampling which involves dividing the population into **strata** or **categories**. Random samples are then taken from each stratum or category.

In many situations, stratified sampling is the best method of choosing a sample. It takes **more time** than simple random sampling but samples should be **more representative** and so **sample error** should be reduced.

Stratified sampling is best demonstrated by means of an example.

4.2.3 Example: Stratified sampling

The number of accountants in each type of work in a particular country are as follows:

Partnerships	500
Public companies	500
Private companies	700
Public practice	800
	2,500

If a sample of 20 was required the sample would be made up as follows:

		Sample
Partnerships	$\frac{500}{2,500} \times 20$	4
Public companies	$\frac{500}{2,500} \times 20$	4
Private companies	$\frac{700}{2,500} \times 20$	6
Public practice	$\frac{800}{2,500} \times 20$	6
		20

4.2.4 Systematic sampling

Systematic sampling is a sampling method which works by selecting every nth item after a random start.

If it were decided to select a sample of 20 from a population of 800, then every 40th (800 ÷ 20) item after a random start in the first 40 should be selected. The starting point could be found using the lottery method or random number tables. If (say) 23 was chosen, then the sample would include the 23rd, 63rd, 103rd, 143rd ... 783rd items. The gap of 40 is known as the **sampling interval**.

It is **cheap** and **easy to use**, but it is possible that a biased sample might be chosen if there is a regular pattern to the population which coincides with the sampling method and it is not completely random since some samples have a zero chance of being selected.

4.2.5 Multistage sampling

Multistage sampling is a probability sampling method which involves dividing the population into a number of sub-populations and then selecting a small sample of these sub-populations at random.

Each sub-population is then divided further, and then a small sample is again selected at random. This process is repeated as many times as is necessary.

The advantages of this method are that fewer investigators are needed and it is not so costly to obtain a sample. However, there is the **possibility of bias** if, for example, only a small number of regions are selected and the method is **not truly random** as once the final sampling areas have been selected the rest of the population cannot be in the sample.

4.2.6 Example: Multistage sampling

A survey of spending habits is being planned to cover the whole of Britain. It is obviously impractical to draw up a sampling frame, so random sampling is not possible. Multistage sampling is to be used instead.

The country is divided into a number of areas and a small sample of these is selected at random. Each of the areas selected is subdivided into smaller units and again, a smaller number of these is selected at random. This process is repeated as many times as necessary and finally, a random sample of the relevant people living in each of the smallest units is taken. A fair approximation to a random sample can be obtained.

Thus, we might choose a random sample of eight areas, and from each of these areas, select a random sample of five towns. From each town, a random sample of 200 people might be selected so that the total sample size is $8 \times 5 \times 200 = 8,000$ people.

4.2.7 Cluster sampling

Cluster sampling is a non-random sampling method that involves selecting one **definable subsection** of the population as the sample, that subsection taken to be representative of the population in question.

For example, the pupils of one school might be taken as a cluster sample of all children at school in one county.

It is a good alternative to multistage sampling if a satisfactory sampling frame does not exist and it is inexpensive to operate. However, there is potential for considerable bias.

4.2.8 Quota sampling

In **quota sampling**, randomness is forfeited in the interests of **cheapness** and **administrative simplicity**. Investigators are told to interview all the people they meet up to a certain quota.

The advantages of quota sampling are that a much larger sample can be studied, and hence more information can be gained at a faster speed for a given outlay than when compared with a fully randomised sampling method. Given suitable, trained and properly briefed field workers, quota sampling yields enough accurate information for many forms of commercial market research.

However, it is not random, any information obtained may be biased and there is no way to check its reliability.

4.2.9 Example: Quota sampling

Consider the figures in Paragraph 4.2.3, but with the following additional information relating to the sex of the accountants.

	Male	*Female*
Partnerships	300	200
Public companies	400	100
Private companies	300	400
Public practice	300	500

PART A   DATA COLLECTION AND ANALYSIS

An investigator's quotas might be as follows.

	Male	Female	Total
Partnerships	30	20	50
Public companies	40	10	50
Private companies	30	40	70
Public practice	30	50	80
			250

Using quota sampling, the investigator would interview the first 30 male accountants in partnerships that he met, the first 20 female accountants in partnerships that he met and so on.

Question   Sampling methods

Sampling methods are frequently used for the collection of data. Five commonly used types of samples are (A) simple random, (B) stratified random, (C) systematic, (D) cluster and (E) quota. State which of these sample types is being described in the following situations.

(i)   One school in an area is selected at random and then all pupils in that school are surveyed.

       Type of sample is [ ]

(ii)   The local authority has a list of all pupils in the area and the sample is selected in such a way that all pupils have an equal probability of selection.

       Type of sample is [ ]

(iii) An interviewer surveys pupils from every school in the area, attempting to question them randomly but in line with specified numbers of boys and girls in the various age groups.

       Type of sample is [ ]

(iv)   The local authority has a list of all pupils in the selected area, categorised according to their gender and age. The sample selected is chosen randomly from the various categories, in proportion to their sizes.

       Type of sample is [ ]

(v)   The local authority has a list of all pupils in the selected area. The first pupil is selected randomly from the list and then every 100th pupil thereafter is selected for the survey.

       Type of sample is [ ]

Answer

(i)   D

(ii)   A

(iii) E

(iv)   B

(v)   C

2: STATISTICAL SOURCES

Question
Systematic sampling

Which of the following are disadvantages of systematic sampling? Tick as appropriate.

- [ ] The sample chosen might be biased
- [ ] Some samples have a zero chance of being selected so sampling method is not completely random
- [ ] Prior knowledge of each item in the population is required

Answer

- [x] The sample chosen might be biased
- [x] Some samples have a zero chance of being selected so sampling method is not completely random
- [ ] Prior knowledge of each item in the population is required

PART A   DATA COLLECTION AND ANALYSIS

Chapter Roundup

- **Data** are the raw materials for data processing. **Information** is data that has been processed.
- **Quantitative data** are data that can be measured. A **'variable'** is something which can be measured.
- **Qualitative data** cannot be measured, but have **attributes** (an attribute is something an object either has or does not have).
- The main **characteristics of good information** are as follows:
    - It should be **relevant** for its purpose.
    - It should be **complete** for its purpose.
    - It should be sufficiently **accurate** for its purpose.
    - It should be **clear** to the user.
    - The user should have **confidence** in it.
    - It should be **communicated** to the right person.
    - It should not be excessive – its **volume** should be manageable.
    - It should be **timely** – in other words communicated at the most appropriate time.
    - It should be communicated by an appropriate **channel** of communication.
    - It should be provided at a **cost** which is less than the value of its benefits.
- Data may be **primary** (collected specifically for the purpose of a survey) or **secondary** (collected for some other purpose).
- The main **secondary external data sources** are Governments, banks, newspapers, trade journals, information bureaux, consultancies, libraries and information services. Many of the sources can be accessed through their websites.
- **Discrete** data/variables can only take on a countable number of values. **Continuous** data/variables can take on any value
- Data are often collected from a **sample** rather than from a population. If the whole population is examined, the survey is called a **census**.

Quick Quiz

1 **Fill in the blanks** in the statements below using the words in the box.

Data can be either (1) .... (have variables) or (2) .... (have (3) ....). Variables can be either (4) .... (eg 0, 1, 2, 3) or (5) .... (eg 0.54, 0.612, 0.117). Data may also be classified as (6) .... (collected for a specific survey) or (7) .... (collected for some other purpose).

• Quantitative	• Continuous	• Attributes	• Primary
• Secondary	• Qualitative	• Discrete	

2 Which of the following statements is/are correct?

☐ Data and information are the same thing

☐ Information is derived from data

☐ Quantitative data are data that can be measured

☐ Data is derived from information

3 Fill in the blanks in the boxes below using the words in the box.

```
                    SAMPLING
                    METHODS
                   /         \
          PROBABILITY       NON-PROBABILITY
          ..........        ..........
          ..........        ..........
          ..........        ..........
          ..........        ..........
          ..........        ..........
          ..........        ..........
```

• multistage	• random	• cluster
• stratified	• quota	• systematic

4 A simple random sample is a sample selected in such a way that every item in the population has an equal chance of being included.

True ☐

False ☐

PART A DATA COLLECTION AND ANALYSIS

5   I   If a sample is selected using random sampling, it will be free from bias
    II   A sampling frame is a numbered list of all items in a sample
    III   Cluster sampling is a non-probability sampling method
    IV   In quota sampling, investigators are told to interview all the people they meet up to a certain quota

Which of the above statements are true?

(a) I, II, III and IV
(b) I, II and IV only
(c) I and II only
(d) I and IV only

6   The essence of systematic sampling is that

(a) Each element of the population has an equal chance of being chosen
(b) Members of various strata are selected by the interviewers up to predetermined limits
(c) Every nth item of the population is selected
(d) Every element of one definable sub-section of the population is selected

Answers to Quick Quiz

1. (1) Quantitative (2) Qualitative (3) Attributes
    (4) Discrete (5) Continuous (6) Primary
    (7) Secondary

2. ☐ Data and information are the same thing
    ☑ Information is derived from data
    ☑ Quantitative data are data that can be measured
    ☐ Data is derived from information

3.
```
                    SAMPLING METHODS
                    /              \
            PROBABILITY          NON-PROBABILITY
                |                      |
             random                  quota
                |
            stratified
                |
            systematic
                |
            multistage
                |
             cluster
```

4. True

5. (d)

6. (c)

End of Chapter Question

Primary data collection (AIA Nov 08, May 09)

(a) Briefly describe four commonly used methods of primary data collection. **(4 marks)**

(b) Questionnaires are commonly used as a method of primary data collection.

   (i) Describe the three main classifications of questions used in questionnaires. **(3 marks)**
   (ii) Provide a list of points to be considered when designing questionnaires. **(5 marks)**

(Total = 12 marks)

Presentation of data

Topic list	Syllabus reference
1 Tables	6.2
2 Charts	6.2
3 Frequency distributions	6.2
4 Histograms	6.2
5 Ogives	6.2
6 Scatter diagrams	6.5

Introduction

We now have to **present** the data we have collected so that they can be of use. This chapter begins by looking at how data can be presented in **tables** and **charts**. Such methods are helpful in presenting key data in a **concise** and **easy to understand way**.

Data that are a mass of numbers can usefully be summarised into a **frequency distribution**. **Histograms** and **ogives** are the **pictorial representation** of grouped and cumulative frequency distributions.

PART A   DATA COLLECTION AND ANALYSIS

1 Tables

1.1 Tables and tabulation

FAST FORWARD Tables are a simple way of presenting information about two variables.

Raw data (for example, a list of results from a survey) need to be **summarised** and **analysed**, to give them meaning. One of the most basic ways is the preparation of a **table**.

Key terms
- **Tabulation** means putting data into tables.
- A **table** is a matrix of data in rows and columns, with the rows and the columns having titles.

Since a table is **two-dimensional**, it can only show **two variables**. To tabulate data, you need to recognise what the two dimensions should represent, prepare **rows** and **columns** accordingly with suitable **titles**, and then **insert the data** into the appropriate places in the table.

1.2 Example: Tables

The total number of employees in a certain trading company is 1,000. They are employed in three departments: production, administration and sales. 600 people are employed in the production department and 300 in administration. There are 110 males under 21 in employment, 110 females under 21, and 290 females aged 21 years and over. The remaining employees are males aged 21 and over.

In the production department there are 350 males aged 21 and over, 150 females aged 21 and over and 50 males under 21, whilst in the administration department there are 100 males aged 21 and over, 110 females aged 21 and over and 50 males aged under 21.

Draw up a table to show all the details of employment in the company and its departments and provide suitable secondary statistics to describe the distribution of people in departments.

Solution

The basic table required has the following two dimensions.

- Departments
- Age/sex analysis

In this example we are going to show the percentage of the total workforce in each department.

Analysis of employees

	Department							
	Production		Administration		Sales		Total	
	No	%	No	%	No	%	No	%
Males 21 yrs +	350	58.4	100	33.3	40 **	40.0	490 *	49.0
Females 21 yrs +	150	25.0	110	36.7	30 **	30.0	290	29.0
Subtotals 21 yrs +	500	83.4	210	70.0	70	70.0	780	78.0
Males under 21	50	8.3	50	16.7	10 **	10.0	110	11.0
Females under 21	50 *	8.3	40 *	13.3	20 **	20.0	110	11.0
Subtotals under 21	100	16.6	90	30.0	30	30.0	220	22.0
Total	600	100.0	300	100.0	100	100.0	1,000	100.0

* Balancing figure to make up the column total
** Balancing figure then needed to make up the row total

1.3 Guidelines for tabulation

The example above illustrates certain guidelines which you should apply when presenting data in tabular form. These are as follows:

- The table should be given a **clear title**
- All columns should be **clearly labelled**
- Where appropriate, there should be **clear sub-totals**
- A **total column** may be presented; this would usually be the right-hand column
- A **total figure** is often advisable at the bottom of each column of figures
- Tables should not be packed with so much data that reading information is difficult
- Non-essential information should be eliminated
- Consider ordering columns/rows by order of importance/magnitude

2 Charts

2.1 Visual display

FAST FORWARD

Charts often convey the meaning or significance of data more clearly than would a table.

Instead of presenting data in a table, it might be preferable to give a **visual display** in the form of a **chart**. The purpose of a chart is to convey the data in a way that will demonstrate its meaning more clearly than a table of data would. Charts are not always more appropriate than tables, and the most suitable way of presenting data will depend on the following:

(a) **What the data are intended to show**. Visual displays usually make one or two points quite forcefully, whereas tables usually give more detailed information.

(b) **Who is going to use the data**. Some individuals might understand visual displays more readily than tabulated data.

2.2 Bar charts

Key term

The **bar chart** is one of the most common methods of presenting data in a visual form. It is a chart in which quantities are shown in the form of bars.

FAST FORWARD

There are three main **types of bar chart: simple**, **component** (including **percentage component**) and **multiple** (or **compound**).

Key term

A **simple bar chart** is a chart consisting of one or more bars, in which the length of each bar indicates the magnitude of the corresponding data item.

2.2.1 Example: A simple bar chart

A company's total sales for the years from 20X1 to 20X6 are as follows.

Year	Sales
	$'000
20X1	800
20X2	1,200
20X3	1,100
20X4	1,400
20X5	1,600
20X6	1,700

The data could be shown on a simple bar chart as follows.

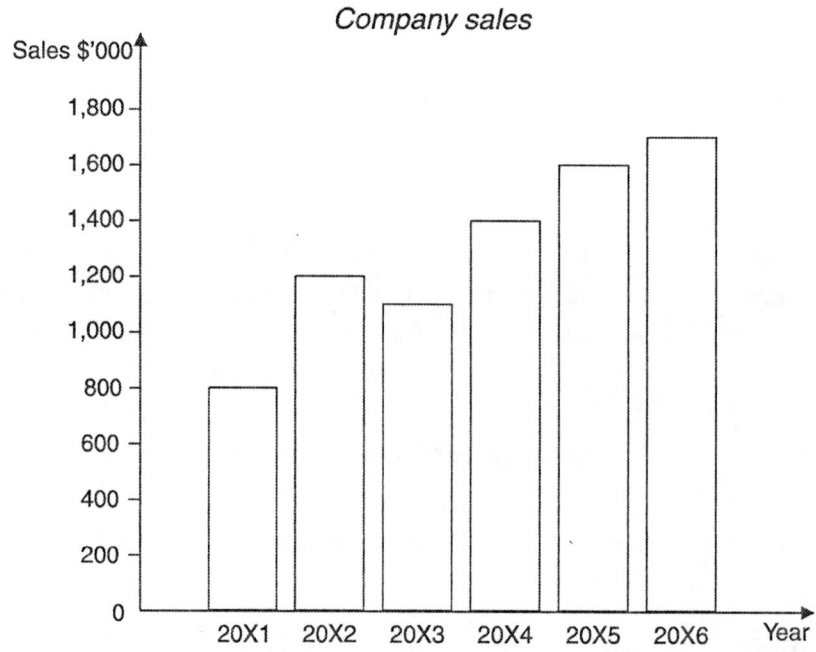

Each axis of the chart must be clearly labelled, and there must be a scale to indicate the magnitude of the data. Here, the y axis includes a scale for the amount of sales, and so readers of the bar chart can see not only that sales have been rising year by year (with 20X3 being an exception), but also what the actual sales have been each year.

2.2.2 Purposes of simple bar charts

Simple bar charts serve two purposes:

- The actual magnitude of each item is shown
- The lengths of bars on the chart allow magnitudes to be compared

Key term

A **component bar chart** is a bar chart that gives a breakdown of each total into its components. The total length of each bar and each component on a component bar chart indicates magnitude (a bigger amount is shown by a longer bar).

2.2.3 Example: A component bar chart

Charbart's sales for the years from 20X7 to 20X9 are as follows:

	20X7	20X8	20X9
	$'000	$'000	$'000
Product A	1,000	1,200	1,700
Product B	900	1,000	1,000
Product C	500	600	700
Total	2,400	2,800	3,400

A component bar chart would show the following:

- How total sales have changed from year to year
- The components of each year's total

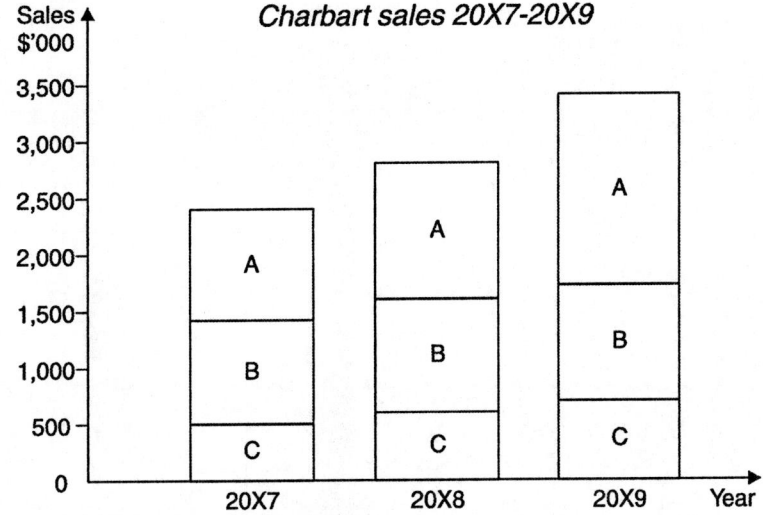

In this diagram the growth in sales is illustrated and the significance of growth in product A sales as the reason for the total sales growth is also fairly clear.

Key term

> A **percentage component bar chart** is a component bar chart which does not show **total magnitudes** – if one or more bars are drawn on the chart, the total length of each bar is the same. The lengths of the sections of the bar however, do vary, and it is these lengths that indicate the **relative sizes** of the components.

2.2.4 Example: A percentage component bar chart

The information in the previous example of sales of Charbart could have been shown in a **percentage component bar chart** as follows.

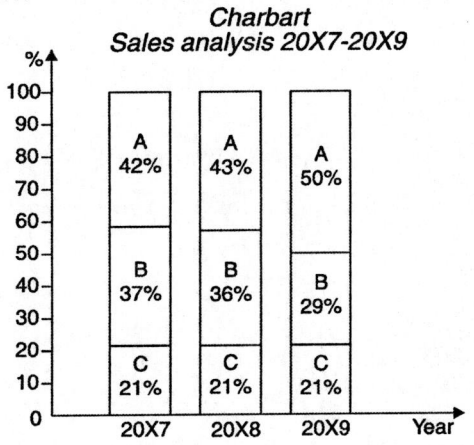

PART A DATA COLLECTION AND ANALYSIS

Working

	20X7		20X8		20X9	
	$'000	%	$'000	%	$'000	%
Product A	1,000	42	1,200	43	1,700	50
Product B	900	37	1,000	36	1,000	29
Product C	500	21	600	21	700	21
Total	2,400	100	2,800	100	3,400	100

This chart shows that sales of C have remained a steady proportion of total sales, but the proportion of A in total sales has gone up quite considerably, while the proportion of B has fallen correspondingly.

Key term

A **multiple bar chart** (or **compound bar chart**) is a bar chart in which two or more separate bars are used to present sub-divisions of data.

2.2.5 Example: A multiple bar chart

The data on Charbart's sales could be shown in a multiple bar chart as follows:

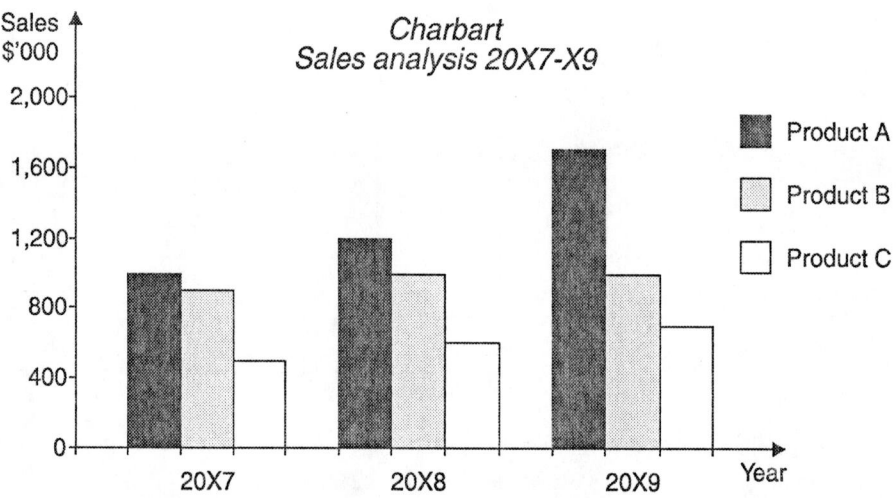

A multiple bar chart uses several bars for each total. In this multiple bar chart, the sales in each year are shown as three separate bars, one for each product, A, B and C.

2.2.6 Information presented by multiple bar charts

Multiple bar charts present similar information to component bar charts, except for the following:

(a) Multiple bar charts do not show the grand total whereas component bar charts do.

(b) Multiple bar charts illustrate the comparative magnitudes of the components more clearly than component bar charts.

Multiple bar charts are sometimes drawn with the bars horizontal instead of vertical.

Multiple bar charts

Income for Canary Bank in 20X0, 20X1 and 20X2 is made up as follows.

	20X0	20X1	20X2
	$'000	$'000	$'000
Interest income	3,579	2,961	2,192
Commission income	857	893	917
Other income	62	59	70

3: PRESENTATION OF DATA

Using the above data complete the following graphs.

(a) *A simple bar chart*

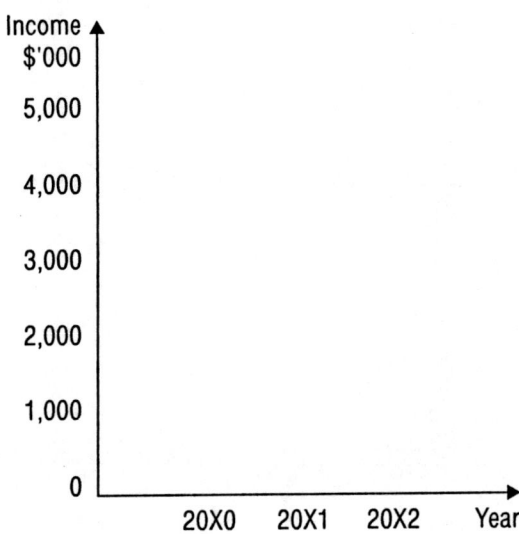

(b) *A multiple bar chart*

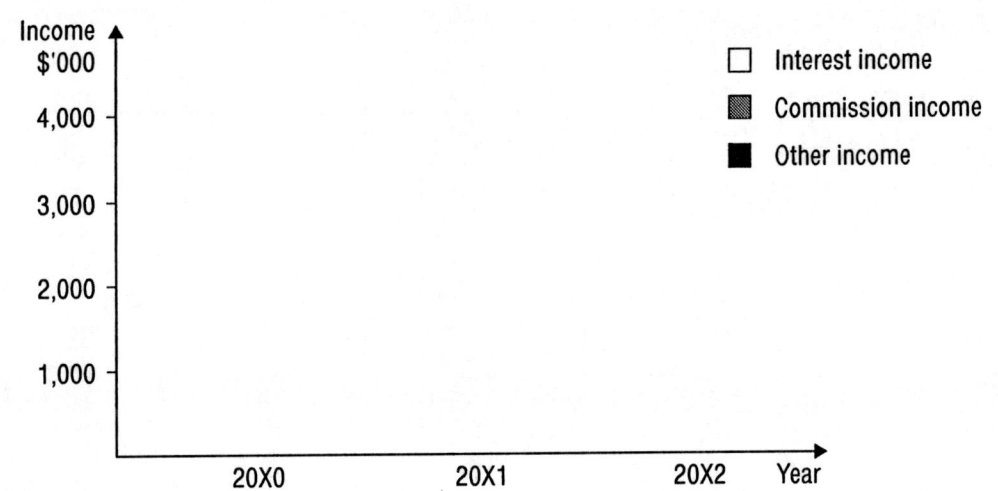

Workings

	20X0	20X1	20X2
	$'000	$'000	$'000
	3,579	2,961	2,192
	857	893	917
	62	59	70
	4,498	3,913	3,179

PART A   DATA COLLECTION AND ANALYSIS

1   *A simple bar chart*

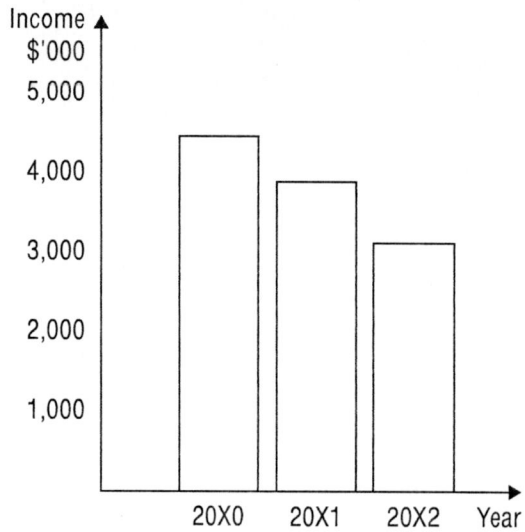

2   *A multiple bar chart*

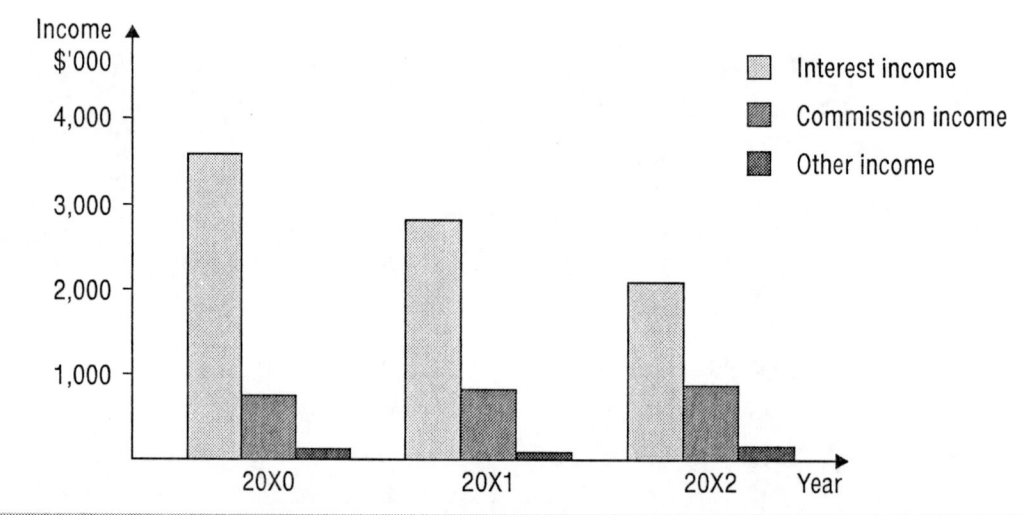

2.3 Pie charts

Key term

A **pie chart** is a chart which is used to show pictorially the relative size of component elements of a total.

It is called a pie chart because it is **circular**, and so has the **shape of a pie** in a round pie dish. The 'pie' is then cut into slices with each slice representing part of the total.

Pie charts have sectors of varying sizes, and you need to be able to draw sectors fairly accurately. To do this, you need a **protractor**. Working out sector sizes involves converting parts of the total into **equivalent degrees of a circle**. A complete 'pie' = 360°: the number of degrees in a circle = 100% of whatever you are showing. An element which is 50% of your total will therefore occupy a segment of 180°, and so on.

2.3.1 Using shading and colour

Two pie charts are shown as follows:

Breakdown of air and noise pollution complaints, 1

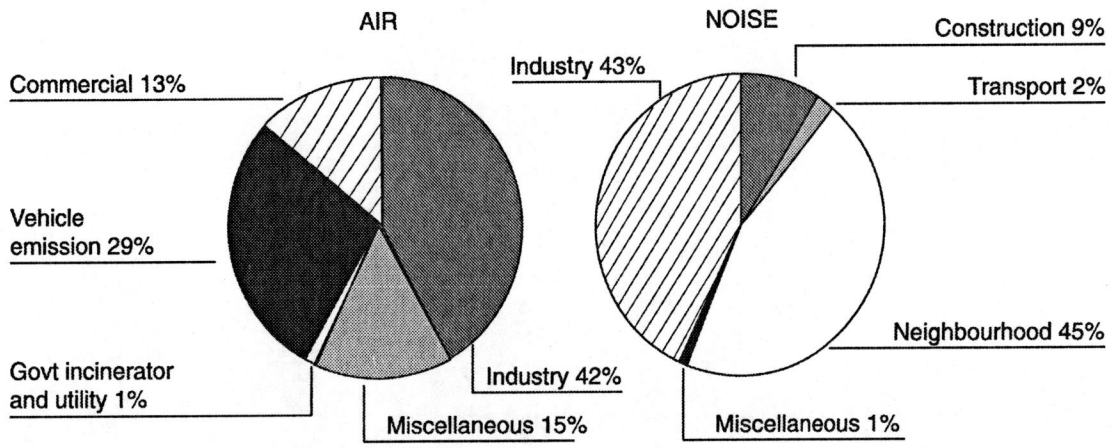

- **Shading** distinguishes the segments from each other
- **Colour** can also be used to distinguish segments

2.3.2 Example: Pie charts

The costs of materials at the Cardiff Factory and the Swansea Factory during January 20X0 were as follows:

	Cardiff factory		Swansea factory	
	$'000	%	$'000	%
Material W	70	35	50	20
Material A	30	15	125	50
Material L	90	45	50	20
Material E	10	5	25	10
	200	100	250	100

Show the costs for the factories in pie charts.

Solution

To convert the components into degrees of a circle, we can use either the **percentage figures** or the **actual cost figures**.

Using the percentage figures

The total percentage is 100%, and the total number of degrees in a circle is 360°. To convert from one to the other, we multiply each percentage value by 360/100% = 3.6.

	Cardiff factory		Swansea factory	
	%	Degrees	%	Degrees
Material W	35	126	20	72
Material A	15	54	50	180
Material L	45	162	20	72
Material E	5	18	10	36
	100	360	100	360

PART A DATA COLLECTION AND ANALYSIS

Using the actual cost figures

	Cardiff factory		Swansea factory	
	$'000	Degrees	$'000	Degrees
Material W (70/200 × 360°)	70	126	50	72
Material A	30	54	125	180
Material L	90	162	50	72
Material E	10	18	25	36
	200	360	250	360

A pie chart could be drawn for each factory.

Cardiff Factory

- Material E 5%
- Material W 35%
- Material L 45%
- Material A 15%

Swansea Factory

- Material E 10%
- Material W 20%
- Material L 20%
- Material A 50%

(a) If the pie chart is drawn manually, a protractor must be used to measure the degrees accurately to obtain the correct sector sizes.

(b) Using a computer makes the process much simpler, especially using a spreadsheet. You just draw up the data in a spreadsheet and click on the chart button to create a visual representation of what you want.

2.3.3 Advantages of pie charts

(a) They give a simple pictorial display of the relative sizes of elements of a total.
(b) They show clearly when one element is much bigger than others.
(c) They can clearly show differences in the elements of two different totals.

2.3.4 Disadvantages of pie charts

(a) They only show the relative sizes of elements. In the example of the two factories, for instance, the pie charts do not show that costs at the Swansea factory were $50,000 higher in total than at the Cardiff factory.

(b) They involve **calculating degrees of a circle** and drawing sectors accurately, and this can be time consuming unless computer software is used.

(c) It is often **difficult to compare sector sizes** easily. For example, suppose that the following two pie charts are used to show the elements of a company's sales.

3: PRESENTATION OF DATA

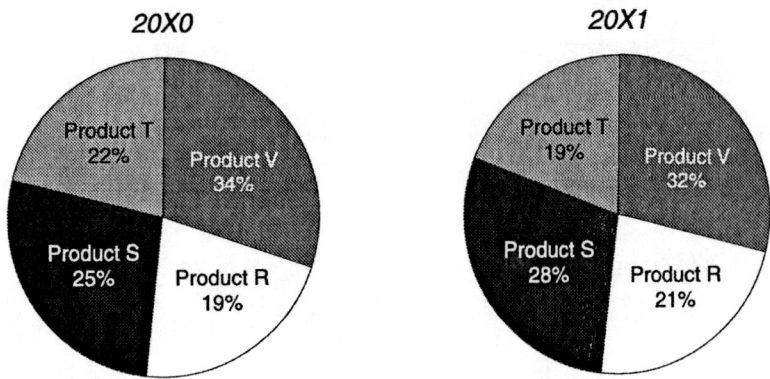

Without the percentage figures, it would not be easy to see how the distribution of sales had changed between 20X0 and 20X1.

Question — Pie charts

The European division of Scent to You, a flower delivery service, has just published its accounts for the year ended 30 June 20X0. The sales director made the following comments.

'Our total sales for the year were $1,751,000, of which $787,000 were made in the United Kingdom, $219,000 in Italy, $285,000 in France and $92,000 in Germany. Sales in Spain and Holland amounted to $189,000 and $34,000 respectively, whilst the rest of Europe collectively had sales of $145,000 in the 12 months to 30 June 20X0.'

Required

Present the above information in the form of a pie chart. Show all of your workings.

Answer

Workings

	Sales $'000		Degrees
United Kingdom	787	(787/1,751 × 360)	162
Italy	219		45
France	285		58
Germany	92		19
Spain	189		39
Rest of Europe	145		30
Holland	34		7
	1,751		360

Scent to You
Sales for the year ended 30 June 20X0

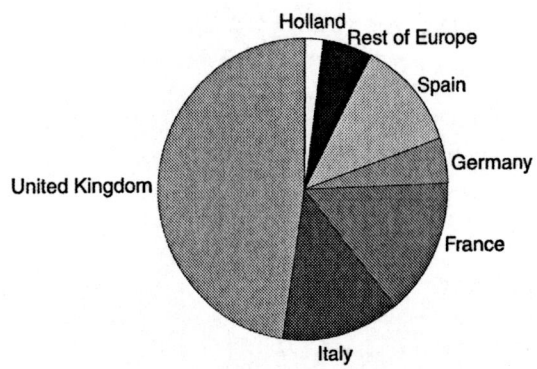

PART A DATA COLLECTION AND ANALYSIS

3 Frequency distributions

3.1 Introduction to frequency distributions

FAST FORWARD

> **Frequency distributions** are used if values of particular variables occur more than once.

Frequently the data collected from a statistical survey or investigation is simply a mass of numbers.

| 65 | 69 | 70 | 71 | 70 | 68 | 69 | 67 | 70 | 68 |
| 72 | 71 | 69 | 74 | 70 | 73 | 71 | 67 | 69 | 70 |

The raw data above yields little information as it stands; imagine how much more difficult it would be if there were hundreds or even thousands of data items. The data could, of course, be arranged in **order size** (an **array**) and the lowest and highest data items, as well as typical items, could be identified.

3.2 Example: Frequency distribution

Many sets of data, however, contain a limited number of data values, even though there may be many occurrences of each value. It can therefore be useful to organise the data into what is known as a **frequency distribution** (or **frequency table**) which records the number of times each value occurs (the **frequency**). A frequency distribution for the data in Paragraph 3.1 (the output in units of 20 employees during one week) is as follows:

Output of employees in one week in units

Output Units	Number of employees (frequency)
65	1
66	0
67	2
68	2
69	4
70	5
71	3
72	1
73	1
74	1
	20

When the data are arranged in this way it is immediately obvious that 69 and 70 units are the most common volumes of output per employee per week.

3.3 Grouped frequency distributions

If there is a large set of data or if every (or nearly every) data item is different, it is often convenient to group frequencies together into **bands** or **classes**. For example, suppose that the output produced by another group of 20 employees during one week was as follows, in units:

1,087	850	1,084	792
924	1,226	1,012	1,205
1,265	1,028	1,230	1,182
1,086	1,130	989	1,155
1,134	1,166	1,129	1,160

3.4 Class intervals

The range of output from the lowest to the highest producer is 792 to 1,265, a **range** of 473 units. This range could be divided into classes of say, 100 units (the **class width** or **class interval**), and the number of employees producing output within each class could then be grouped into a single frequency, as follows:

Output Units	Number of employees (frequency)
700 – 799	1
800 – 899	1
900 – 999	2
1,000 – 1,099	5
1,100 – 1,199	7
1,200 – 1,299	4
	20

Note. Once items have been 'grouped' in this way their individual values are lost.

As well as being used for **discrete variables** (as above), grouped frequency distributions (or grouped frequency tables) can be used to present data for **continuous variables**.

3.5 Example: A grouped frequency distribution for a continuous variable

Suppose we wish to record the heights of 50 different individuals. The information might be presented as a grouped frequency distribution, as follows:

Height cm	Number of individuals (frequency)
Up to and including 154	1
Over 154, up to and including 163	3
Over 163, up to and including 172	8
Over 172, up to and including 181	16
Over 181, up to and including 190	18
Over 190	4
	50

Notes

1   It would be wrong to show the ranges as 0 – 154, 154 – 163, 163 – 172 and so on, because 154 cm and 163 cm would then be values in 2 classes, which is not permissible. Although each value should only be in 1 class, we have to make sure that each possible value can be included. Classes such as 154 – 162, 163 – 172 would not be suitable since a height of 162.5 cm would not belong in either class. Such classes could be used for discrete variables, however.

2   **There is an open ended class at each end of the range.** This is because heights up to 154 cm and over 190 cm are thought to be uncommon, so that a single 'open ended' class is used to group all the frequencies together.

3.6 Guidelines for preparing grouped frequency distributions

To prepare a grouped frequency distribution, a decision must be made about how wide each class should be. You should observe the following guidelines if you are not told how many classes to use or what the class interval should be.

(a)   The size of each class should be appropriate to the nature of the data being recorded, and the most appropriate class interval varies according to circumstances.

(b) The upper and lower limits of each class interval should be suitable 'round' numbers for class intervals which are in multiples of 5, 10, 100, 1,000 and so on. For example, if the class interval is 10, and data items range in value from 23 to 62 (discrete values), the class intervals should be 20–29, 30–39, 40–49, 50–59 and 60–69, rather than 23–32, 33–42, 43–52 and 53–62.

(c) With **continuous variables**, either:

(i) The **upper limit** of a class should be **'up to and including ...'** and the **lower limit** of the next class should be **'over ...'**; or

(ii) The **upper limit** of a class should be **'less than...'**, and the **lower limit** of the next class should be **'at least ...'**.

Question — Grouped frequency distributions

The commission earnings for May 20X0 of the assistants in a department store were as follows (in dollars).

60	35	53	47	25	44	55	58	47	71
63	67	57	44	61	48	50	56	61	42
43	38	41	39	61	51	27	56	57	50
55	68	55	50	25	48	44	43	49	73
53	35	36	41	45	71	56	40	69	52
36	47	66	52	32	46	44	32	52	58
49	41	45	45	48	36	46	42	52	33
31	36	40	66	53	58	60	52	66	51
51	44	59	53	51	57	35	45	46	54
46	54	51	39	64	43	54	47	60	45

Required

Prepare a grouped frequency distribution classifying the commission earnings into categories of $5 commencing with '$25 and under $30'.

Answer

We are told what classes to use, so the first step is to identify the lowest and highest values in the data. The lowest value is $25 (in the first row) and the highest value is $73 (in the fourth row). This means that the class intervals must go up to '$70 and under $75'.

We can now set out the classes in a column, and then count the number of items in each class using tally marks.

Class interval	Tally marks	Total
$25 and less than $30	///	3
$30 and less than $35	////	4
$35 and less than $40	⩘ ⩘	10
$40 and less than $45	⩘ ⩘ ⩘	15
$45 and less than $50	⩘ ⩘ ⩘ ///	18
$50 and less than $55	⩘ ⩘ ⩘ ⩘	20
$55 and less than $60	⩘ ⩘ ///	13
$60 and less than $65	⩘ ///	8
$65 and less than $70	⩘ /	6
$70 and less than $75	///	3
	Total	100

3.7 Cumulative frequency distributions

A cumulative frequency distribution (or cumulative frequency table) can be used to show the total number of times that a value above or below a certain amount occurs.

There are two possible cumulative frequency distributions for the grouped frequency distribution in Paragraph 3.4.

	Cumulative frequency		Cumulative frequency
≥ 700	20	< 800	1
≥ 800	19	< 900	2
≥ 900	18	<1,000	4
≥1,000	16	<1,100	9
≥1,100	11	<1,200	16
≥1,200	4	<1,300	20

(a) The symbol > means 'greater than' and ≥ means 'greater than or equal to'. The symbol < means 'less than' and ≤ means 'less than or equal to'. These symbols provide a convenient method of stating classes.

(b) The first cumulative frequency distribution shows that of the total of 20 employees, 19 produced 800 units or more, 18 produced 900 units or more, 16 produced 1,000 units or more and so on.

(c) The second cumulative frequency distribution shows that, of the total of 20 employees, one produced under 800 units, two produced under 900 units, four produced under 1,000 units and so on.

3.8 Frequency distributions – a summary

Students often find frequency distributions tricky. The following summary might help to clarify the different types of frequency distribution we have covered in this section.

(a) **Frequency distribution.** Individual data items are arranged in a table showing the frequency each **individual** data item occurs.

(b) **Grouped frequency distribution – discrete variables.** Data items which are discrete variables, (eg the number of marks obtained in an examination) are divided into classes of say 10 marks. The numbers of students (frequencies) scoring marks within each band are then grouped into a single frequency.

(c) **Grouped frequency distribution – continuous variables.** These are similar to the grouped frequency distributions for discrete variables (above). However, as they are concerned with **continuous** variables note the following points:

   (i) There is an open-ended class at the end of the range.

   (ii) Class intervals must be carefully considered so that they capture all of the data once (and only once).

(d) **Cumulative frequency distribution.** These distributions are used to show the number of times that a value above or below a certain amount occurs. Cumulative frequencies are obtained by adding the individual frequencies together.

4 Histograms

> A **frequency distribution** can be represented pictorially by means of a **histogram**. The number of observations in a class is represented by the **area** covered by the bar, rather than by its height.

4.1 Histograms of frequency distributions with equal class intervals

If all the class intervals are the same, as in the frequency distribution in Paragraph 3.4, **the bars of the histogram all have the same width and the heights will be proportional to the frequencies.** The histogram looks almost identical to a bar chart except that **the bars are joined together.** Because the bars are joined together, when presenting discrete data the data must be treated as continuous so that there are no gaps between class intervals. For example, for a cricketer's scores in various games the classes would have to be ≥ 0 but < 10, ≥ 10 but < 20 and so on, instead of 0–9, 10–19 and so on.

A histogram of the distribution in Paragraph 3.4 would be drawn as follows:

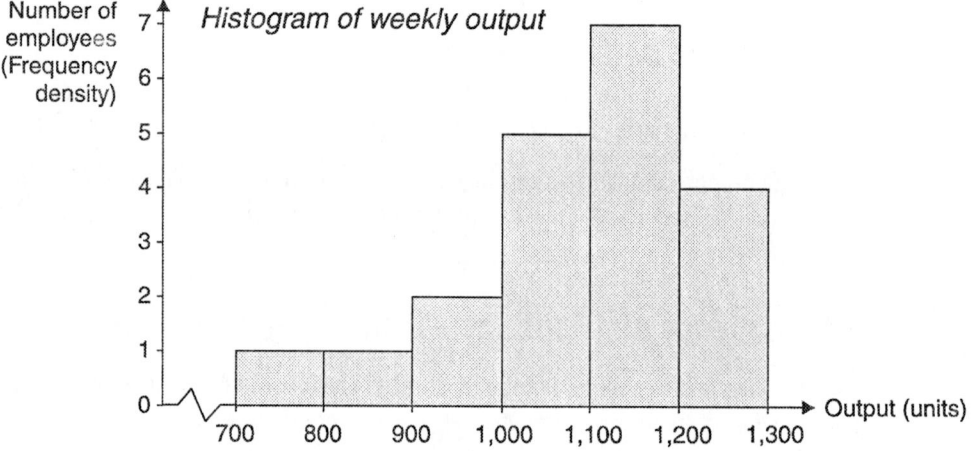

Note. That the discrete data have been treated as continuous, the intervals being changed to >700 but ≤ 800, >800 but ≤ 900 and so on.

4.2 Histograms of frequency distributions with unequal class intervals

If a distribution has **unequal class intervals**, the **heights** of the bars have to be **adjusted** for the fact that the bars do not have the same width.

4.2.1 Example: A histogram with unequal class intervals

The weekly wages of employees of Salt Lake Company are as follows:

Wages per employee	Number of employees
Up to and including $600	4
> $600 $\leq$ $800	6
> $800 $\leq$ $900	6
> $900 $\leq$ $1,200	6
More than $1,200	3

The class intervals for wages per employee are not all the same, and range from $100 to $300.

Solution

A histogram is drawn as follows.

(a) **The width of each bar on the chart must be proportionate to the corresponding class interval.** In other words, the bar representing wages of >$600 ≤$800, a range of $200, will be twice as wide as the bar representing wages of >$800 ≤$900, a range of only $100.

(b) **A standard width of bar must be selected.** This should be the size of class interval which occurs most frequently. In our example, class intervals $100, $200 and $300 each occur once. An interval of $200 will be selected as the standard width.

(c) **Open-ended classes must be closed off.** It is usual for the width of such classes to be the same as that of the adjoining class. In this example, the class 'up to and including $600' will become >$400 ≤$600 and the class 'more than $1,200' will become >$1,200 ≤$1,500.

(d) Each frequency is then multiplied by (standard class width ÷ actual class width) to obtain the height of the bar in the histogram.

Formula to learn

$$\text{Adjustment factor} = \frac{\text{Standard class width}}{\text{Current class width}}$$

(e) The height of bars no longer corresponds to **frequency** but rather to **frequency density** and hence the vertical axis should be labelled **frequency density**.

(f) Note that the data is considered to be **continuous** since the gap between, for example, $799.99 and $800.00 is very, very small.

Class interval	Size of interval	Frequency	Adjustment	Height of bar
> $400 ≤ $600	200	4	× 200/200	4
> $600 ≤ $800	200	6	× 200/200	6
> $800 ≤ $900	100	6	× 200/100	12
> $900 ≤ $1,200	300	6	× 200/300	4
> $1,200 ≤ $1,500	300	3	× 200/300	2

(i) The first two bars will be of normal height.

(ii) The third bar will be twice as high as the class frequency (6) would suggest, to compensate for the fact that the class interval, $100, is only half the standard size.

(iii) The fourth and fifth bars will be two thirds as high as the class frequencies (6 and 3) would suggest, to compensate for the fact that the class interval, $300, is 150% of the standard size.

Histogram of weekly earnings: Salt Lake

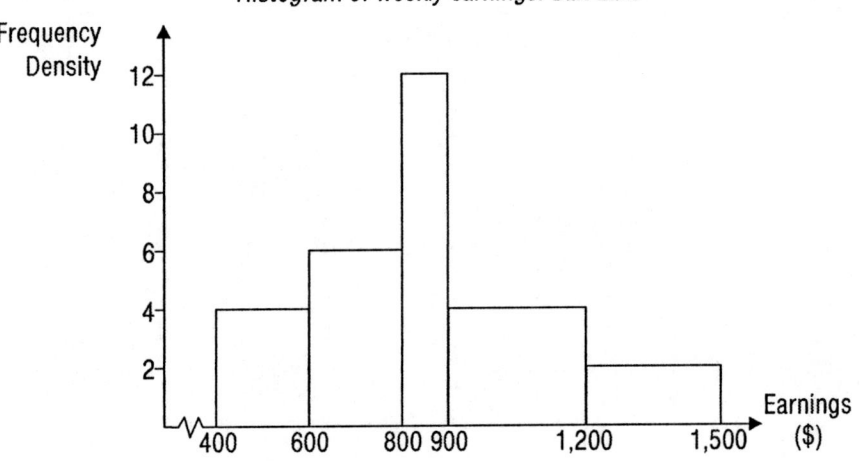

PART A DATA COLLECTION AND ANALYSIS

Question
Histogram (1)

In a histogram in which one class interval is one and a half times as wide as the remaining classes, the height to be plotted in relation to the frequency for that class is

(a) × 1.5
(b) × 1.00
(c) × 0.75
(d) × 0.67

Answer

If a distribution has unequal class intervals, the heights of the bars have to be adjusted for the fact that the bars do not have the same width. If the width of one bar is one and a half times the standard width, we must divide the frequency by one and a half, ie multiply by 0.67 (1/1.5 = 2/3 = 0.67).

The correct answer is (d).

Question
Histogram (2)

The following grouped frequency distribution shows the performances of individual sales staff in one month.

Sales	Number of sales staff
Up to $10,000	1
> $10,000 ≤ $12,000	10
> $12,000 ≤ $14,000	12
> $14,000 ≤ $18,000	8
> $18,000 ≤ $22,000	4
> $22,000	1

Required

Draw a histogram from this information

Answer

This is a grouped frequency distribution for continuous variables.

Before drawing the histogram, we must decide on the following.

(a) A **standard class width**: $2,000 will be chosen.

(b) An **open-ended class width**. In this example, the open-ended class width will therefore be $2,000 for class 'up to $10,000' and $4,000 for the class '> $22,000'.

Class interval	Size of interval $	Frequency	Adjustment	Height of bar
Up to $10,000	2,000	1	× 2/2	1
> $10,000 ≤ $12,000	2,000	10	× 2/2	10
> $12,000 ≤ $14,000	2,000	12	× 2/2	12
> $14,000 ≤ $18,000	4,000	8	× 2/4	4
> $18,000 ≤ $22,000	4,000	4	× 2/4	2
> $22,000	4,000	1	× 2/4	½

3: PRESENTATION OF DATA

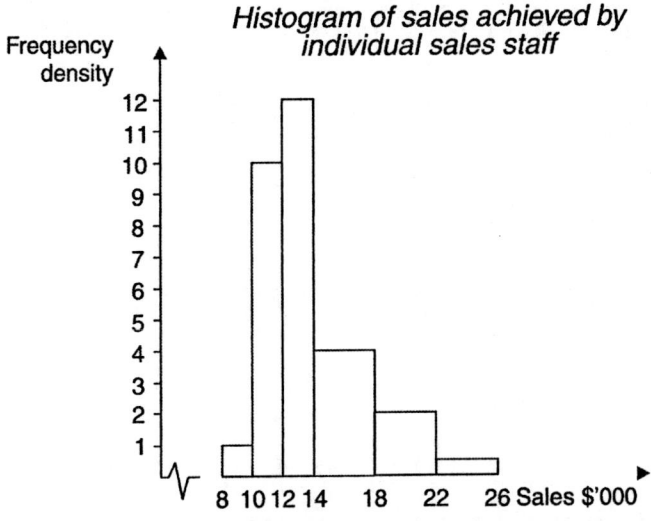

5 Ogives

Just as a grouped frequency distribution can be graphed as a histogram, a cumulative frequency distribution can be graphed as an ogive.

FAST FORWARD

An **ogive** shows the cumulative number of items with a value less than or equal to, or alternatively greater than or equal to, a certain amount.

5.1 Example: Ogives

Consider the following frequency distribution.

Number of faulty units rejected on inspection	Frequency	Cumulative frequency
> 0, ≤ 1	5	5
> 1, ≤ 2	5	10
> 2, ≤ 3	3	13
> 3, ≤ 4	1	14
	14	

An ogive would be drawn as follows:

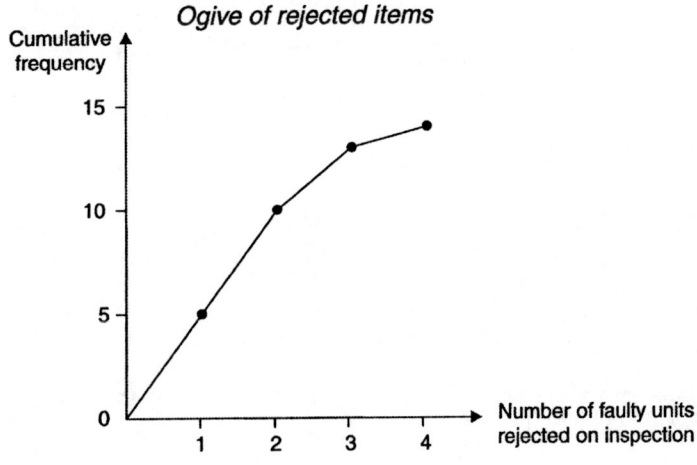

PART A   DATA COLLECTION AND ANALYSIS

The ogive is drawn by plotting the cumulative frequencies on the graph, and joining them with straight lines. Although many ogives are more accurately curved lines, you can use straight lines to make them easier to draw. **An ogive drawn with straight lines may be referred to as a cumulative frequency polygon (or cumulative frequency diagram) whereas one drawn as a curve may be referred to as a cumulative frequency curve.**

For grouped frequency distributions, where we work up through values of the variable, the cumulative frequencies are plotted against the **upper limits** of the classes. For example, for the class 'over 2, up to and including 3', the cumulative frequency should be plotted against 3.

Question Ogives

A grouped frequency distribution for the volume of output produced at a factory over a period of 40 weeks is as follows.

Output (units)	Number of times output achieved
> 0 ≤ 200	4
> 200 ≤ 400	8
> 400 ≤ 600	12
> 600 ≤ 800	10
> 800 ≤ 1,000	6
	40

Required

Draw an appropriate ogive, and estimate the number of weeks in which output was 550 units or less.

Answer

Upper limit of interval	Frequency	Cumulative frequency
200	4	4
400	8	12
600	12	24
800	10	34
1,000	6	40

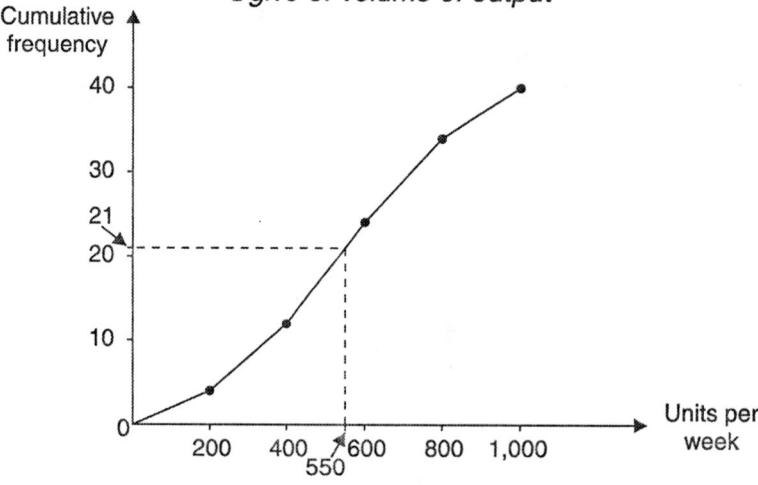

Ogive of volume of output

The dotted lines indicate that output of up to 550 units was achieved in 21 out of the 40 weeks.

5.2 Downward-sloping ogives

We can also draw ogives to show the cumulative number of items with values greater than or equal to some given value.

5.3 Example: Downward-sloping ogives

Output at a factory over a period of 80 weeks is shown by the following frequency distribution.

Output per week Units	Number of times output achieved
> 0 ≤ 100	10
> 100 ≤ 200	20
> 200 ≤ 300	25
> 300 ≤ 400	15
> 400 ≤ 500	10
	80

Required

Present this information in the form of a downward-sloping ogive.

Solution

If we want to draw an ogive to show the number of weeks in which output **exceeded** a certain value, the cumulative total should begin at 80 and drop to 0. In drawing an ogive when we work down through values of the variable, the **descending cumulative frequency** should be plotted against the **lower limit** of each class interval.

Lower limit of interval	Frequency	Cumulative ('more than') frequency
0	10	80
100	20	70
200	25	50
300	15	25
400	10	10
500	0	0

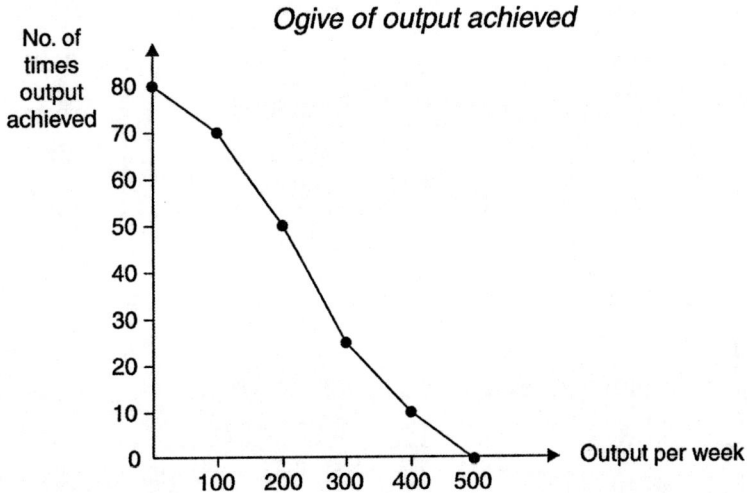

Make sure that you understand what this curve shows. For example, 350 on the x axis corresponds with about 18 on the y axis. This means that output of 350 units or more was achieved 18 times out of the 80 weeks.

PART A DATA COLLECTION AND ANALYSIS

6 Scatter diagrams

Exam focus point: Scatter diagrams have come up a few times in exams.

FAST FORWARD: **Scatter diagrams** are graphs which are used to exhibit data, (rather than equations) in order to compare the way in which two variables vary with each other.

6.1 Constructing a scatter diagram

The x axis of a scatter diagram is used to represent the independent variable and the y axis represents the dependent variable.

To construct a scatter diagram or scattergraph, we must have several pairs of data, with each pair showing the value of one variable and the corresponding value of the other variable. Each pair is plotted on a graph. The resulting graph will show a number of pairs, scattered over the graph. The scattered points might or might not appear to follow a trend.

6.2 Example: Scatter diagram

The output at a factory each week for the last ten weeks, and the cost of that output, were as follows:

Week	1	2	3	4	5	6	7	8	9	10
Output (units)	10	12	10	8	9	11	7	12	9	14
Cost ($)	42	44	38	34	38	43	30	47	37	50

Required

Plot the data given on a scatter diagram.

Solution

The data could be shown on a scatter diagram as follows:

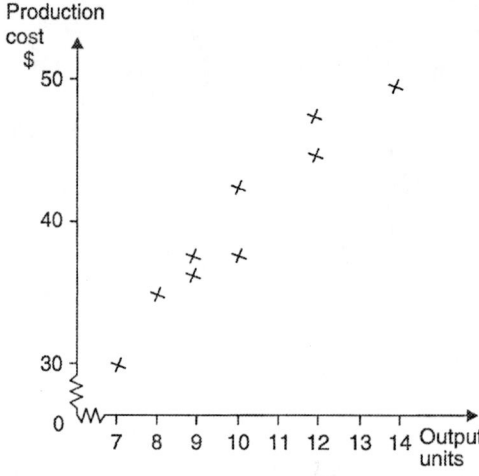

(a) The cost depends on the volume of output: volume is the independent variable and is shown on the x axis.

(b) You will notice from the graph that the plotted data, although scattered, lie approximately on a rising trend line, with higher total costs at higher output volumes. (The lower part of the axes have been omitted, so as not to waste space. The break in the axes is indicated by the jagged lines.)

6.3 The trend line

For the most part, scatter diagrams are used to try to identify **trend lines**.

If a trend can be seen in a scatter diagram, the next step is to try to draw a trend line.

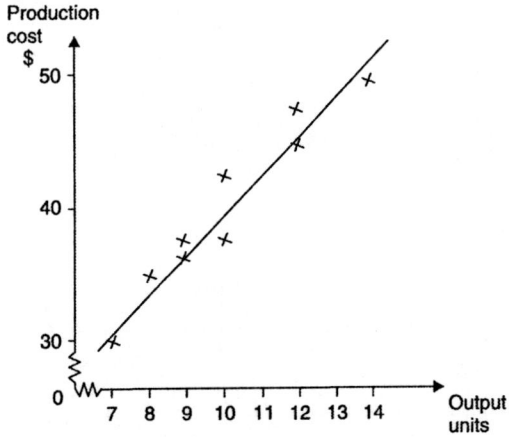

6.3.1 Using trend lines to make predictions

(a) In the previous example, we have drawn a trend line from the scatter diagram of output units and production cost. This trend line might turn out to be, say, y = 10 + 3x. We could then use this trend line to establish what we think costs ought to be, approximately, if output were, say, 10 units or 15 units in any week. (These 'expected' costs could subsequently be compared with the actual costs, so that managers could judge whether actual costs were higher or lower than they ought to be.)

(b) If a scatter diagram is used to record sales over time, we could draw a trend line, and use this to forecast sales for next year.

6.3.2 Adding trend lines to scatter diagrams

The trend line could be a straight line, or a curved line. The simplest technique for drawing a trend line is to make a visual judgement about what the closest-fitting trend line seems to be, the 'line of best fit'.

Here is another example of a scatter diagram with a trend line added.

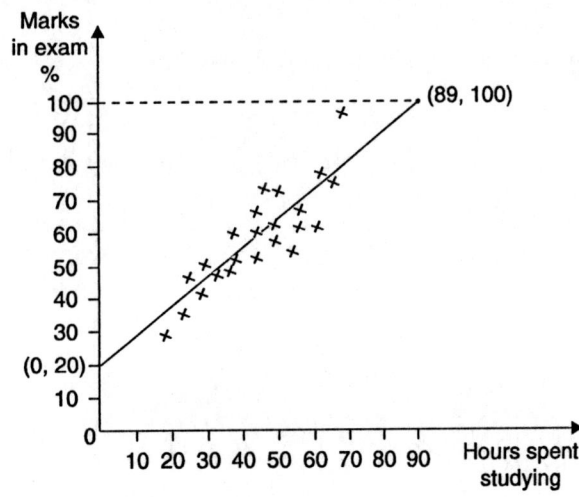

The equation of a straight line is given by **y = a + bx**, where **a** is the **intercept** on the y axis and **b** is the **gradient**.

The line passes through the point x = 0, y = 20, so a = 20. The line also passes through x = 89, y = 100, so:

100 = 20 + (b × 89)

b = $\frac{(100-20)}{89}$

= 0.9

The line is y = 20 + 0.9x

We will look at this in more detail in Chapter 6.

Question — Definite variables

The quantities of widgets produced by WDG Co during the year ended 31 October 20X9 and the related costs were as follows.

Month	Production Thousands	Factory cost $'000
20X8		
November	7	45
December	10	59
20X9		
January	13	75
February	14	80
March	11	65
April	7	46
May	5	35
June	4	30
July	3	25
August	2	20
September	1	15
October	5	35

You may assume that the value of money remained stable throughout the year.

Required

(a) Draw a scatter diagram related to the data provided above, and plot on it the line of best fit.

(b) Now answer the following questions:

  (i) What would you expect the factory cost to have been if 12,000 widgets had been produced in a particular month?

  (ii) What is your estimate of WDG's monthly fixed cost?

Answer

Your answers to parts (b)(i) and (ii) may have been slightly different from those given here, but they should not have been very different, because the data points lay very nearly along a straight line.

(a) WDG Co – Scatter diagram of production and factory costs, November 20X8–October 20X9

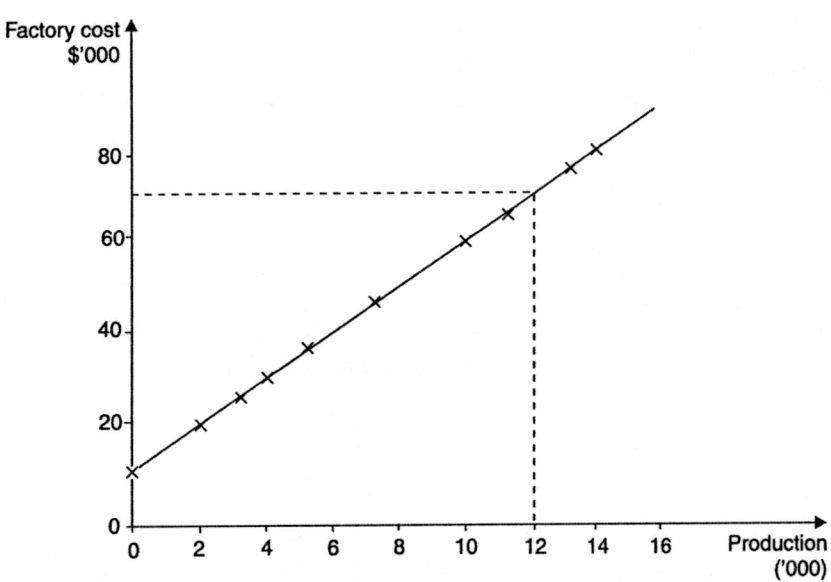

(b) (i) The estimated factory cost for a production of 12,000 widgets is $70,000.

(ii) The monthly fixed costs are indicated by the point where the line of best fit meets the vertical axis (costs at zero production). The fixed costs are estimated as $10,000 a month.

Chapter Roundup

- **Tables** are a simple way of presenting information about two variables.
- **Charts** often convey the meaning or significance of data more clearly than would a table.
- There are three main **types of bar chart**: **simple**, **component** (including **percentage component**) and **multiple** (or **compound**).
- **Frequency distributions** are used if values of particular variables occur more than once.
- A **frequency distribution** can be represented pictorially by means of a **histogram**. The number of observations in a class is represented by the **area** covered by the bar, rather than by its height.
- An **ogive** shows the cumulative number of items with a value less than or equal to, or alternatively greater than or equal to, a certain amount.
- **Scatter diagrams** are graphs which are used to exhibit data, (rather than equations) in order to compare the way in which two variables vary with each other.

Quick Quiz

1. Which of the following is not recommended when producing a table of information?

    (a) Keeping accuracy to a maximum
    (b) Clearly labelling all columns
    (c) Eliminating unnecessary information
    (d) Ordering columns and rows by order of importance and magnitude

2. When selecting a standard width of bar in a histogram you would select the size of the class interval which occurs most frequently.

    True ☐
    False ☐

3. A grouped frequency distribution can be drawn as a(n) **histogram/ogive**, whereas a cumulative frequency distribution can be graphed as a(n) **ogive/histogram**.

4. A scatter diagram has an x axis and a y axis which represent dependent and independent variables as follows.

    x axis ⎤
            ? ⎡ independent variable
    y axis ⎦   ⎣ dependent variable

5. In a histogram, one class is ¾ the width of the other classes. If the score in that class is 33, the correct height to plot on the histogram is ☐

6. A pie chart is used to display the following data:

Sales	%
Region A	26
Region B	41
Region C	33

    What angle on the pie chart will be used to represent Region C's share of sales?

    (a) 33
    (b) 237.6
    (c) 118.8
    (d) 59.4

7. A cumulative frequency distribution of output of employees is as follows:

Weekly output Units	Cumulative frequency
Less than 150	90
Less than 200	250
Less than 300	310
Less than 400	340
Less than 600	350

    How many employees produced more than 200 units? ☐

    How many employees produced between 200 and 300 units? ☐

PART A   DATA COLLECTION AND ANALYSIS

Answers to Quick Quiz

1. (a) Maximising accuracy would make the table too detailed and hard to understand.

2. True

3. A grouped frequency distribution can be drawn as a **histogram**, whereas a cumulative frequency distribution can be graphed as an **ogive**.

4. x axis ⟶ independent variable
   y axis ⟶ dependent variable

5. $\boxed{44}$

   $$\frac{33}{0.75} = 44$$

6. (c) Region C's angle is given by 33% × 360 = 118.8

7. $\boxed{100}$ produced more than 200 units
   $\boxed{60}$ produced between 200 and 300 units

End of Chapter Question

Presentation of data (AIA Nov 09, Nov 08)

The director of a business believes that the sales of one of its products are directly related to the average price that competitors are charging for the identical product. Over a 12 month period the monthly sales has been recorded of his product alongside the average price charged by his competitors as follows.

Month	Price (£)	Sales
1	1.75	48
2	2.10	64
3	1.80	53
4	1.75	45
5	2.00	60
6	1.60	35
7	1.40	38
8	1.75	25
9	1.85	55
10	1.80	50
11	1.70	38
12	1.60	40

Required

(a) Plot the scatter diagram of the above data and comment on the possible relationship between the variables. **(6 marks)**

The ages, rounded to the nearest year, of a group of employees in the business have been recorded as follows:

Age, years	Frequency
16 – 20	5
21 – 25	20
26 – 30	24
31 – 35	30
36 – 40	27
41 – 45	22
46 – 50	18
51 – 55	12
56 – 60	8
61 – 65	3

(b) Plot a cumulative frequency graph for this distribution and comment on its possible uses.
(6 marks)

(Total = 12 marks)

PART A DATA COLLECTION AND ANALYSIS

Summary statistics – averages

Topic list	Syllabus reference
1 The arithmetic mean	6.3
2 The mode	6.3
3 The median	6.3

Introduction

In Chapter 3 we saw how data can be summarised and presented in tabular, chart and graphical formats. Sometimes you might need more information than that provided by diagrammatic representations of data. In such circumstances you may need to apply some sort of numerical analysis, for example you might wish to calculate a **measure of centrality** and a **measure of dispersion**. In Chapter 4b we will look at measures of dispersion, in this chapter measures of centrality, or averages.

An **average** is a representative figure that is used to give some impression of the size of all the items in the population. There are three main types of average:

- **Arithmetic mean**
- **Mode**
- **Median**

We will be looking at each of these averages in turn, their calculation, advantages and disadvantages. In the next chapter we will move on to the second type of numerical measure, measures of dispersion.

PART A DATA COLLECTION AND ANALYSIS

1 The arithmetic mean

1.1 Arithmetic mean of ungrouped data

FAST FORWARD

The **arithmetic mean** is the best known type of average and is widely understood. It is used for further statistical analysis.

Arithmetic mean of ungrouped data = $\dfrac{\text{Sum of values of items}}{\text{Number of items}}$

The arithmetic mean of a variable x is shown as $\bar{x}$ ('x bar').

1.1.1 Example: The arithmetic mean

The demand for a product on each of 20 days was as follows (in units).

3 12 7 17 3 14 9 6 11 10 1 4 19 7 15 6 9 12 12 8

The arithmetic mean of daily demand is $\bar{x}$.

$\bar{x} = \dfrac{\text{Sum of demand}}{\text{Number of days}} = \dfrac{185}{20} = 9.25$ units

In this example, demand on any one day is never actually 9.25 units. The arithmetic mean is merely an **average representation** of demand on each of the 20 days.

1.2 Arithmetic mean of data in a frequency distribution

It is more likely in an assessment that you will be asked to calculate the arithmetic mean of a **frequency distribution**. In our previous example, the frequency distribution would be shown as follows:

Daily demand x	Frequency f	Demand × frequency fx
1	1	1
3	2	6
4	1	4
6	2	12
7	2	14
8	1	8
9	2	18
10	1	10
11	1	11
12	3	36
14	1	14
15	1	15
17	1	17
19	1	19
	20	185

$\bar{x} = \dfrac{185}{20} = 9.25$

1.3 Sigma, Σ

Key term

Σ means 'the sum of' and is used as shorthand to mean 'the sum of a set of values'.

In the previous example:

(a) Σf would mean the sum of all the frequencies, which is 20

(b) Σfx would mean the sum of all the values of 'frequency multiplied by daily demand', that is, all 14 values of fx, so Σfx = 185

1.4 Arithmetic mean of grouped data in class intervals

FAST FORWARD

The **arithmetic mean of grouped data**, $\bar{x} = \dfrac{\Sigma fx}{\Sigma f}$ where n is the number of values recorded, or the number of items measured.

Exam focus point

This formula will be given to you in your exam.

There are a couple of different formulae given in the exam formulae sheet in the real exam. We recommend you use the formula above both for ease and consistency.

You might also be asked to calculate (or at least approximate) the arithmetic mean of a frequency distribution, where the frequencies are shown in class intervals.

1.4.1 Example: The arithmetic mean of grouped data

Using the example in Paragraph 1.2, the frequency distribution might have been shown as follows:

Daily demand	Frequency
>0 ≤ 5	4
>5 ≤ 10	8
>10 ≤ 15	6
>15 ≤ 20	2
	20

There is, of course, an extra difficulty with finding the average now; as the data have been collected into classes, a **certain amount of detail has been lost** and the values of the variables to be used in the calculation of the mean are **not clearly specified**.

1.4.2 The midpoint of class intervals

To calculate the arithmetic mean of grouped data we therefore need to decide on **a value which best represents all of the values in a particular class interval**. This value is known as the **midpoint**.

The **midpoint** of each class interval is conventionally taken, on the assumption that the frequencies occur **evenly** over the class interval range. In the example above, the variable is **discrete**, so the first class includes 1, 2, 3, 4 and 5, giving a midpoint of 3. With a **continuous** variable, the mid-points would have been 2.5, 7.5 and so on. Once the value of x has been decided, the mean is calculated using the formula for the arithmetic mean of grouped data.

PART A   DATA COLLECTION AND ANALYSIS

Daily demand	Midpoint x	Frequency f	fx
>0 ≤ 5	3	4	12
>5 ≤ 10	8	8	64
>10 ≤ 15	13	6	78
>15 ≤ 20	18	2	36
		Σf = 20	Σfx = 190

Arithmetic mean $\bar{x} = \dfrac{\Sigma fx}{\Sigma f} = \dfrac{190}{20} = 9.5$ units

Because the assumption that frequencies occur evenly within each class interval is not quite correct in this example, our approximate mean of 9.5 is not exactly correct, and is in error by 0.25 (9.5 – 9.25). **As the frequencies become larger, the size of this approximating error should become smaller.**

1.5 Example: The arithmetic mean of combined data

Suppose that the mean age of a group of 5 people is 27 and the mean age of another group of 8 people is 32. How would we find the mean age of the whole group of 13 people?

Arithmetic mean = $\dfrac{\text{Sum of values of items}}{\text{Number of items}}$

The sum of the ages in the first group is 5 × 27 = 135

The sum of the ages in the second group is 8 × 32 = 256

The sum of all 13 ages is 135 + 256 = 391

The mean age is therefore $\dfrac{391}{13}$ = 30.08 years.

Question   Mean

The mean weight of 10 units at 5 kg, 10 units at 7 kg and 20 units at X kg is 8 kg.

The value of X is [   ]

Answer

The value of X is [10]

Workings

Mean = $\dfrac{\text{Sum of values of items}}{\text{Number of items}}$

Sum of first 10 units = 5 × 10 = 50 kg

Sum of second 10 units = 7 × 10 = 70 kg

Sum of third 20 units = 20 × X = 20X

Sum of all 40 units = 50 + 70 + 20X = 120 + 20X

∴ Arithmetic mean = 8 = $\frac{120 + 20X}{40}$

∴ 8 × 40 = 120 + 20X

320 = 120 + 20X (subtract 120 from both sides)

320 − 120 = 20X

200 = 20X

10 = X (divide both sides by 20)

1.6 The advantages and disadvantages of the arithmetic mean

Advantages of the arithmetic mean

- It is easy to calculate
- It is widely understood
- It is representative of the whole set of data
- It is supported by mathematical theory and is suited to further statistical analysis

Disadvantages of the arithmetic mean

- **Its value may not correspond to any actual value.** For example, the 'average' family might have 2.3 children, but no family has exactly 2.3 children.

- **An arithmetic mean might be distorted by extremely high or low values.** For example, the mean of 3, 4, 4 and 6 is 4.25, but the mean of 3, 4, 4, 6 and 15 is 6.4. The high value, 15, distorts the average and in some circumstances the mean would be a misleading and inappropriate figure.

Question — Definite variables

For the week ended 15 November, the wages earned by the 69 operators employed in the machine shop of Mermaid Co were as follows.

Wages	Number of operatives
under $600	3
Over $600 and under $700	11
$700 and under $800	16
$800 and under $900	15
$900 and under $1,000	10
$1,000 and under $1,100	8
$1,100	6
	69

Required

Calculate the arithmetic mean wage of the machine operators of Mermaid Co for the week ended 15 November.

Answer

The midpoint of the range 'under $600' is assumed to be $550 and that of the range over $1,100 to be $1,150, since all other class intervals are $100. This is obviously an approximation which might result in a loss of accuracy, but there is no better alternative assumption to use. Because wages can vary in steps of 1c, they are virtually a continuous variable and hence the mid-points of the classes are halfway between their end points.

PART A DATA COLLECTION AND ANALYSIS

Midpoint of class x $	Frequency f	fx
550	3	1,650
650	11	7,150
750	16	12,000
850	15	12,750
950	10	9,500
1,050	8	8,400
1,150	6	6,900
	69	58,350

Arithmetic mean $= \dfrac{\Sigma fx}{\Sigma f} = \dfrac{58,350}{69} = \$845.65$

2 The mode

2.1 The modal value

The **mode** or **modal value** is an average which means 'the most frequently occurring value'.

2.2 Example: The mode

The daily demand for inventory in a ten day period is as follows:

Demand Units	Number of days
6	3
7	6
8	1
	10

The mode is 7 units, because it is the value which occurs most frequently.

2.3 The mode of a grouped frequency distribution

The **mode of a grouped frequency distribution** can be calculated from a histogram.

2.4 Example: Finding the mode from a histogram

Consider the following grouped frequency distribution:

Class interval			Frequency
0	and less than	10	0
10	and less than	20	50
20	and less than	30	150
30	and less than	40	100

(a) The modal class (the one with the highest frequency) is '20 and less than 30'. But how can we find a single value to represent the mode?

(b) What we need to do is draw a histogram of the frequency distribution.

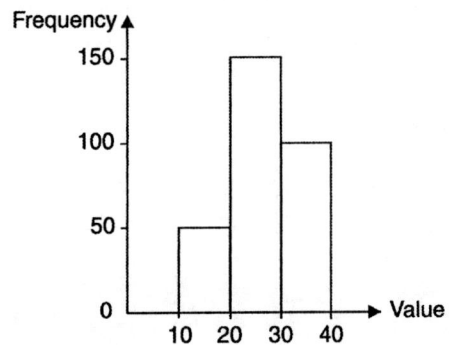

The **modal class is always the class with the tallest bar**. This may not be the class with the highest frequency if the classes do not all have the same width.

(c) We can estimate the mode graphically as follows:

Step 1 Join with a straight line the top left hand corner of the bar for the modal class and the top left hand corner of the next bar to the right.

Step 2 Join with a straight line the top right hand corner of the bar for the modal class and the top right hand corner of the next bar to the left.

(d) Where these two lines intersect, we find the **estimated modal value**. In this example it is approximately 26.7.

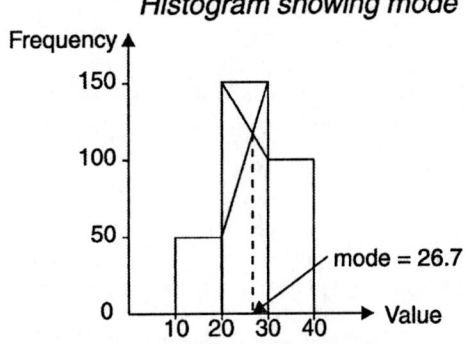
Histogram showing mode

(e) We are assuming that the frequencies occur evenly within each class interval but this may not always be correct. It is unlikely that the 150 values in the modal class occur evenly. Hence **the mode in a grouped frequency distribution is only an estimate.**

2.5 The advantages and disadvantages of the mode

Advantages of the mode

- It is easy to find
- It is not influenced by a few extreme values
- It can be used for data which are not even numerical (unlike the mean and median)
- It can be the value of an actual item in the distribution

Disadvantages of the mode

- It may be unrepresentative; it takes no account of a high proportion of the data, only representing the most common value
- It does not take every value into account
- There can be two or more modes within a set of data
- If the modal class is only very slightly bigger than another class, just a few more items in this other class could mean a substantially different result, suggesting some instability in the measure

PART A   DATA COLLECTION AND ANALYSIS

3 The median

3.1 The middle item of a distribution

The median of a set of ungrouped data is found by arranging the items in ascending or descending order of value, and selecting the item in the middle of the range. **A list of items in order of value is called an array.**

> **FAST FORWARD**
>
> The **median** is the value of the middle member of an array. The middle item of an odd number of items is calculated as the $\left(\dfrac{n+1}{2}\right)^{th}$ item.

3.2 Example: The median

(a) The median of the following nine values:

    8   6   9   12   15   6   3   20   11

is found by taking the middle item (the fifth one) in the array:

    3   6   6   8   9   11   12   15   20

The median is 9.

(b) Consider the following array.

    1   2   2   2   3   5   6   7   8   11

The median is 4 because, with an even number of items, we have to take the arithmetic mean of the two middle ones (in this example, (3 + 5)/2 = 4).

Question   Median (1)

The following times taken to produce a batch of 100 units of Product X have been noted.

21 mins	17 mins	24 mins	11 mins	37 mins	27 mins
20 mins	15 mins	17 mins	23 mins	29 mins	30 mins
24 mins	18 mins	17 mins	21 mins	24 mins	20 mins

What is the median time?

Answer

The times can be arranged as follows:

11 15 17 17 17 18 20 20 21 21 23 24 24 24 27 29 30 37

There are 18 items which is an even number, therefore the median is the arithmetic mean of the two middle items (ie ninth and tenth items) = 21 mins.

4a: SUMMARY STATISTICS – AVERAGES

Question Median (2)

The following scores are observed for the times taken to complete a task, in minutes:

12,   34,   14,   15,   21,   24,   9,   17,   11,   8

What is the median score?

(a) 14.00
(b) 14.10
(c) 14.50
(d) 14.60

Answer

The first thing to do is to arrange the scores in order of magnitude.

8,   9,   11,   12,   14,   15,   17,   21,   24,   34

There are ten items, and so median is the arithmetic mean of the 5th and 6th items.

$$= \frac{14 + 15}{2} = \frac{29}{2} = 14.50$$

The correct answer is therefore (c).

You could have eliminated options B and D straight away. Since there are ten items, and they are all whole numbers, the average of the 5th and 6th items is either going to be a whole number (14.00) or 'something and a half' (14.50).

3.3 Finding the median of an ungrouped frequency distribution

The median of an ungrouped frequency distribution is found in a similar way. Consider the following distribution.

Value x	Frequency f	Cumulative frequency
8	3	3
12	7	10
16	12	22
17	8	30
19	5	35
	35	

The median would be the (35 + 1)/2 = 18th item. The 18th item has a value of 16, as we can see from the cumulative frequencies in the right hand column of the above table.

3.4 Finding the median of a grouped frequency distribution

FAST FORWARD The **median of a grouped frequency distribution** can be established from an ogive.

Finding the median of a grouped frequency distribution from an ogive is best explained by means of an example.

3.5 Example: The median from an ogive

Construct an ogive of the following frequency distribution and hence establish the median.

Class $	Frequency	Cumulative frequency
≥ 340, < 370	17	17
≥ 370, < 400	9	26
≥ 400, < 430	9	35
≥ 430, < 460	3	38
≥ 460, < 490	2	40
	40	

Solution

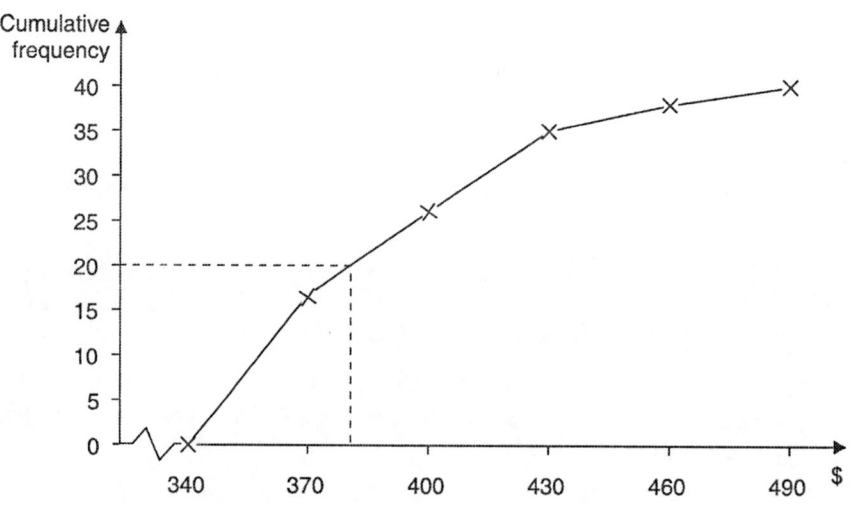

The median is at the $1/2 \times 40 = 20$th item. Reading off from the horizontal axis on the ogive, the value of the median is approximately $380.

Note. Because we are assuming that the values are spread evenly within each class, the median calculated is only approximate.

3.6 The advantages and disadvantages of the median

Advantages of the median

- It is easy to understand
- It is unaffected by extremely high or low values
- It can be the value of an actual item in the distribution

Disadvantages of the median

- It fails to reflect the full range of values
- It is unsuitable for further statistical analysis
- Arranging data into order of size can be tedious

Chapter Roundup

- The **arithmetic mean** is the best known type of average and is widely understood. It is used for further statistical analysis.

- The **arithmetic mean of ungrouped data** = $\dfrac{\text{Sum of values of items}}{\text{Number of items}}$

- The **arithmetic mean of grouped data**, $\bar{x} = \dfrac{\sum fx}{n}$ or $\dfrac{\sum fx}{\sum f}$ where n is the number of values recorded, or the number of items measured.

- The **mode or modal value** is an average which means 'the most frequently occurring value'.

- The **mode of a grouped frequency distribution** can be calculated from a histogram.

- The **median** is the value of the middle member of an array. The middle item of an odd number of items is calculated as the $\dfrac{(n+1)^{th}}{2}$ item.

- The **median of a grouped frequency distribution** can be established from an ogive.

PART A   DATA COLLECTION AND ANALYSIS

Quick Quiz

1. Insert the formulae in the box below into the correct position.

   (a) The arithmetic mean of ungrouped data =

   (b) The arithmetic mean of grouped data =   or

   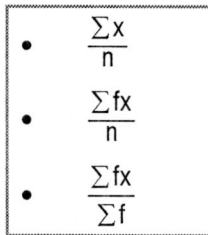

   - $\dfrac{\sum x}{n}$
   - $\dfrac{\sum fx}{n}$
   - $\dfrac{\sum fx}{\sum f}$

2. What is the name given to the average which means 'the most frequently occurring value'?

(a) Arithmetic mean
(b) Median
(c) Mode

3. The mean weight of a group of components has been calculated as 133.5. The individual weights of the components were 143, 96, x, 153.5, 92.5, y, 47. When y = 4x;

   What is the value of x?

4. Calculate the mid-points for both discrete and continuous variables in the table below.

Class interval	Midpoint (Discrete data)	Midpoint (Continuous data)
25 < 30		
30 < 35		
35 < 40		
40 < 45		
45 < 50		
50 < 55		
55 < 60		
60 < 65		

5. (a) The mode of a grouped frequency distribution can be found from a(n) **histogram/ogive**.
   (b) The median of a grouped frequency distribution can be found from a(n) **histogram/ogive**.

6. A group of children have the following ages in years: 10, 8, 6, 9, 13, 12, 7, 11.

   What is the median age?

Answers to Quick Quiz

1. (a) $\dfrac{\sum x}{n}$

   (b) $\dfrac{\sum fx}{n}$ or $\dfrac{\sum fx}{\sum f}$

2. (c) Mode

3. $\boxed{80.5}$

   Mean = $\dfrac{\text{Total}}{7}$

   So Total = 7×133.5
   = 934.5

   $934.5 = 143 + 96 + x + 153.5 + 92.5 + y + 47$
   $934.5 = 532 + x + y$
   $y = 4x$

   So $934.5 = 532 + x + 4x$
   $5x = 934.5 - 532$
   $5x = 402.5$
   $x = 80.5$

4.

Class interval	Midpoint (Discrete data)	Midpoint (Continuous data)
25 < 30	27	27.5
30 < 35	32	32.5
35 < 40	37	37.5
40 < 45	42	42.5
45 < 50	47	47.5
50 < 55	52	52.5
55 < 60	57	57.5
60 < 65	62	62.5

5. (a) Histogram
   (b) Ogive

6. $\boxed{9½}$ 6, 7, 8, 9, 10, 11, 12, 13

   The median is 9½.

PART A DATA COLLECTION AND ANALYSIS

End of Chapter Question

Averages (AIA Nov 08)

The ages, rounded to the nearest year, of a group of employees in a company have been recorded as follows.

Age, years	Frequency
16 – 20	5
21 – 25	20
26 – 30	24
31 – 35	30
36 – 40	27
41 – 45	22
46 – 50	18
51 – 55	12
56 – 60	8
61 – 65	3

Required

(a) Plot a cumulative frequency graph for this distribution and comment on its possible uses.

(6 marks)

(b) Estimate values of the mean, mode and median of this distribution. **(8 marks)**

(Total = 14 marks)

Summary statistics – dispersion

4b

Topic list	Syllabus reference
1 The range	6.3
2 Quartiles and the semi-interquartile range	6.3
3 The mean deviation	6.3
4 The variance and the standard deviation	6.3
5 The coefficient of variation	6.3
6 Skewness	6.3

Introduction

In Chapter 4a we introduced the first type of statistic that can be used to describe certain aspects of a set of data – **averages**. Averages are a method of determining the **'location'** or **central point** of a distribution, but they give no information about the **dispersion** of values in the distribution.

Measures of dispersion give some idea of the **spread of a variable about its average**. The main measures are as follows:

- **The range**
- **The semi-interquartile range**
- **The standard deviation**
- **The variance**
- **The coefficient of variation**

PART A   DATA COLLECTION AND ANALYSIS

1 The range

FAST FORWARD The **range** is the difference between the highest and lowest observations.

1.1 Main properties of the range as a measure of spread

- It is easy to find and to understand
- It is easily affected by one or two extreme values
- It gives no indication of spread between the extremes
- It is not suitable for further statistical analysis

Question Mean and range

Calculate the mean and the range of the following set of data.

4   8   7   3   5   16   24   5

Mean	Range

Answer

Mean	Range
9	21

Workings

1   Mean $\bar{x} = \dfrac{72}{8} = 9$

2   Range = 24 − 3 = 21

2 Quartiles and the semi-interquartile range

2.1 Quartiles

FAST FORWARD The **quartiles** and the **median** divide the population into four groups of equal size.

Key terms

Quartiles are one means of identifying the range within which most of the values in the population occur.

- The **lower quartile** (Q_1) is the value below which 25% of the population fall
- The **upper quartile** (Q_3) is the value above which 25% of the population fall
- The **median** (Q_2) is the value of the middle member of an array

2.1.1 Example: Quartiles

If we had 11 data items:

- $Q_1 = 11 \times 1/4 = 2.75 = $ 3rd item
- $Q_3 = 11 \times 3/4 = 8.25 = $ 9th item
- $Q_2 = 11 \times 1/2 = 5.5 = $ 6th item

2.2 The semi-interquartile range

FAST FORWARD

The **semi-interquartile range** is half the difference between the upper and lower quartiles.

The lower and upper quartiles can be used to calculate a measure of spread called the **semi-interquartile range**.

Key term

The **semi-interquartile range** is half the difference between the lower and upper quartiles and is sometimes called the **quartile deviation**, $\frac{(Q_3-Q_1)}{2}$

For example, if the lower and upper quartiles of a frequency distribution were 6 and 11, the semi-interquartile range of the distribution would be $(11 - 6)/2 = 2.5$ units. This shows that the average distance of a quartile from the median is 2.5. The smaller the quartile deviation, the less dispersed is the distribution.

As with the range, the quartile deviation may be misleading as a measure of spread. If the majority of the data are towards the lower end of the range then the third quartile will be considerably further above the median than the first quartile is below it, and when the two distances from the median are averaged the difference is disguised. Therefore it is often better to quote the actual values of the two quartiles, rather than the quartile deviation.

2.3 The inter-quartile range

FAST FORWARD

The **inter-quartile range** is the difference between the values of the upper and lower quartiles $(Q_3 - Q_1)$ and hence shows the range of values of the middle half of the population.

2.4 Example: Using ogives to find the semi-interquartile range

Construct an ogive of the following frequency distribution and hence establish the semi-interquartile range.

Class $	Frequency	Cumulative frequency
$\geq 340, < 370$	17	17
$\geq 370, < 400$	9	26
$\geq 400, < 430$	9	35
$\geq 430, < 460$	3	38
$\geq 460, < 490$	2	40
	40	

Solution

Establish which items are Q_1 and Q_3 (the lower and upper quartiles respectively).

Upper quartile $(Q_3) = 3/4 \times 40 = $ 30th value

Lower quartile $(Q_1) = 1/4 \times 40 = $ 10th value

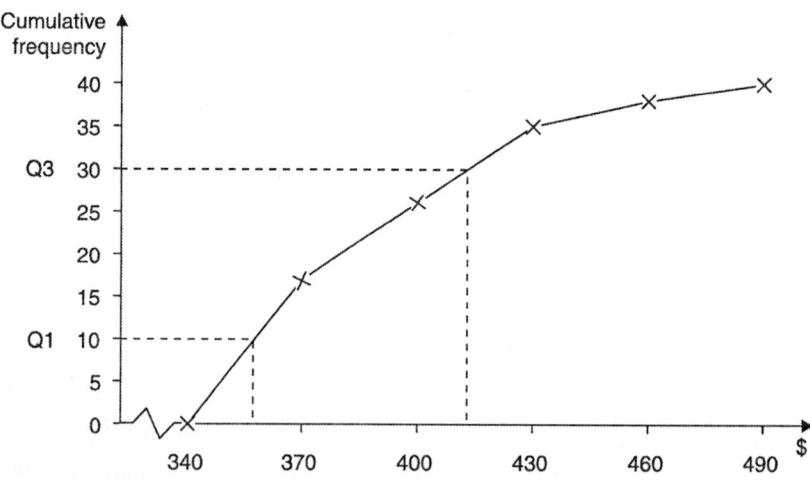

Reading off the values from the ogive, approximate values are as follows.

Q_3 (upper quartile) = $412

Q_1 (lower quartile) = $358

$$\text{Semi-interquartile range} = \frac{Q_3 - Q_1}{2}$$

$$= \frac{\$(412 - 358)}{2}$$

$$= \frac{\$54}{2}$$

$$= \$27$$

> **Exam Focus point**
>
> Remember that the median is equal to Q_2 (the point above which, and below which, 50% of the population fall). In the example in Paragraph 2.4 the median would be the 40/2 = 20th item which could be found from reading off the ogive (approximately 385).

2.5 Deciles

As we have seen, quartiles divide a cumulative distribution into quarters. We can also divide the cumulative distribution into tenths to produce **deciles**. For example, the first decile will have 10% of values below it and 90% above it.

4b: SUMMARY STATISTICS – DISPERSION

3 The mean deviation

3.1 Measuring dispersion

Because it only uses the middle 50% of the population, the inter-quartile range is a useful measure of dispersion if there are **extreme values** in the distribution. If there are no extreme values which could potentially distort a measure of dispersion, however, it seems unreasonable to exclude 50% of the data. The mean deviation (the topic of this section), and the standard deviation (the topic of Section 4) are often more useful measures.

FAST FORWARD

> The **mean deviation** is a measure of the average amount by which the values in a distribution differ from the arithmetic mean.

Mean deviation = $\dfrac{\Sigma f |x - \bar{x}|}{n}$

You will need to know this formula for your assessment but we are using it to build up your understanding of this topic.

3.2 Explaining the mean deviation formula

(a) $|x - \bar{x}|$ is the difference between each value (x) in the distribution and the arithmetic mean $\bar{x}$ of the distribution. When calculating the mean deviation for grouped data the deviations should be measured to the midpoint of each class: that is, x is the midpoint of the class interval. The vertical bars mean that all differences are taken as positive since the total of all of the differences, if this is not done, will always equal zero. Thus if x = 3 and $\bar{x}$ = 5, then $x - \bar{x}$ = –2 but $|x - \bar{x}|$ = 2.

(b) $f |x - \bar{x}|$ is the value in (a) above, multiplied by the frequency for the class.

(c) $\Sigma f |x - \bar{x}|$ is the sum of the results of all the calculations in (b) above.

(d) n (which equals Σf) is the number of items in the distribution.

3.3 Example: The mean deviation

The hours of overtime worked in a particular quarter by the 60 employees of ABC Co are as follows.

Hours		
More than	Not more than	Frequency
0	10	3
10	20	6
20	30	11
30	40	15
40	50	12
50	60	7
60	70	6
		60

Required

Calculate the mean deviation of the frequency distribution shown above.

PART A DATA COLLECTION AND ANALYSIS

Solution

Midpoint x	f	fx	$|x - \bar{x}|$	$f|x - \bar{x}|$
5	3	15	32	96
15	6	90	22	132
25	11	275	12	132
35	15	525	2	30
45	12	540	8	96
55	7	385	18	126
65	6	390	28	168
	$\Sigma f = 60$	$\Sigma fx = 2{,}220$		780

Arithmetic mean $\bar{x} = \dfrac{\Sigma fx}{\Sigma f} = \dfrac{2{,}220}{60} = 37$

Mean deviation $= \dfrac{780}{60} = 13$ hours

Question — Mean deviation

Complete the following table and then calculate the arithmetic mean and the mean deviation of the following frequency distribution (to one decimal place).

Value	Frequency of occurrence
5	4
15	6
25	8
35	20
45	6
55	6
	50

x	f	fx	$|x - \bar{x}|$	$f|x - \bar{x}|$
5				
15				
25				
35				
45				
55				

Arithmetic mean $\bar{x} = \boxed{} = \boxed{}$

Mean deviation $= \boxed{} = \boxed{}$

Answer

x	f	fx	$|x - \bar{x}|$	$f|x - \bar{x}|$
5	4	20	27.2	108.8
15	6	90	17.2	103.2
25	8	200	7.2	57.6
35	20	700	2.8	56.0
45	6	270	12.8	76.8
55	6	330	22.8	136.8
	50	1,610		539.2

Arithmetic mean $\bar{x} = \dfrac{1{,}610}{50} = 32.2$

Mean deviation $= \dfrac{539.2}{50} = 10.8$

3.4 Summary of the mean deviation

(a) It is a measure of dispersion which shows by how much, on average, each item in the distribution differs in value from the arithmetic mean of the distribution.

(b) Unlike quartiles, it uses all values in the distribution to measure the dispersion, but it is not greatly affected by a few extreme values because an average is taken.

(c) It is not, however, suitable for further statistical analysis.

4 The variance and the standard deviation

4.1 The variance

FAST FORWARD

The **variance**, s^2, is the average of the squared mean deviation for each value in a distribution.

Instead of s, σ is the Greek letter sigma (in lower case) is sometimes used. The variance is therefore called 'sigma squared'.

4.2 Calculation of the variance for ungrouped data

Step 1	Difference between value and mean	$x - \bar{x}$
Step 2	Square of the difference	$(x - \bar{x})^2$
Step 3	Sum of the squares of the difference	$\Sigma(x - \bar{x})^2$
Step 4	Average of the sum (= variance = s^2)	$\dfrac{\Sigma(x - \bar{x})^2}{n}$

4.3 Calculation of the variance for grouped data

Step 1	Difference between value and mean	$(x - \bar{x})$
Step 2	Square of the difference	$(x - \bar{x})^2$
Step 3	Sum of the squares of the difference	$\Sigma f(x - \bar{x})^2$
Step 4	Average of the sum (= variance = s^2)	$\dfrac{\Sigma f(x - \bar{x})^2}{\Sigma f}$

4.4 The standard deviation

The units of the variance are the square of those in the original data because we squared the differences. We therefore need to take the square root to get back to the units of the original data. **The standard deviation = square root of the variance.**

The standard deviation measures the spread of data around the mean. In general, the larger the standard deviation value in relation to the mean, the more dispersed the data.

FAST FORWARD

The **standard deviation**, which is the square root of the variance, is the most important measure of spread used in statistics. Make sure you understand how to calculate the standard deviation of a set of data.

There are a number of formulae which you may use to calculate the standard deviation; use whichever one you feel comfortable with. For our examples we will use the following formulae:

$$\text{Standard deviation (for ungrouped data)} = \sqrt{\frac{\Sigma(x - \bar{x})^2}{n}} = \sqrt{\frac{\Sigma x^2}{n} - \bar{x}^2}$$

$$\text{Standard deviation (for grouped data)} = \sqrt{\frac{\Sigma f(x - \bar{x})^2}{\Sigma f}} = \sqrt{\frac{\Sigma fx^2}{\Sigma f} - \left(\frac{\Sigma fx}{\Sigma f}\right)^2}$$

The key to these calculations is to set up a table with totals as shown below and then use the totals in the formulae given to you.

4.5 Example: The variance and the standard deviation

Calculate the variance and the standard deviation of the frequency distribution in the example in Paragraph 3.3.

Solution

Using the formula provided in the assessment, the calculation is as follows.

Midpoint x	f	fx	x^2	fx^2
5	3	15	25	75
15	6	90	225	1,350
25	11	275	625	6,875
35	15	525	1,225	18,375
45	12	540	2,025	24,300
55	7	385	3,025	21,175
65	6	390	4,225	25,350
	$\Sigma f = 60$	$\Sigma fx = 2,220$		$\Sigma fx^2 = 97,500$

Mean = $\dfrac{\Sigma fx}{\Sigma f} = \dfrac{2{,}220}{60} = 37$

Variance = $\dfrac{\Sigma fx^2}{\Sigma f} - \left(\dfrac{\Sigma fx}{\Sigma f}\right)^2 = \dfrac{97{,}500}{60} - (37)^2 = 256$ hours

Standard deviation = $\sqrt{256} = 16$ hours

Question — Variance and standard deviation

Calculate the variance and the standard deviation of the frequency distribution in the question entitled: mean deviation.

Answer

x	f	fx	x^2	fx^2
5	4	20	25	100
15	6	90	225	1,350
25	8	200	625	5,000
35	20	700	1,225	24,500
45	6	270	2,025	12,150
55	6	330	3,025	18,150
	$\Sigma f = 50$	$\Sigma fx = 1610$		$\Sigma fx^2 = 61{,}250$

Mean = $\dfrac{1{,}610}{50} = 32.2$

Variance = $\dfrac{61{,}250}{50} - (32.2)^2 = 188.16$

Standard deviation = $\sqrt{188.16} = 13.72$

Exam focus point

In the exam you will be given an exam formulae sheet. This gives the formula for variances. Remember that the variance is simply the standard deviation squared.

Standard deviation (for ungrouped data)

$s^2 = \dfrac{\Sigma(x - \bar{x})^2}{n}$ therefore $s = \sqrt{\dfrac{\Sigma(x - \bar{x})^2}{n}} = \sqrt{\dfrac{\Sigma x^2}{n} - \bar{x}^2}$

Standard deviation (for grouped data)

$s^2 = \dfrac{\Sigma fx^2}{\Sigma f} - \left(\dfrac{\Sigma fx}{\Sigma f}\right)^2$ therefore $s = \sqrt{\dfrac{\Sigma fx^2}{\Sigma f} - \left(\dfrac{\Sigma fx}{\Sigma f}\right)^2}$

PART A DATA COLLECTION AND ANALYSIS

4.6 The main properties of the standard deviation

The standard deviation's main properties are as follows:

(a) It is based on **all the values in the distribution** and so is more comprehensive than dispersion measures based on quartiles, such as the quartile deviation.

(b) It is suitable for **further statistical analysis**.

(c) It is **more difficult to understand** than some other measures of dispersion.

The importance of the standard deviation lies in its **suitability for further statistical analysis** (we shall consider this further when we study the normal distribution in Chapter 5).

4.7 The variance and the standard deviation of several items together

You may need to calculate the variance and standard deviation for n items together, given the variance and standard deviation for one item alone.

4.8 Example: Several items together

The daily demand for an item of inventory has a mean of 6 units, with a variance of 4 and a standard deviation of 2 units. Demand on any one day is unaffected by demand on previous days or subsequent days.

Required

Calculate the arithmetic mean, the variance and the standard deviation of demand for a five day week.

Solution

If we let:

- Arithmetic mean = $\bar{x}$ = 6
- Variance = σ^2 = 4
- Standard deviation = σ = 2
- Number of days in week = n = 5

The following rules apply to $\bar{x}$, σ^2 and σ when we have several items together:

- **Arithmetic mean** = $n\bar{x}$ = 5 × 6 = 30 units
- **Variance** = $n\sigma^2$ = 5 × 4 = 20 units
- **Standard deviation** = $\sqrt{n\sigma^2}$ = $\sqrt{20}$ = 4.47 units

5 The coefficient of variation

5.1 Comparing the spreads of two distributions

FAST FORWARD

The spreads of two distributions can be compared using the **coefficient of variation**.

Formula to learn

Coefficient of variation (coefficient of relative spread) = $\dfrac{\text{Standard deviation}}{\text{mean}}$

The bigger the coefficient of variation, the wider the spread. For example, suppose that two sets of data, A and B, have the following means and standard deviations.

	A	B
Mean	120	125
Standard deviation	50	51
Coefficient of variation (50/120)	0.417	(51/125) 0.408

Although B has a higher standard deviation in absolute terms (51 compared to 50) its relative spread is less than A's since the coefficient of variation is smaller.

Question — Coefficient of variation

Calculate the coefficient of variation of the distribution in the questions on Mean deviation and Variance and standard deviation.

Answer

$$\text{Coefficient of variation} = \frac{\text{standard deviation}}{\text{mean}} = \frac{13.72}{32.2} = 0.426$$

Question — Variance

The number of new orders received by five salesmen last week is: 1, 3, 5, 7, 9. The variance of the number of new orders received is:

(a) 2.40
(b) 2.83
(c) 6.67
(d) 8.00

Answer

x	$(x - \bar{x})^2$
1	16
3	4
5	0
7	4
9	16
$\Sigma x = 25$	$\Sigma(x-\bar{x})^2 = 40$

$$\bar{x} = \frac{25}{5} = 5$$

$$\frac{\Sigma(x-\bar{x})^2}{n} = \frac{40}{5} = 8$$

The correct answer is therefore (d).

6 Skewness

6.1 Skewed distributions

As well as being able to calculate the average and spread of a frequency distribution, you should be aware of the **skewness** of a distribution.

Skewness is the asymmetry of a frequency distribution curve.

6.2 Symmetrical frequency distributions

A **symmetrical frequency distribution** (a normal distribution) can be drawn as follows:

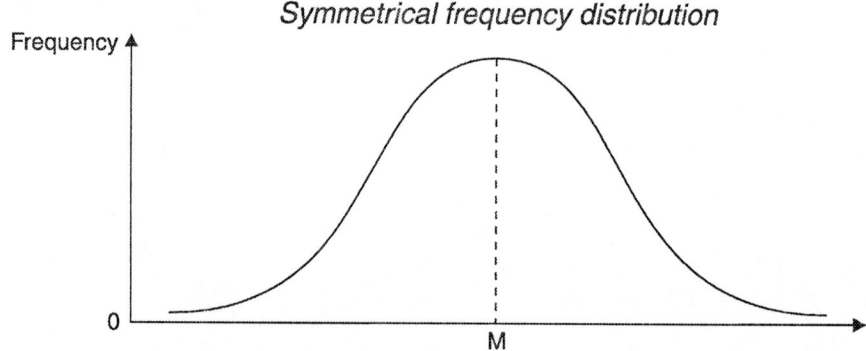

Properties of a symmetrical distribution

- Its mean, mode and median all have the same value, M.
- Its two halves are mirror images of each other.

6.3 Positively skewed distributions

A **positively skewed** distribution's graph will lean towards the **left hand side**, with a tail stretching out to the right, and can be drawn as follows.

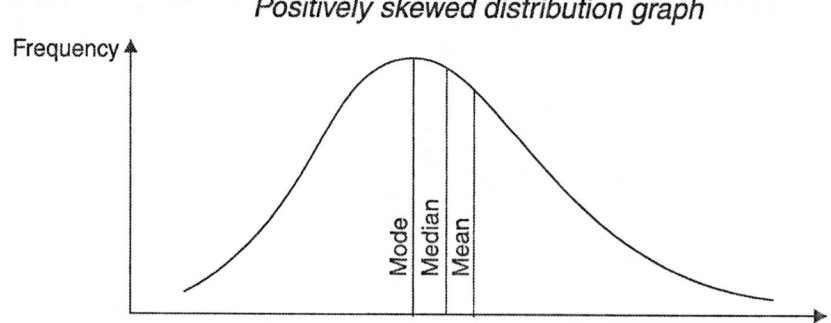

Properties of a positively skewed distribution

- Its mean, mode and median all have different values
- The mode will have a lower value than the median
- Its mean will have a higher value than the median (and than most of the distribution)
- It does not have two halves which are mirror images of each other

6.4 Negatively skewed distributions

A **negatively skewed distribution's** graph will lean towards the **right hand side**, with a tail stretching out to the left, and can be drawn as follows:

Negatively skewed distribution graph

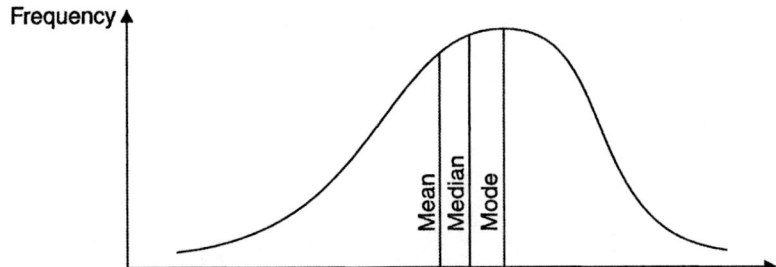

Properties of a negatively skewed distribution

- Its mean, median and mode all have different values
- The mode will be higher than the median
- The mean will have a lower value than the median (and than most of the distribution)

Since the mean is affected by extreme values, it may not be representative of the items in a very skewed distribution.

6.5 Example: Skewness

In a quality control test, the weights of standard packages were measured to give the following grouped frequency table:

Weights in grams	Number of packages
198 and less than 199	3
199 and less than 200	8
200 and less than 201	93
201 and less than 202	148
202 and less than 203	48

Required

(a) Calculate the mean, standard deviation and median of the weights of the packages.
(b) Explain whether or not you think that the distribution is symmetrical.

Solution

(a)

Weight g	Midpoint x	f	fx	$x - \bar{x}$	$f(x - \bar{x})^2$
198 and less than 199	198.5	3	595.5	−2.77	23.0187
199 and less than 200	199.5	8	1,596.0	−1.77	25.0632
200 and less than 201	200.5	93	18,646.5	−0.77	55.1397
201 and less than 202	201.5	148	29,822.0	0.23	7.8292
202 and less than 203	202.5	48	9,720.0	1.23	72.6192
		300	60,380.0		183.6700

Mean $= \dfrac{\Sigma fx}{\Sigma f} = \dfrac{60{,}380}{300} = 201.27\text{g}$

Standard deviation $= \sqrt{\dfrac{183.67}{300}} = 0.78\text{g}$

The **median** (the 150th item) could be estimated as:

$201 + \dfrac{(150 - 93 - 8 - 3)}{148} = 201.31\text{g}$

(b) The distribution appears not to be symmetrical, but negatively skewed.

The mean is in the higher end of the range of values at 201.27g.

The median has a higher value than the mean, and the mode has a higher value than the median. This suggests that the frequency distribution is negatively skewed.

Question — Skewness

Which of these options is true where data is highly positively skewed?

(a) The least representative average is the median
(b) The mode will overestimate the average
(c) The mean will tend to overestimate the average
(d) The mean, mode and median will produce equally representative results

Answer

(c) The mean will tend to overstate the average, and the mode will underestimate it.

Chapter Roundup

- The **range** is the difference between the highest and lowest observations.
- The **quartiles** and the **median** divide the population into four groups of equal size.
- The **semi-interquartile range** is half the difference between the upper and lower quartiles.
- The **inter-quartile range** is the difference between the upper and lower quartiles ($Q_3 - Q_1$) and hence shows the range of values of the middle half of the population.
- The **mean deviation** is a measure of the average amount by which the values in a distribution differ from the arithmetic mean.
- The **variance**, σ^2, is the average of the squared mean deviation for each value in a distribution.
- The **standard deviation**, which is the square root of the variance, is the most important measure of spread used in statistics. Make sure you understand how to calculate the standard deviation of a set of data.
- The spreads of two distributions can be compared using the **coefficient of variation**.
- **Skewness** is the asymmetry of a frequency distribution curve.

Quick Quiz

1 Fill in the blanks in the statements below using the words in the box.

   (a) [_____] quartile = Q_1 = value [_____] which 25% of the population fall.

   (b) [_____] quartile = Q_3 = value [_____] which 25% of the population fall.

   | Upper | Above | Below | Lower |

2 (a) The formula for the semi-interquartile range is [_____]

   (b) The semi-interquartile range is also known as the [_____]

3 In a negatively skewed distribution:

   (a) The mean is the same as the median
   (b) The mean is smaller than the median
   (c) The mean lies between the median and the mode
   (d) The mean is larger than the median

4 The standard deviation of a sample of data is 36. What is the value of the variance? [_____]

PART A   DATA COLLECTION AND ANALYSIS

Answers to Quick Quiz

1. (a) **Lower** quartile = Q_1 = value **below** which 25% of the population fall
   (b) **Upper** quartile = Q_3 = value **above** which 25% of the population fall

2. (a) $\dfrac{Q_3 - Q_1}{2}$
   (b) Quartile deviation

3. (b) The mean is smaller than the median.

4. $\boxed{1{,}296}$ The variance is the square of the standard deviation.
   $36^2 = 1{,}296$

End of Chapter Question

Dispersion   (AIA May 09)

The number of contracts completed during a particular month by a team of 12 sales consultants was as follows.

6, 10, 13, 7, 8, 14, 20, 8, 8, 9, 12, 7

Required

(a) Determine values of the mean, mode and median of the data.   **(6 marks)**

(b) Based on these values comment on the skewness or symmetry of the data.   **(2 marks)**

(c) Explain which measure of variation would be most suitable to calculate for this data.   **(2 marks)**

(d) When summary measures are calculated for grouped frequency distributions rather than for raw data, explain why the values are described as estimates.   **(2 marks)**

(Total = 12 marks)

Applying probability to decision making

Topic list	Syllabus reference
1 The concept of probability	6.4
2 The rules of probability	6.4
3 Expected values	6.4
4 Expectation and decision making	6.4
5 Decision trees	6.4
6 Probability distributions	6.4
7 The normal distribution	6.4
8 The standard normal distribution	6.4
9 Using the normal distribution to calculate probabilities	6.4
10 Binomial distribution	6.4
11 Poisson distribution	6.4

Introduction

'The likelihood of rain this afternoon is 50%' warns the weather report from your radio. 'There's no chance of you catching that bus' grunts the helpful soul as you puff up the hill. The headline on your newspaper screams 'Odds of Paperclip Party winning the election rise to one in four'.

'Likelihood' and **'chance'** are expressions used in our everyday lives to denote a **level of uncertainty**. **Probability**, is the mathematical term used when we need to calculate the likelihood of an event happening.

This chapter will therefore explain various techniques for assessing probability and look at how it can be applied in business decision making.

The chapter then concludes by looking at distribution and probability.

PART A DATA COLLECTION AND ANALYSIS

1 The concept of probability

1.1 Introducing probability

> **FAST FORWARD**
>
> Probability is a measure of **likelihood** and can be stated as a percentage, a ratio, or more usually as a number from 0 to 1.

Consider the following:

- Probability = 0 = impossibility
- Probability = 1 = certainty
- Probability = 1/2 = a 50% chance of something happening
- Probability = 1/4 = a 1 in 4 chance of something happening

1.2 Expressing probabilities

In statistics, **probabilities** are more commonly expressed as **proportions** than as **percentages**. Consider the following possible outcomes.

Possible outcome	Probability as a percentage %	Probability as a proportion
A	15.0	0.150
B	20.0	0.200
C	32.5	0.325
D	7.5	0.075
E	12.5	0.125
F	12.5	0.125
	100.0	1.000

It is useful to consider how probability can be quantified. A businessman might estimate that if the selling price of a product is raised by 20p, there would be a 90% probability that demand would fall by 30%, but how would he have reached his estimate of 90% probability?

1.3 Assessing probabilities

There are several ways of assessing probabilities.

- They may be measurable with **mathematical certainty**

  - If a coin is tossed, there is a 0.5 probability that it will come down heads, and a 0.5 probability that it will come down tails

  - If a die is thrown, there is a one-sixth probability that a 6 will turn up

- They may be measurable from an analysis of **past experience**

- Probabilities can be estimated from **research** or **surveys**

Note. Probability is a measure of the likelihood of an event happening in the long run, or over a large number of times.

The rules of probability in section 2 will go through in detail how to calculate probabilities in various situations.

2 The rules of probability

2.1 Setting the scene

It is the year 2030 and a computer software program generates examinations that are equally likely to be easy or difficult. There is no link between the number of questions on each paper, which is arrived at on a fair basis by the computer software, and the standard of the paper. You are about to take five examinations.

2.2 Simple probability

It is vital that the first examination is easy as it covers a subject which you have tried, but unfortunately failed, to understand. What is the probability that it will be an easy examination?

Obviously the probability of an easy paper is 1/2 (or 50% or 0.5). This reveals a very important principle (which holds if each result is equally likely).

Formula to learn

$$\text{Probability of achieving the desired result} = \frac{\text{Number of ways of achieving desired result}}{\text{Total number of possible outcomes}}$$

Let us apply the principle to our example.

Total number of possible outcomes = 'easy' or 'difficult' = 2
Total number of ways of achieving the desired result (which is 'easy') = 1
The probability of an easy examination, or P(easy examination) = 1/2

2.2.1 Example: Simple probability

Suppose that a die is rolled. What is the probability that it will show a six?

Solution

$$P(6) = \frac{\text{Number of ways of achieving desired result}}{\text{Total number of possible outcomes}}$$

$$= \frac{1}{6} \text{ or } 16.7\% \text{ or } 0.167$$

2.3 Venn diagrams

A Venn diagram is a pictorial method of showing probability. We can show all the possible outcomes (E) and the outcome we are interested in (A).

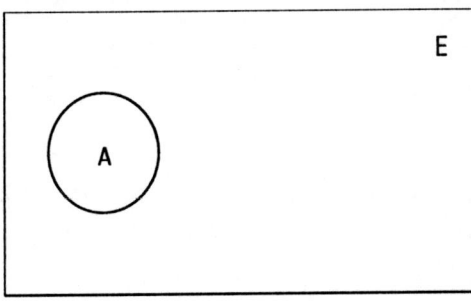

2.4 Complementary outcomes

You are desperate to pass more of the examinations than your rival but, unlike you, they are more likely to pass the first examination if it is difficult. What is the probability of the first examination being more suited to your rival's requirements?

We know that the probability of certainty is one. The certainty in this scenario is that the examination will be easy or difficult.

P(easy or difficult examination) = 1
From Paragraph 2.2, P(easy examination) = 1/2
P(not easy examination) = P(difficult examination)
= 1 − P(easy examination)
= 1 − 1/2
= 1/2

Formula to learn

$P(\overline{A}) = 1 - P(A)$, where $\overline{A}$ is 'not A'.

2.4.1 Venn diagram: Complementary outcomes

The probability of **not** A is shown by the shaded region.

2.4.2 Example: Complementary outcomes

If there is a 25% chance of the Paperclip Party winning the next general election, use the law of complementary events to calculate the probability of the Paperclip Party **not** winning the next election.

Solution

P(winning) = 25% = 1/4
P(not winning) = 1 − P(winning) = 1 − 1/4 = 3/4

2.5 The simple addition or OR law

FAST FORWARD

The **simple addition law** for two mutually exclusive events, A and B, is as follows:

$P(A \text{ or } B) = P(A \cup B) = P(A) + P(B)$

The time pressure in the second examination is enormous. The computer will produce a paper which will have between five and nine questions. You know that, easy or difficult, the examination must have six questions at the most for you to have any hope of passing it.

What is the probability of the computer producing an examination with six or fewer questions? In other words, what is the probability of an examination with five **or** six questions?

Don't panic. Let us start by using the basic principle.

$$P(5 \text{ questions}) = \frac{\text{Total number of ways of achieving a five question examination}}{\text{Total number of possible outcomes } (= 5, 6, 7, 8 \text{ or } 9 \text{ questions})}$$

$$= \frac{1}{5}$$

Likewise $P(6 \text{ questions}) = \frac{1}{5}$

Either five questions or six questions would be acceptable, so the probability of you passing the examination must be greater than if just five questions or just six questions (but not both) were acceptable. We therefore add the two probabilities together so that the probability of passing the examination has increased.

So $P(5 \text{ or } 6 \text{ questions}) = P(5 \text{ questions}) + P(6 \text{ questions})$

$$= \frac{1}{5} + \frac{1}{5} = \frac{2}{5}$$

FAST FORWARD

Mutually exclusive outcomes are outcomes where the occurrence of one of the outcomes excludes the possibility of any of the others happening.

In the example the outcomes are **mutually exclusive** because it is impossible to have five questions *and* six questions in the same examination.

2.5.1 Venn diagram: Mutually exclusive outcomes

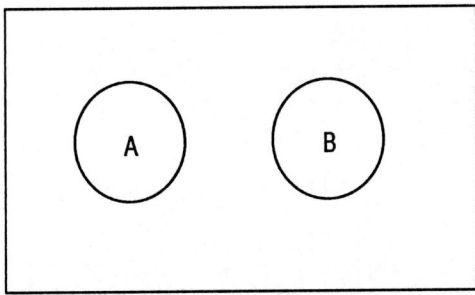

2.5.2 Example: Mutually exclusive outcomes

The delivery of an item of raw material from a supplier may take up to six weeks from the time the order is placed. The probabilities of various delivery times are as follows:

Delivery time	Probability
≤ 1 week	0.10
> 1, ≤ 2 weeks	0.25
> 2, ≤ 3 weeks	0.20
> 3, ≤ 4 weeks	0.20
> 4, ≤ 5 weeks	0.15
> 5, ≤ 6 weeks	0.10
	1.00

Required

Calculate the probability that a delivery will take the following times:

(a) Two weeks or less
(b) More than three weeks

Solution

(a) P(≤ 1 or > 1, ≤ 2 weeks) = P(≤ 1 week) + P(>1, ≤ 2 weeks)
                              = 0.10 + 0.25
                              = 0.35

(b) P(> 3, ≤ 6 weeks) = P(> 3, ≤ 4 weeks) + P(> 4, ≤ 5 weeks) + P(> 5, ≤ 6 weeks)
                       = 0.20 + 0.15 + 0.10
                       = 0.45

2.6 The simple multiplication or AND law

FAST FORWARD

The **simple multiplication law** for two independent events, A and B, is as follows:

P(A and B) = P(A ∩ B) = P(A)P(B)

Important!

P(A and B) = 0 when A and B have mutually exclusive outcomes.

You still have three examinations to sit: astrophysics, geography of the moon and computer art. Stupidly, you forgot to revise for the astrophysics examination, which will have between 15 and 20 questions. You think that you may scrape through this paper if it is easy **and** if there are only 15 questions.

What is the probability that the paper the computer produces will exactly match your needs? Do not forget that there is no link between the standard of the examination and the number of questions ie they are **independent** events.

The best way to approach this question is diagrammatically, showing all the possible outcomes.

	Number of questions					
Type of paper	15	16	17	18	19	20
Easy (E)	E and 15*	E and 16	E and 17	E and 18	E and 19	E and 20
Difficult (D)	D and 15	D and 16	D and 17	D and 18	D and 19	D and 20

The diagram shows us that, of the 12 possible outcomes, there is only one 'desired result' (which is asterisked). We can therefore calculate the probability as follows:

P(easy paper **and** 15 questions) = 1/12.

The answer can be found more easily as follows:

P(easy paper **and** 15 questions) = P(easy paper) × P(15 questions) = 1/2 × 1/6 = 1/12.

The number of questions has no effect on, nor is it affected by whether it is an easy or difficult paper.

FAST FORWARD

Independent events are events where the outcome of one event in no way affects the outcome of the other events.

2.6.1 Example: Independent events

A die is thrown and a coin is tossed simultaneously. What is the probability of throwing a 5 and getting heads on the coin?

Solution

The probability of throwing a 5 on a die is 1/6
The probability of a tossed coin coming up heads is 1/2
The probability of throwing a 5 and getting heads on a coin is 1/2 × 1/6 = 1/12

2.7 The general rule of addition

> **FAST FORWARD**
>
> The **general rule of addition** for two events, A and B, which are not mutually exclusive, is as follows:
> P(A or B) = P (A ∪ B) = P(A) + P(B) − P(A and B)

The three examinations you still have to sit are placed face down in a line in front of you at the final examination sitting. There is an easy astrophysics paper, a difficult geography of the moon paper and a difficult computer art paper. Without turning over any of the papers you are told to choose one of them. What is the probability that the first paper that you select is difficult or is the geography of the moon paper?

Let us think about this carefully.

There are two difficult papers, so P(difficult) = 2/3

There is one geography of the moon paper, so P(geography of the moon) = 1/3

If we use the OR law and add the two probabilities then we will have double counted the difficult geography of the moon paper. It is included in the set of difficult papers **and** in the set of geography of the moon papers. In other words, we are **not** faced with mutually exclusive outcomes because the occurrence of a geography of the moon paper does not exclude the possibility of the occurrence of a difficult paper. We therefore need to take account of this **double counting**.

P(difficult paper or geography of the moon paper) = P(difficult paper) + P(geography of the moon paper) − P(difficult paper and geography of the moon paper).

Using the AND law, P(difficult paper or geography of the moon paper) = 2/3 + 1/3 − (1/3) = 2/3.

Since it is **not** impossible to have an examination which is difficult **and** about the geography of the moon, these two events are not mutually exclusive.

2.7.1 Venn diagram: General rule of addition

We can show how to calculate P(A ∪ B) from three diagrams.

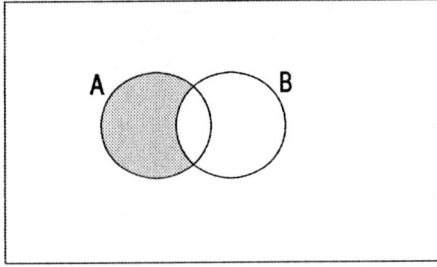

The shaded area is the probability of A and **not** B = P(A) − P(A ∩ B)

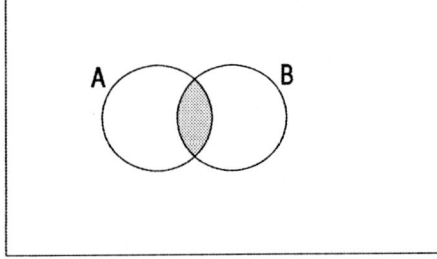

The shaded area is the probability of A **and** B = P (A ∩ B)

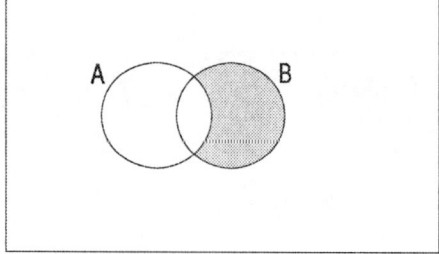

The shaded area is the probability of B and **not** A = P(B) − (A ∩ B)

If we add these three sections together we get the formula for the probability of A **or** B =
P(A) + P(B) − P(A ∩ B)

 Question   General rule of addition

If one card is drawn from a normal pack of 52 playing cards, what is the probability of getting an ace or a spade?

Probability

Ace	Spade	Ace of spades	Ace or spade

Answer

Probability

Ace	Spade	Ace of spades	Ace or spade
$\frac{4}{52}$	$\frac{13}{52}$	$\frac{1}{52}$	$\frac{4}{13}$

Working

P(ace or spade) = $\frac{4}{52} + \frac{13}{52} - \frac{1}{52} = \frac{16}{52} = \frac{4}{13}$

2.8 The general rule of multiplication

FAST FORWARD

The **general rule of multiplication** for two dependent events, A and B, is as follows:

P(A and B) = P(A ∩ B) P(A) × P(B/A)
          = P(B) × P(A/B)

Computer art is your last examination. Understandably you are very tired and you are uncertain whether you will be able to stay awake. You believe that there is a 70% chance of your falling asleep if it becomes too hot and stuffy in the examination hall. It is well known that the air conditioning system serving the examination hall was installed in the last millennium and is therefore extremely unreliable. There is a 1 in 4 chance of it breaking down during the examination, thereby causing the temperature in the hall to rise. What is the likelihood that you will drop off?

The scenario above has led us to face what is known as **conditional probability**. We can rephrase the information provided as 'the probability that you will fall asleep, given that it is too hot and stuffy, is equal to 70%' and we can write this as follows.

5: APPLYING PROBABILITY TO DECISION MAKING

P(fall asleep/too hot and stuffy) = 70%.

FAST FORWARD

> **Dependent** or **conditional** events are events where the outcome of one event depends on the outcome of the others.

Whether you fall asleep is **conditional** upon whether the hall becomes too hot and stuffy. The events are not, therefore, independent and so we cannot use the simple multiplication law. So:

P(it becomes too hot and stuffy and you fall asleep)

= P(too hot and stuffy) × P(fall asleep/too hot and stuffy)
= 25% × 70% = 0.25 × 0.7 = 0.175 = $17\frac{1}{2}$%

Important!

> When A and B are independent events, then P(B/A) = P(B) since, by definition, the occurrence of B (and therefore P(B)) does not depend upon the occurrence of A. Similarly P(A/B) = P(A).

2.8.1 Example: Conditional probability

The board of directors of Shuttem Co has warned that there is a 60% probability that a factory will be closed down unless its workforce improves its productivity. The factory's manager has estimated that the probability of success in agreeing a productivity deal with the workforce is only 30%.

Required

Determine the likelihood that the factory will be closed.

Solution

If outcome A is the shutdown of the factory and outcome B is the failure to improve productivity:

P(A and B) = P(B) × P(A/B)
= 0.7 × 0.6
= 0.42

FAST FORWARD

> **Contingency tables** can be useful for dealing with **conditional probability**.

2.8.2 Example: Contingency tables

A cosmetics company has developed a new anti-dandruff shampoo which is being tested on volunteers. Seventy percent of the volunteers have used the shampoo whereas others have used a normal shampoo, believing it to be the new anti-dandruff shampoo. Of those using the new shampoo, 2/7 showed no improvement whereas 1/3 of those using the normal shampoo had less dandruff.

Required

A volunteer shows no improvement. What is the probability that he used the normal shampoo?

Solution

The problem is solved by drawing a contingency table, showing 'improvement' and 'no improvement', volunteers using normal shampoo and volunteers using the new shampoo.

Let us suppose that there were 1,000 volunteers (we could use any number). We could depict the results of the test on the 1,000 volunteers as follows.

	New shampoo	Normal shampoo	Total
Improvement	***500	****100	600
No improvement	**200	200	400
	*700	***300	1,000

* $70\% \times 1{,}000$ ** $\frac{2}{7} \times 700$

*** Balancing figure **** $\frac{1}{3} \times 300$

We can now calculate P (shows no improvement)

$P(\text{shows no improvement}) = \frac{400}{1{,}000}$

$P(\text{used normal shampoo/shows no improvement}) = \frac{200}{400} = \frac{1}{2}$

Other probabilities are just as easy to calculate.

$P(\text{shows improvement/used new shampoo}) = \frac{500}{700} = \frac{5}{7}$

$P(\text{used new shampoo/shows improvement}) = \frac{500}{600} = \frac{5}{6}$

Question — Independent events

The independent probabilities that the three sections of a management accounting department will encounter one computer error in a week are respectively 0.1, 0.2 and 0.3. There is never more than one computer error encountered by any one section in a week. Calculate the probability that there will be the following number of errors encountered by the management accounting department next week.

(a) At least one computer error
(b) One and only one computer error

Answer

(a) The probability of at least one computer error is 1 minus the probability of no error. The probability of no error is $0.9 \times 0.8 \times 0.7 = 0.504$.

(Since the probability of an error is 0.1, 0.2 and 0.3 in each section, the probability of no error in each section must be 0.9, 0.8 and 0.7 respectively.)

The probability of at least one error is $1 - 0.504 = 0.496$.

(b) Y = yes, N = no

		Section 1	Section 2	Section 3
(i)	Error?	Y	N	N
(ii)	Error?	N	Y	N
(iii)	Error?	N	N	Y

		Probabilities
(i)	$0.1 \times 0.8 \times 0.7 =$	0.056
(ii)	$0.9 \times 0.2 \times 0.7 =$	0.126
(iii)	$0.9 \times 0.8 \times 0.3 =$	0.216
	Total	0.398

The probability of only one error only is 0.398.

5: APPLYING PROBABILITY TO DECISION MAKING

Question
General rule of addition

In a student survey, 60% of the students are male and 75% are AIA candidates. The probability that a student chosen at random is either female or a AIA candidate is:

(a) 0.85
(b) 0.30
(c) 0.40
(d) 1.00

Answer

P(male) = 60% = 0.6
P(female) = 1 − 0.6 = 0.4
P(AIA candidate) = 75% = 0.75

We need to use the general rule of addition to avoid double counting.

∴ P(female or AIA candidate) = P(female) + P(AIA candidate) − P(female *and* AIA candidate)

$\quad$ = 0.4 + 0.75 − (0.4 × 0.75)
$\quad$ = 1.15 − 0.3
$\quad$ = 0.85

The correct answer is (a).

You should have been able to eliminate options C and D immediately. 0.4 is the probability that the candidate is female and 1.00 is the probability that something will definitely happen – neither of these options are likely to correspond to the probability that the candidate is either female or a AIA candidate.

3 Expected values

FAST FORWARD

An **expected value** (or **EV**) is a weighted average value, based on probabilities. The expected value for a single event can offer a helpful guide for management decisions.

3.1 How to calculate expected values

If the probability of an outcome of an event is p, then the expected number of times that this outcome will occur in n events (the expected value) is equal to n × p.

For example, suppose that the probability that a transistor is defective is 0.02. How many defectives would we expect to find in a batch of 4,000 transistors?

EV = 4,000 × 0.02
$\quad$ = 80 defectives

Formula to learn

Expected value (EV) = $\sum$np

Where $\quad$ $\sum$ = sum of
$\qquad\quad$ n = outcome
$\qquad\quad$ p = probability of outcome occurring

3.2 Example: Expected values

The daily sales of Product T may be as follows.

Units	Probability
1,000	0.2
2,000	0.3
3,000	0.4
4,000	0.1
	1.0

Required

Calculate the expected daily sales.

Solution

The EV of daily sales may be calculated by multiplying each possible outcome (volume of daily sales) by the probability that this outcome will occur.

Units	Probability	Expected value Units
1,000	0.2	200
2,000	0.3	600
3,000	0.4	1,200
4,000	0.1	400
		EV of daily sales 2,400

In the long run the expected value should be approximately the actual average, if the event occurs many times over. In the example above, we do not expect sales on any one day to equal 2,400 units, but in the long run, over a large number of days, average sales should equal 2,400 units a day.

3.3 Expected values and single events

The point made in the preceding paragraph is an important one. An **expected value** can be calculated when the **event will only occur once or twice**, but it will not be a true long-run average of what will actually happen, because there is no long run.

3.4 Example: Expected values and single events

Suppose, for example, that a businessman is trying to decide whether to invest in a project. He estimates that there are three possible outcomes.

Outcome	Profit/(loss) $	Probability
Success	10,000	0.2
Moderate success	2,000	0.7
Failure	(4,000)	0.1

The expected value of profit may be calculated as follows:

Profit/(loss) $	Probability	Expected value $
10,000	0.2	2,000
2,000	0.7	1,400
(4,000)	0.1	(400)
		Expected value of profit 3,000

In this example, the project is a one-off event, and as far as we are aware, it will not be repeated. The actual profit or loss will be $10,000, $2,000 or $(4,000), and the average value of $3,000 will not actually happen. There is no long-run average of a single event.

Nevertheless, the expected value can be used to help the manager decide whether or not to invest in the project.

Question — Expected values

A company manufactures and sells product D. The selling price of the product is $6 per unit, and estimates of demand and variable costs of sales are as follows:

Probability	Demand Units	Probability	Variable cost per unit $
0.3	5,000	0.1	3.00
0.6	6,000	0.3	3.50
0.1	8,000	0.5	4.00
		0.1	4.50

The unit variable costs do not depend on the volume of sales.

Fixed costs will be $10,000.

Required

Calculate the expected profit.

Answer

The EV of demand is as follows:

Demand Units	Probability	Expected value Units
5,000	0.3	1,500
6,000	0.6	3,600
8,000	0.1	800
		EV of demand 5,900

The EV of the variable cost per unit is as follows:

Variable costs $	Probability	Expected value $
3.00	0.1	0.30
3.50	0.3	1.05
4.00	0.5	2.00
4.50	0.1	0.45
		EV of unit variable costs 3.80

		$
Sales	5,900 units × $6.00	35,400
Less: variable costs	5,900 units × $3.80	22,420
Contribution		12,980
Less: fixed costs		10,000
Expected profit		2,980

PART A DATA COLLECTION AND ANALYSIS

4 Expectation and decision making

4.1 Decision making

FAST FORWARD

> Probability and expectation should be seen as an aid to decision making.

The concepts of probability and expected value are vital in **business decision making**. The expected values for single events can offer a helpful guide for management decisions.

- A project with a positive EV should be accepted.
- A project with a negative EV should be rejected.

Another decision rule involving expected values that you are likely to come across is the choice of an option or alternative which has the **highest EV of profit** (or the **lowest EV of cost**).

Choosing the option with the highest EV of profit is a decision rule that has both merits and drawbacks, as the following simple example will show.

4.2 Example: The expected value criterion

Suppose that there are two mutually exclusive projects with the following possible profits.

Project A		Project B	
Probability	Profit	Probability	Profit/(loss)
	$		$
0.8	5,000	0.1	(2,000)
0.2	6,000	0.2	5,000
		0.6	7,000
		0.1	8,000

Required

Determine which project should be chosen.

Solution

The EV of profit for each project is as follows.

$

(a) Project A $(0.8 \times 5,000) + (0.2 \times 6,000)$ = 5,200
(b) Project B $(0.1 \times (2,000)) + (0.2 \times 5,000) + (0.6 \times 7,000) + (0.1 \times 8,000)$ = 5,800

Project B has a higher EV of profit. This means that on the balance of probabilities, it could offer a better return than A, and so is arguably a better choice.

On the other hand, the minimum return from project A would be $5,000 whereas with B there is a 0.1 chance of a loss of $2,000. So project A might be a safer choice.

Question — Expected values 2

A company is deciding whether to invest in a project. There are three possible outcomes of the investment:

Outcome	Profit/(Loss)
	$'000
Optimistic	19.2
Most likely	12.5
Pessimistic	(6.7)

There is a 30% chance of the optimistic outcome, and a 60% chance of the most likely outcome arising. The expected value of profit from the project is

(a) $7,500
(b) $12,590
(c) $13,930
(d) $25,000

Answer

(b) Since the probabilities must total 100%, the probability of the pessimistic outcome = 100% − 60% − 30% = 10%.

Outcome	Profit/(Loss) $	Probability	Expected value $
Optimistic	19,200	0.3	5,760
Most likely	12,500	0.6	7,500
Pessimistic	(6,700)	0.1	(670)
		1.0	12,590

If you selected option A, you calculated the expected value of the most likely outcome instead of the entire project.

If you selected option C, you forgot to treat the 6,700 as a loss, ie as a negative value.

If you selected option D, you forgot to take into account the probabilities of the various outcomes arising.

4.3 Payoff tables

Decisions have to be taken about a wide variety of matters (capital investment, controls on production, project scheduling and so on) and under a wide variety of conditions from **virtual certainty** to **complete uncertainty**.

There are, however, certain common factors in many business decisions:

(a) When a decision has to be made, there will be a range of possible **actions**.

(b) Each action will have certain **consequences**, or **payoffs** (for example, profits, costs, time).

(c) The payoff from any given action will depend on the **circumstances** (for example, high demand or low demand), which may or may not be known when the decision is taken. Frequently each circumstance will be assigned a probability of occurrence. The circumstances are **not** dependent on the action taken.

For a decision with these elements, a **payoff table** can be prepared.

> **FAST FORWARD**
>
> A payoff table is simply a table with **rows for circumstances** and **columns for actions** (or vice versa), and the payoffs in the cells of the table.

For example, a decision on the level of advertising expenditure to be undertaken given different states of the economy, would have payoffs in $'000 of profit after advertising expenditure as follows:

Circumstances: the state of the economy	Actions: expenditure		
	High	Medium	Low
Boom	+50	+30	+15
Stable	+20	+25	+5
Recession	0	−10	−35

4.4 Example: Payoff table

A cinema has to decide how many programmes to print for a premiere of a film. From previous experience of similar events, it is expected that the probability of sales will be as follows:

Number of programmes demanded	Probability of demand
250	0.1
500	0.2
750	0.4
1,000	0.1
1,250	0.2

The best print quotation received is $2,000 plus 20 pence per copy. Advertising revenue from advertisements placed in the programme totals $2,500. Programmes are sold for $2 each. Unsold programmes are worthless.

Required

(a) Construct a payoff table.
(b) Find the most profitable number of programmes to print.

Solution

(a)

Circumstances: demand levels	Actions: print levels				
	250	500	750	1,000	1,250
250 (p = 0.1)	950	900	850	800	750
500 (p = 0.2)	950	1,400	1,350	1,300	1,250
750 (p = 0.4)	950	1,400	1,850	1,800	1,750
1,000 (p = 0.1)	950	1,400	1,850	2,300	2,250
1,250 (p = 0.2)	950	1,400	1,850	2,300	2,750

These figures are calculated as the profit under each set of circumstances. For example, if the cinema produces 1,000 programmes and 1,000 are demanded, the profit is calculated as follows.

Total revenue = advertising revenue + sale of programmes
= $2,500 + $(1,000 × 2)
= $4,500

Total costs = $2,000 + $(0.20 × 1,000)
= $2,000 + $200
= $2,200

Profit = total revenue − total costs = $4,500 − $2,200 = $2,300

Similarly, if the cinema produces 750 programmes, but only 500 are demanded, the profit is calculated as follows.

Total revenue = $2,500 + $(500 × 2)
= $2,500 + $1,000 = $3,500

Total costs = $2,000 + $(0.20 × 750)
= $2,000 + $150
= $2,150

Profit = total revenue − total costs = $3,500 − $2,150 = $1,350

Note. Whatever the print level, the maximum profit that can be earned is determined by the demand. This means that when 250 programmes are printed, the profit is $950 when demand is 250. Profit is also $950 when demand is 500, 750, 1,000 or 1,250.

(b) The expected profits from each of the possible print levels are as follows:

Print 250

Expected profit = $((950 × 0.1) + (950 × 0.2) + (950 × 0.4) + (950 × 0.1) + (950 × 0.2)) = $950

Print 500

Expected profit = $((900 × 0.1) + (1,400 × (0.2 + 0.4 + 0.1 + 0.2))) = $1,350

Print 750

Expected profit = $((850 × 0.1) + (1,350 × 0.2) + (1,850 × 0.7)) = $1,650

Print 1,000

Expected profit = $((800 × 0.1) + (1,300 × 0.2) + (1,800 × 0.4) + (2,300 × 0.3)) = $1,750

Print 1,250

Expected profit = $((750 × 0.1) + (1,250 × 0.2) + (1,750 × 0.4) + (2,250 × 0.1) + (2,750 × 0.2)) = $1,800

1,250 programmes should therefore be printed in order to **maximise expected profit**.

Formula to learn

E(X) = Expected value = Probability × Payoff

Question — Payoff tables

In a restaurant there is a 30% chance of 5 apple pies being ordered a day and a 70% chance of 10 being ordered. Each apple pie sells for $2. It costs $1 to make an apple pie. Using a payoff table, decide how many apple pies the restaurant should prepare each day, bearing in mind that unsold apple pies must be thrown away at the end of each day.

Answer

		Prepared	
		Five	Ten
Demand	Five (P = 0.3)	5	0
	Ten (P = 0.7)	5	10

Prepare five, profit = ($5 × 0.3) + ($5 × 0.7) = $5
Prepare ten, profit = ($0 × 0.3) + ($10 × 0.7) = $7

Ten pies should be prepared.

4.5 Limitations of expected values

Evaluating decisions by using expected values have a number of limitations.

(a) The **probabilities** used when calculating expected values are likely to be estimates. They may therefore be **unreliable** or **inaccurate**.

(b) Expected values are **long-term averages** and may not be suitable for use in situations involving **one-off decisions**. They may therefore be useful as a **guide** to decision making.

(c) Expected values do not consider the **attitudes to risk of** the people involved in the decision-making process. They do not, therefore, take into account all of the factors involved in the decision.

(d) The time value of money may not be taken into account: $100 now is worth more than $100 in ten years' time.

4.6 Risk and uncertainty

Probability is used to help to calculate **risk** in decision making.

Risk involves situations or events which may or may not occur, but whose probability of occurrence can be calculated statistically and the frequency predicted.

Uncertainty involves situations or events whose outcome cannot be predicted with statistical confidence.

5 Decision trees

Decision trees are diagrams which illustrate the choices and possible outcomes of a decision.

5.1 Definition

A **decision tree** is a pictorial method of showing a sequence of interrelated decisions and their expected outcomes. Decision trees can incorporate both the probabilities of, and values of, expected outcomes, and are used in decision-making.

A probability problem such as 'what is the probability of throwing a six with one throw of a die?' is fairly straightforward and can be solved using the basic principles of probability.

More complex probability questions, although solvable using the basic principles, require a clear logical approach to ensure that all possible choices and outcomes of a decision are taken into consideration. **Decision trees** are a useful means of interpreting such probability problems.

Exactly how does the use of a decision tree permit a clear and logical approach?

- All the possible **choices** that can be made are shown as **branches** on the tree.
- All the possible **outcomes** of each choice are shown as **subsidiary branches** on the tree.

5.1.1 Constructing a decision tree

There are two stages in preparing a decision tree:

- Drawing the tree itself to show all the choices and outcomes
- Putting in the numbers (the probabilities, outcome values and EVs)

Every **decision tree starts** from a **decision point** with the **decision options** that are currently being considered.

(a) It helps to identify the **decision point**, and any subsequent decision points in the tree, with a symbol. Here, we shall use a **square shape**.

(b) There should be a **line**, or **branch**, for each **option** or **alternative**.

It is conventional to draw decision trees from left to right, and so a decision tree will start as follows:

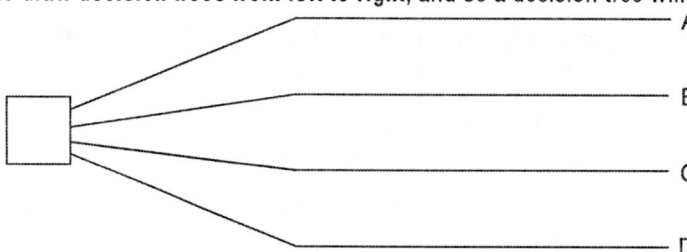

The **square** is the **decision point**, and A, B, C and D represent **four alternatives** from which a choice must be made (such as buy a new machine with cash, hire a machine, continue to use existing machine, raise a loan to buy a machine).

If the outcome from any choice is certain, the branch of the decision tree for that alternative is complete.

If the outcome of a particular choice is uncertain, the various possible outcomes must be shown.

We show the various possible outcomes on a decision tree by inserting an **outcome point** on the **branch** of the tree. Each possible outcome is then shown as a **subsidiary branch**, coming out from the outcome point. The probability of each outcome occurring should be written on to the branch of the tree which represents that outcome.

To distinguish decision points from outcome points, **a circle will be used as the symbol for an outcome point**:

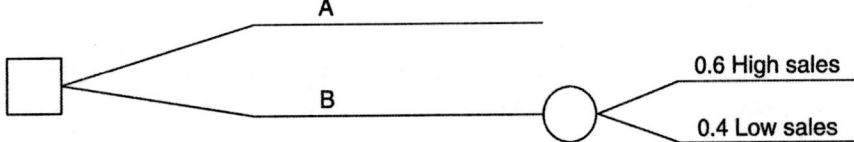

In the example above, there are two choices facing the decision-maker, A and B. The outcome if A is chosen is known with certainty, but if B is chosen, there are two possible outcomes, high sales (0.6 probability) or low sales (0.4 probability).

When several outcomes are possible, it is usually simpler to show two or more stages of outcome points on the decision tree.

5.1.2 Example: several possible outcomes

A company can choose to launch a new product XYZ or not. If the product is launched, expected sales and expected unit costs might be as follows:

Sales		Unit costs	
Units	Probability	$	Probability
10,000	0.8	6	0.7
15,000	0.2	8	0.3

(a) The decision tree could be drawn as follows:

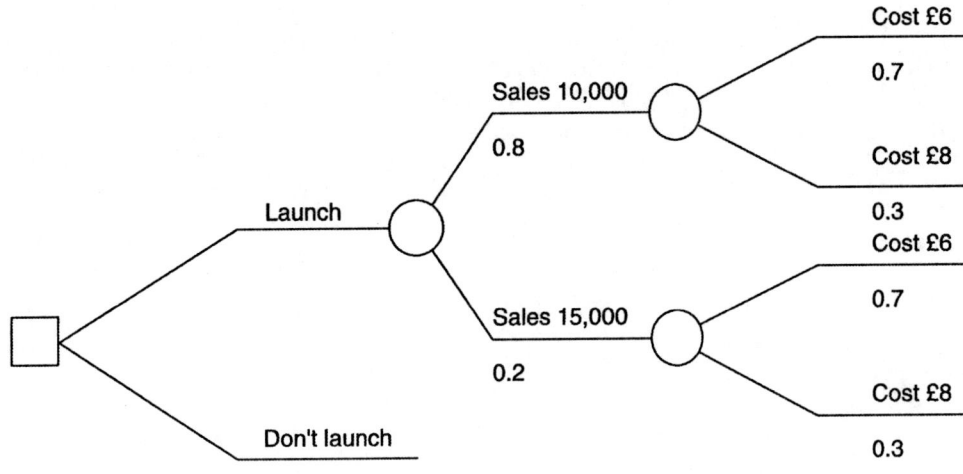

(b) The layout shown above will usually be easier to use than the alternative way of drawing the tree, which is as follows:

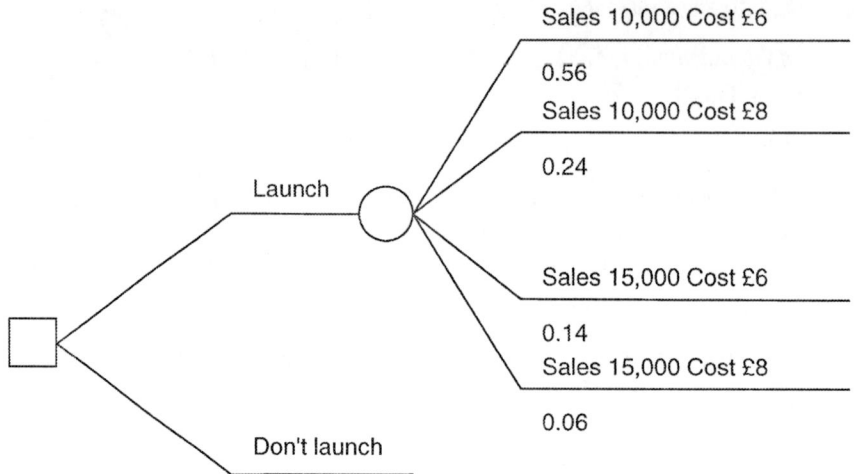

Sometimes, a **decision taken now** will lead to **other decisions to be taken in the future**. When this situation arises, the decision tree can be drawn as a **two-stage tree**, as follows:

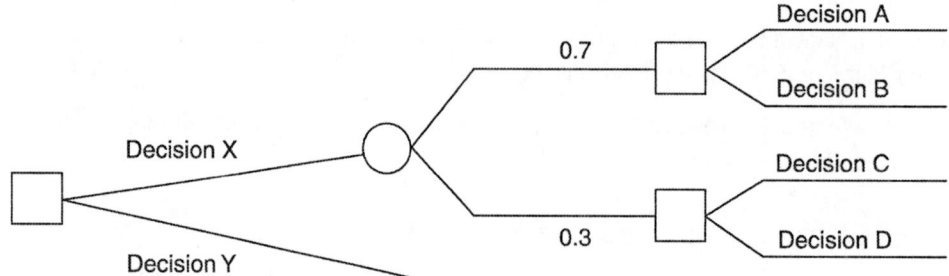

In this tree, either a choice between A and B or else a choice between C and D will be made, depending on the outcome which occurs after choosing X.

The decision tree should be in **chronological order** from **left to right**. When there are two-stage decision trees, the first decision in time should be drawn on the left.

5.1.3 Example: a decision tree

Beethoven has a new wonder product, the vylin, of which it expects great things. At the moment the company has two courses of action open to it, to test market the product or abandon it.

If the company test markets it, the cost will be $100,000 and the market response could be positive or negative with probabilities of 0.60 and 0.40.

If the response is positive the company could either abandon the product or market it full scale.

If it markets the vylin full scale, the outcome might be low, medium or high demand, and the respective net gains/(losses) would be (200), 200 or 1,000 in units of $1,000 (the result could range from a net loss of $200,000 to a gain of $1,000,000). These outcomes have probabilities of 0.20, 0.50 and 0.30 respectively.

If the result of the test marketing is negative and the company goes ahead and markets the product, estimated losses would be $600,000.

If, at any point, the company abandons the product, there would be a net gain of $50,000 from the sale of scrap. All the financial values have been discounted to the present.

Required

(a) Draw a decision tree.
(b) Include figures for cost, loss or profit on the appropriate branches of the tree.

Solution

The starting point for the tree is to **establish what decision has to be made now**. What are the options?

(a) To test market
(b) To abandon

The outcome of the 'abandon' option is known with certainty. There are two possible outcomes of the option to test market, positive response and negative response.

Depending on the outcome of the test marketing, another decision will then be made, to abandon the product or to go ahead.

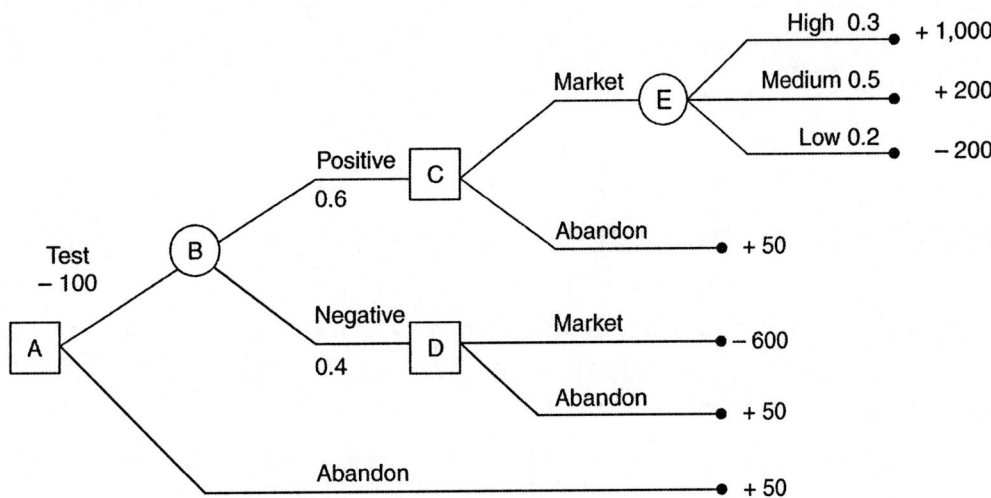

5.1.4 Evaluating the decision with a decision tree

Rollback analysis evaluates the EV of each decision option. You have to work from right to left and calculate EVs at each outcome point.

The expected value (EV) of each decision option can be evaluated, using the decision tree to help with keeping the logic properly sorted out. The basic rules are as follows:

(a) We start on the **right hand side** of the tree and **work back** towards the left-hand side and the current decision under consideration. This is sometimes known as the '**rollback technique**' or '**rollback analysis**'.

(b) Working from **right to left**, we calculate the **EV of revenue, cost, contribution or profit** at each outcome point on the tree.

In the above example, the right-hand-most outcome point is point E, and the EV is as follows:

	Profit x $'000	Probability p		px $'000
High	1,000	0.3		300
Medium	200	0.5		100
Low	(200)	0.2		(40)
			EV	360

PART A DATA COLLECTION AND ANALYSIS

This is the EV of the decision to market the product if the test shows positive response. It may help you to write the EV on the decision tree itself, at the appropriate outcome point (point E).

(a) **At decision point C**, the **choice** is as follows:

    (i)   Market, EV = + 360 (the EV at point E)
    (ii)   Abandon, value = + 50

The choice would be to market the product, and so the EV at decision point C is +360.

(b) **At decision point D**, the **choice** is as follows:

    (i)   Market, value = – 600
    (ii)   Abandon, value = +50

The choice would be to abandon, and so the EV at decision point D is +50.

The second stage decisions have therefore been made. If the original decision is to test market, the company will market the product if the test shows positive customer response, and will abandon the product if the test results are negative.

The evaluation of the decision tree is completed as follows:

(a) **Calculate the EV at outcome point B.**

    0.6 × 360   (EV at C)
  +   0.4 × 50   (EV at D)
  =   216 + 20 = 236

(b) **Compare the options at point A**, which are as follows:

    (i)   Test: EV = EV at B minus test marketing cost = 236 – 100 = 136
    (ii)   Abandon: Value = 50

The choice would be to test market the product, because it has a **higher EV of profit**.

Evaluating decisions by using **decision trees has a number of limitations**.

(a) The time value of money may not be taken into account.

(b) Decision trees are not very suitable for use in complex situations.

(c) The outcome with the highest EV may have the greatest risks attached to it. Managers may be reluctant to take risks which may lead to losses.

(d) The probabilities associated with different branches of the 'tree' are likely to be estimates, and possibly unreliable or inaccurate.

6 Probability distributions

6.1 Converting frequency distributions into probability distributions

FAST FORWARD

If we convert the frequencies in a frequency distribution table into proportions, we get a **probability distribution**.

Marks out of 10 (statistics test)	Number of students (frequency distribution)	Proportion or probability (probability distribution)
0	0	0.00
1	0	0.00
2	1	0.02*
3	2	0.04
4	4	0.08
5	10	0.20
6	15	0.30
7	10	0.20
8	6	0.12
9	2	0.04
10	0	0.00
	50	1.00

* 1/50 = 0.02

Key term

A **probability distribution** is an analysis of the proportion of times each particular value occurs in a set of items.

6.2 Graphing probability distributions

A graph of the probability distribution would be the same as the graph of the frequency distribution, but with the **vertical axis marked in proportions** rather than in numbers.

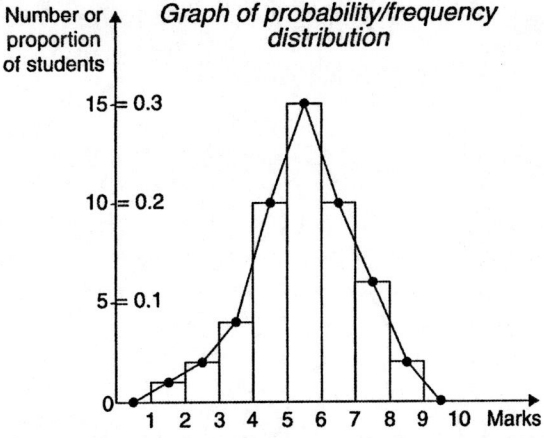

(a) The area under the curve in the frequency distribution represents the total number of students whose marks have been recorded, 50 people.

(b) **The area under the curve in a probability distribution is 100%, or 1** (the total of all the probabilities).

7 The normal distribution

> **FAST FORWARD**
>
> The **normal distribution** is a probability distribution which usually applies to **continuous variables**, such as distance and time.

7.1 Introduction

In calculating P(x), x can be any value, and does not have to be a whole number.

The normal distribution can also apply to **discrete variables** which can take **many possible values**. For example, the volume of sales, in units, of a product might be any whole number in the range 100 – 5,000 units. There are so many possibilities within this range that the variable is for all practical purposes **continuous**.

7.2 Graphing the normal distribution

The normal distribution can be drawn as a graph, and it would be a **bell-shaped curve**.

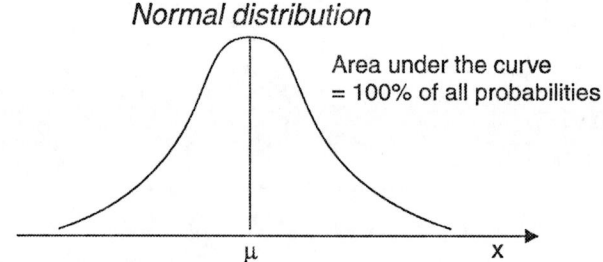

7.3 Properties of the normal distribution

> **FAST FORWARD**
>
> Properties of the normal distribution are as follows:
>
> - It is symmetrical and bell-shaped
> - It has a mean, μ (pronounced mew)
> - The area under the curve totals exactly 1
> - The area to the left of μ = area to the right of μ = 0.5

7.4 Importance of the normal distribution

The normal distribution is important because in the practical application of statistics, it has been found that **many probability distributions are close enough to a normal distribution** to be treated as one without any significant loss of accuracy. This means that the normal distribution can be used as a tool in business decision making involving probabilities.

8 The standard normal distribution

8.1 Introduction

For any normal distribution, the **dispersion** around the mean (μ) of the frequency of occurrences can be measured exactly in terms of the **standard deviation** (σ) (a concept we covered in Chapter 4b).

The **standard** normal distribution has a mean (μ) of 0 and a standard deviation (σ) of 1.

(a) The entire frequency curve represents all the possible outcomes and their frequencies of occurrence. Since the normal curve is **symmetrical**, 50% of occurrences have a value greater than the mean value (μ), and 50% of occurrences have a value less than the mean value (μ).

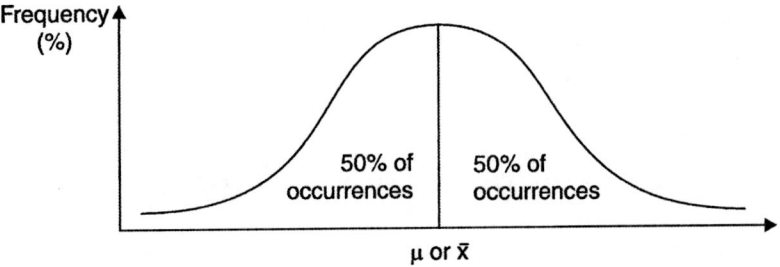

(b) About 68% of frequencies have a value within one standard deviation either side of the mean.

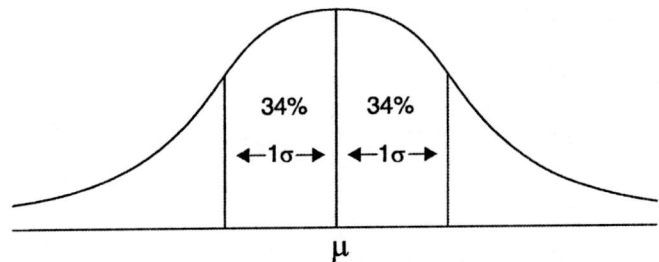

(c) 95% of the frequencies in a normal distribution occur in the range ± 1.96 standard deviations from the mean.

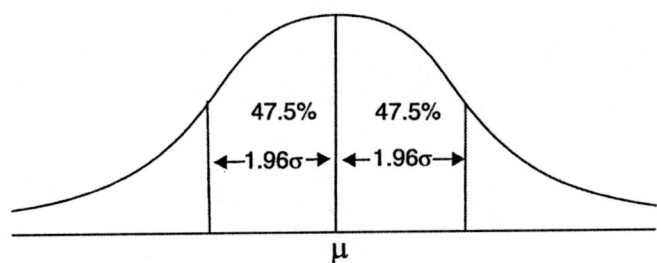

You will not need to remember these precise figures as a **normal distribution table** can be used to find the relevant proportions and this will be given to you in the exam.

8.2 Normal distribution tables

Although there is an infinite number of normal distributions, depending on values of the mean μ and the standard deviation σ, **the relative dispersion of frequencies around the mean, measured as proportions of the total population, is exactly the same for all normal distributions**. In other words, whatever the normal distribution, 47.5% of outcomes will always be in the range between the mean and 1.96 standard deviations below the mean, 49.5% of outcomes will always be in the range between the mean and 2.58 standard deviations below the mean and so on.

A **normal distribution table**, shown at the end of this Study Text, gives the proportion of the total between the mean and a point above or below the mean for any multiple of the standard deviation.

8.2.1 Example: Normal distribution tables

What is the probability that a randomly picked item will be in the shaded area of the diagram below?

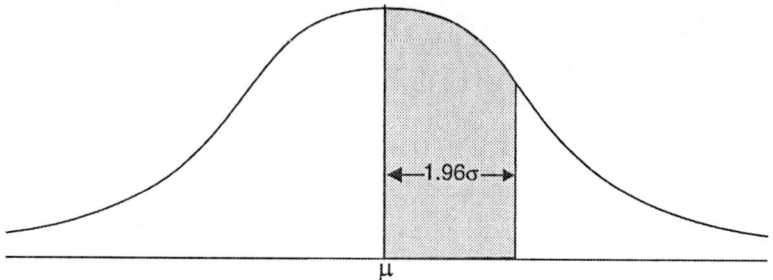

Look up 1.96 in the normal distribution table and you will obtain the value .475. This means there is a 47.5% probability that the item will be in the shaded area.

Since the normal distribution is symmetrical 1.96σ below the mean will also correspond to an area of 47.5%.

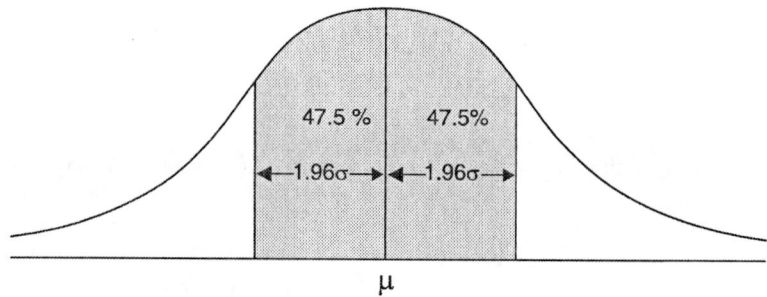

The total shaded area = 47.5% × 2 = 95%

In Paragraph 8.1(c) we said that 95% of the frequencies in a normal distribution lie in the range ± 1.96 standard deviations from the mean but we did not say what this figure was based on. It was of course based on the corresponding value in the normal distribution tables (when z = 1.96) as shown above.

We can also show that 99% of the frequencies occur in the range ± 2.58 standard deviation from the mean.

Using the normal distribution table, a z score of 2.58 corresponds to an area of 0.4949 (or 49.5%). Remember, the normal distribution is symmetrical.

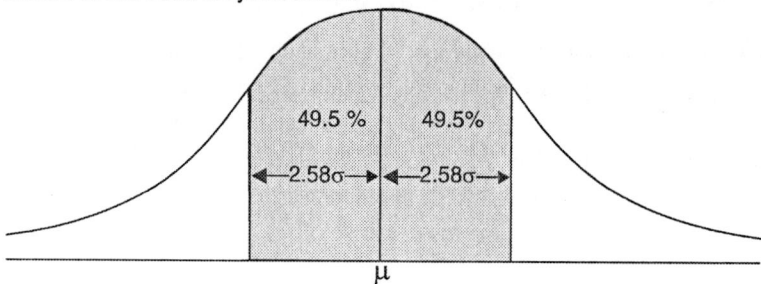

49.5% × 2 = 99%

If mean, μ + 2.58σ = 49.5% and
mean, μ − 2.58σ = 49.5%
Range = mean ± 2.58σ = 99.0%

Therefore, 99% of frequencies occur in the range mean (μ) ± 2.58 standard deviations (σ), as proved by using normal distribution tables.

Question

68% of frequencies

Prove that approximately 68% of frequencies have a value within one standard deviation either side of the mean, μ.

Answer

One standard deviation corresponds to z = 1

If z = 1, we can look this value up in normal distribution tables to get a value (area) of 0.3413. One standard deviation above the mean can be shown on a graph as follows:

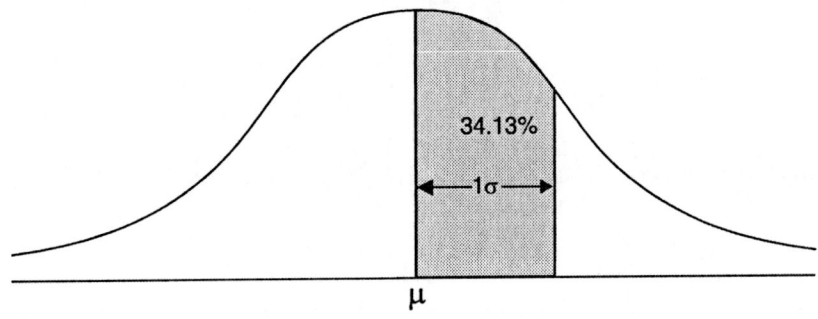

The normal distribution is symmetrical, and we must therefore show the area corresponding to one standard deviation below the mean on the graph also.

① The area one standard deviation **below** the mean

② The area one standard deviation **above** the mean

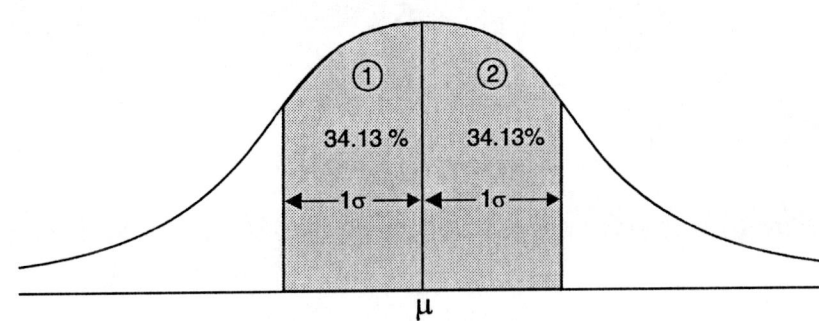

Area one standard deviation above **and** below the mean

= ① + ②

= 34.13% + 34.13%

= 68.26% + 68%

PART A DATA COLLECTION AND ANALYSIS

9 Using the normal distribution to calculate probabilities

$z = \dfrac{x - \mu}{\sigma}$ This formula is given to you in the exam formulae sheet

FAST FORWARD

The normal distribution can be used to calculate probabilities. Sketching a graph of a normal distribution curve often helps in normal distribution problems.

$$z = \dfrac{x - \mu}{\sigma}$$

where z = the number of standard deviations above or below the mean (z score)
       x = the value of the variable under consideration
       μ = the mean
       σ = the standard deviation.

9.1 Introduction

In order to calculate probabilities, we need to **convert** a normal distribution (X) with a mean μ and standard deviation σ to the standard normal distribution (z) before using the table to find the probability figure.

9.2 Example: Calculating z

Calculate the following z scores and identify the corresponding proportions using normal distribution tables.

(a) $x = 100, \mu = 200, \sigma = 50$
(b) $x = 1{,}000, \mu = 1{,}200, \sigma = 200$
(c) $x = 25, \mu = 30, \sigma = 6$

Solution

(a) $z = \dfrac{x - \mu}{\sigma}$

   $= \dfrac{100 - 200}{50}$

   $= 2$

   A z score of 2 corresponds to a proportion of 0.4772 or 47.72%.

(b) $z = \dfrac{x - \mu}{\sigma}$

   $= \dfrac{1{,}000 - 1{,}200}{200}$

   $= 1$

   A z score of 1 corresponds to a proportion of 0.3413 or 34.13%.

(c) $z = \dfrac{x - \mu}{\sigma}$

$= \dfrac{25 - 30}{6}$

$= 0.8333$

0.8333 corresponds to a proportion of 0.2967 or 29.67%

9.3 Example: Using the normal distribution to calculate probabilities

A frequency distribution is normal, with a mean of 100 and a standard deviation of 10.

Required

Calculate the proportion of the total frequencies which will be:

(a) above 80
(b) above 90
(c) above 100
(d) above 115
(e) below 85
(f) below 95
(g) below 108
(h) in the range 80 – 110
(i) in the range 90 – 95

Solution

(a) If the value (x) is **below** the mean (μ), the total proportion is 0.5 plus proportion between the value and the mean (area (a)).

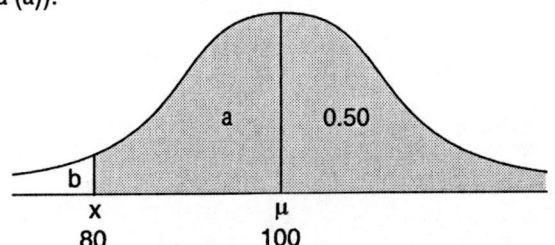

The proportion of the total frequencies which will be above 80 is calculated as follows.

$\dfrac{80 - 100}{10}$ = 2 standard deviations **below** the mean.

From the tables, where z = 2 the proportion is 0.4772.

The proportion of frequencies above 80 is 0.5 + 0.4772 = 0.9772.

(b) The proportion of the total frequencies which will be above 90 is calculated as follows.

$\dfrac{90 - 100}{10}$ = 1 standard deviation **below** the mean.

From the tables, when z = 1, the proportion is 0.3413.

The proportion of frequencies above 90 is 0.5 + 0.3413 = 0.8413.

(c) 100 is the mean. The proportion above this is 0.5. (The normal curve is symmetrical and 50% of occurrences have a value greater than the mean, and 50% of occurrences have a value less than the mean.)

(d) If the value is **above** the mean, the proportion (b) is 0.5 minus the proportion between the value and the mean (area (a)).

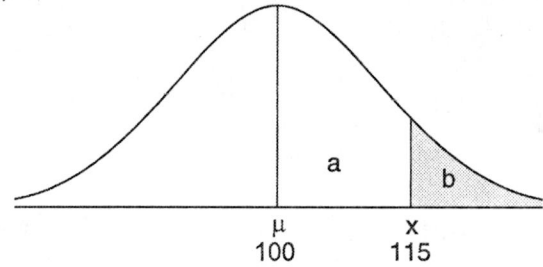

The proportion of the total frequencies which will be above 115 is calculated as follows.

$\dfrac{115 - 100}{10} = 1.5$ standard deviations **above** the mean.

From the tables, where z = 1.5, the proportion is 0.4332.

The proportion of frequencies above 115 is therefore 0.5 − 0.4332 = 0.0668.

(e) If the value is **below** the mean, the proportion (b) is 0.5 minus the proportion between the value and the mean (area (a)).

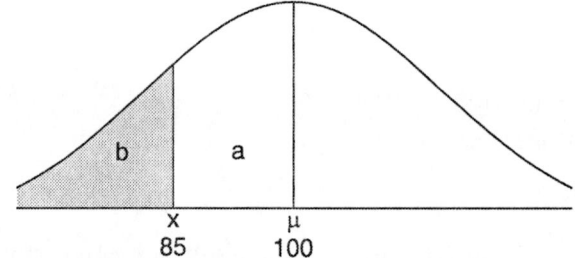

The proportion of the total frequencies which will be below 85 is calculated as follows.

$\dfrac{85 - 100}{10} = 1.5$ standard deviations **below** the mean.

The proportion of frequencies below 85 is therefore the same as the proportion above 115 = 0.0668.

(f) The proportion of the total frequencies which will be below 95 is calculated as follows.

$\dfrac{95 - 100}{10} = 0.5$ standard deviations **below** the mean.

When z = 0.5, the proportion from the tables is 0.1915. The proportion of frequencies below 95 is therefore 0.5 − 0.1915 = 0.3085.

(g) If the value is **above** the mean, the proportion required is 0.5 plus the proportion between the value and the mean (area (a)).

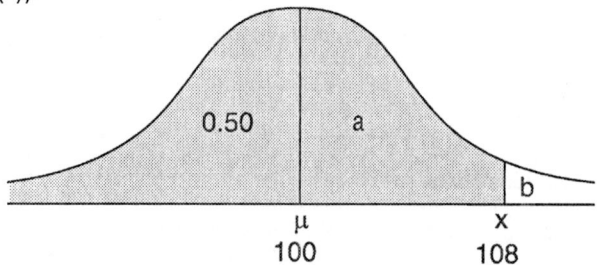

The proportion of the total frequencies which will be below 108 is calculated as follows.

$\dfrac{108 - 100}{10} = 0.8$ standard deviations **above** the mean.

From the tables for z = 0.8 the proportion is 0.2881.

The proportion of frequencies below 108 is 0.5 + 0.2881 = 0.7881.

(h) The proportion of the total frequencies which will be in the range 80–110 is calculated as follows. The range 80 to 110 may be divided into two parts:

(i) 80 to 100 (the mean)
(ii) 100 to 110.

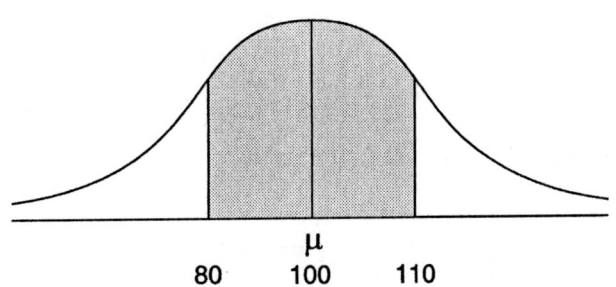

The proportion in the range 80 to 100 is (2 standard deviations) 0.4772

The proportion in the range 100 to 110 is (1 standard deviation) 0.3413

The proportion in the total range 80 to 110 is 0.4772 + 0.3413 = 0.8185.

(i) The range 90 to 95 may be analysed as:

(i) the proportion above 90 and below the mean
(ii) minus the proportion above 95 and below the mean

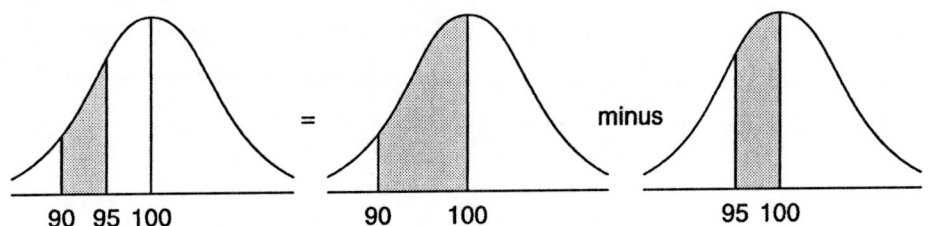

Proportion above 90 and below the mean (1 standard deviation)	0.3413
Proportion above 95 and below the mean (0.5 standard deviations)	0.1915
Proportion between 90 and 95	0.1498

Question — Normal distribution and proportions

The salaries of employees in an industry are normally distributed, with a mean of $14,000 and a standard deviation of $2,700.

Required

(a) Calculate the proportion of employees who earn less than $12,000.
(b) Calculate the proportion of employees who earn between $11,000 and $19,000.

Answer

(a)

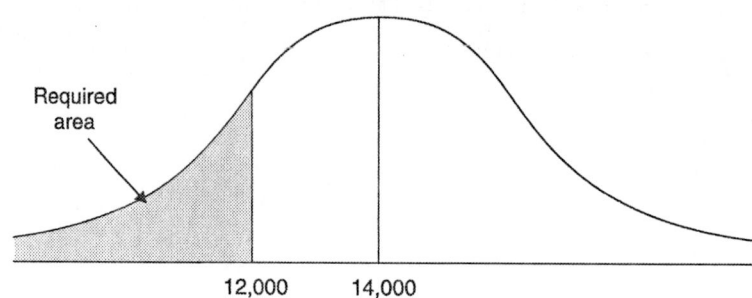

$$z = \frac{12{,}000 - 14{,}000}{2{,}700}$$

$$= -0.74$$

From normal distribution tables, the proportion of salaries between $12,000 and $14,000 is 0.2704 (from tables). The proportion of salaries less than $12,000 is therefore $0.5 - 0.2704 = 0.2296$.

(b)

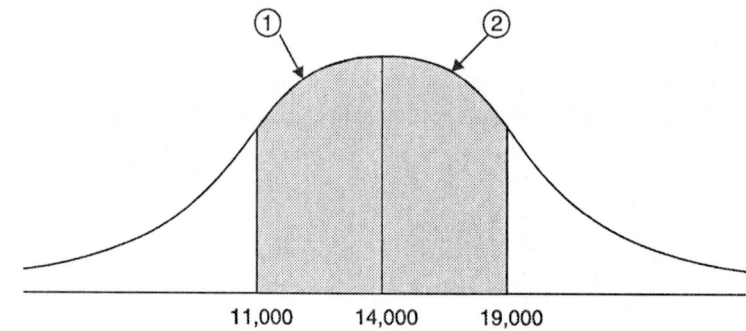

① $z = \dfrac{11{,}000 - 14{,}000}{2{,}700}$

$= 1.11$

② $z = \dfrac{19{,}000 - 14{,}000}{2{,}700}$

$= 1.85$

The proportion with earnings between $11,000 and $14,000 is 0.3665 (from tables where z = 1.11).

The proportion with earnings between $14,000 and $19,000 is 0.4678 (from tables where z = 1.85).

The required proportion is therefore $0.3665 + 0.4678 = 0.8343$.

Note. The normal distribution is, in fact, a way of calculating probabilities. In this question, for example, the **probability** that an employee earns less than $12,000 (part (a)) is 0.2296 (or 22.96%) and the probability that an employee earns between $11,000 and $19,000 is 0.8343 (or 83.43%).

Exam focus point: Make sure you always draw a sketch of a normal distribution to identify the areas that you are concerned with.

FAST FORWARD: If you are given the **variance** of a distribution, remember to first calculate the standard deviation by taking its square root.

5: APPLYING PROBABILITY TO DECISION MAKING

Question — Normal distribution

The specification for the width of a widget is a minimum of 42mm and a maximum of 46.2mm. A normally distributed batch of widgets is produced with a mean of 45mm and a variance of 4mm.

Required

(a) Calculate the percentage of parts that are too small
(b) Calculate the percentage of parts that are too big

Answer

(a)

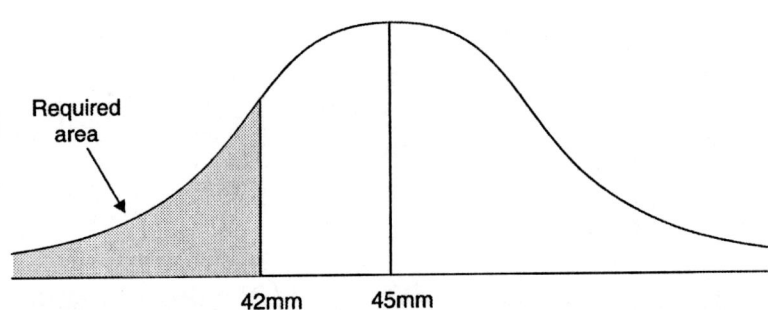

$\sigma = \sqrt{4} = 2$

$z = \dfrac{42 - 45}{2} = -1.5$

Proportion of widgets between 42mm and 45mm = 0.4332.
Proportion of widgets smaller than 42mm = 0.5 − 0.4332 = 0.0668
= 6.68%

(b)

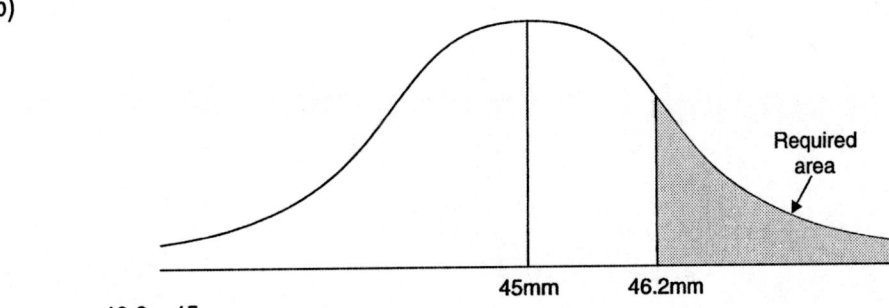

$z = \dfrac{46.2 - 45}{2} = 0.6$

Proportion of widgets between 45mm and 46.2mm = 0.2257.
Proportion of widgets bigger than 46.2mm = 0.5 − 0.2257 = 0.2743
= 27.43%

Exam focus point

You may need to work backwards from a % of population to calculate the z score and then the x value.

Question — Standard deviation

A normal distribution has a mean of 120 and a standard deviation of 15. 75% of the population is therefore below what value?

PART A DATA COLLECTION AND ANALYSIS

Answer

50% of the population is below 120.

25% of the population is below x.

From the normal distribution table, a value of 0.25 equates to a z value of 0.67.

$$z = \frac{x - \mu}{\sigma}$$

$$0.67 = \frac{x - 120}{15}$$

$0.67 \times 15 = x - 120$

$10.05 = x - 120$

$x = 10.05 + 120$

$= 130.05$

75% of the population is below 130.05

Exam focus point

Your aim should be to set aside enough time to work through as many calculations as you can in this area. Calculations on the material in this chapter have come up in most exams!

10 Binomial distribution

General term: $\frac{n!}{x!\,(n-x)!} Q^{n-x} P^x$

This formula is given to you in the exam formulae sheet.

FAST FORWARD

The binomial distribution is used to calculate the probability of a specified number of events (x) either happening or not happening.

Where: $\frac{n!}{x!\,(n-x)!} Q^{n-x} P^x$

- n = the number of trials
- x = the value of the event we are interested in
- P = the expected probability of the event happening
- Q = the expected probability of the event NOT happening.

10.1 Introduction

The binomial distribution looks at the probability of an event happening or not happening so there are only **TWO possible outcomes**. An example would be in manufacturing a product, where a unit that is produced is EITHER defective or NOT defective. A binomial distribution could be used to examine the probability of a given number of defects (x) if a certain number of items (n) were produced.

This is different from the normal distribution where the outcome of a trial covers a **wide range** of values (for example, the width of the units being manufactured, in our example in Section 9.)

10.2 Criteria for using a binomial distribution

To use the binomial distribution, the following criteria must be met:

- Each trial consists of TWO possible outcomes.
- The trials are independent and identical. (The outcome of one trial doesn't affect the outcome of other trials.)
- We are interested in the probability of a specified number of successes or failures in the number of trials.
- The probability of success or failure is the same for each trial.

10.3 Example: using the formula

$$\frac{n!}{x!(n-x)!} Q^{n-x} P^x$$

The formula is not actually as complicated as it looks at first sight.

Let's imagine that we are interested in the probability of exactly 1 defective unit being produced out of a total of 4 units produced. The probability of a defective unit is 50%.

Solution

Using our understanding of probability from earlier in this chapter we can estimate the probability of exactly one defective unit as follows:

Possible outcomes of the production of 4 units (where x = defective, o = not defective):

xxxx	xxxo	xxoo	**xooo**
xoxx	xoxo	xoox	xxox
oxxx	oxxo	oooo	**oxoo**
ooxx	**ooxo**	**ooox**	oxox

There are 16 possible outcomes, of which 4 correspond to one defect, giving a probability of 4 / 16 = 25%.

It is quicker to **use the binomial distribution formula** to obtain this result:

- n is the number of trials, here this is 4.
- n! is a mathematical notation called a factorial. For example here there are 4 units produced; 4! means $4 \times 3 \times 2 \times 1 = 24$.
- x is the number of occurrences of an event that we are interested in. Here this is 1.
- (n − x) is the number of trials minus the number of occurrences of an event that we are interested in. For example here (n − x) = (4 − 1) = 3 and (n − x)! = 3! or $3 \times 2 \times 1 = 6$.
- The probability of failure (P) is 0.5 so the probability of success (Q) = 1 − 0.5 = 0.5.

So the formula becomes

$$\frac{4!}{1!(3)!} 0.5^3 \, 0.5^1 = \frac{24}{6} \times 0.125 \times 0.5 = 0.25$$

There is a **further shortcut** because the expression $\frac{n!}{x!(n-x)!}$ appears on many calculators as nCr.

To use this function you input the number of trials (n) first, then press the nCr button, then enter the number of events you are interested in (x), and finally press the equals button.

So here this would be **4** then **nCr** then **1** then press = and this should give 4.

This short-cut will save a lot of time in the exam **and will be used from here on**.

Question
More than 1 event

What is the probability of less than 2 defective units being produced out of a total of 4 units produced? The probability of a defective unit is 50%.

Answer

We are being asked to calculate the probability of the number of events (defects) being either 0 or 1.

From the earlier example we know the probability of 1 defect is 0.25.

The probability of 0 defects (using the short-cut approach) can be calculated as:

4 nCr 0 × 0.5^4 × 0.5^0

This equals 1 × 0.0625 × 1 = 0.0625

So the probability of the number of defects being EITHER 0 OR 1 = 0.0625 + 0.25 = 0.3125.

Exam focus point: In the exam you may have to identify whether it is appropriate to apply the binomial distribution

11 Poisson distribution

General term: $\dfrac{e^{-m} m^x}{x!}$

This formula is given to you in the exam formulae sheet.

FAST FORWARD

The Poisson distribution is used to calculate the probability that a specified number of events ('x') will occur during a specific interval of time or in a specific distance, area or volume

Where: $\dfrac{e^{-m} m^x}{x!}$

- m = the mean value
- x = the value of the event we are interested in (the random variable)
- e = a mathematical constant (the base of natural logarithms)

11.1 Introduction

The Poisson distribution looks at the probability of a given number of occurrences happening in a given interval where the occurrences occur at random and are independent.

In order to use the Poisson distribution, the mean (or average) value must be known. The probability of a different value occurring can then be calculated, in relation to the mean.

11.2 Example: using the formula

$$\frac{e^{-m} m^x}{x!}$$

Again the formula is not actually as complicated as it looks at first sight.

Let's imagine that we are interested in the probability of an employee at a call centre receiving

(a) no queries per period
(b) **more than** 3 queries in a given period.

The mean number of queries per period is 2.

Solution

Let 'x' be the random variable denoting the number of queries.

(a) The probability of 0 queries (so x = 0) is:

$$\frac{e^{-m} m^x}{x!} = \frac{e^{-2} 2^0}{0!} = \frac{0.1353 \times 1}{1} = 0.1353$$

Note: Mathematical convention dictates that the factorial of 0 is 1.

(b) The probability of more than 3 queries is the same as $1 - P(x \le 3)$:

$$P(x>3) = 1 - P(x \le 3)$$
$$= 1 - [P(x=0) + P(x=1) + P(x=2) + P(x=3)]$$
$$= 1 - \left[\frac{e^{-2} 2^0}{0!} + \frac{e^{-2} 2^1}{1!} + \frac{e^{-2} 2^2}{2!} + \frac{e^{-2} 2^3}{3!} \right]$$
$$= 1 - [0.1353 + 0.2707 + 0.2707 + 0.1804]$$
$$= 1 - 0.8571$$
$$= 0.1429$$

Question

A tour operator has identified that its holiday brochure has 10 typing errors in its 50 pages.

(a) What is the probability that page 40 has no errors?
(b) What is the probability that page 20 has 2 errors or fewer?

Answer

First we need to calculate the mean number of errors per page.

Mean = 10 / 50 = 0.2

Let x be the random variable denoting the number of errors per page.

(a) $P(x = 0) = \dfrac{e^{-m} m^x}{x!} = \dfrac{e^{-0.2} 0.2^0}{0!} = \dfrac{0.8187 \times 1}{1} = 0.8187$

PART A   DATA COLLECTION AND ANALYSIS

(b) $P(x \leq 2) = P(x = 0) + P(x = 1) + P(x = 2)$

$$= \frac{e^{-0.2} 0.2^0}{0!} + \frac{e^{-0.2} 0.2^1}{1!} + \frac{e^{-0.2} 0.2^2}{2!}$$

$= 0.8187 + 0.1637 + 0.0164$

$= 0.9988$

Exam focus point In the exam you may have to identify whether it is appropriate to apply the Poisson distribution

Chapter Roundup

- Probability is a measure of **likelihood** and can be stated as a percentage, a ratio, or more usually as a number from 0 to 1.

- The **simple addition law** for two mutually exclusive events, A and B, is as follows:

    P(A or B) = P(A∪B) = P(A) + P(B)

- **Mutually exclusive outcomes** are outcomes where the occurrence of one of the outcomes excludes the possibility of any of the others happening.

- The **simple multiplication law** for two independent events A and B, is as follows:

    P(A and B) = P(A) P(B)

- **Independent events** are events where the outcome of one event in no way affects the outcome of the other events.

- The **general rule of addition** for two events, A and B, which are not mutually exclusive, is as follows:

    P(A or B) = P(A ∪ B) = P(A) + P(B) − P(A and B)

- The **general rule of multiplication** for two dependent events, A and B, is as follows:

    P(A and B) = P(A ∩ B) P(A) × P(B/A)
    = P(B) × P(A/B)

- **Dependent** or **conditional** events are events where the outcome of one event depends on the outcome of the others.

- **Contingency tables** can be useful for dealing with **conditional probability**.

- An **expected value** (or **EV**) is a weighted average, based on probabilities. The expected value for a single event can offer a helpful guide for management decisions.

- **Probability and expectation should be seen as an aid to decision making**.

- A payoff table is simply a table with **rows for circumstances** and **columns for actions** (or vice versa), and the payoffs in the cells of the table.

- Probability is used to help to calculate **risk** in decision making.

- A **decision tree** is a pictorial method of showing a sequence of interrelated decisions and their expected outcomes. Decision trees can incorporate both the probabilities of, and values of, expected outcomes, and are used in decision-making.

- If we convert the frequencies in a frequency distribution table into proportions, we get a **probability distribution**.

- The **normal distribution** is a probability distribution which usually applies to **continuous variables**, such as distance and time.

- Properties of the normal distribution are as follows:
    - It is symmetrical and bell-shaped
    - It has a mean, μ (pronounced mew)
    - The area under the curve totals exactly 1
    - The area to the left of μ = area to the right of μ = 0.5

PART A   DATA COLLECTION AND ANALYSIS

- The normal distribution can be used to calculate probabilities. Sketching a graph of a normal distribution curve often helps in normal distribution problems.

  $$z = \frac{x - \mu}{\sigma}$$

  where z = the number of standard deviations above or below the mean (z score)
  x = the value of the variable under consideration
  μ = the mean
  σ = the standard deviation.

- If you are given the **variance** of a distribution, remember to first calculate the standard deviation by taking its square root.

- The binomial distribution is used to calculate the probability of a specified number of events (x) either happening or not happening.

  $$\frac{n!}{x!(n-x)!} Q^{n-x} P^x$$

  where n = the number of trials
  x = the value of the event we are interested in
  P = the expected probability of the event happening
  Q = the expected probability of the event NOT happening.

- The Poisson distribution is used to calculate the probability that a specified number of events ('x') will occur during a specific interval of time or in a specific distance, area or volume.

  $$\frac{e^{-m} m^x}{x!}$$

  where m = the mean value
  x = the value of the event we are interested in (the random variable)
  e = a mathematical constant (the base of natural logarithms)

Quick Quiz

1   Complete the following equations

(a) $P(\overline{X}) = 1 - \boxed{}$

(b) Simple addition/OR law

   $P(A \text{ or } B \text{ or } C) = \boxed{}$

   where A, B and C are $\boxed{}$

(c) Simple multiplication/AND law

   $P(A \text{ and } B) = \boxed{}$

   where A and B are $\boxed{}$

(d) General rule of addition

   $P(A \text{ or } B) = \boxed{}$

   where A and B are $\boxed{}$

(e) General rule of multiplication

P(A and B) = ☐

where A and B are ☐

2   Match the terms (1)–(3) with the definitions (a)–(c).

(1) Mutually exclusive outcomes
(2) Independent events
(3) Conditional events

(a) The occurrence of one of the outcomes excludes the possibility of any of the others happening
(b) Events where the outcome of one event depends on the outcome of the others
(c) Events where the outcome of one event in no way affects the outcome of the other events

3   An analysis of 480 working days in a factory shows that on 360 days there were no machine breakdowns. Assuming that this pattern will continue, what is the probability that there will be a machine breakdown on a particular day?

(a) 0%
(b) 25%
(c) 35%
(d) 75%

4   A production director is responsible for overseeing the operations of three factories – North, South and West. He visits one factory per week. He visits the West factory as often as he visits the North factory, but he visits the South factory twice as often as he visits the West factory.

What is the probability that in any one week he will visit the North factory?

(a) 0.17
(b) 0.20
(c) 0.25
(d) 0.33

5   A project may result in profits of $15,000 or $20,000, or in a loss of $5,000. The probabilities of each profit are 0.2, 0.5 and 0.3 respectively.

What is the expected profit? ☐

PART A   DATA COLLECTION AND ANALYSIS

Answers to Quick Quiz

1. (a) $1 - P(X)$
    (b) $P(A) + P(B) + P(C)$ — Mutually exclusive outcomes
    (c) $P(A) \times P(B)$ — Independent events
    (d) $P(A) + P(B) - P(A \text{ and } B)$ — Not mutually exclusive outcomes
    (e) $P(A) \times P(B/A) = P(B) \times P(A/B)$ — Dependent events

2. (a) = 1
    (b) = 3
    (c) = 2

3. (b) The data tells us that there was a machine breakdown on 120 days (480 – 360) out of a total of 480.

    $P(\text{machine breakdown}) = 120/480 \times 100\%$
    $= 25\%$

    You should have been able to eliminate option A immediately since a probability of 0% = impossibility.

    If you selected option C, you calculated the probability of a machine breakdown as 120 out of a possible 365 days instead of 480 days.

    If you selected option D, you incorrectly calculated the probability that there was **not** a machine breakdown on any particular day.

4.
Factory	Ratio of visits
North	1
South	2
West	$\frac{1}{4}$

    Pr(visiting North factory) = 1/4 = 0.25

    If you didn't select the correct option, make sure that you are clear about how the correct answer has been arrived at. Remember to look at the **ratio** of visits since no actual numbers of visits are given.

5. $\boxed{11{,}500}$

    $EV = (15{,}000 \times 0.2) + (20{,}000 \times 0.5) + (-5{,}000 \times 0.3)$
    $= 3{,}000 + 10{,}000 - 1{,}500$
    $= 11{,}500$

End of Chapter Question

Applying probability to decision making (AIA Nov 08)

(a) Distinguish between discrete and continuous probability distributions. **(2 marks)**

(b) A Building Society claims that, during the last three months, three quarters of all applications for new loans have been successful. In a certain period seven applications for new loans are expected to be assessed.

Required

(i) Determine the probability that six or more of the applications will be successful. **(5 marks)**

(ii) Determine the probability that exactly three applications will be unsuccessful. **(3 marks)**

(c) In a Building Society the time taken by a supervisor to carry out an initial assessment to determine whether an application for a new loan can be recommended for further consideration is thought to be normally distributed with a mean value of 20 minutes and a standard deviation of 6 minutes.

Required

(i) Determine the probability that an assessment will last longer than 30 minutes. **(3 marks)**

(ii) Determine the probability that an assessment will take between 18 and 23 minutes. **(3 marks)**

(iii) Determine the duration such that 90% of assessments will take less than that time. **(4 marks)**

(Total = 20 marks)

PART A DATA COLLECTION AND ANALYSIS

Measuring the relationship between two variables

Topic list	Syllabus reference
1 Correlation	6.5
2 The correlation coefficient and the coefficient of determination	6.5
3 Spearman's rank correlation coefficient	6.5
4 Lines of best fit	6.5
5 The scattergraph method	6.5
6 Linear regression analysis	6.5

Introduction

We looked at scatter diagrams in Chapter 3. We are now going to look at how the inter-relationship shown between variables in a scatter diagram can be described and calculated. The first three sections deal with **correlation**, which is concerned with assessing the strength of the relationship between two variables.

We will then see how, if we assume that there is a **linear relationship** between two variables (such as selling costs and sales volume) we can determine the equation of a straight line to represent the relationship between the variables and use that equation to make **forecasts** or **predictions**.

PART A DATA COLLECTION AND ANALYSIS

Exam focus point

The contents of this chapter have been examined frequently.

1 Correlation

FAST FORWARD

When the value of one variable is related to the value of another, they are said to be **correlated**.

Key term

Two variables are said to be correlated if a change in the value of one variable is accompanied by a change in the value of another variable. This is what is meant by **correlation**.

1.1 Examples of variables which might be correlated

- A person's height and weight
- The distance of a journey and the time it takes to make it

1.2 Scatter diagrams

One way of showing the correlation between two related variables is on a scatter diagram (see Chapter 3), plotting a number of pairs of data on the graph. For example, a scatter diagram showing monthly selling costs against the volume of sales for a 12-month period might be as follows:

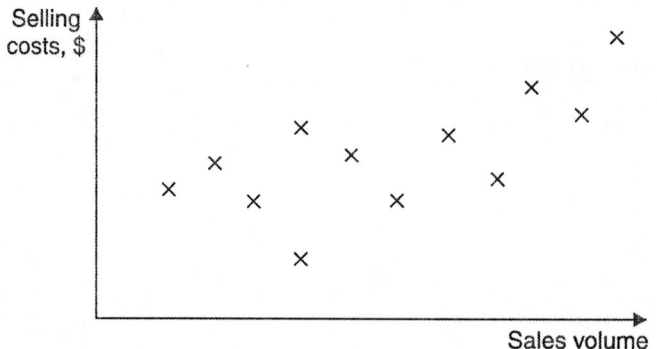

The **independent** variable (the cause) is plotted on the **horizontal** (x) axis and the **dependent** variable (the effect) is plotted on the **vertical** (y) axis.

This scattergraph suggests that there is some correlation between selling costs and sales volume, so that as sales volume rises, selling costs tend to rise as well.

Exam focus point

Many students find the maths in this chapter quite tricky. Many questions, however, have a part requiring the drawing of a scatter graph. These are easy marks for anyone.

6: MEASURING THE RELATIONSHIP BETWEEN TWO VARAIABLES

1.3 Degrees of correlation

FAST FORWARD — Two variables might be **perfectly correlated**, **partly correlated** or **uncorrelated**. Correlation can be positive or negative.

These differing degrees of correlation can be illustrated by scatter diagrams.

Perfect correlation

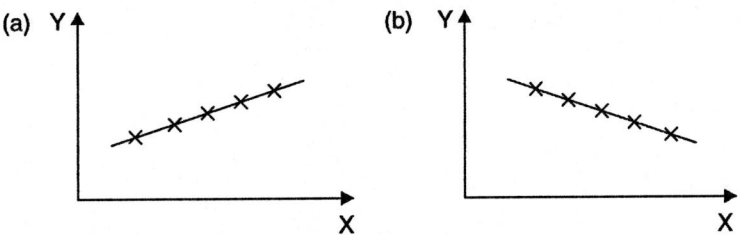

All the pairs of values lie on a straight line. An exact **linear relationship** exists between the two variables.

Partial correlation

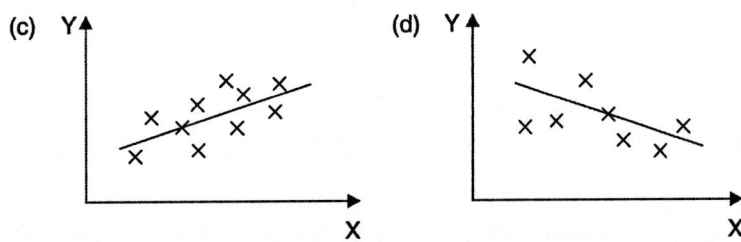

In (c), although there is no exact relationship, low values of X tend to be associated with low values of Y, and high values of X with high values of Y.

In (d) again, there is no exact relationship, but low values of X tend to be associated with high values of Y and vice versa.

No correlation

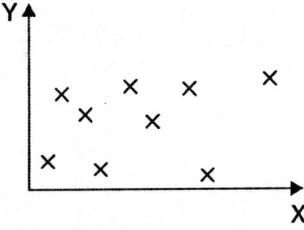

The values of these two variables are not correlated with each other.

1.4 Positive and negative correlation

Correlation, whether perfect or partial, can be **positive** or **negative**.

Key terms

- **Positive correlation** means that low values of one variable are associated with low values of the other, and high values of one variable are associated with high values of the other.

- **Negative correlation** means that low values of one variable are associated with high values of the other, and high values of one variable with low values of the other.

PART A   DATA COLLECTION AND ANALYSIS

2 The correlation coefficient and the coefficient of determination

FAST FORWARD

The **degree of correlation** between two variables is measured by **Pearson's correlation coefficient, r**. The nearer r is to +1 or –1, the stronger the relationship.

2.1 The correlation coefficient

Pearson's correlation coefficient, r (also known as the **product moment** correlation coefficient) is used to measure how strong the connection is between two variables, known as the degree of correlation.

It is calculated using a formula which will be given to you in the exam. It looks complicated but with a systematic approach and plenty of practice, you will be able to answer correlation questions in the exam.

Correlation coefficient, $r = \dfrac{n\Sigma XY - \Sigma X \Sigma Y}{\sqrt{[n\Sigma X^2 - (\Sigma X)^2][n\Sigma Y^2 - (\Sigma Y)^2]}}$

Where X and Y represent pairs of data for two variables X and Y

n = the number of pairs of data used in the analysis

2.2 The correlation coefficient range

The correlation coefficient, r must always fall between –1 and +1. If you get a value outside this range you have made a mistake.

- r = +1 means that the variables are **perfectly positively correlated**
- r = –1 means that the variables are **perfectly negatively correlated**
- r = 0 means that the variables are **uncorrelated**

2.3 Example: The correlation coefficient

The cost of output at a factory is thought to depend on the number of units produced. Data have been collected for the number of units produced each month in the last six months, and the associated costs, as follows:

Month	Output '000s of units X	Cost $'000 Y
1	2	9
2	3	11
3	1	7
4	4	13
5	3	11
6	5	15

Required

Assess whether there is there any correlation between output and cost.

Solution

$$r = \frac{n\sum XY - \sum X \sum Y}{\sqrt{[n\sum X^2 - (\sum X)^2][n\sum Y^2 - (\sum Y)^2]}}$$

We need to find the values for the following.

(a) $\sum XY$ Multiply each value of X by its corresponding Y value, so that there are six values for XY. Add up the six values to get the total.

(b) $\sum X$ Add up the six values of X to get a total. $(\sum X)^2$ will be the square of this total.

(c) $\sum Y$ Add up the six values of Y to get a total. $(\sum Y)^2$ will be the square of this total.

(d) $\sum X^2$ Find the square of each value of X, so that there are six values for X^2. Add up these values to get a total.

(e) $\sum Y^2$ Find the square of each value of Y, so that there are six values for Y^2. Add up these values to get a total.

Set out your workings in a table.

Workings

X	Y	XY	X^2	Y^2
2	9	18	4	81
3	11	33	9	121
1	7	7	1	49
4	13	52	16	169
3	11	33	9	121
5	15	75	25	225
$\sum X = 18$	$\sum Y = 66$	$\sum XY = 218$	$\sum X^2 = 64$	$\sum Y^2 = 766$

$(\sum X)^2 = 18^2 = 324$

$(\sum Y)^2 = 66^2 = 4{,}356$

$n = 6$

$$r = \frac{(6 \times 218) - (18 \times 66)}{\sqrt{[(6 \times 64) - 324] \times [(6 \times 766) - 4{,}356]}}$$

$$= \frac{1{,}308 - 1{,}188}{\sqrt{(384 - 324) \times (4{,}596 - 4{,}356)}}$$

$$= \frac{120}{\sqrt{60 \times 240}} = \frac{120}{\sqrt{14{,}400}} = \frac{120}{120} = 1$$

There is **perfect positive correlation** between the volume of output at the factory and costs which means that there is a perfect linear relationship between output and costs.

PART A   DATA COLLECTION AND ANALYSIS

 Question   Correlation

A company wants to know if the money they spend on advertising is effective in creating sales. The following data have been collected.

Monthly advertising expenditure $'000	Sales in following month $'000
1.2	132.5
0.9	98.5
1.6	154.3
2.1	201.4
1.6	161.0

Required

Calculate Pearson's correlation coefficient for the data and explain the result.

Answer

Monthly advertising expenditure	Sales			
X	Y	X²	Y²	XY
1.2	132.5	1.44	17,556.25	159.00
0.9	98.5	0.81	9,702.25	88.65
1.6	154.3	2.56	23,808.49	246.88
2.1	201.4	4.41	40,561.96	422.94
1.6	161.0	2.56	25,921.00	257.60
7.4	747.7	11.78	117,549.95	1175.07

$(\Sigma X)^2 = 7.4^2 = 54.76$

$(\Sigma Y)^2 = 747.7^2 = 559,055.29$

$$r = \frac{(5 \times 1,175.07) - (7.4 \times 747.7)}{\sqrt{[(5 \times 11.78) - 54.76] \times [(5 \times 117,549.95) - 559,055.29]}}$$

$$= \frac{5,875.35 - 5,532.98}{\sqrt{4.14 \times 28,694.46}}$$

$$= \frac{342.37}{\sqrt{118,795.06}}$$

$$= \frac{342.37}{344.67} = 0.993$$

0.993 is very close to 1, therefore there is a strong positive correlation and sales are dependent on advertising expenditure.

2.4 The coefficient of determination, r^2

FAST FORWARD

The **coefficient of determination** r^2 measures the proportion of the total variation in the value of one variable that can be explained by variations in the value of the other variable.

Unless the correlation coefficient r is exactly or very nearly +1, –1 or 0, its meaning or significance is a little unclear. For example, if the correlation coefficient for two variables is +0.8, this would tell us that the variables are positively correlated, but the correlation is not perfect. It would not really tell us much else. A more meaningful analysis is available from **the square of the correlation coefficient, r**, which is called the **coefficient of determination**, r^2.

2.5 Interpreting r^2

In the question above, r = –0.992, therefore r^2 = 0.984. This means that over 98% of variations in sales can be explained by the passage of time, leaving 0.016 (less than 2%) of variations to be explained by other factors.

Similarly, if the correlation coefficient between a company's output volume and maintenance costs was 0.9, r^2 would be 0.81, meaning that 81% of variations in maintenance costs could be explained by variations in output volume, leaving only 19% of variations to be explained by other factors (such as the age of the equipment).

Note, however, that if r^2 = 0.81, we would say that 81% of **the variations in y can be explained by variations in x**. We do not necessarily conclude that 81% of variations in y are *caused* by the variations in x. We must beware of reading too much significance into our statistical analysis.

2.6 Correlation and causation

If two variables are well correlated, either positively or negatively, this may be due to **pure chance** or there may be a **reason** for it. The larger the number of pairs of data collected, the less likely it is that the correlation is due to chance, though that possibility should never be ignored entirely.

If there is a reason, it may not be **causal**. For example, monthly net income is well correlated with monthly credit to a person's bank account, for the logical (rather than causal) reason that for most people the one equals the other.

Even if there is a causal explanation for a correlation, it does not follow that variations in the value of one variable cause variations in the value of the other. For example, sales of ice cream and of sunglasses are well correlated, not because of a direct causal link but because the weather influences both variables.

3 Spearman's rank correlation coefficient

3.1 Coefficient of rank correlation

In the examples considered above, the data were given in terms of the values of the relevant variables, such as the number of hours. Sometimes however, they are given in terms of order or **rank** rather than actual values.

FAST FORWARD

Spearman's rank correlation coefficient is used when data is given in terms of order or rank, rather than actual values.

PART A   DATA COLLECTION AND ANALYSIS

> **Coefficient of rank correlation**, $R = 1 - \left[\dfrac{6\sum d^2}{n(n^2-1)}\right]$
>
> Where n is the number of pairs of data
>
> d is the difference between the rankings in each set of data.
>
> This formula will be given to you in the exam

The coefficient of rank correlation can be **interpreted** in exactly the same way as the ordinary correlation coefficient. Its value can range from −1 to +1.

3.2 Example: The rank correlation coefficient

The examination placings of seven students were as follows:

Student	Statistics placing	Economics placing
A	2	1
B	1	3
C	4	7
D	6	5
E	5	6
F	3	2
G	7	4

Required

Judge whether the placings of the students in statistics correlate with their placings in economics.

Solution

Correlation must be measured by **Spearman's coefficient** because we are given the **placings** of students, and not their actual marks.

$$R = 1 - \dfrac{6\sum d^2}{n(n^2-1)}$$

where d is the difference between the rank in statistics and the rank in economics for each student.

Student	Rank Statistics	Rank Economics	d	d^2
A	2	1	1	1
B	1	3	2	4
C	4	7	3	9
D	6	5	1	1
E	5	6	1	1
F	3	2	1	1
G	7	4	3	9
			$\sum d^2 =$	26

$$R = 1 - \dfrac{6 \times 26}{7 \times (49-1)} = 1 - \dfrac{156}{336} = 0.536$$

The correlation is **positive**, 0.536, but the correlation is **not strong**.

3.3 Tied ranks

If in a problem some of the items **tie for a particular ranking**, these must be given an **average place** before the coefficient of rank correlation is calculated. Here is an example:

Position of students in examination		Express as
A	1 = average of 1 and 2	1.5
B	1 =	1.5
C	3	3
D	4	4
E	5 =	6
F	5 = average of 5, 6 and 7	6
G	5 =	6
H	8	8

Question — Spearman's coefficient

Five artists were placed in order of merit by two different judges as follows:

Artist	Judge P rank	Judge Q rank
A	1	4 =
B	2 =	1
C	4	3
D	5	2
E	2 =	4 =

Required

Assess how the two sets of rankings are correlated.

Answer

Artist	Judge P rank	Judge Q rank	d	d²
A	1.0	4.5	3.5	12.25
B	2.5	1.0	1.5	2.25
C	4.0	3.0	1.0	1.00
D	5.0	2.0	3.0	9.00
E	2.5	4.5	2.0	4.00
				28.50

$$R = 1 - \frac{6 \times 28.5}{5 \times (25-1)} = -0.425$$

There is a **slight negative correlation** between the rankings.

4 Lines of best fit

4.1 Strength of a relationship

Correlation enables us to determine the **strength of any relationship between two variables** but it does not offer us any method of **forecasting** values for one variable, Y, given values of another variable, X.

4.2 Equation of a straight line

If we assume that there is a **linear relationship** between the two variables and we determine the **equation of a straight line (Y = a + bX)** which is a good fit for the available data plotted on a scattergraph, we can use the equation for forecasting. We do this by substituting values for X into the equation and deriving values for Y.

4.3 Estimating the equation

There are a number of techniques for estimating the equation of a line of best fit. We will be looking at the **scattergraph method** and **simple linear regression analysis**. Both provide a technique for estimating values for a and b in the equation, y = a + bx.

5 The scattergraph method

FAST FORWARD

The **scattergraph method** involves the use of judgement to draw what seems to be a line of best fit through plotted data.

5.1 Example: The scattergraph method

Suppose we have the following pairs of data about output and costs.

Month	Output '000 units	Costs $'000
1	20	82
2	16	70
3	24	90
4	22	85
5	18	73

(a) These pairs of data can be plotted on a **scattergraph** (the **horizontal** axis representing the **independent** variable and the **vertical** axis the **dependent**) and a line of best fit might be judged as the one shown below. It is drawn to pass through the middle of the data points, thereby having as many data points below the line as above it.

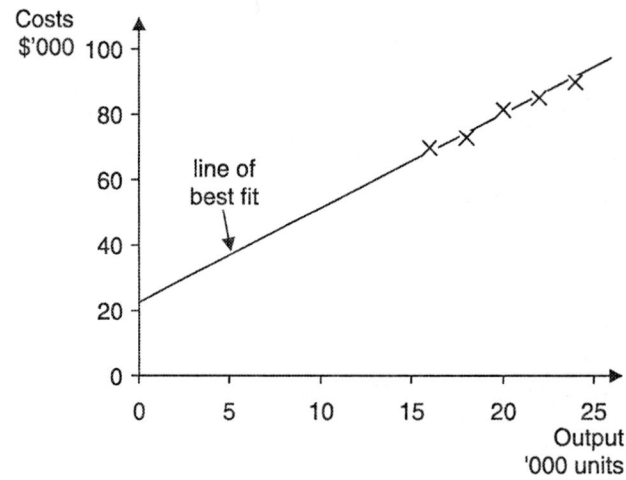

(b) A **formula for the line of best fit** can be found. In our example, suppose that we read the following data from the graph.

   (i) When X = 0, Y = 22,000. This must be the value of **a** in the formula Y = a + bX.

   (ii) When X = 20,000, Y = 82,000. Since Y = a + bX, and a = 22,000, 82,000 = 22,000 + (b × 20,000)

   b × 20,000 = 60,000
   b = 3

(c) In this example the estimated equation from the scattergraph is Y = 22,000 + 3X.

5.2 Forecasting and scattergraphs

If the company to which the data in Paragraph 5.1 relates wanted to predict costs at a certain level of output (say 13,000 units), the value of 13,000 could be substituted into the equation Y = 22,000 + 3X and an estimate of costs made.

If X = 13, Y = 22,000 + (3 × 13,000)

∴ Y = $61,000

Predictions can be made directly from the scattergraph, but this will usually be less accurate.

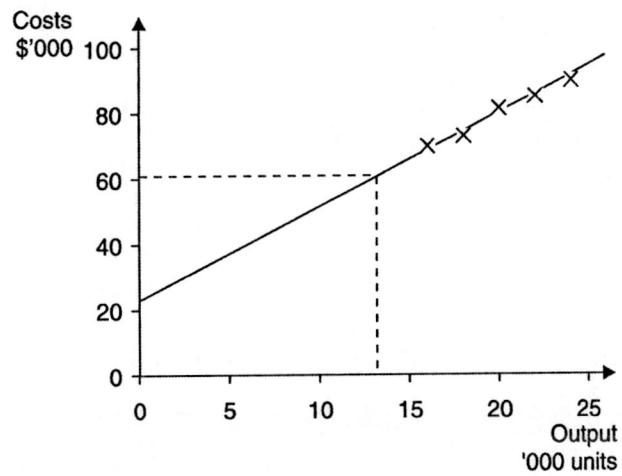

The prediction of the cost of producing 13,000 units from the scattergraph is $61,000.

6 Linear regression analysis

FAST FORWARD

Linear regression analysis (the least squares method) is one technique for estimating a line of best fit. Once an equation for a line of best fit has been determined, forecasts can be made.

Formula to learn

The **least squares method of linear regression analysis** involves using the following formulae for a and b in Y = a + bX.

$$b = \frac{n\sum XY - \sum X \sum Y}{n\sum X^2 - (\sum X)^2}$$

$$a = \overline{Y} - b\overline{X}$$

where n is the number of pairs of data
$\overline{X}$ is the mean X value of all the pairs of data
$\overline{Y}$ is the mean Y value of all the pairs of data

PART A DATA COLLECTION AND ANALYSIS

6.1 Some helpful hints

(a) The value of b must be calculated first as it is needed to calculate a.

(b) $\overline{X}$ is the mean of the X values = $\dfrac{\Sigma X}{n}$

$\overline{Y}$ is the mean of the Y values = $\dfrac{\Sigma Y}{n}$

(c) Remember that X is the independent variable and Y is the dependent variable

(d) Set your workings out in a table to find the figures to put into the formulae.

6.2 Example: Linear regression analysis

(a) Given that there is a fairly high degree of correlation between the output and the costs detailed in Paragraph 5.1 (so that a linear relationship can be assumed), calculate an equation to determine the expected level of costs, for any given volume of output, using the least squares method.

(b) Prepare a budget for total costs if output is 22,000 units.

(c) Confirm that the degree of correlation between output and costs is high by calculating the correlation coefficient.

Solution

(a) *Workings*

X	Y	XY	X^2	Y^2
20	82	1,640	400	6,724
16	70	1,120	256	4,900
24	90	2,160	576	8,100
22	85	1,870	484	7,225
18	73	1,314	324	5,329
$\Sigma X = 100$	$\Sigma Y = 400$	$\Sigma XY = 8,104$	$\Sigma X^2 = 2,040$	$\Sigma Y^2 = 32,278$

n = 5 (There are five pairs of data for x and y values)

$$b = \dfrac{n\Sigma XY - \Sigma X \Sigma Y}{n\Sigma X^2 - (\Sigma X)^2} = \dfrac{(5 \times 8,104) - (100 \times 400)}{(5 \times 2,040) - 100^2}$$

$$= \dfrac{40,520 - 40,000}{10,200 - 10,000} = \dfrac{520}{200} = 2.6$$

$$a = \overline{Y} - b\overline{X} = \dfrac{400}{5} - 2.6 \times \left(\dfrac{100}{5}\right) = 28$$

Y = 28 + 2.6X

where Y = total cost, in thousands of pounds
      X = output, in thousands of units

Compare this equation to that determined in Paragraph 5.1.

Note. The fixed costs are $28,000 (when X = 0 costs are $28,000) and the variable cost per unit is $2.60.

(b) If the output is 22,000 units, we would expect costs to be

28 + (2.6 × 22) = 85.2 = $85,200.

(c) $r = \dfrac{520}{\sqrt{200 \times (5 \times 32{,}278 - 400^2)}} = \dfrac{520}{\sqrt{200 \times 1{,}390}} = \dfrac{520}{527.3} = +0.986$

Question — Linear regression analysis

If $\Sigma x = 79$, $\Sigma y = 1{,}466$, $\Sigma x^2 = 1{,}083$, $\Sigma y^2 = 363{,}076$, $\Sigma xy = 19{,}736$ and $n = 6$, then the value of b, the gradient, to two decimal places, is:

(a) 10.12
(b) 111.03
(c) 13.62
(d) −8.53

Answer

(a)

$r = \dfrac{(6 \times 19{,}736) - (79 \times 1{,}466)}{(6 \times 1{,}083) - 79^2}$

$= \dfrac{118{,}416 - 115{,}814}{6{,}498 - 6{,}241} = \dfrac{2{,}602}{257} = 10.12$

Question — Forecasting

In a forecasting model based on $y = a + bx$, the intercept is $262. If the value of y is $503 and x is 23, then the value of the gradient, to two decimal places, is:

(a) −20.96
(b) −10.48
(c) 10.48
(d) 20.96

Answer

(c) $y = a + bx$
 $503 = 262 + (b \times 23)$
 $241 = b \times 23$
 $b = 10.48$

6.3 Interpolation and extrapolation

FAST FORWARD

To forecast a value of Y related to X, if the value of X is within the range of X values used to determine the relationship then the forecasting is said to be interpolation.

If the value of X is outside the given range used to develop the model then the forecasting process is said to be extrapolation.

Exam focus point

The difference between interpolation and extrapolation have been examined more than once in this paper.

PART A DATA COLLECTION AND ANALYSIS

Chapter Roundup

- When the value of one variable is related to the value of another, they are said to be **correlated**.
- Two variables might be **perfectly correlated, partly correlated** or **uncorrelated**. Correlation can be **positive** or **negative**.
- The **degree of correlation** between two variables is measured by the **Pearson's correlation coefficient**, r. The nearer r is to +1 or –1, the stronger the relationship.
- The **coefficient of determination, r^2**, measures the proportion of the total variation in the value of one variable that can be explained by variations in the value of the other variable.
- **Spearman's rank correlation coefficient** is used when data is given in terms of order or rank, rather than actual values.
- The **scattergraph method** involves the use of judgement to draw what seems to be a line of best fit through plotted data.
- **Linear regression analysis** (the **least squares method**) is one technique for estimating a line of best fit. Once an equation for a line of best fit has been determined, forecasts can be made.
- To forecast a value of Y related to X, if the value of X is within the range of X values used to determine the relationship then the forecasting is said to be interpolation.
- If the value of X is outside the given range used to develop the model then the forecasting process is said to be extrapolation.

Quick Quiz

1. _____ correlation means that low values of one variable are associated with low values of the other, and high values of one variable are associated with high values of the other.

2. _____ correlation means that low values of one variable are associated with high values of the other, and high values of one variable with low values of the other.

3.
   - Perfect positive correlation, r = ⬜
   - Perfect negative correlation, r = ⬜
   - No correlation, r = ⬜

   The correlation coefficient, r, must always fall within the range ⬜ to ⬜

4. If the correlation coefficient of a set of data is 0.95, what is the coefficient of determination? ⬜

5. If Y = a + bX, it is best to use the regression of Y upon X where X is the dependent variable and Y is the independent variable.

   True ⬜
   False ⬜

6. If Σx = 30, Σy = 62, Σx² = 238, Σy² = 1,014, Σxy = 485, n = 4

   What is the correlation coefficient? (to 2 decimal places) ⬜

Answers to Quick Quiz

1. Positive correlation

2. Negative correlation

3. - $r = +1$
   - $r = -1$
   - $r = 0$

   The correlation coefficient, r, must always fall within the range –1 to +1.

4. Correlation coefficient = r = 0.95

   Coefficient of determination = r^2 = 0.95^2 = 0.9025 or 90.25%

   This tells us that over 90% of the variations in the dependent variable (Y) can be explained by variations in the independent variable, X.

5. False. When using the regression of Y upon X, X is the independent variable and Y is the dependent variable (the value of Y will depend upon the value of X).

6. $\boxed{0.76}$

   $$r = \frac{n\Sigma xy - \Sigma x \Sigma y}{\sqrt{[n\Sigma x^2 - (\Sigma x)^2][n\Sigma y^2 - (\Sigma y)^2]}}$$

   $$= \frac{(4 \times 485) - (30 \times 62)}{\sqrt{[(4 \times 238) - 30^2] \times [(4 \times 1{,}014) - 62^2]}}$$

   $$= \frac{1{,}940 - 1{,}860}{\sqrt{52 \times 212}}$$

   $$= \frac{80}{104.995}$$

   $$= 0.76$$

PART A   DATA COLLECTION AND ANALYSIS

End of Chapter Question

Factory Manager (AIA Nov 08)

A Factory Manager is interested in investigating whether it is the experience of the machine operator or the amount of training that the operator has received which has the greater influence on the output from the machine. Over the last month the average daily output from 10 identical machines at the factory has been recorded (on a scale from 0 to 100) and this is tabulated below together with the experience of the relevant machine operator, in terms of weeks spent operating that machine, and the number of training programmes undertaken. The Manager has already calculated the value of the correlation coefficient between Output and Amount of Training as 0.724.

Machine	Output	Experience (weeks)	Amount of Training
A	80	36	2
B	65	25	1
C	78	34	4
D	67	38	2
E	90	43	5
F	58	15	2
G	65	32	4
H	77	39	4
I	80	38	4
J	93	55	5

Required

(a) By calculating a suitable correlation coefficient between Output and Experience determine whether it is the Experience of the operator or the Amount of Training which is the better predictor of Machine Output. **(10 marks)**

(b) Using the information from part (a) determine the best fit equation to predict Machine Output. **(6 marks)**

(c) Distinguish between interpolation and extrapolation in forecasting. **(4 marks)**

(Total = 20 marks)

Time series analysis

Topic list	Syllabus reference
1 The components of time series	6.6
2 Finding the trend	6.6
3 Finding the seasonal variations	6.6
4 Forecasting	6.6
5 The reliability of time series analysis forecasts	6.6

Introduction

In some situations, there are no independent variables from which to forecast a dependent variable. In this chapter we will be looking at a technique called **time series analysis**. With this **forecasting** method we look at **past data** about the variable which we want to forecast (such as sales levels) to see if there are **any patterns**. We then assume that these patterns will continue into the future. We are then able to forecast what we believe will be the value of a variable at some particular point of time in the future.

PART A DATA COLLECTION AND ANALYSIS

1 The components of time series

A **time series** is a series of figures or values recorded over time. Any pattern found in the data is then assumed to continue into the future and an **extrapolative forecast** is produced.

1.1 Examples of time series

- Output at a factory each day for the last month
- Monthly sales over the last two years
- Total annual costs for the last ten years
- The Retail Prices Index/Consumer Prices Index each month for the last ten years
- The number of people employed by a company each year for the last 20 years

There are four components of a time series: **trend**, **seasonal variations**, **cyclical variations** and **random variations**.

1.2 The trend

The **trend** is the underlying long-term movement over time in the values of the data recorded.

1.3 Example: Preparing time series graphs and identifying trends

	Output per labour hour Units	Cost per unit $	Number of employees
20X4	30	1.00	100
20X5	24	1.08	103
20X6	26	1.20	96
20X7	22	1.15	102
20X8	21	1.18	103
20X9	17	1.25	98
	(A)	(B)	(C)

(a) In time series (A) there is a **downward trend** in the output per labour hour. Output per labour hour did not fall every year, because it went up between 20X5 and 20X6, but the long-term movement is clearly a downward one.

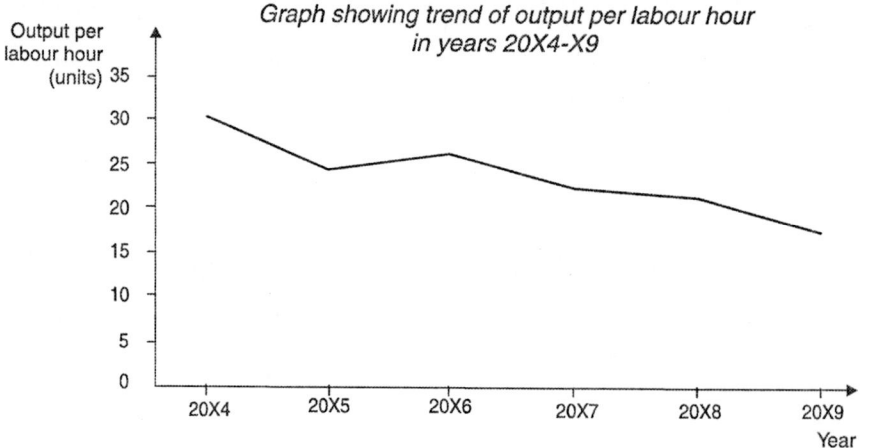

(b) In time series (B) there is an **upward trend** in the cost per unit. Although unit costs went down in 20X7 from a higher level in 20X6, the basic movement over time is one of rising costs.

Graph showing trend of costs per unit in years 20X4-X9

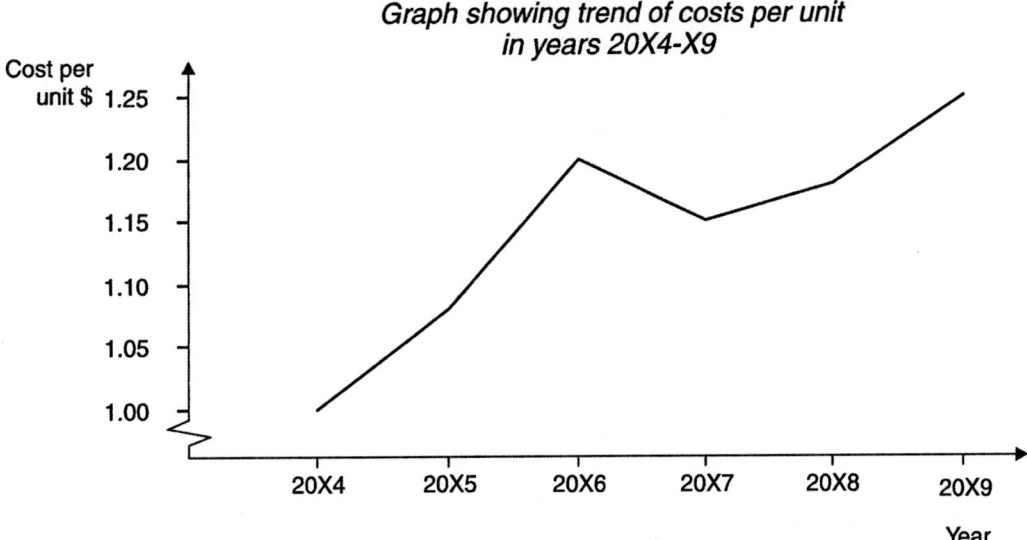

(c) In time series (C) there is no clear movement up or down, and the number of employees remained fairly constant around 100. The trend is therefore a **static**, or **level** one.

Graph showing trend of number of employees in years 20X4-X9

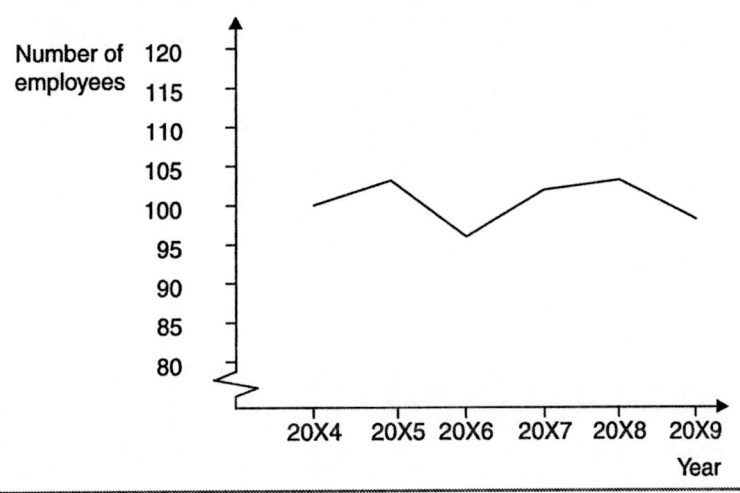

Exam focus point

The November 13 and May 14 exams had questions on time series analysis. Both questions asked, among other requirements, for a time series graph to be drawn.

1.4 Seasonal variations

Key term

Seasonal variations are short-term fluctuations in recorded values, due to different circumstances which affect results at different times of the year, on different days of the week or at different times of day etc.

1.5 Examples of seasonal variations

(a) Sales of ice cream will be higher in summer than in winter, and sales of overcoats will be higher in autumn than in spring.

(b) Shops might expect higher sales shortly before Christmas, or in their winter and summer sales.

(c) Sales might be higher on Friday and Saturday than on Monday.

(d) The telephone network may be heavily used at certain times of the day (such as mid-morning and mid-afternoon) and much less used at other times (such as in the middle of the night).

1.6 Example: The trend and seasonal variations

The number of customers served by a company of travel agents over the past four years is shown in the following **historigram** (time series graph).

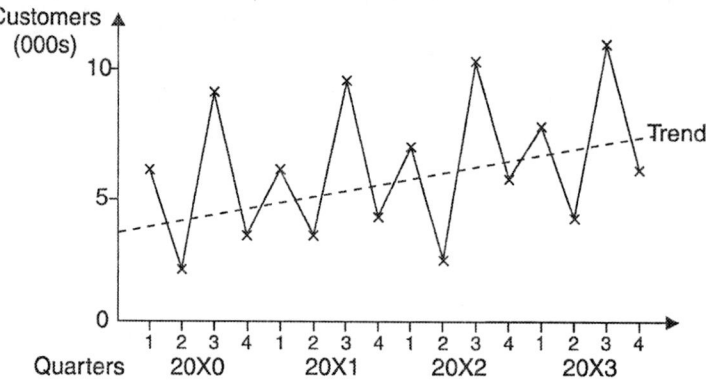

In this example, there would appear to be large **seasonal fluctuations in demand,** but there is also a basic **upward trend.**

1.7 Cyclical variations

FAST FORWARD

> **Cyclical variations** are medium-term changes in results caused by circumstances which repeat in cycles.

In business, cyclical variations are commonly associated with **economic cycles**, successive **booms** and **slumps** in the economy. Economic cycles may last a few years. Cyclical variations are **longer** term than seasonal variations.

Though you should be aware of the cyclical component, you will not be expected to carry out any calculation connected with isolating it. The mathematical models which we will use, therefore exclude any reference to C.

1.8 Summarising the components

The components of a time series **combine** to produce a variable in one of two ways:

Key terms

Additive model:	Series = Trend + Seasonal + Random
	Y = T + S + R
Multiplicative model:	Series = Trend × Seasonal × Random
	Y = T × S × R

2 Finding the trend

2.1 Methods of finding the trend

The main problem we are concerned with in time series analysis is how to **identify the trend** and **seasonal variations**.

Main methods of finding a trend

(a) A **line of best fit** (the **trend line**) can be drawn by eye on a graph.
(b) **Linear regression analysis** can be used. (We covered this in Chapter 6.)
(c) A technique known as **moving averages** can be used.

2.2 Finding the trend by moving averages

One method of finding the trend is by the use of **moving averages**.

Key terms

- A **moving average** is an average of the results of a fixed number of periods
- The **moving averages method** attempts to remove seasonal variations from actual data by a process of averaging

2.3 Example: Moving averages of an odd number of results

Year	Sales Units
20X0	390
20X1	380
20X2	460
20X3	450
20X4	470
20X5	440
20X6	500

Required

Take a moving average of the annual sales over a period of three years.

Solution

(a) Average sales in the three year period 20X0 – 20X2 were:

$$\left(\frac{390 + 380 + 460}{3}\right) = \frac{1{,}230}{3} = 410$$

This average relates to the middle year of the period, 20X1.

(b) Similarly, average sales in the three year period 20X1 – 20X3 were:

$$\left(\frac{380 + 460 + 450}{3}\right) = \frac{1{,}290}{3} = 430$$

This average relates to the middle year of the period, 20X2.

(c) The average sales can also be found for the periods 20X2–20X4, 20X3–20X5 and 20X4–20X6, to give the following.

Year	Sales	Moving total of 3 years' sales	Moving average of 3 years' sales (÷ 3)
20X0	390		
20X1	380	1,230	410
20X2	460	1,290	430
20X3	450	1,380	460
20X4	470	1,360	453
20X5	440	1,410	470
20X6	500		

Notes

1 The moving average series has five figures relating to the years from 20X1 to 20X5. The original series had seven figures for the years from 20X0 to 20X6.

2 There is an upward trend in sales, which is more noticeable from the series of moving averages than from the original series of actual sales each year.

2.4 Over what period should a moving average be taken?

The above example averaged over a three-year period. Over what period should a moving average be taken? The answer to this question is that **the moving average which is most appropriate will depend on the circumstances and the nature of the time series**.

Notes

1. A moving average which takes an average of the results in many time periods will represent results over a longer term than a moving average of two or three periods.

2. On the other hand, with a moving average of results in many time periods, the last figure in the series will be out of date by several periods. In our example, the most recent average related to 20X5. With a moving average of five years' results, the final figure in the series would relate to 20X4.

3. When there is a known cycle over which seasonal variations occur, such as all the days in the week or all the seasons in the year, the most suitable moving average would be one which covers one full cycle.

Question — Three-month moving average

Using the following data, complete the following table in order to determine the three-month moving average for the period January-June.

Month	No of new houses finished	Moving total 3 months new houses finished	Moving average of 3 months new houses finished
January	500		
February	450		
March	700		
April	900		
May	1,250		
June	1,000		

Answer

Month	No of new houses finished	Moving total 3 months new houses finished	Moving average of 3 months new houses finished
January	500		
February	450	1,650	550
March	700	2,050	683
April	900	2,850	950
May	1,250	3,150	1,050
June	1,000		

2.5 Moving averages of an even number of results

FAST FORWARD

When finding the moving average of an **even number of results**, a second moving average has to be calculated so that trend values can relate to specific actual figures.

In the previous example, moving averages were taken of the results in an **odd number of time periods**, and the average then related to the **midpoint of the overall period**. If a moving average were taken of results in an **even number of time periods**, the basic technique would be the same, but **the midpoint of the overall period would not relate to a single period**. For example, suppose an average were taken of the following four results:

Spring	120	
Summer	90	average 115
Autumn	180	
Winter	70	

The average would relate to the midpoint of the period, between summer and autumn. The trend line average figures need to relate to a particular time period; otherwise, seasonal variations cannot be calculated. To overcome this difficulty, we take a **moving average of the moving average**. An example will illustrate this technique.

2.6 Example: Moving averages over an even number of periods

Calculate a moving average trend line of the following results:

Year	Quarter	Volume of sales '000 units
20X5	1	600
	2	840
	3	420
	4	720
20X6	1	640
	2	860
	3	420
	4	740
20X7	1	670
	2	900
	3	430
	4	760

PART A DATA COLLECTION AND ANALYSIS

Solution

A moving average of **four** will be used, since the volume of sales would appear to depend on the season of the year, and each year has four **quarterly** results.

The moving average of four does not relate to any specific period of time; therefore a second moving average of two will be calculated on the first moving average trend line.

Year	Quarter	Actual volume of sales '000 units (A)	Moving total of 4 quarters' sales '000 units (B)	Moving average of 4 quarters' sales '000 units (B ÷ 4)	Midpoint of 2 moving averages Trend line '000 units (C)
20X5	1	600			
	2	840			
			2,580	645.0	
	3	420			650.00
			2,620	655.0	
	4	720			657.50
			2,640	660.0	
20X6	1	640			660.00
			2,640	660.0	
	2	860			662.50
			2,660	665.0	
	3	420			668.75
			2,690	672.5	
	4	740			677.50
			2,730	682.5	
20X7	1	670			683.75
			2,740	685.0	
	2	900			687.50
			2,760	690.0	
	3	430			
	4	760			

By taking **a midpoint** (a moving average of two) of the original moving averages, we can relate the results **to specific quarters** (from the third quarter of 20X5 to the second quarter of 20X7).

The time series information and moving average trend can be shown on a graph.

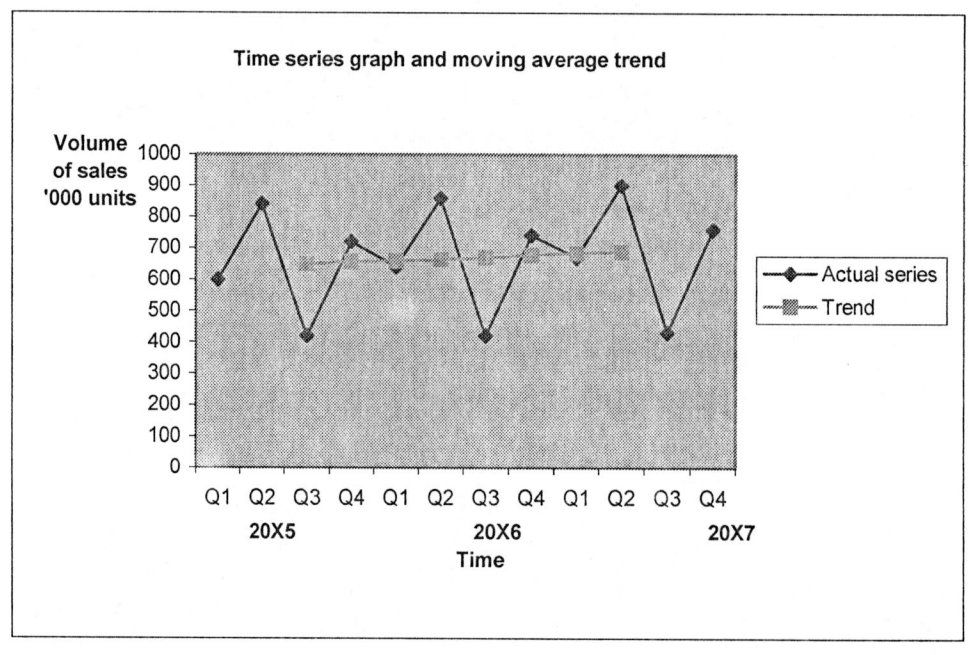

3 Finding the seasonal variations

FAST FORWARD

Seasonal variations are the difference between actual and trend figures. An average of the seasonal variations for each time period within the cycle must be determined and then adjusted so that the total of the seasonal variations sums to zero. Seasonal variations can be estimated using the **additive model (Y = T + S + R, with seasonal variations = Y – T)** or the **multiplicative model (Y = T × S × R, with seasonal variations = Y ÷ T)**.

3.1 Finding the seasonal component using the additive model

Once a trend has been established, by whatever method, we can find the **seasonal variations**.

Step 1   The additive model for time series analysis is Y = T + S + R.

Step 2   If we deduct the trend from the additive model, we get Y – T = S + R.

Step 3   If we assume that R, the random, component of the time series is relatively small and therefore negligible, then S = Y – T.

Therefore, the seasonal component, **S = Y – T** (the de-trended series).

3.2 Example: The trend and seasonal variations

Output at a factory appears to vary with the day of the week. Output over the last three weeks has been as follows.

	Week 1 '000 units	Week 2 '000 units	Week 3 '000 units
Monday	80	82	84
Tuesday	104	110	116
Wednesday	94	97	100
Thursday	120	125	130
Friday	62	64	66

Required

Find the seasonal variation for each of the 15 days, and the average seasonal variation for each day of the week using the moving averages method.

Solution

Actual results fluctuate up and down according to the day of the week and so a **moving average of five** will be used. The **difference** between the actual result on any one day (Y) and the trend figure for that day (T) will be the **seasonal variation (S)** for the day. The seasonal variations for the 15 days are as follows:

PART A DATA COLLECTION AND ANALYSIS

		Actual (Y)	Moving total of five days' output	Trend (T)	Seasonal variation (Y–T)
Week 1	Monday	80			
	Tuesday	104			
	Wednesday	94	460	92.0	+2.0
	Thursday	120	462	92.4	+27.6
	Friday	62	468	93.6	–31.6
Week 2	Monday	82	471	94.2	–12.2
	Tuesday	110	476	95.2	+14.8
	Wednesday	97	478	95.6	+1.4
	Thursday	125	480	96.0	+29.0
	Friday	64	486	97.2	–33.2
Week 3	Monday	84	489	97.8	–13.8
	Tuesday	116	494	98.8	+17.2
	Wednesday	100	496	99.2	+0.8
	Thursday	130			
	Friday	66			

You will notice that the variation between the actual results on any one particular day and the trend line average is not the same from week to week. This is because Y – T contains not only seasonal variations but **random** variations, and an **average** of these variations can be taken.

	Monday	Tuesday	Wednesday	Thursday	Friday
Week 1			+2.0	+27.6	–31.6
Week 2	–12.2	+14.8	+1.4	+29.0	–33.2
Week 3	–13.8	+17.2	+0.8		
Average	–13.0	+16.0	+1.4	+28.3	–32.4

Variations around the basic trend line should cancel each other out, and **add up to 0.** At the moment they do not. **The average seasonal estimates must therefore be corrected so that they add up to zero** and so we spread the total of the daily variations (0.30) across the five days (0.3 ÷ 5) so that the final total of the daily variations goes to zero.

	Monday	Tuesday	Wednesday	Thursday	Friday	Total
Estimated average daily variation	–13.00	+16.00	+1.40	+28.30	–32.40	0.30
Adjustment to reduce total variation to 0	–0.06	–0.06	–0.06	–0.06	–0.06	–0.30
Final estimate of average daily variation	–13.06	+15.94	+1.34	+28.24	–32.46	0.00

These might be rounded up or down as follows.

Monday –13; Tuesday +16; Wednesday +1; Thursday +28; Friday –32; Total 0.

Question Four-quarter moving average trend

Calculate a four-quarter moving average trend centred on actual quarters and then find seasonal variations from the following:

	Sales in $'000			
	Spring	Summer	Autumn	Winter
20X7	200	120	160	280
20X8	220	140	140	300
20X9	200	120	180	320

Answer

		Sales (Y)	4-quarter total	8-quarter total	Moving average (T)	Seasonal variation (Y–T)
20X7	Spring	200				
	Summer	120				
			760			
	Autumn	160		1,540	192.5	–32.5
			780			
	Winter	280		1,580	197.5	+82.5
			800			
20X8	Spring	220		1,580	197.5	+22.5
			780			
	Summer	140		1,580	197.5	–57.5
			800			
	Autumn	140		1,580	197.5	–57.5
			780			
	Winter	300		1,540	192.5	+107.5
			760			
20X9	Spring	200		1,560	195.0	+5.0
			800			
	Summer	120		1,620	202.5	–82.5
			820			
	Autumn	180				
	Winter	320				

We can now average the seasonal variations.

	Spring	Summer	Autumn	Winter	Total
20X7			–32.5	+82.5	
20X8	+22.5	–57.5	–57.5	+107.5	
20X9	+5.0	–82.5			
	+27.5	–140.0	–90.0	+190.0	
Average variations (in $'000)	+13.75	–70.00	–45.00	+95.00	–6.25
Adjustment so sum is zero	+1.5625	+1.5625	+1.5625	+1.5625	+6.25
Adjusted average variations	+15.3125	–68.4375	–43.4375	+96.5625	0

These might be rounded up or down to:

Spring $15,000, Summer –$68,000, Autumn –$43,000, Winter $97,000

3.3 Finding the seasonal component using the multiplicative model

The method of estimating the seasonal variations in the additive model is to use the differences between the trend and actual data. **The additive model assumes that the components of the series are independent of each other**, an increasing trend not affecting the seasonal variations for example.

The alternative is to use the **multiplicative model** whereby **each actual figure is expressed as a proportion of the trend**. Sometimes this method is called the **proportional model**.

PART A DATA COLLECTION AND ANALYSIS

3.4 Example: Multiplicative model

The additive model example above (in Paragraph 3.2) can be reworked on this alternative basis. The trend is calculated in exactly the same way as before but we need a different approach for the seasonal variations.

The multiplicative model is $Y = T \times S \times R$ and, just as we calculated $S = Y - T$ for the additive model we can calculate $S = Y/T$ for the multiplicative model.

		Actual (Y)	Trend (T)	Seasonal variation (Y/T)
Week 1	Monday	80		
	Tuesday	104		
	Wednesday	94	92.0	1.022
	Thursday	120	92.4	1.299
	Friday	62	93.6	0.662
Week 2	Monday	82	94.2	0.870
	Tuesday	110	95.2	1.155
	Wednesday	97	95.6	1.015
	Thursday	125	96.0	1.302
	Friday	64	97.2	0.658
Week 3	Monday	84	97.8	0.859
	Tuesday	116	98.8	1.174
	Wednesday	100	99.2	1.008
	Thursday	130		
	Friday	66		

The summary of the seasonal variations expressed in **proportional terms** is as follows.

	Monday	Tuesday	Wednesday	Thursday	Friday
Week 1			1.022	1.299	0.662
Week 2	0.870	1.155	1.015	1.302	0.658
Week 3	0.859	1.174	1.008		
Total	1.729	2.329	3.045	2.601	1.320
Average	0.8645	1.1645	1.0150	1.3005	0.6600

Instead of summing to zero, as with the absolute approach, these should **sum** (in this case) **to 5 (an average of 1)**.

They actually sum to 5.0045 so 0.0009 has to be deducted from each one. This is too small to make a difference to the figures above, so we should deduct 0.002 and 0.0025 to each of two seasonal variations. We could arbitrarily decrease Monday's variation to 0.8625 and Tuesday's to 1.162.

3.5 When to use the multiplicative model

The multiplicative model is better than the additive model for forecasting when the trend is increasing or decreasing over time. In such circumstances, seasonal variations are likely to be increasing or decreasing too. The additive model simply adds absolute and unchanging seasonal variations to the trend figures whereas the multiplicative model, by multiplying increasing or decreasing trend values by a constant seasonal variation factor, takes account of changing seasonal variations.

3.6 Summary

We can summarise the steps to be carried out when calculating the seasonal variation as follows:

Step 1 Calculate the moving total for an appropriate period.

Step 2 Calculate the moving average (the trend) for the period. (Calculate the midpoint of two moving averages if there are an even number of periods.)

Step 3 Calculate the seasonal variation. For an additive model, this is Y – T. For a multiplicative model, this is Y/T.

Step 4 Calculate an average of the seasonal variations.

Step 5 Adjust the average seasonal variations so that they add up to **zero** for an **additive model**. When using the **multiplicative model**, the average seasonal variations should add up to an **average of 1**.

Question — Average seasonal variations

Find the average seasonal variations for the sales data in the previous question (entitled: Four-quarter moving average trend) using the **multiplicative** model.

Answer

	Spring	Summer	Autumn	Winter	Total
20X7			0.83*	1.42	
20X8	1.11	0.71	0.71	1.56	
20X9	1.03	0.59			
	2.14	1.30	1.54	2.98	

	Spring	Summer	Autumn	Winter	Total
Average variations	1.070	0.650	0.770	1.490	3.980
Adjustment to sum to 4	+ 0.005	+ 0.005	+ 0.005	+ 0.005	0.020
Adjusted average variations	1.075	0.655	0.775	1.495	4.000

* Seasonal variation $Y/T = \dfrac{160}{192.5} = 0.83$

Question — Multiplicative model

In a time series analysis, the multiplicative model is used to forecast sales and the following seasonal variations apply.

	Quarters			
	1	2	3	4
Seasonal variation	0.8	1.9	0.75	?

The actual sales value for the last two quarters of 20X1 were:

Quarter 3 = $250,000
Quarter 4 = $260,000

(a) The seasonal variation for the fourth quarter is:

    A   0.55
    B   –3.45
    C   1.00
    D   1.45

PART A   DATA COLLECTION AND ANALYSIS

(b)   The trend line for sales:

A   Remained constant between quarter 3 and quarter 4
B   Increased between quarter 3 and quarter 4
C   Decreased between quarter 3 and quarter 4
D   Cannot be determined from the information given

Answer

(a)   **The correct answer is A.**

As this is a multiplicative model, the seasonal variations should sum (in this case) to 4 (an average of 1) as there are four quarters.

Let x = seasonal variation in quarter 4.

$0.8 + 1.9 + 0.75 + x = 4$

$\therefore 3.45 + x = 4$
$x = 4 - 3.45$
$x = 0.55$

(b)   **The correct answer is B.**

For a multiplicative model, the seasonal component is as follows:

$S = Y/T$

$\therefore T = Y/S$

	Quarter 3	Quarter 4
Seasonal component (S)	0.75	0.55
Actual sales (Y)	$250,000	$260,000
Trend (T) (= Y/S)	$333,333	$472,727

The trend line for sales has therefore increased between quarter 3 and quarter 4.

3.7 Seasonally-adjusted data

Key term

Seasonally-adjusted data (deseasonalised) is data which have had any seasonal variations taken out, so leaving a figure which might indicate the trend. Seasonally-adjusted data should indicate whether the overall trend is rising, falling or stationary.

3.8 Example: Seasonally-adjusted data

Actual sales figures for four quarters, together with appropriate seasonal adjustment factors derived from previous data, are as follows.

Quarter	Actual sales $'000	Seasonal adjustments Additive model $'000	Multiplicative model
1	150	+3	1.02
2	160	+4	1.05
3	164	−2	0.98
4	170	−5	0.95

Required

Deseasonalise these data.

Solution

We are reversing the normal process of applying seasonal variations to trend figures.

The rules for deseasonalising data are as follows.

- **Additive model** – subtract positive seasonal variations from and add negative seasonal variations to actual results.
- **Multiplicative model** – divide the actual results by the seasonal variation factors.

		Deseasonalised sales	
Quarter	Actual sales	Additive model	Multiplicative model
	$'000	$'000	$'000
1	150	147	147
2	160	156	152
3	164	166	167
4	170	175	179

Question — Seasonally-adjusted figures

Unemployment numbers actually recorded in a town for the first quarter of 20X9 were 4,700. The underlying trend at this point was 4,400 people and the seasonal factor is 0.85. Using the multiplicative model for seasonal adjustment, the seasonally-adjusted figure (in whole numbers) for the quarter is:

(a) 5,529
(b) 5,176
(c) 3,995
(d) 3,740

Answer

The correct answer is A.

If you remembered the ruling that you need to **divide** by the seasonal variation factor to obtain seasonally-adjusted figures (using the multiplicative model), then you should have been able to eliminate options C and D. This might have been what you did if you weren't sure whether you divided the **actual results** or the **trend** by the seasonal variation factor.

$$\text{Seasonally adjusted data} = \frac{\text{Actual results}}{\text{Seasonal factor}} = \frac{4,700}{0.85} = 5,529$$

4 Forecasting

FAST FORWARD

Forecasts can be made by **extrapolating the trend** and **adjusting for seasonal variations**. Remember, however, that all forecasts are subject to error.

PART A   DATA COLLECTION AND ANALYSIS

4.1 Making a forecast

Step 1 **Plot a trend line**: use the line of best fit method, linear regression analysis or the moving averages method.

Step 2 **Extrapolate the trend line**. This means extending the trend line outside the range of known data and forecasting future results from historical data.

Step 3 **Adjust forecast trends** by the applicable average seasonal variation to obtain the actual forecast.

    (a) **Additive model** – add positive variations to and subtract negative variations from the forecast trends.

    (b) **Multiplicative model** – multiply the forecast trends by the seasonal variation.

4.2 Example: Forecasting

Use the trend values and the estimates of seasonal variations calculated in Paragraph 3.2 to forecast sales in week 4.

Solution

We begin by plotting the trend values on a graph and extrapolating the trend line.

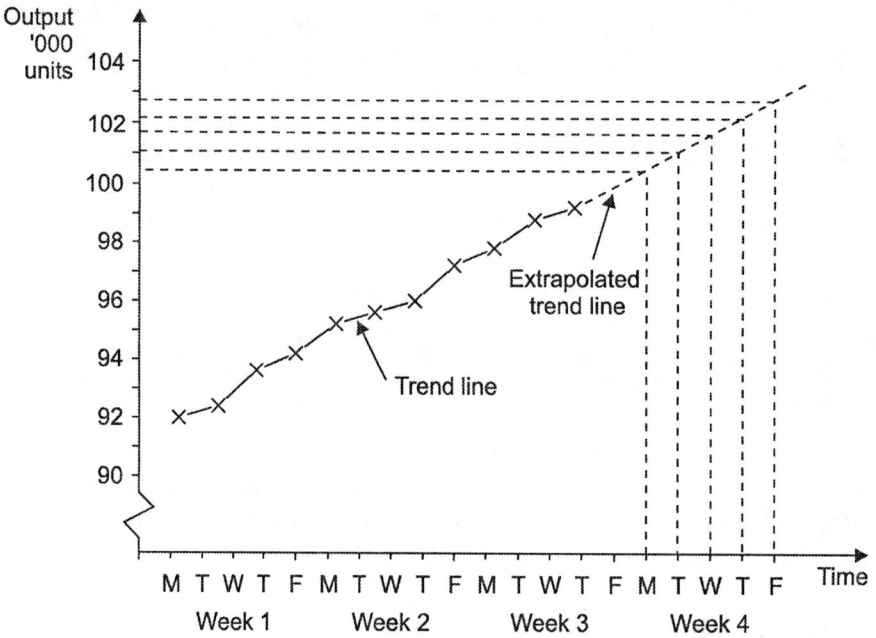

From the extrapolated trend line we can take the following readings and adjust them by the seasonal variations.

Week 4	Trend line readings	Seasonal variations	Forecast
Monday	100.5	−13	87.5
Tuesday	101.5	+16	117.1
Wednesday	101.7	+1	102.7
Thursday	102.2	+28	130.2
Friday	102.8	−32	70.8

If we had been using the multiplicative model the forecast for Tuesday, for example, would be 101.1 × 1.1645 = 117.7 (from Paragraph 3.4).

Question Forecasting

Over a 36-month period, sales have been found to have an underlying linear trend of Y = 14.224 + 7.898X, where Y is the number of items sold and X represents the month. Monthly deviations from trend have been calculated and month 37 is expected to be 1.28 times the trend value.

The forecast number of items to be sold in month 37 is approximately

(a) 389
(b) 390
(c) 391
(d) 392

Answer

This is typical of multiple choice questions that you must work through fully if you are to get the right answer.

Y = 14.224 + 7.898X

If X = 37, trend in sales for month 37 = 14.224 + (7.898 × 37)
= 306.45

∴ Seasonally-adjusted trend value = 306.45 × 1.28
= 392.256

∴ The correct answer is 392, option D.

4.3 Residuals

Key term

A **residual** is the difference between the results which would have been predicted (for a past period for which we already have data) by the trend line adjusted for the average seasonal variation and the actual results.

The residual is therefore the difference which is not explained by the trend line and the average seasonal variation. The residual gives some indication of how much actual results were affected by other factors. Large residuals suggest that any forecast is likely to be unreliable.

In the example in Paragraph 3.2, the 'prediction' for Wednesday of week 2 would have been 95.6 + 1 = 96.6. As the actual value was 97, the residual was only 97 – 96.6 = 0.4.

5 The reliability of time series analysis forecasts

FAST FORWARD

Remember that all forecasts are subject to error. There are a number of factors which will affect the reliability of forecasts.

All forecasts are subject to error, but the likely errors vary from case to case.

(a) The further into the future the forecast is for, the more unreliable it is likely to be.
(b) The less data available on which to base the forecast, the less reliable the forecast.
(c) The pattern of trend and seasonal variations cannot be guaranteed to continue in the future.
(d) There is always the danger of random variations upsetting the pattern of trend and seasonal variation.
(e) The extrapolation of the trend line is done by judgement and can introduce error.

PART A   DATA COLLECTION AND ANALYSIS

Chapter Roundup

- A **time series** is a series of figures or values recorded over time. Any pattern found in the data is then assumed to continue into the future and an **extrapolative forecast** is produced.
- There are four components of a time series: **trend**, **seasonal variations**, **cyclical variations** and **random variations**.
- The **trend** is the underlying long-term movement over time in the values of the data recorded.
- **Seasonal variations** are short-term fluctuations in recorded values, due to different circumstances which affect results at different times of the year, on different days of the week or at different times of the day etc.
- **Cyclical variations** are medium-term changes in results caused by circumstances which repeat in cycles.
- One method of finding the trend is by the use of **moving averages**.
- When finding the moving average of an **even number of results**, a second moving average has to be calculated so that trend values can relate to specific actual figures.
- **Seasonal variations are the difference between actual and trend figures.** An average of the seasonal variations for each time period within the cycle must be determined and then adjusted so that the total of the seasonal variations sums to zero. Seasonal variations can be estimated using the **additive model** ($Y = T + S + R$, with seasonal variations = $Y - T$) or the **multiplicative model** ($Y = T \times S \times R$, with seasonal variations = Y/T).
- **Forecasts** can be made by **extrapolating the trend** and **adjusting for seasonal variations**.
- Remember that all forecasts are subject to error. There are a number of factors which will affect the reliability of forecasts.

Quick Quiz

1. If the trend is increasing or decreasing over time, it is better to use the additive model for forecasting.

   True ☐

   False ☐

2. **Results** | **Method**

   Odd number of time periods ⎤ | ⎡ Calculate 1 moving average

   ?

   Even number of time periods ⎦ | ⎣ Calculate 2 moving averages

3. When deseasonalising data, the following rules apply to the additive model.

   I   Add positive seasonal variations
   II Subtract positive seasonal variations
   III Add negative seasonal variations
   IV Subtract negative seasonal variations

   (a) I and II
   (b) II and III
   (c) II and IV
   (d) I only

4. Cyclical variation is the term used for the difference which is not explained by the trend line and the average seasonal variation.

   True ☐

   False ☐

5. The trend for profit (y) is related to time (t) by the equation $y = 50 + 1.5t$.

   What is the estimate of the profit to the nearest $ at time $t = 21$ if the seasonal component at that point is 0.9 using a multiplicative model? ☐

6. Unemployment last quarter was 738,000. The trend figure for that quarter was 700,000 and the seasonal factor using the additive model was −17,500.

   What is the seasonally adjusted unemployment figure for the last quarter? ☐

PART A   DATA COLLECTION AND ANALYSIS

Answers to Quick Quiz

1. False
2. Odd number of time periods = calculate 1 moving average
   Even number of time periods = calculate 2 moving averages
3. (b)
4. False. The residual is the term used to explain the difference which is not explained by the trend line and the average seasonal variation.
5. $\boxed{73}$ $y = 50 + (1.5 \times 21)$
   $= 81.5$
   Forecast $= 81.5 \times 0.9$
   $= 73.35$
6. $\boxed{755,500}$ The seasonally adjusted value is an estimate of the trend.
   Trend = Actual value − Seasonal component
   $= 738,000 − (−17,500)$
   $= 755,500$

End of Chapter Question

Time series analysis   (AIA 5/09)

The sales of a product have been recorded on a quarterly basis over the last four years as follows:

Year	Quarter	Sales
20X4	1	56
	2	48
	3	45
	4	67
20X5	1	60
	2	51
	3	46
	4	69
20X6	1	62
	2	53
	3	47
	4	70
20X7	1	64
	2	57
	3	52
	4	80

Required

(a) Plot the time series on a graph and comment on any trend or seasonal effect.   (6 marks)
(b) Estimate the trend by calculating a suitable moving average.   (6 marks)
(c) Using an additive model, estimate the average seasonal effects.   (8 marks)

(Total = 20 marks)

Index numbers

Topic list	Syllabus reference
1 Basic terminology	6.7
2 Index relatives	6.7
3 Time series of index relatives	6.7
4 Time series deflation	6.7
5 Composite index numbers	6.7
6 Weighted index numbers	6.7
7 Laspeyre and Paasche indices	6.7
8 The Retail Prices Index for the United Kingdom	6.7

Introduction

A number of methods of data presentation looked at in Chapter 3 can be used to identify visually the **trends** in data over a period of time. It may also be useful, however, to identify trends using statistical rather than visual means. This is frequently achieved by constructing a set of **index numbers**.

Index numbers provide a **standardised way of comparing the values**, over time, of prices, wages, volume of output and so on. They are used extensively in business, government and commerce.

PART A DATA COLLECTION AND ANALYSIS

1 Basic terminology

1.1 Price indices and quantity indices

FAST FORWARD

An **index** is a measure, over time, of the average changes in the values (price or quantity) of a group of items.

Key terms

An index comprises a series of index numbers and may be a price index or a quantity index.
- A **price index** measures the change in the money value of a group of items over time.
- A **quantity index** (also called a volume index) measures the change in the non-monetary values of a group of items over time.

It is possible to prepare an index for a single item, but such an index would probably be unnecessary. An index is a most useful measure of comparison when there is a **group of items**.

1.2 Index points

The term **'points'** refers to the difference between the index values in two years.

1.3 Example: Index points

For example, suppose that the index of food prices in 20X1 – 20X6 was as follows:

Year	Index
20X1	180
20X2	200
20X3	230
20X4	250
20X5	300
20X6	336

The index has risen 156 points between 20X1 and 20X6 (336 – 180). This is an increase of:

$$\left(\frac{156}{180}\right) \times 100 = 86.7\%.$$

Similarly, the index rose 36 points between 20X5 and 20X6 (336 – 300), a rise of 12%.

1.4 The base period, or base year

Index numbers normally take the value for a **base date as 100**. The base period is usually the starting point of the series, though this is not always the case.

2 Index relatives

2.1 Assessment formulae

FAST FORWARD

An **index relative** (sometimes just called a relative) is the name given to an index number which measures the change in a single distinct commodity.

8: INDEX NUMBERS

Formula to learn

- A **price relative** is calculated as $100 \times \dfrac{P_1}{P_0}$
- A **quantity relative** is calculated as $100 \times \dfrac{Q_1}{Q_0}$

2.2 Example: Single-item indices

(a) **Price index number**

If the price of a cup of coffee was 40c in 20X0, 50c in 20X1 and 76c in 20X2, then using 20X0 as a base year the **price index numbers** for 20X1 and 20X2 would be as follows:

20X1 price index = $100 \times \dfrac{50}{40} = 125$

20X2 price index = $100 \times \dfrac{76}{40} = 190$

(b) **Quantity index number**

If the number of cups of coffee sold in 20X0 was 500,000, in 20X1 700,000 and in 20X2 600,000, then using 20X0 as a base year, the **quantity index numbers** for 20X1 and 20X2 would be as follows:

20X1 quantity index = $100 \times \dfrac{700{,}000}{500{,}000} = 140$

20X2 quantity index = $100 \times \dfrac{600{,}000}{500{,}000} = 120$

Question — Price index

The price of a kilogram of raw material was $80 in Year 1 and $120 in Year 2. Using Year 1 as a base year, the price index number for Year 2 is:

(a) 67
(b) 140
(c) 150
(d) 167

Answer

(c) Year 2 price index = 120/80 × 100 = 150

Option (c) is therefore correct.

If you selected option (a), you have confused the numerator with the denominator and calculated 80/120 instead of 120/80.

If you selected option (b), you simply took the price difference of $40 ($120 − $80 = $40) and added this to 100.

If you selected option (d), you added 80/120 × 100% = 67% to 100 which equals 167 which is incorrect.

PART A   DATA COLLECTION AND ANALYSIS

Question — Quantity index

A company used 20,000 litres of a raw material in Year 1. In Year 5 the usage of the same raw material amounted to 25,000 litres. Using Year 1 as a base year, the quantity index number for Year 5 is

(a) 105
(b) 120
(c) 125
(d) 180

Answer

(c) Year 5 quantity index = $\dfrac{25{,}000}{20{,}000} \times 100 = 125$

If you selected option (a), you took the difference in litres (25,000 – 20,000 = 5,000) and interpreted this as a five point increase, ie 100 + 5 = 105.

If you selected option (d) you calculated $\dfrac{20{,}000}{25{,}000} \times 100 = 80$ and added this to 100 which is not the correct method to use.

3 Time series of index relatives

FAST FORWARD Index relatives can be calculated using the **fixed base method** or the **chain base method**.

(a) The **fixed base method**. A base year is selected (index 100), and all subsequent changes are measured against this base. Such an approach should only be used if **the basic nature of the commodity is unchanged over time**.

Formula to learn

Fixed base index = $\dfrac{\text{Value in any given year}}{\text{Value in base year}} \times 100$

(b) The **chain base method**. Changes are calculated with respect to the value of the commodity in the period immediately before. This approach can be used for any set of commodity values but must be used if **the basic nature of the commodity is changing over time**.

Formula to learn

Chain base index = $\dfrac{\text{This year's value}}{\text{Last year's value}} \times 100$

3.1 Example: Fixed base method

The price of a commodity was $2.70 in 20X0, $3.11 in 20X1, $3.42 in 20X2 and $3.83 in 20X3. Construct a **fixed base index** for the years 20X0 to 20X3 using 20X0 as the base year.

Solution

Fixed base index	20X0	100	
	20X1	115	(3.11/2.70 × 100)
	20X2	127	(3.42/2.70 × 100)
	20X3	142	(3.83/2.70 × 100)

3.2 Example: Chain base method

Using the information in Paragraph 3.1 construct a chain base index for the years 20X0 to 20X3 using 20X0 as the base year.

Solution

Chain base index	20X0	100	
	20X1	115	(3.11/2.70 × 100)
	20X2	110	(3.42/3.11 × 100)
	20X3	112	(3.83/3.42 × 100)

Important!

> The chain base relatives show the rate of change in prices from year to year, whereas the fixed base relatives show changes relative to prices in the base year.

3.3 Splicing a single index

> **Splicing** involves redefining the base year of an index in a particular year and then restating the index values in previous years.

It is sometimes necessary to change the base of a time series (to **rebase**) of fixed base relatives, perhaps because the **base time point is too far in the past**. The following table shows a price index which rebased its base year to 2000.

Year	Price index
	(1975 = 100)
1998	320
1999	325
2000	331
	(2000 = 100)
2001	104
2002	108

We need to change the base of the original index to 2000.

1998 $100 \times \dfrac{320}{331} = 97$

1999 $100 \times \dfrac{325}{331} = 98$

The index now becomes:

Year	Price index
	(2000 = 100)
1998	97
1999	98
2000	100
2001	104
2002	108

PART A   DATA COLLECTION AND ANALYSIS

Question   Rebased index

In 2001 a price index based on 1990 = 100 had a value of 132. In 2001 it was rebased at 2001 = 100. The value of the new index in 2006 was 111.

For a continuous estimate of price changes since 1990, how should the new index be expressed in terms of the old index (to 2 decimal places)?

(a) 118.92
(b) 146.52
(c) 132.00
(d) 121.50

Answer

The correct answer is B.

$\dfrac{111}{100} \times 132 = 146.52$

3.4 Comparing sets of fixed base relatives

(a) You may be required to compare two sets of time series relatives. For example, an index of the annual number of advertisements placed by an organisation in the press and the index of the number of the organisation's product sold per annum might be compared. If the base years of the two indices differ, however, comparison is extremely difficult (as the illustration below shows).

	20W8	20W9	20X0	20X1	20X2	20X3	20X4
Number of advertisements placed (20X0 = 100)	90	96	100	115	128	140	160
Volumes of sales (20W0 = 100)	340	347	355	420	472	515	572

(b) From the figures above it is impossible to determine whether sales are increasing at a greater rate than the number of advertisements placed, or vice versa. This difficulty can be overcome by **rebasing** one set of relatives so that the **base dates are the same**. For example, we could rebase the index of volume of sales to 20X0.

	20W8	20W9	20X0	20X1	20X2	20X3	20X4
Number of advertisements placed (20X0 = 100)	90	96	100	115	128	140	160
Volumes of sales (20X0 = 100)	96	98*	100	118	133**	145	161

* $\dfrac{347}{355} \times 100$

** $\dfrac{472}{355} \times 100$

(c) The two sets of relatives are now much easier to compare. They show that volume of sales is increasing at a slightly faster rate, in general, than the number of advertisements placed.

4 Time series deflation

4.1 Real value of a commodity

FAST FORWARD

The real value of a commodity can only be measured in terms of some **'indicator'** such as the **rate of inflation** (historically represented in the UK by the Retail Prices Index (RPI)).

For example the cost of a commodity may have been $10 in 20X0 and $11 in 20X1, representing an increase of 10%. However, if we are told the prices **in general** (as measured by the RPI) increased by 12% between 20X0 and 20X1, we can argue that the **real** cost of the commodity has decreased.

FAST FORWARD

Time series deflation is a technique used to obtain a set of index relatives that measure the changes in the real value of some commodity with respect to some given indicator.

4.2 Example: Deflation

Mack Johnson works for Pound of Flesh Co. Over the last five years he has received an annual salary increase of $500. Despite his employer assuring him that $500 is a reasonable annual salary increase, Mack is unhappy because, although he agrees $500 is a lot of money, he finds it difficult to maintain the standard of living he had when he first joined the company.

Consider the figures below:

Year	(a) Wages $	(b) RPI	(c) Real wages $
1	12,000	250	12,000
2	12,500	260	12,019
3	13,000	275	11,818
4	13,500	295	11,441
5	14,000	315	11,111

(a) This column shows Mack's wages over the five-year period.

(b) This column shows the current RPI.

(c) This column shows what Mack's wages are worth taking prices, as represented by the RPI, into account. The wages have been deflated relative to the new base period (Year 1). Economists call these deflated wage figures **real wages**. The real wages for Years 2 and 4, for example, are calculated as follows:

Year 2: $\$12,500 \times \dfrac{250}{260} = \$12,019$

Year 4: $\$13,500 \times \dfrac{250}{295} = \$11,441$

Conclusion

The real wages index shows that the real value of Mack's wages has fallen by 7.4% over the five-year period is ($= \dfrac{12,000 - 11,111}{12,000} \times 100\%$). In real terms he is now earning $11,111 compared to $12,000 in Year 1. He is probably justified, therefore, in being unhappy.

Formula to learn

$$\text{Deflated/inflated cash flow} = \text{Actual cash flow in given year} \times \dfrac{\text{Index number for base year}}{\text{Index number for given year}}$$

5 Composite index numbers

FAST FORWARD — Composite index numbers cover more than one item.

5.1 Example: Composite index numbers

Suppose that the cost of living index is calculated from only three commodities: bread, tea and caviar, and that the prices for 20X1 and 20X2 were as follows.

Commodity	20X1	20X2
Bread	20c a loaf	40c a loaf
Tea	25c a packet	30c a packet
Caviar	450c a jar	405c a jar

(a) A simple index could be calculated by adding the prices for single items in 20X2 and dividing by the corresponding sum relating to 20X1 (if 20X1 is the base year). In general, if the sum of the prices in the base year is ΣP_0 and the sum of the prices in the new year is ΣP_1, the index is $100 \times \dfrac{\Sigma P_1}{\Sigma P_0}$. The index, known as a **simple aggregate price index**, would therefore be calculated as follows:

Commodity	P_0 20X1 $	P_1 20X2 $
Bread	0.20	0.40
Tea	0.25	0.30
Caviar	4.50	4.05
	$\Sigma P_0 = 4.95$	$\Sigma P_1 = 4.75$

Year	$\dfrac{\Sigma P_1}{\Sigma P_0}$	Simple aggregate price index
20X1	$\dfrac{4.95}{4.95} = 1.00$	100
20X2	$\dfrac{4.75}{4.95} = 0.96$	96

(b) The simple aggregate price index has a number of **disadvantages**.

(i) It ignores the **amounts** of bread, tea and caviar consumed (and hence the importance of each item).

(ii) It ignores the **units** to which the prices refer. If, for example, we had been given the price of a cup of tea rather than a packet of tea, the index would have been different.

5.2 Average relatives indices

To overcome the problem of different units we consider the changes in prices as **ratios** rather than absolutes so that all price movements, whatever their absolute values, are treated as equally important. Price changes are considered as ratios rather than absolutes by using the **average price relatives index**. Quantity changes are considered as ratios by using the **average quantity relatives index**.

- Average price relatives index = $100 \times \frac{1}{n} \times \Sigma \left(\frac{P_1}{P_0} \right)$

- Average quantity relatives index = $100 \times \frac{1}{n} \times \Sigma \left(\frac{Q_1}{Q_0} \right)$

where n is the number of goods.

The price relative P_1/P_0 (so called because it gives the new price level of each item relative to the base year price) for a particular commodity will have the same value whatever the unit for which the price is quoted.

5.3 Example: Average relatives indices

Using the information in the example in Paragraph 5.1, we can construct the **average price relatives index** as follows.

Commodity	P_0	P_1	$\frac{P_1}{P_0}$
	$	$	
Bread	0.20	0.40	2.00
Tea	0.25	0.30	1.20
Caviar	4.50	4.05	0.90
			4.10

Year	$\frac{1}{n} \Sigma \left(\frac{P_1}{P_0} \right)$	Average price relatives index
20X1	$\frac{1}{3} \times 3.00 = 1.00$	100
20X2	$\frac{1}{3} \times 4.10 = 1.37$	137

There has therefore been an average price increase of 37% between 20X1 and 20X2.

No account has been taken of the **relative importance** of each item in this index. Bread is probably more important than caviar. To overcome both the problem of quantities in different units and the need to attach importance to each item, we can use **weighting** which reflects the **importance of each item**. To decide the weightings of different items in an index, it is necessary to obtain information, perhaps by market research, about the **relative importance** of each item. The next section of this chapter looks at **weighted index numbers**.

6 Weighted index numbers

6.1 Weighting

FAST FORWARD

Weighting is used to reflect the importance of each item in the index.

There are two types of index which give different weights to different items:

- Weighted average of relatives indices
- Weighted aggregate indices

The weighted average of relatives index is the one that you need to be able to calculate in your assessment.

6.2 Weighted aggregate indices

This method of weighting involves multiplying each component value by its corresponding weight and adding these products to form an aggregate. This is done for both the base period and the period in question. The aggregate for the period under consideration is then divided by the base period aggregate.

The general form of a **weighted aggregate index** is:

$$\frac{\Sigma wv_n}{\Sigma wv_o}$$

where w is the weighting factor
v_o is the value of the commodity in the base period
v_n is the value of the commodity in the period in question

Price indices are usually weighted by quantities and quantity indices are usually weighted by prices.

Question — Weighted aggregate indexes

What are the formulae for calculating price and quantity weighted aggregate indices if base year weights are used?

Answer

Price index: $\dfrac{\Sigma Q_o P_n}{\Sigma Q_o P_o} \times 100$

where P_0 represents the prices of items in the base year
P_n represents the prices of items in the new year
Q_0 represents the quantities of the items consumed in the base year

Quantity index: $\dfrac{\Sigma P_o Q_n}{\Sigma P_o Q_o} \times 100$

where Q_0 represents the quantities consumed in the base year
Q_n represents the quantities consumed in the new year
P_0 represents the prices in the base year

6.3 Example: a price index

In the previous example of the cost of living index (Paragraph 5.1), the 20X2 index value could have been calculated as follows, assuming the quantities purchased by each household were as given below.

Item	Quantity Q_0	Price in 20X1 P_0	$P_0 Q_0$	Price in 20X2 P_n	$P_n Q_0$
Bread	6	20	120	40	240
Tea	2	25	50	30	60
Caviar	0.067	450	30	405	27
			200		327

Index in 20X2 = $\dfrac{327}{200} \times 100 = 163.5$

We will now look at an example of a **quantity index**, which measures **changes in quantities** and uses **prices as weights**.

6.4 Example: a quantity index

The Falldown Construction Company uses four items of materials and components in a standard production job.

In 20X0 the quantities of each material or component used per job and their cost were as follows:

Item	Quantity Units	Price per unit $
Material A	20	2
Material B	5	10
Component C	40	3
Component D	15	6

In 20X2 the quantities of materials and components used per job were as follows:

Item	Quantity Units
Material A	15
Material B	6
Component C	36
Component D	25

Using 20X0 as a base year, calculate the quantity index value in 20X2 for the amount of materials used in a standard job.

6.5 Solution

Item	Price P_o	Quantity used in 20X0 Q_o	P_oQ_o ($)	Quantity used in 20X2 Q_n	P_oQ_n ($)
Material A	$2	20	40	15	30
Material B	$10	5	50	6	60
Component C	$3	40	120	36	108
Component D	$6	15	90	25	150
			300		348

Quantity index = $\frac{348}{300} \times 100 = 116$

This would suggest that the company is using 16% more materials in 20X2 than in 20X0 on a standard job.

7 Laspeyre and Paasche indices

Laspeyre and Paasche indices are special cases of weighed aggregate indices.

7.1 Laspeyre indices

Laspeyre indices use weights from the base period and are therefore sometimes called base weighted indices.

7.2 Laspeyre price index

A **Laspeyre price index** uses **quantities** consumed in the base period as weights. In the notation already used it can be expressed as follows.

PART A   DATA COLLECTION AND ANALYSIS

Formula to learn

$$\text{Laspeyre price index} = \frac{P_n Q_o}{P_o Q_o} \times 100$$

7.3 Laspeyre quantity index

A **Laspeyre quantity index** uses **prices** from the base period as weights and can be expressed as follows.

Formula to learn

$$\text{Laspeyre quantity index} = \frac{P_o Q_n}{P_o Q_o} \times 100$$

7.4 Paasche indices

Paasche indices use **current time period weights**. In other words the weights are changed every time period.

7.4.1 Paasche price index

A **Paasche price index** uses **quantities** consumed in the current period as weights and can be expressed as follows.

Formula to learn

$$\text{Paasche price index} = \frac{P_n Q_n}{P_o Q_n} \times 100$$

7.4.2 Paasche quantity index

A **Paasche quantity index** uses **prices** from the current period as weights and can be expressed as follows.

Formula to learn

$$\text{Paasche quantity index} = \frac{P_n Q_n}{P_n Q_o} \times 100$$

Exam focus point

Index numbers were tested in the May 13 and May 14 exams. These questions asked, amongst other requirements, for calculations of the Laspeyre and Paasche indices. **The indices formulae are not given in the exam formulae sheet.** Make sure you know them!

7.5 Example: Laspeyre and Paasche price indices

The wholesale price index in Ruritania is made up from the prices of five items. The price of each item, and the average quantities purchased by manufacturing and other companies each week were as follows, in 20X0 and 20X2.

Item	Quantity 20X0 '000 units	Price per unit 20X0 Roubles	Quantity 20X2 '000 units	Price per unit 20X2 Roubles
P	60	3	80	4
Q	30	6	40	5
R	40	5	20	8
S	100	2	150	2
T	20	7	10	10

Required

Calculate the price index in 20X2, if 20X0 is taken as the base year, using the following.

(a) A Laspeyre index
(b) A Paasche index

7.6 Solution

Item	Q_o	P_o	Q_n	P_n	Laspeyre P_oQ_o	P_nQ_o	Paasche P_nQ_n	P_oQ_n
P	60	3	80	4	180	240	320	240
Q	30	6	40	5	180	150	200	240
R	40	5	20	8	200	320	160	100
S	100	2	150	2	200	200	300	300
T	20	7	10	10	140	200	100	70
					900	1,110	1,080	950

20X2 index numbers are as follows.

(a) Laspeyre index $= 100 \times \dfrac{1,110}{900} = 123.3$

(b) Paasche index $= 100 \times \dfrac{1,080}{950} = 113.7$

The Paasche index for 20X2 reflects the decline in consumption of the relatively expensive items R and T since 20X0. The Laspeyre index for 20X2 fails to reflect this change.

Question — Indexes

A baker has listed the ingredients he used and their prices, in 20X3 and 20X4, as follows.

Ingredients	Kg used 20X3 '000s	Price per kg 20X3 $	Kg used 20X4 '000s	Price per kg 20X4 $
Milk	3	1.20	4	1.50
Eggs	6	0.95	5	0.98
Flour	1	1.40	2	1.30
Sugar	4	1.10	3	1.14

Required

Calculate the following quantity indices for 20X4 (with 20X3 as the base year).

(a) A Laspeyre index
(b) A Paasche index

Answer

Workings

	Q_o	P_o	Q_n	P_n	Laspeyre P_oQ_o	P_oQ_n	Paasche P_nQ_n	P_nQ_o
Milk	3	1.20	4	1.50	3.60	4.80	6.00	4.50
Eggs	6	0.95	5	0.98	5.70	4.75	4.90	5.88
Flour	1	1.40	2	1.30	1.40	2.80	2.60	1.30
Sugar	4	1.10	3	1.14	4.40	3.30	3.42	4.56
					15.10	15.65	16.92	16.24

PART A DATA COLLECTION AND ANALYSIS

Quantity index numbers for 20X4 are as follows.

(a) **Laspeyre method** = $100 \times \dfrac{15.65}{15.10}$ = 103.64

(b) **Paasche method** = $100 \times \dfrac{16.92}{16.24}$ = 104.19

7.7 Which to use – Paasche or Laspeyre ?

Both patterns of consumption and prices change and a decision therefore has to be made as to whether a Paasche or a Laspeyre index should be used.

The following points should be considered when deciding which type of index to use:

(a) A **Paasche index requires quantities to be ascertained each year**. A Laspeyre index only requires them for the base year. Constructing a Paasche index may therefore be costly.

(b) For the **Paasche index the denominator has to be recalculated each year** because the quantities/prices must be changed to current year consumption/price levels.

For the **Laspeyre index, the denominator is fixed**. The Laspeyre index can therefore be calculated as soon as current prices/quantities are known. The Paasche index, on the other hand, cannot be calculated until the end of a period, when information about current quantities/prices becomes available.

(c) The denominator of a Laspeyre index is fixed and therefore the Laspeyre index numbers for several different years can be **directly compared**. With the Paasche index, on the other hand, comparisons can only be drawn directly between the current year and the base year (although indirect comparisons can be made).

(d) The weights for a Laspeyre index become **out of date**, whereas those for the Paasche index are updated each year.

(e) A **Laspeyre price index** implicitly assumes that, whatever the price changes, the quantities purchased will remain the same. In terms of economic theory, no substitution of cheaper alternative goods and services is allowed to take place. Even if goods become relatively more expensive, it assumes that the same quantities are bought. As a result, the **index tends to overstate inflation**.

(f) The effect of current year weighting when using the Paasche price index means that greater importance is placed on goods that are relatively cheaper now than they were in the base year. As a consequence, the **Paasche price index** tends to **understate inflation**.

In practice, it is common to use a Laspeyre index and revise the weights every few years. (Where appropriate, a new base year may be created when the weights are changed.)

8 The Retail Prices Index for the United Kingdom

FAST FORWARD

The **Retail Prices Index** (RPI) is a measure which can be used to **measure price inflation** and can be used to **deflate data** and for **index linking**. Widespread usage of the RPI has reduced as it has been replaced by the **Consumer Price Index** (CPI).

8.1 Items included in the RPI calculation

We will conclude our study of index numbers by looking at the construction of the UK Retail Prices Index (RPI). On one particular day of each month, data was collected about prices of the following groups of items:

- Food and catering
- Alcohol and tobacco
- Housing and household expenditure
- Personal expenditure
- Travel and leisure

(a) Each group was sub-divided into sections: for example 'food' was sub-divided into bread, butter, potatoes and so on. These sections could then in turn be sub-divided into more specific items. The groups did not cover every item of expenditure.

(b) The weightings given to each group, section and sub-section were based on information provided by the *Living Costs and Food Survey*, which was based on a survey of households over the year.

8.2 Using the RPI

The RPI can be used to measure price inflation. We saw in Section 4 how it can be used to **deflate** time-related data so that change in **real values** can be measured.

It can also be used for **index linking**. For example, pensions can be increased in line with increases in the RPI.

In 2013, the UK Office of National Statistics announced that in future it would place greater emphasis on the Consumer Price Index (CPI), which is an alternative measure of inflation.

Question — Index linking

At the start of 20X3, Doris's index-linked pension was $5,200 per year and the RPI was at 360. At the start of the following year, the RPI had increased to 375. What pension can Doris now expect to receive?

Answer

The percentage increase in the RPI $= \dfrac{\text{Change}}{\text{Original value}} \times 100$

$= \dfrac{(375 - 360)}{360} \times 100$

$= 4.17\%$

Pension increase $= 4.17\% \times \$5,200$
$= \$216.84$

New pension $= \$(5,200 + 216.84)$
$= \$5,416.84$

PART A　DATA COLLECTION AND ANALYSIS

Chapter Roundup

- An **index** is a measure, over time, of the average changes in the value (price or quantity) of a group of items.
- An **index relative** (sometimes just called a relative) is the name given to an index number which measures the change in a single distinct commodity.
- Index relatives can be calculated using the **fixed base method** or the **chain base method**.
- **Splicing** involves redefining the base year of an index in a particular year and then restating the index values in previous years.
- The **real value** of a commodity can only be measured in terms of some '**indicator**', such as the **rate of inflation** (historically represented by the Retail Prices Index (RPI)).
- **Time series deflation** is a technique used to obtain a set of index relatives that measure the changes in the real value of some commodity with respect to some given indicator.
- **Composite index numbers** cover more than one item.
- **Weighting** is used to reflect the importance of each item in the index.
- **Weighted average of relatives indices** are found by calculating indices and then applying weights.
- The **Retail Prices Index** (RPI) is a measure which can be used to **measure price inflation** and can be used to **deflate data** and for **index linking**. Widespread usage of the RPI has reduced as it has been replaced by the **Consumer Price Index (CPI)**.

Quick Quiz

1. Complete the following equations using the symbols in the box below.

   (a) **Price index** = ☐ × 100

   (b) **Quantity index** = ☐ × 100

P_1	P_0
Q_1	Q_0

2. An index relative is the name given to an index number which measures the change in a group of items.

   True ☐

   False ☐

3. Fixed base method ⎤ ⎡ Changes are measured against base period

   Chain base method ⎦ ? ⎣ Changes are measured against the previous period

4. In 2006 the retail price index was 198 with 1987 = 100. Convert a weekly wage of $421 back to 1987 prices. ☐

5. The chain base index for an item last year was 130. The price of the item has risen by 10% between last year and this year.

   What is the chain base index for this year? ☐

6. In 2008, a price index based on 1994 = 100 stood at 139. In that year it was rebased at 2008 = 100. By 2010, the new index stood at 120. For a continuous estimate of price changes since 1994, the new index may be expressed in terms of the old as (to 1 decimal place) ☐

7. What are the formulae for Laspeyre quantity index, Laspeyre price index, Paasche price index and Paasche quantity index?

Answers to Quick Quiz

1. (a) Price index = $\dfrac{P_1}{P_0} \times 100$

   (b) Quantity index = $\dfrac{Q_1}{Q_0} \times 100$

2. False. An index relative is an index number which measures the change in a **single distinct commodity**.

3. Fixed base method ⟶ Changes are measured against the base period
   Chain base method ⟶ Changes are measured against the previous period

4. $\boxed{212.63}$ Deflated cash flow = Actual cash flow in given year × $\dfrac{\text{Index number for base year}}{\text{Index number for given year}}$

   $= \$421 \times \dfrac{100}{198}$

   $= \$212.63$

5. $\boxed{143}$ $130 \times (1 + 10\%)$
   $= 130 \times 1.1 = 143$

6. $\boxed{166.8}$

	1994	2008	2010
1994 = 100	100	139	
2008 = 100		100	120

   Between 2008 and 2010, prices increased by 20%. The price index for 2010 with 1994 as the base year should also show a 20% increase on the 2008 index of 139.

   $= 139 \times 120\% = 139 \times 1.2$
   $= 166.8$

7. **Laspeyre price index** = $\dfrac{P_n Q_0}{P_0 Q_0} \times 100$

   Laspeyre quantity index = $\dfrac{P_0 Q_n}{P_0 Q_0} \times 100$

   Paasche price index = $\dfrac{P_n Q_n}{P_0 Q_n} \times 100$

   Paasche quantity index = $\dfrac{P_n Q_n}{P_n Q_0} \times 100$

End of Chapter Question

Index numbers (AIA Nov 08)

The average monthly quantities purchased of five major food items and the corresponding prices were recorded for the years 20X1 and 20X7, in relevant units, as follows:

Food	Year 20X1		Year 20X7	
	Price	Quantity	Price	Quantity
V	17	25	19	30
W	13	15	18	18
X	5	20	6	26
Y	12	14	16	15
Z	22	19	24	17

Required

(a) Calculate values of the Laspeyres and Paasche price index numbers. **(8 marks)**

(b) Define what the Laspeyres and Paasche price index numbers, calculated in (a) above, represent and comment on their disadvantages. **(6 marks)**

(c) Briefly describe how the Retail Price index was calculated and how it was used. **(6 marks)**

(Total = 20 marks)

PART A DATA COLLECTION AND ANALYSIS

Business information technology

Overview of information systems

Topic list	Syllabus reference
1 General systems theory	–
2 Information theory	–
3 Information systems	6.8
4 The systems development life cycle and project management	6.8

Introduction

In this chapter we look at **systems and information theory**.

Much of the material in this chapter is theoretical. In the exam you may be required to show you have learnt and understood the theory.

It is important to ensure you learn the theory. As with many topics, the key is extensive question practice during the revision phase of your studies.

PART B BUSINESS INFORMATION TECHNOLOGY

1 General systems theory

The term **system** is widely used – the 'respiratory system', the 'political system', the 'long ball system', and so on. Any definition of a 'system' must therefore be wide ranging.

FAST FORWARD

Any system can be thought of in terms of **inputs, processing** and **outputs**.

Key terms

A **system** is set of interacting components that operate together to accomplish a purpose.

A **business system** is a collection of people, machines and methods organised to accomplish a set of specific functions.

Information systems (IS) include all systems and procedures involved in the collection, storage, production and distribution of information.

Information technology (IT) describes the equipment used to capture, store, transmit or present information. IT provides a large part of the information systems infrastructure.

1.1 The component parts of a system

A system has three component parts: inputs, processes and outputs. Other key characteristics of a system are the environment and the system boundary – as shown in the following diagram.

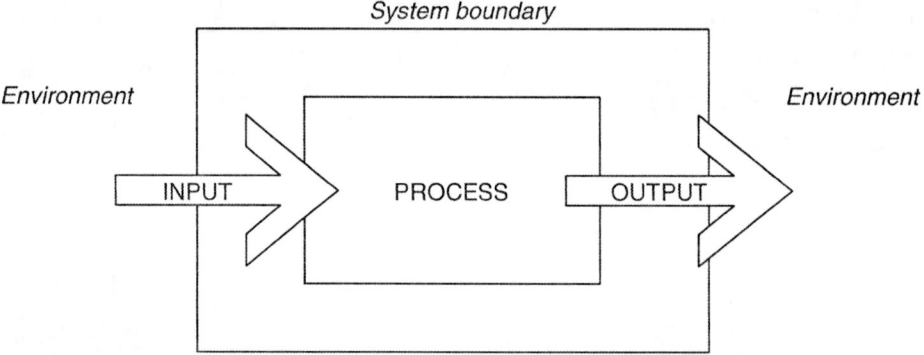

1.1.1 Inputs

Inputs **provide the system with what it needs** to be able to operate. Input may vary from matter, energy or human actions, to information.

- Matter might include, in a manufacturing operation, adhesives or rivets.
- Human input might consist of typing an instruction booklet or starting up a piece of machinery.

Inputs may be **outputs from other systems**, for example, the output from a transactions processing system forms the input for a management information system.

1.1.2 Processes

A process **transforms an input into an output**. Processes may involve tasks performed by humans, plant, computers, chemicals and a wide range of other actions.

Processes may consist of **assembly**, for example where electronic consumer goods are being manufactured, or **disassembly**, for example where oil is refined.

There is **not necessarily a clear relationship** between the number of inputs to a process and the number of outputs.

1.1.3 Outputs

Outputs are the **results of the processing**. They could be said to represent the **purpose** for which the system exists.

Many outputs are used as **inputs to other systems**.

Alternatively outputs may be discarded as **waste** (an input to the ecological system) or **re-input** to the system which has produced them, for example, in certain circumstances, defective products.

1.1.4 The system boundary

FAST FORWARD

A system exists in an environment. An environment surrounds the system but is not part of it. A **system boundary** separates the system from its environment.

The concept of the system boundary is explained above. For example, a cost accounting department's boundary can be expressed in terms of who works in it and what work it does. This boundary will separate it from other departments, such as the financial accounts department.

System boundaries may be natural or artificially created (an organisation's departmental structures are artificially created).

There may be **interfaces** between various systems, both internal and external to an organisation, to allow the exchange of resources. In a commercial context, this is most likely to be a reciprocal exchange, for example money for raw materials.

1.1.5 The environment

Anything which is outside the system boundary belongs to the system's environment and not to the system itself. A system **accepts inputs** from the environment and **provides outputs** into the environment. The parts of the environment from which the system receives inputs may not be the same as those to which it delivers outputs.

The environment exerts a considerable influence on the behaviour of a system; at the same time the system can do little to **control** the behaviour of the environment.

Question — The environment

The environment affects the performance of a system. Using a business organisation as an example of a system, give five examples of environmental factors which might affect it.   **(5 marks)**

Answer

(a) Policies adopted by the government or ruling political body.
(b) The strength of the domestic currency of the organisation's country of operation.
(c) Social attitudes: concern for the natural environment.
(d) The regulatory and legislative framework within which the company operates.
(e) The number of competitors in the marketplace and the strategies they adopt (eg products, price, quality).

You may have thought of other valid factors.

1.2 Subsystems

A system itself may contain a number of systems, called **subsystems**. Each subsystem consists of a process whereby component parts interact to achieve an objective. Separate subsystems **interact** with each other, and **respond** to each other by means of **communication** or observation. The goals of subsystems must be consistent with the goal of the overall system.

Often, whether something is a system or a subsystem is a matter of definition, and depends on the context of the **observer**. For example, an organisation is a social system, and its 'environment' may be seen as society as a whole. Another way of looking at an organisation would be to regard it as a subsystem of the entire social system. **Information** links up the different subsystems in an organisation.

1.3 The systems approach

The theory we have covered in this section may applied to a wide range of situations. For example, a computerised information system may also be thought of in terms of inputs, processed outputs and subsystems.

Organisations can also be viewed as a system. **Inputs** are received and **processed** to produce **outputs** of goods and services. The **objectives** of the organisation are thereby fulfilled.

The systems approach uses three steps:

1. Identify what the **whole system** is
2. Identify the overall **objectives** of the system as a whole
3. Make **plans** with these objectives in mind

1.4 Socio-technical systems

Another point of view suggests that an organisation is a 'structured **socio-technical** system', that is, it consists of at least **three subsystems**:

1. A structure.
2. A technological system (concerning the work to be done, and the machines, tools and other facilities available to do it).
3. A social system (concerning the people within the organisation, the ways they think and the ways they interact with each other).

2 Information theory

2.1 Why do organisations need information?

> **FAST FORWARD**
>
> Organisations require **information** for a range of **purposes**:
>
> - Planning
> - Controlling
> - Recording transactions
> - Performance measurement
> - Decision making

2.1.1 Planning

Once any decision has been made, it is necessary to plan **how to implement** the steps necessary to make it effective. Planning requires a knowledge of, among other things, available **resources**, possible **time-scales** for implementation and the likely **outcome under alternative scenarios**.

2.1.2 Controlling

Once a plan is implemented, its actual performance must be controlled. Information is required to assess **whether it is proceeding as planned** or whether there is some unexpected deviation from plan. It may consequently be necessary to take some form of corrective action.

2.1.3 Recording transactions

Information about **each transaction or event** is required for a number of reasons. Documentation of transactions can be used as **evidence** in a case of dispute. There may be a **legal requirement** to record transactions, for example for accounting and audit purposes. Detailed information on production costs can be built up, allowing a better **assessment of profitability**. Similarly, labour utilised in providing a particular service can be measured. Structured systems can be installed to capture transactions data.

2.1.4 Performance measurement

Just as individual operations need to be controlled, so overall performance must be measured in order to enable **comparisons against budget or plan** to be carried out. This may involve the collection of information on, for example, costs, revenues, volumes, time-scale and profitability.

2.1.5 Decision making

Information is also required to make informed decisions. This completes the full circle of organisational activity.

2.2 Internal information

> **FAST FORWARD**
>
> Data can be **collected** from **within** and **beyond an organisation**. **Information systems** are used to convert this **data into information** and to **communicate** it to management at all levels.

Data and information come from sources both inside and outside an organisation, and an information system should be designed so as to obtain – or **capture** – all the relevant data and information from whatever source. Capturing data/information from **inside** the organisation involves the following:

(a) A **system** for collecting or measuring **transactions** data – for example sales, purchases, stock (inventory) turnover etc – which sets out procedures for **what** data is **collected**, how frequently, by whom, and by what methods, and how it is **processed**, and **filed** or **communicated**.

(b) **Informal communication** of information between **managers and staff** (for example, by word of mouth or at meetings).

(c) **Communication between managers**.

2.3 Internal data sources

2.3.1 The accounting records

Accounts receivable ledgers, accounts payable ledgers, general ledgers and cash books etc hold information that may be of great value outside the accounts department, for example, sales information for the marketing function.

To maintain the integrity of its accounting records, an organisation operates **controls** over transactions. These also give rise to valuable information. A stock control system for example will include details of purchase orders, goods received notes, goods returned notes and so on, which can be analysed to **provide management information** about speed of delivery, say, or the quality of supplies.

2.3.2 Other internal sources

Organisations record information to enable them to carry out operations and administrative functions.

(a) Information about **employees** will be held, possibly linked to the **payroll** system. Additional information may be obtained from this source if, say, a project is being costed and it is necessary to ascertain the availability and rate of pay of different levels of staff, or the need for and cost of recruiting staff from outside the organisation.

(b) Much information will be produced by a **production** department about machine capacity, fuel consumption, movement of people, materials, work in progress, set up times, maintenance requirements and so on.

(c) Many **service** businesses, notably accountants and solicitors, need to keep detailed records of the **time spent** on various activities, both to justify fees to clients and to assess the efficiency and profitability of operations.

Staff themselves are one of the primary sources of internal information. Information may be obtained either informally in the course of day to day business or through meetings, interviews or questionnaires.

2.4 External information

Capturing information from **outside** the organisation might be entrusted to particular individuals, or might be 'informal'.

Routine formal collection of data from outside sources includes the following:

(a) A company's **tax specialists** will be expected to gather information about changes in tax law and how this will affect the company.

(b) Obtaining information about any new legislation on health and safety at work, or employment regulations, must be the responsibility of a particular person – for example, the company's **legal expert** or **company secretary** – who must then pass on the information to other managers affected by it.

(c) **Research and development (R & D)** work often relies on information about other R & D work being done by another company or by government institutions.

(d) **Marketing managers** need to know about the opinions and buying attitudes of potential customers. To obtain this information, they might carry out market research exercises.

Informal gathering of information from the environment **goes on all the time, consciously or unconsciously**, because the employees of an organisation learn **what is going on in the world around** them – perhaps from the internet, newspapers, television reports, meetings with business associates or the trade press.

2.5 External data sources

We looked at primary external and secondary external data sources in Chapter 2, Section 3.

Key term

> The phrase **environmental scanning** is often used to describe the process of gathering external information, which is available from a wide range of sources.

Question — Information

(a) Think about the relative importance of internally-produced and external information. What sort of problems might, say, Marks and Spencer face if it decided **not** to collect external information?

(b) Also think about how information needs vary for different types of organisation, such as commercial, public sector and charities.

Answer

(a) Both internal and external information can be very important. Internal information in a profit seeking organisation would cover items like, sales, costs, receivables, payables, cash flow forecasts, employee skills and inventory. It would be difficult to see how an organisation could operate without information like this. However, no organisation operates in a vacuum. They all receive information and resources from outside and produce products, deliver services and generate information for outside parties. So, a retailing company like Marks and Spencer needs external information such as the following:

- Supplier information
- Latest fashion trends
- Competitors' products and prices
- Information from manufacturers about costs and delivery times
- Feedback from customers on products
- Legal information, such as minimum wage rates and tax rates

If Marks and Spencer did not collect this information then its activities would become increasingly irrelevant (and perhaps illegal). Financial problems would soon follow.

(b) Information that is needed by commercial organisations is primarily aimed at the production of profits. So the information set out in part (a) is typical of both the internal and external information needed.

The public sector is primarily concerned with delivering services, such and education and health. It receives money from government and needs information that will allow it to budget carefully. It needs information about its efficiency to ensure that the money is wisely spent. Instead of sales, the public sector usually provides services free of charge. However, there should be an attempt to collect information about the benefits provided by an item of expenditure as budgets are limited and public sector organisations often have to choose between different expenditures. For example, a council might have to decide whether to repair roads or extend a school.

Charities are somewhat like the public sector insofar as they need information that can help them decide how their donations can be spent. They will need information too about where their funds come from, such as government grants that might be available, or the success of charity appeals in raising money.

3 Information systems

3.1 Types of information system

FAST FORWARD

Different **types of information systems** exist with different characteristics – reflecting the different roles they perform.

3.1.1 Executive Information Systems (EIS)

Key term

An **Executive Information System (EIS)** pools data from internal and external sources and makes information available to senior managers in an easy to use form. EIS help senior managers make strategic, unstructured decisions.

An EIS should provide senior managers with easy access to key **internal** and **external** information. The system summarises and tracks strategically critical information, possibly drawn from internal MIS and

DSS (see below), but also including data from external sources eg competitors, legislation, and external databases such as Reuters.

Executive Information Systems are sometimes referred to as **Executive Support Systems** (ESS). An ESS/EIS is likely to have the following **features**:

- Flexibility
- Quick response time
- Sophisticated data analysis and modelling tools

A model of a typical EIS follows:

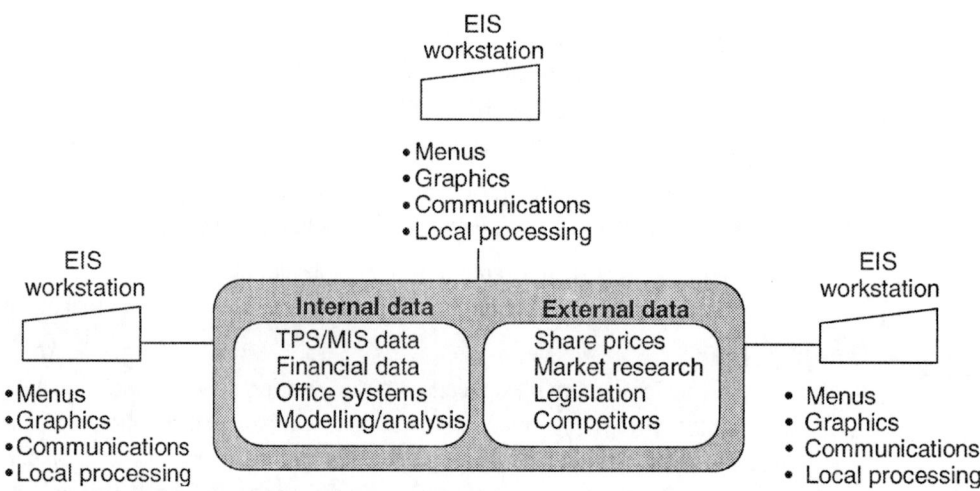

3.1.2 Management Information Systems (MIS)

Key term

Management Information Systems (MIS) convert data from mainly internal sources into information (eg summary reports, exception reports). This information enables managers to make timely and effective decisions for planning, directing and controlling the activities for which they are responsible.

An MIS provides regular reports and (usually) online access to the organisation's current and historical performance.

MIS usually transform data from underlying transaction processing systems (TPS) into summarised files that are used as the basis for management reports.

MIS have the following characteristics:

- Support **structured** decisions at operational and management control levels
- Designed to report on **existing** operations
- Have little analytical capability
- Relatively **inflexible**
- Have an **internal** focus
- Not suitable for **strategic planning** and **decision-making**

You may see the term **Management Information System** used as an umbrella term for **all information systems** within an organisation.

3.1.3 Decision Support Systems (DSS)

Key term

Decision Support Systems (DSS) combine data and analytical models or data analysis tools to support semi-structured and unstructured decision making.

DSS are used by management to assist in making decisions on issues which are subject to high levels of uncertainty, the various **responses** which management could undertake, or the likely **impact** of those actions.

Decision support systems are intended to provide a wide range of alternative information gathering and analytical tools with a major emphasis upon **flexibility** and **user-friendliness**.

DSS have more analytical power than other systems, enabling them to analyse and condense large volumes of data into a form that aids managers' decision making. The objective is to allow the manager to consider a number of **alternatives** and evaluate them under a variety of potential conditions.

3.1.4 Knowledge Work Systems (KWS)

Key terms

> **Knowledge Work Systems (KWS)** are information systems that facilitate the creation and integration of new knowledge into an organisation.
>
> **Knowledge Workers** are people whose jobs primarily involve creating new information and knowledge. They are often members of a profession such as doctors, engineers, lawyers and scientists.

KWS help knowledge workers create new knowledge and expertise. Examples include:

- Computer Aided Design (CAD)
- Computer Aided Manufacturing (CAM)
- Specialised financial software that analyses trading situations

KWS are information systems that facilitate the creation and integration of new knowledge into an organisation. They provide knowledge workers with tools such as:

- Analytical tools
- Powerful graphics facilities
- Communication tools
- Access to external databases
- A user-friendly interface

The workstations of knowledge workers are often designed for the specific tasks they perform. For example, a design engineer would require sufficient graphics power to manipulate 3D Computer Aided Design (CAD) images; a financial analyst would require a powerful desktop computer to access and manipulate a large amount of financial data (an **investment workstation**).

Virtual reality systems are another example of KWS. These systems create computer generated simulations that emulate real-world activities. Interactive software and hardware (eg special headgear) provide simulations so realistic that users experience sensations that would normally only occur in the real world.

Supermarkets now use virtual reality programmes to test shelf planning, using the technology to improve efficiency and increase sales through better product display.

3.1.5 Office Automation Systems (OAS)

Key term

> **Office Automation Systems (OAS)** are computer systems designed to increase the productivity of data and information workers.

OAS support the major activities performed in a typical office such as document management, facilitating communication and managing data. Examples include:

- Word processing, desktop publishing, and digital filing systems
- Email, voice mail, videoconferencing, webinars, groupware, intranets, schedulers
- Spreadsheets, desktop databases

PART B BUSINESS INFORMATION TECHNOLOGY

3.1.6 Transaction Processing Systems (TPS)

Key term

A **Transaction Processing System (TPS)** performs and records routine transactions.

TPS are used for **routine tasks** in which data items or transactions must be processed so that operations can continue. TPS support most business functions in most types of organisation. They include accounting systems such as the sales and purchase ledger and operational systems such as delivery tracking systems. The main TPS that you are likely to encounter regularly is the EPOS (Electronic Point of Sale system) in a supermarket, which scans the barcodes on products and communicates with the in-house system to retrieve the current price. It will also record all the data to do with the sale and update the inventory records. The following table shows a range of TPS applications.

	Transaction processing systems				
	Sales/ marketing systems	Manufacturing/ production systems	Finance/ accounting systems	Human resources systems	Other types (eg university)
Major functions of system	• Sales management • Market research • Promotion pricing • New products	• Scheduling • Purchasing • Shipping/ receiving • Engineering • Operations	• Budgeting • General ledger • Billing • Management accounting	• Employee records • Benefits • Salaries • Labour relations • Training	• Admissions • Student academic records • Course records • Graduates
Major application systems	• Sales order information system • Market research system • Pricing system	• Materials resource planning • Purchase order control • Engineering • Quality control	• General ledger • Accounts receivable /payable • Budgeting • Funds management	• Payroll • Employee records • Employee benefits • Career path systems	• Registration • Student record • Curriculum/ class control systems • Benefactor information system

3.1.7 Expert systems

Expert systems are a form of DSS that allow users to benefit from expert knowledge and information. The system will consist of a **database** holding specialised data and **rules** about what to do in, or how to interpret, a given set of circumstances.

For example, many financial institutions now use expert systems to process straightforward **loan applications**. The user enters certain key facts into the system such as the loan applicant's name and most recent addresses, their income and monthly outgoings, and details of other loans. The system will then:

(a) **Check the facts** given against its database to see whether the applicant has a good credit record.

(b) **Perform calculations** to see whether the applicant can afford to repay the loan.

(c) **Match up other criteria**, such as whether the security offered for the loan or the purpose for which the loan is wanted is acceptable, and to what extent the loan applicant fits the lender's profile of a good risk (based on the lender's previous experience).

A decision is then suggested, based on the results of this processing. This is why it is now often possible to get a loan or arrange insurance **over the telephone or online**, whereas in the past it would have been necessary to go and speak to a bank manager or send details to an actuary and then wait for him or her to come to a decision.

There are many other **business applications** of expert systems.

(a) **Legal** advice.

(b) **Tax** advice.

(c) **Forecasting** of economic or financial developments, or of market and customer behaviour.

(d) **Surveillance**, for example of the number of customers entering a supermarket, to decide what shelves need restocking and when more checkouts need to be opened, or of machines in a factory, to determine when they need maintenance.

(e) **Diagnostic systems**, to identify causes of problems, for example in production control in a factory, or in healthcare.

(f) **Project management**.

(g) **Education** and **training**, diagnosing a student's or worker's weaknesses and providing or recommending extra instruction as appropriate.

An organisation can use an expert system when a number of conditions are met.

(a) The problem is **reasonably well-defined**.

(b) The expert can define some **rules** by which the problem can be solved.

(c) The problem cannot be solved by **conventional** transaction processing or data handling.

(d) The **expert could be released** to more difficult problems. Experts are often highly paid, meaning the value of even small time savings is likely to be significant.

(e) The **investment** in an expert system is **cost-justified**.

Question — Expert systems

Explain why organisations use expert systems for decision-making tasks which humans are naturally better able to perform than computers? **(5 marks)**

Answer

The primary reason has to do with the relative costs. A 'human' expert is likely to be more expensive either to employ or to use on a consultancy basis.

Second, enshrining an expert's accumulated wisdom in a computer system means that this wisdom can be accessed by more people. Thus, the delivery of complicated services to customers, decisions whether or not to extend credit and so forth, can be made by less experienced members of staff. If a manufacturing company has a complicated mixture of plant and machinery, then the repair engineer may accumulate a lot of knowledge over a period of time about the way it behaves: if a problem occurs, the engineer will be able to make a reasoned guess as to where the likely cause is to be found. If this accumulated expert information is made available to less experienced staff, it means that some of their learning curve is avoided.

An expert system is advantageous because it saves time, like all computer systems (in theory at least) but it is particularly useful as it possesses both knowledge and limited reasoning ability.

3.1.8 Intranets and Extranets

Organisations are increasingly using **intranets** and **extranets** to **disseminate information**.

(a) An **intranet** is an internal network used to share information. Intranets use a combination of the organisation's own networked computers and internet technology. The idea behind an 'intranet' is that organisations set up their own **mini version of the internet**. Organisation members use networked computers to access information held on a server. The user interface is a browser – similar to those used on the internet. The intranet offers access to information on a wide variety of topics. Potential applications include company news, induction material, online procedure and policy manuals, employee web pages where individuals post details of their activities and progress, and **internal databases** of the corporate information store.

(b) An **extranet** is an intranet that is accessible to **authorised outsiders**, using a valid username and password. The username will have access rights attached – determining which parts of the extranet can be viewed. An extranet can link parts of the intranets of related organisations – for example within a supply chain – for their mutual benefit. Extranets can be used to share inventory and price information. Extranets are becoming a very popular means for business partners to exchange information.

Key terms

> An **intranet** is a private network inside a company or organisation accessed through web-browser like software. Intranets are for the use of staff only, they are not accessible by the public. Intranets are used to provide and distribute information.
>
> An **extranet** allows customers and suppliers to gain limited access to an intranet in order to enhance the speed and efficiency of their business relationship. Put another way, it is an intranet that allows some access by authorised outsiders.

Question — Types of systems

Which of the following statements is **incorrect**?

(a) Expert systems exist that can help decide credit worthiness.
(b) A management information system is normally capable of producing exception reports.
(c) Batch processing systems are not appropriate if information is required to be up to date at all times.
(d) An expert system always provides the correct solution to a problem.

Answer

(d) An expert system can produce an incorrect answer. The answer produced by the system depends on the quality of the data and rules held by the system. The other statements are all correct.

Exam focus point

> This area of the syllabus is developing quickly. Ensure you keep up to date by wide reading of print and web based publications.

4 The systems development life cycle and project management

In the **early days** of computing, systems were developed in a fairly **haphazard** fashion and poorly planned. The consequences were often **badly designed** systems, which cost too much to make and which were not suited to users' needs.

As early as the 1960s, developers attempted to bring order to the development process. Since then, a number of **systems development life cycle** (SDLC) models have been created. The original 'typical' SDLC is sometimes referred to as the **waterfall model** – this is because it involves a **sequence** of stages in which the **output of each stage** becomes the **input for the next stage**.

> **Exam focus point**
>
> There are a number of different SDLC models, the syllabus does not specify which one the examiner prefers.

An example of a 'typical' SDLC model is explained below (this one has seven stages, some analysts prefer to combine various stages such as Analysis and Design).

Stage	Comment
Identification of a problem or opportunity	This starts with the initial suggestion that 'things could be done better' and may involve an analysis of the organisation's information requirements.
Feasibility study	This involves a review of the existing system and the identification of a range of possible alternative solutions. A feasible (technical, operational, economic, social) solution will be selected – or a decision not to proceed made.
System investigation	A fact finding exercise which investigates the existing system to assess its problems and requirements and to obtain details of data volumes, response times and other key indicators.
System analysis	Once the workings of the existing system have been documented, they can be analysed. This process examines why current methods are used, what alternatives might achieve the same, or better, results, and what performance criteria are required from a new system.
System design	System design will examine existing computerised and manual procedures, addressing, in particular, inputs, outputs, program design, file design and security. New processes will also be considered allowing a detailed specification of the new system to be produced.
System implementation	This stage carries development through from design to operations. It involves the acquisition (or writing) of software, program testing, file conversion or set-up, acquisition and installation of hardware and 'going live'.
Review, maintenance and operations	This is an ongoing process which ensures that the system meets the objectives set during the feasibility study, that it is accepted by users and that its performance is satisfactory.

4.1 Project management

Developing a new system, even with a framework such as the SDLC to go by, is no small or easy undertaking and it is important for the project to be **carefully managed** to ensure a successful result.

Projects are usually deemed successful if they are completed at the **specified level of quality, on time** and **within budget**.

Constraint	Comment
Quality	The end result should conform to the project specification. In other words, the result should achieve what the project was supposed to do.
Budget	The project should be completed without exceeding authorised expenditure.
Timescale	The progress of the project must follow the planned process, so that the 'result' is ready for use at the agreed date. As time is money, proper time management can help contain costs.

It is possible to add a fourth constraint: **scope** or **functionality**. This means that all the work that was specified has been done and all the deliverables have, in fact, been delivered.

An article in *Financial Management* (June 2006) helpfully summarises the factors that contribute to successful project delivery as follows:

(a) **Proper planning** with regard to time, cost and resource constraints.

(b) The **involvement of users** (among other key stakeholders) in development and delivery processes, to ensure that their needs are met (without subsequent changes).

(c) **Competent** and **committed project staff**, with the right skills.

(d) **Ownership by senior managers** on the basis of a clear business case.

(e) **Careful management of constraints**: control procedures for monitoring the pace, money/resource usage and conformance of the project.

(f) **Risk assessment and management**, allowing for risk reduction and contingency planning.

(g) **Clear criteria for business case** and **precise measurements of performance**, so that project success can be evaluated and lessons learned.

4.2 Controlling a project

Project managers often make use of sophisticated **software** and **systems** which enable them to control project activities, an example is **PRINCE** which was developed by the UK Government. The acronym PRINCE stands for PRojects IN Controlled Environments.

4.3 PRINCE2

The latest version of PRINCE, **PRINCE2** is now the *de facto* UK standard for systems project management and is widely used in other countries. The wide acceptance PRINCE has achieved is itself an important advantage to its use for managing projects, since it provides a common language for all participants.

Stage control is the process undertaken by the project manager to ensure that any given stage of the project remains on course. A project might consist of just one stage, of course.

PRINCE2 project control (Prince2, Axelos Ltd) includes a structure of reports and meetings as follows:

(a) A **project initiation** meeting agrees the scope and objectives of the project and gives approval for it to start.

(b) The completion of each project stage is marked by an **end stage assessment**, which includes reports from the project manager and the project assurance team. The next stage does not commence until its plans have been reviewed and approved.

(c) **Mid stage assessments** are optional and may arise if, for example, a stage runs for a particularly long time or it is necessary to start a new stage before the current one is complete.

(d) **Highlight reports** are submitted regularly by the project manager to their superiors. These reports are the main overall routine control mechanism and their frequency (often monthly) is agreed at project initiation. They are essentially progress reports and should include brief summaries of project schedule and budget status.

(e) The **checkpoint** is the main control device used by the project team itself. Meetings are held more frequently than highlight reports are prepared (possibly weekly) and provide a basis for continuing progress review by team leaders and members.

4.4 Project changes

Sometimes projects need to change, for example where a particular stage is **delayed** or **unforeseeable problems** occur. Other possible causes of changes to the original project plan include:

(a) The availability of **new technology**.
(b) **Changes** in **staff**.
(c) A realisation that **user requirements were misunderstood**.
(d) **Changes** in the **business environment**.
(e) **New legislation** eg on data protection.

The **earlier** a change is made the **less expensive** it should prove. However, changes will cost time and money and should not be undertaken lightly.

When considering a change **an investigation** should be conducted to discover:

(a) The **consequences** of **not implementing** the proposed change.
(b) The **impact** of the change on **time, cost** and **quality**.
(c) The **expected costs** and **benefits** of the change.
(d) The **risks associated with the change**, and with the status quo.

The process of ensuring that proper consideration is given to the impact of proposed changes is known as **change control**.

Another type of project management called **Agile** project management is better suited to projects that are susceptible to a lot of change. Traditional waterfall project management is increasingly being eschewed in favour of **Agile** project management, especially in software development. In agile project management, various small sections of the overall project called 'iterations' are completed at the same time over a relatively short period. These iterations can be re-worked and improved upon over the duration of the project, enabling continuous improvement. This approach makes it easier to change the scope of the project as a result of changing requirements, since it allows the project team to go back and modify work already done. It is harder to go back and change work in a waterfall project since each phase of the project needs to be completed before the next phase can occur.

Chapter Roundup

- Any system can be thought of in terms of **inputs**, **processing** and **outputs**.
- A system exists in an environment. An environment surrounds the system but is not part of it. A **system boundary** separates the system from its environment.
- Organisations require information for a range of purposes.
  - Planning
  - Controlling
  - Recording transactions
  - Performance measurement
  - Decision making
- Data can be **collected** from **within and beyond an organisation**. **Information systems** are used to convert this **data into information** and to **communicate** it to management at all levels.
- Different **types of information systems** exist with different characteristics – reflecting the different roles they perform.

Quick Quiz

1 What are the three component parts of a system?

   (1) ....

   (2) ....

   (3) ....

2 What do the following initials stand for?

   - EIS
   - MIS
   - DSS
   - KWS
   - OAS
   - TPS

3 Which of the following statements is **incorrect**?

   (a) Expert systems exist that can help decide credit worthiness.

   (b) A management information system is normally capable of producing exception reports.

   (c) Batch processing systems are not appropriate if information is required to be up to date at all times.

   (d) An expert system always provides the correct solution to a problem.

4 Which of the following is not a type of information system?

   (a) EIS
   (b) MIS
   (c) DWS
   (d) OAS

5 Put these elements of the SDLC into order:

   - Feasibility study
   - Identification of a problem or opportunity
   - System analysis
   - System design
   - System implementation
   - System investigation
   - Review, maintenance and operations

PART B BUSINESS INFORMATION TECHNOLOGY

Answers to Quick Quiz

1. Inputs, processes and outputs.

2.
   - Executive Information Systems (EIS)
   - Management Information Systems (MIS)
   - Decision Support Systems (DSS)
   - Knowledge Work Systems (KWS)
   - Office Automation Systems (OAS)
   - Transaction Processing Systems (TPS)

3. (d) An expert system can produce an incorrect answer. The answer produced by the system depends on the quality of the data and rules held by the system. The other statements are all correct.

4. (c) The others are: Executive Information System, Management Information System and Office Automation System.

5. Correct order:

   (i) Identification of a problem or opportunity
   (ii) Feasibility study
   (iii) System investigation
   (iv) System analysis
   (v) System design
   (vi) System implementation
   (vii) Review, maintenance and operations

End of Chapter Question

Systems Development Life Cycle (AIA May 09)

As part of an induction course for some new recruits to your organisation you have been asked to prepare some notes for a talk on the Systems Development Life Cycle. Describe the various stages of the Cycle to inform the new recruits.

(20 marks)

Computer hardware and software

Topic list	Syllabus reference
1 Hardware	6.9
2 Software	6.10

Introduction

Accounting staff do not need to have expert knowledge of computer hardware, and software to perform their roles effectively. However, since so much accounting work is now performed using computers, it is useful to have a working knowledge of the **tools of your trade**.

PART B   BUSINESS INFORMATION TECHNOLOGY

1 Hardware

1.1 A computer

FAST FORWARD

A computer may be defined as a device which will accept **input** data, **process** it according to certain rules and stores or **outputs** data.

Computers have traditionally been classified as supercomputers, mainframes, minicomputers and microcomputers (or **PCs**), but the distinctions are less distinct with modern systems.

Key term

A **computer** is a device which will accept input data, process it, and store or output the results.

Let's look more closely at the definition above.

(a) The **device** is actually a group of mechanical and electronic devices working together to accept **inputs**, **process** them and produce **output**.

(b) A computer processes data according to **rules**.

(c) A computer's operations are performed 'according to programmed **logical** and **arithmetic** rules.' The **arithmetic** element might be as simple as $x + y = z$. An example of a **logical rule** is 'if x does not contain a value then display an error message'.

A **computer** is therefore a mixture of physical, **tangible** things like keyboards, screens, circuits and cables (**hardware**) and **intangible** arithmetic and logical rules (**software**). Using electrical impulses, the two are connected and communicate with each other. A **peripheral** is a piece of equipment, such as a printer, that can be connected to a computer.

1.2 Computer hardware

Key term

Hardware means the various physical components which comprise a computer system, as opposed to the non-tangible software elements.

1.3 Types of computer

Computers can be **classified** as follows, starting with the most powerful:

- Supercomputers
- Mainframe computers, now sometimes called 'enterprise servers'
- Minicomputers (also called 'mid-range' computers)
- Microcomputers (also called Personal Computers – PCs, laptops, mobile devices)

Question   Computer systems experience

If you are studying at a university or college, discuss the types of computer systems fellow students have encountered. They will probably all have used PCs, laptops, and mobile devices such as a smartphone or tablet, but there may be some who have experience of larger systems.

> **Answer**
>
> There are a vast range of software products available. Fellow students may have experience of systems they have found to be particularly good, or particularly bad. Discussing system qualities and types should help your overall systems knowledge, and may prove useful when system purchases are being considered.

1.3.1 Supercomputers

Supercomputers are the most powerful computers. They are quite rare, and are not used in business. Supercomputers are able to process very **large amounts** of **data** very quickly. They are used for very complex calculations, particular in the fields of science and engineering, for example by astronomers tracking the movement of objects in outer space. Manufacturers of supercomputers include Cray and Fujitsu.

1.3.2 Mainframes

After supercomputers, the next most powerful computers are mainframes. A mainframe is a **very powerful** computer often used at the centre of a large computer system. The mainframe is linked by cable or other telecommunications links to a number of terminals. A mainframe has significantly **more processing power than a PC** and offers very **extensive data storage** facilities. Some people now refer to mainframes as 'Enterprise servers'. IBM is a well-known manufacturer of mainframe computers.

1.3.3 Minicomputers (midrange computers)

The term 'minicomputer' (also known as a 'midrange computer') is sometimes used to describe a computer that has **more processing power than a PC**, but **less than a mainframe**.

The term minicomputer isn't used very often now, as with the development of more powerful PCs and physically smaller mainframes, it is difficult to define exactly what a minicomputer is. Price, power and number of users supported are sometimes used as distinguishing features.

The most likely computer to fall in this category is a **network server**. This is a midrange computer in an organisation that acts a central source of data and programs which can be shared with other computer users in a network.

1.3.4 Personal computers (PCs)

The most common type of computer is the **Personal Computer** or PC. A PC is a general-purpose, single-user computer designed to be operated by one person at a time. The technical name for a PC is a **microcomputer**.

PCs are now the norm for small to medium-sized business computing and for home computing and provide access to the internet. Often they are linked together in a **network** to enable **sharing** of information between users.

The **physical components** of a typical Personal Computer (PC) are shown in the following diagram:

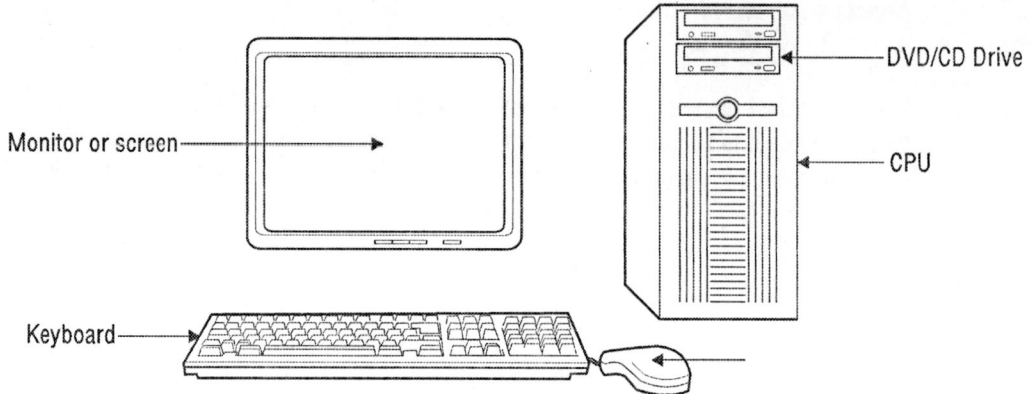

1.4 Other common descriptions of computers

We have described the four main categories of computers. You may also hear other descriptions of computers that relate to their role or some other characteristic. Some common example are:

- File servers
- Portables (or laptops)
- Macs
- Workstations

1.4.1 File servers

A file server is more powerful than the average desktop PC, although many file servers are in fact very powerful PCs. The file server provides **additional services** for users of networked PCs. We shall discuss these in more detail later in this chapter.

A very large network is likely to use a 'mainframe' computer as its server. Many mainframes are now often referred to as **'enterprise servers'**.

1.4.2 Portables (or laptops)

Laptop computers are popular as they are easy to transport, and therefore allow people to use their computer on the move or in a number of **different locations**. They also save desk **space**.

Laptops, are powered either from the mains electricity supply or through the use of a rechargeable battery. Laptops offer full functionality and many models include all the features of desktop PCs.

The availability of fast broadband internet access in many countries has enabled workers to work remotely away from the office, and 'on the move' using a laptop, rather than having to be fixed to their office desk. In addition to having internet access, workers can log on to their organisation's intranet, where they can access files and information in the company's servers, and communicate through a variety of methods including email, video calling, and webinars (live meetings held over the internet that included shared presentations, documents and software applications).

Laptops have some disadvantages, such as the following:

- Keyboard **ergonomics** (ie keys which are too small, or too close together for quick typing).
- **Battery power** is often limited.

1.4.2.1 Mobile devices

Mobile devices include smartphones (eg an Apple iPhone) and tablets (eg an Apple iPad). These are handheld devices with powerful processors that offer a range of functions using mobile friendly applications or 'apps'. **Touch-sensitive screens** on these devices allow the screen to be used as an input device. Selections are made by users touching areas of the screen. Sensors, built into the screen surround, detect which area has been touched. Although not as broadly functional as laptops, mobile devices are highly practical when users need access to information or need to communicate when they are on the move. For example, apps are available that facilitate voice calling, video calling, emailing, document viewing and editing. Hybrid laptops also exist that are laptops with a 'screen' that can also function as a tablet.

1.4.3 Workstations

The term workstation is sometimes used to describe a high performance personal computer used for a specialised purpose. However, the term is also now also often used to describe a person's desk, chair and computer – their immediate **working environment**.

1.4.4 Macs (Apple Macintosh computers)

Computers made by Apple Macintosh are often referred to as **Macs**. Introduced in 1984, the **Macintosh** or Mac is essentially a PC, although people generally don't include Macs when using the term PC. In the past, the Mac distinguished itself from other PCs by providing a user-friendly operating system that utilised windows, icons, and a mouse. The operating system called 'Windows' used on other PCs, copied many features from the Mac. There are now many different Macintosh models, with varying degrees of power. The operating system used by Macs is called 'Mac OS'.

1.5 PC parts and specifications

FAST FORWARD

> The **processor** is at the heart of any computer. It consists of an arithmetic and logic unit and a control unit. Important concepts are clock speed (MHz) and RAM.

1.5.1 The processor or CPU

Key term

> The **processor** or Central Processing Unit (CPU) is the collection of circuitry and registers that performs the processing in a computer. The processor is sometimes described as the 'brain' of the computer.

Two important components of the CPU are:

- The arithmetic and logic unit (ALU) which performs arithmetic and logical operations
- The control unit, which extracts instructions from memory and decodes and executes them

The set of operations that the processor performs is known as the **instruction set**.

1.5.2 Chips

On large machines, CPUs require one or more circuit boards. On personal computers and small workstations, the CPU is housed in a single **chip**. A chip is a small piece of silicon upon which is etched an integrated circuit, which consists of transistors and their interconnecting patterns on an extremely small scale. The chip is mounted on a carrier unit which in turn is 'plugged' on to a circuit board – called the **motherboard** – with other chips, each with their own functions, such as sound (a 'sound card') and video (a 'video card').

Many PCs carry a sticker saying 'Intel inside' – referring to the chips made by the Intel company. The other major manufacturer is AMD.

1.5.3 MHz, cycles and clock speed

The signals are co-ordinated by a **clock** which sends out a 'pulse' – a sort of tick-tock sequence called a **cycle** – at regular intervals. Processor speed is measured in the number of these cycles produced per second.

This speed is expressed in MegaHertz (MHz) or GigaHertz (GHz):

- 1 MHz = one **million** cycles per **second**
- 1 GHz = one **billion** cycles per **second**

1.5.4 The bus

A signal travels along an electronic path that is called a **bus** in computer jargon. A 'local bus' is a particularly fast route.

1.6 Memory

The computer's **memory** is also known as main store or internal store. Memory is used to store data within the processing unit while the computer is operating. The reason for holding programs in the memory is to **speed up processing**. However, a computer's memory is limited in its size, and can only hold a certain volume of data at any time.

The memory will hold the following:

(a) **Programs**. The control unit acts on program instructions that are held in the store; these program instructions include the operating system.

(b) Some **input data**. A small area of internal store is needed to take in the data that will be processed next.

(c) A **working area**. The computer will need an area of store to hold data that is currently being processed or is used for processing other data.

(d) Some **output data**. A small area of store is needed to hold temporarily the data or information that is ready for output to an output device.

1.6.1 Bits and bytes

Each individual storage element in the computer's memory consists of a simple circuit which can be switched **on** or **off**. These two states can be conveniently expressed by the numbers **1** and **0** respectively. Any piece of data or instruction must be coded in these symbols before processing can commence.

Each 1 or 0 is a **bit**. Bits are grouped together in groups of eight to form **bytes**. Most PCs use **32 bit** or **64 bit** processors. This means that data travels around from one place to another in groups of 32 or 64 bits.

The processing capacity of a computer is in part dictated by the capacity of its memory. Capacity is calculated in **kilobytes** (1 kilobyte = 2^{10} (1,024) bytes), **megabytes** (1 megabyte = 2^{20} bytes), **gigabytes** (2^{30}) and **terabytes** (2^{40}). These are abbreviated to Kb, Mb, Gb and Tb.

Question — Kilobytes, megabytes, gigabytes and terabytes

For convenience a kilobyte (1,024 bytes) is generally thought of as 1,000 bytes (hence the name **kilo**).

(a) Approximately how many bytes are there in a megabyte?
(b) Approximately how many megabytes are there in a gigabyte?
(c) Approximately how many gigabytes are there in a terabyte?

Answer

(a) 1 million or, more accurately, (2^{20} = 1,048,576)
(b) 1,000 or, more accurately, 1,024. ($2^{30}/2^{20}$ = 1,024)
(c) 1,000 or, more accurately, 1,024. ($2^{40}/2^{30}$ = 1,024)

1.7 Types of memory

A distinction can be made between two main types of memory, **RAM** and **ROM**. The term **cache** is also important.

1.7.1 RAM

Key term

> **RAM** (random access memory) is memory that is directly available to the processing unit. It holds the data and programs in current use. Data can be written on to or read from random access memory.

RAM can be defined as memory with the ability to access any location in the memory in any order with the same speed. **Random access** is an essential requirement for the main memory of a computer. RAM in microcomputers is **'volatile'** which means that the contents of the memory are **erased** when the computer's power is switched off.

The RAM on a typical modern business PC is likely to be around eight gigabytes. The size of the RAM is extremely important. A computer with a 3 GHz clock speed but only 4 GB of RAM will not be as efficient as a 3 GHz PC with 8Gb of RAM.

Question — Noise and light

When you start up a program on a PC you may hear a crackling noise, and see a little light flickering on the front of the base unit. What is happening?

Answer

The program is being read from the PC's hard disk into the Random Access Memory (RAM).

1.7.2 ROM

Key term

> **ROM** (read-only memory) is a memory chip into which fixed data is written permanently at the time of its manufacture. New data cannot be written into the memory – the data on the memory chip can't be changed.

ROM is **'non-volatile'** memory, which means that its contents do not disappear when the computer's power source is switched off. A computer's **start-up program**, known as a 'bootstrap' program, is always held in a form of a ROM. 'Booting up' means running this program.

When you turn on a PC you will usually see a reference to **BIOS** (basic input/output system). This is part of the ROM chip containing all the programs needed to control the keyboard, screen, disk drives and so on.

1.7.3 Cache

The **cache** is a small capacity but **extremely fast** memory chip which saves a second copy of the pieces of data most recently read from or written to main memory. When the cache is full, older entries are 'flushed out' to make room for new ones.

The principle is that if a piece of data is accessed once it is highly likely that it will be accessed again soon afterwards, and so keeping it readily to hand will speed up processing.

1.8 Input devices

1.8.1 The keyboard

Data may be input manually via a **keyboard**. Alternatively, data may be input using some **automated system**. The ideal method of data input in a given application is one which minimises input time, cost and errors.

The keyboard is the tool most often used for computer input. Keying data into a computer using a keyboard can be a **labour-intensive** process. In many cases the process of inputting data is speeded up through some form of automated **data capture**. We will look at automatic input devices later in this section.

1.8.2 Touch-sensitive screens

In section 1.4.2.1 we looked at the touch-sensitive screen of mobile devices such as smartphones, tablets and hybrid laptops/tablets. The touch-sensitive screen is both an output device which displays text and graphics, and an input device that allows the user to enter and select data by touching the screen.

1.8.3 Optical mouse

An **optical mouse** has a small light-emitting diode (LED) that bounces light off the surface the mouse is moved across. The mouse contains sensors that convert this movement into co-ordinates the computer can understand.

A typical mouse has two or three **buttons** which can be pressed (**clicked**) to send specific signals. For example, a 'click' on the left hand button can be used to send the cursor to a new cell in a spreadsheet and a 'double click' can select a particular application from a Windows menu. Most mice also have a **wheel** used to scroll within pages or documents that can't all be displayed on a single screen.

1.9 Automatic input devices

In the following paragraphs we explain some of the most common document reading methods. Document reading methods reduce the manual work involved in data input. This **saves time and money** and also **reduces errors**.

1.9.1 Magnetic ink character recognition (MICR)

Magnetic ink character recognition **(MICR)** involves the recognition by a machine of special formatted characters printed in magnetic ink. The characters are read using a specialised reading device. The main advantage of MICR is its speed and accuracy, but MICR documents are expensive to produce. The main commercial application of MICR is in the banking industry – on cheques and deposit slips.

1.9.2 Optical mark reading (OMR)

OMR involves the marking of a pre-printed form with a ballpoint pen or typed line or cross in an appropriate box. The card is then read by an OMR device which senses the mark in each box using an electric current and translates it into machine code. Applications in which OMR is used include **National Lottery** entry forms, and answer sheets for multiple choice questions in exams.

1.9.3 Scanners and Optical Character Recognition (OCR)

A scanner is device that can **read text or illustrations printed on paper** and translate the information into a **form the computer can use**. To edit text read by a scanner, you need **optical character recognition (OCR)** software to translate the image into text. Businesses may use a scanner and OCR to obtain 'digital' versions of documents they have only paper copies of. To enable the OCR software to recognise the characters correctly, the paper copy of the document must be good quality.

1.9.4 Bar coding and EPOS

Bar codes are groups of marks which, by their spacing and thickness, indicate specific codes or values. Electronic Point of Sale (EPOS) devices, which include bar code readers, enable supermarkets and other retailers to record and manage inventory movements – and provide detailed sales information.

1.9.5 EFTPOS

Many retailers use EFTPOS systems (**Electronic Funds Transfer** at the **Point of Sale**). An EFTPOS system involves making payment electronically using a customers debit or credit card. A small terminal is used which reads the customers details and processes payment from their bank account or credit card account.

1.9.6 Magnetic stripe cards

Credit and debit cards, and some other cards, contain data held on a thin strip of magnetic recording tape stuck to the back of the card. The magnetic card reader converts this information into directly computer-sensible form. The most common use of magnetic stripe cards is as bank credit or service cards. However the magnetic strip in these cards is becoming redundant due to the prevalence of smart chips contained in the cards.

1.9.7 Smart cards

Because of security concerns, magnetic stripe technology has been replaced by smart cards. The data on magnetic strip cards can be read, written, deleted or changed with equipment that is reasonably easy to obtain.

A smart card is a plastic card in which is embedded **a microprocessor chip**. The microprocessor replaces the 'usual' magnetic tape. The microprocessor is under a gold contact pad on one side of the card. The chip enables much **more effective security** checks to be made. The most common smart card applications include credit and debit cards. These have a microchip and require the user to enter a personal identification number (PIN) to authorise a transaction – referred to as 'chip and pin'. Some credit and debit smart cards have a contactless payment facility which allows the customer to make small purchases by simply touching the card on an electronic reader at the till in a shop. This facility is also available on 'prepaid' cards, which are similar to credit and debit cards but are pre-loaded with money.

Some smartphones enable contactless payment to be made in a similar way to smart cards, eg the Apple Pay app (application) for an iPhone. The consumer touches their phone on a reader at the till which actions payment from their credit/debit/prepaid card without having to present the card itself.

Another application of smart card technology is access and security systems. For example, access to buildings such as offices, universities and gyms is controlled by barriers or doors which require an authorised person to place a smart card on a reader for the barriers or doors to open. The smart card contains all relevant information about the person, including their level of access to different parts of the building. Often, a single card is used as an identity card and a smart card to gain access to buildings.

1.9.8 Voice recognition

Computer software has been developed that can convert speech into computer-sensible form via a microphone. Users are required to speak clearly and reasonably slowly.

1.10 Output devices

> **FAST FORWARD**
>
> **Output** is usually sent to either the **screen**, to a **printer**, or to another **computer file** – possibly for processing by another computer.

The commonest methods of computer output are printers and screen display. Sometimes output is produced in the form of a computer file.

1.10.1 Printers

Laser printers are now widespread. They print a whole page at a time, rather than line by line. The **quality** of output with laser printers is very **high**. Laser printers are relatively expensive to purchase, but compared with inkjet printers, running costs are relatively low.

Inkjet printers are small and reasonably cheap, making them popular where a 'private' output device is required. They work by sending a jet of ink on to the paper to produce the required characters. They are fairly quiet and fast, but they may produce smudged output if the paper is not handled carefully. The price and regularity with which ink cartridges need to be replaced mean that running costs can be high.

Multi-functional devices or MFDs are common in larger businesses. They are machines that have many features such as printing, photocopying and scanning to email. MFDs can be linked to the business's IT network which allows users within the company to send their printing to the machine from any device logged into the company's network.

1.10.2 The VDU or monitor

A VDU (visual display unit) or 'monitor' displays text and graphics. The screen's **resolution** is the number of pixels that are lit up. A **pixel** is a picture element – a 'dot' on the screen, as it were. The fewer the pixels on screen, the larger each individual pixel will be, so fewer pixels mean lower resolution or image quality. A larger number of smaller pixels will provide a higher resolution, better quality display. Touch-sensitive screens are both an output and an input device, as we saw earlier in the chapter.

1.10.3 The choice of output medium

Choosing a suitable output medium depends on a number of factors:

Factor	Comment
Hard copy	Is a printed version of the output needed?
Quantity	For example, a VDU screen can hold a certain amount of data, but it becomes more difficult to read when information goes 'off-screen' and can only be read a 'page' at a time.
Speed	For example if a single enquiry is required it may be quicker to make notes from a VDU display.
Suitability for further use	Output to a file would be appropriate if the data will be processed further, maybe in a different system.
Cost	The 'best' output device may not be justifiable on the grounds of cost – another output medium should be chosen.

10: COMPUTER HARDWARE AND SOFTWARE

Question
Manufacturers

The next time you are in a shop that sells computer equipment, identify two manufacturers for each of the following:

(a) PCs
(b) Printers and multi-functional devices

Answer

Major manufacturers include the following:

(a) PCs – Dell, Compaq, IBM, Sony
(b) Printers and multi-functional devices – Canon, Epson, Hewlett Packard, Lexmark

There are many others.

1.11 Storage devices

FAST FORWARD The most common type of storage is hard disk drives (HDD).

1.11.1 Hard disks

A modern business PC invariably has an **internal hard disk**. The disk is covered on both sides with a **magnetic** material. Data is held on a number of circular, concentric **tracks** on the surfaces of the disk, and is read or written by rotating the disk past read/write heads. The mechanism that causes the disk to rotate is called the hard disk drive (HDD). At the time of writing the average new **PC** has a hard disk size of around 1 Terabyte. Larger systems may use a stack of **removable hard disks**.

In larger businesses data is stored centrally on multiple hard drives of servers. This works on the same principle as a PC and a hard disk. As discussed earlier a server is a computer that acts a central source of data and programs which can be shared with other computer users in a network. The server has a number of hard disk drives for storage. A user can save file and from their PC to a folder in a networked server drive in the same way as saving to their internal hard drive.

1.11.2 Memory sticks

The memory stick (also known as a 'flash drive') is a small portable storage medium which can typically hold between 2 and 128 Gb of data (although 1Tb memory sticks are available). It is useful for storage and for moving files between computers. The memory stick is inserted into one of the computer's USB ports.

1.11.3 Optical disks

With the rise of affordable larger capacity storage mediums, the use of optical disks is becoming increasingly redundant. The main types of optical disks are **CD-ROM** (Compact Disc – Read Only Memory), **DVD** (Digital Versatile Disc) and **Blu-ray**. Optical disks are read from and written to using lasers. Blu-ray disks hold the highest amount of storage of optical disks.

1.11.4 Tape storage

Although hard disks are a more popular form of data storage, **Magnetic tape cartridges** have a **relatively large capacity** and are still widely used as a **backing storage** medium. Tapes are generally measured in terms of tape width and length. The width and length of the tape has a bearing on the amount of data that can be stored on the tape. Fast tapes which can be used to create a back-up file very quickly are known as **tape streamers**.

Tape storage is a cheaper form of storage than hard disk. However data has to be recorded **along the length** of a computer tape and so it is **more time consuming** to access a particular file than data on disk (ie direct access is not possible with tape – the tape has to be forwarded or rewound to the required location).

In 2015, IBM and Fujifilm announced they had developed storage tape able to hold up to 220 terabytes (TB) of data per cartridge.

1.11.5 Cloud storage

A more recent development is online storage or **cloud storage**. The person wanting to store data does not need to own the necessary hardware to do so. Instead they can buy cloud storage space and access from companies who own servers to hold the data. The customer uploads data to these servers, and accesses it as needed, via the internet. This is useful as data can be retrieved from any location, and even if the office burns down.

Cloud storage is often linked to **cloud computing**, whereby software applications are provided to computers and other devices over the internet. Data files that are created using the software are saved to the cloud and automatically backed up. Dedicated file storage or hosting services, such as DropBox, manage this data and give users access via the internet. They also offer services which allow data to be easily shared between authorised users and devices.

> **Exam focus point**
> Computer hardware is a key topic. Ensure that you know the different types of input and output devices.

2 Software

> **FAST FORWARD**
> **Operating system software** manages computer resources and supervises the running of other programs. It provides a 'bridge' between software programs and the hardware.

> **Key term**
> **Software** is the name given to programs or sets of programs that tell the computer what to do.

We now turn our attention to the sets of instructions (programs) used with computers. These are referred to as software.

There are two main types of software.

- The **operating system** provides the link between hardware and software, and it controls the interaction between the user and the computer, via the human-computer interface, or HCI.

- **Applications software** is any computer program designed to help the user perform a task — rather than to control the operation of the computer.

10: COMPUTER HARDWARE AND SOFTWARE

Question — Software packages

Name three software packages and state the role or type of the package.

Answer

There are many examples to choose from. Here are four.

(a) Microsoft Windows – the operating system for most PCs
(b) Microsoft Word – word processing software
(c) Microsoft Excel – spreadsheet software
(d) Sage 50 Accounts – an accounting package

2.1 The operating system

Key term

The **operating system** is concerned with the operation of the computer. It provides the link between the computer hardware, the user and other software.

An **operating system** is a program that provides the 'bridge' between **applications** software (such as word processing packages, spreadsheets or accounting packages) and the **hardware**. For example, access to data files held on disk during the processing of a business application would be managed by the operating system.

An operating system will typically perform the following tasks.

(a) Initial **set-up** of the computer once it has 'booted up' via the BIOS.
(b) Checking that **hardware** (including peripherals) is functioning properly.
(c) Calling up of program files and data files into **memory**.
(d) **Opening and closing** of files.
(e) Maintenance of **directories** (folders) in storage.
(f) Controlling **input and output** devices.
(g) Controlling system **security** (for example, monitoring the use of passwords).
(h) Handling of **interruptions** (for example, program abnormalities or machine failure).
(i) Managing **multitasking** (ie using more than one application at one time, for example printing out a Word document while you work on an Excel spreadsheet).

2.1.1 Microsoft Windows

FAST FORWARD

The most widely used operating system is **Microsoft Windows**, which is available in a range of versions for both PCs and networks. Other operating systems include the Mac OS system, Unix and Linux.

The most popular computer operating system, particularly for PCs and small networks, is Microsoft Windows.

Microsoft Windows includes the following features:

(a) A **'Desktop'**, which is a general area from which programs etc may be accessed. Shortcuts to disk drives, folders (directories), applications and files can all be placed on the Desktop.

(b) A **'Taskbar'** which includes the **Start** menu (from which applications may be launched) and which enables buttons to be added for chosen applications, providing quick access to the applications.

(c) A **Recycle Bin** for easy deletion and recovery of files.

(d) Easy integration with **networking** software.

(e) **Multitasking** is available, allowing more than one program to be active at one time.

(f) The **Internet Explorer and Edge** browsers are included.

Although (as with almost all software) it does contain bugs and irritations, Microsoft Windows provides a **comprehensive working environment**, managing programs specifically written for it. This makes it **easier for beginners** to learn, as applications tend to look and 'feel' the same.

Other features of Windows are explained in the table below:

Feature/area	Comment
User-friendly	User interface enhancements include easier navigation, such as **single-click launching** of applications, icon highlighting, forward/backward buttons, and an easy to customise Start Menu. Application packages written for Windows are generally **similar in design** providing a familiar look and feel. This **reduces training time** and costs and makes **skills transferable**.
Reliability	(a) Windows can be set up to regularly **test** the user's hard disk, system files, and configuration information to increase the system reliability, and in many cases fix problems automatically. (b) Enhanced **backup** and **restore** functions.
Web integration	**There are a variety of features designed to enhance internet access and use of internet facilities and technologies, and integrate them with the user's system.**
Multimedia	Windows has **graphics** and **video capabilities** and support for **games** hardware such as joysticks.
Graphical user interface (GUI)	Windows has a **user-friendly** GUI (some say this was copied from the Macintosh Operating System). Most dialogue between the user and software is conducted through the mouse and on-screen images rather than typed text. The GUI has certain features, explained below, which can be remembered by the abbreviation **WIMP** (which stands for 'Windows, Icons, Mouse and Pull-down menu').

2.2 Other operating systems

2.2.1 Mac OS

Apple Macintosh computers or **Macs** use a completely different operating system called **Mac OS**. Recent versions of the Mac OS and recent versions of Windows are increasingly able to use data files created on the 'other' system. Other competitors to Windows and the Mac OS exist, such as **Unix** and **Linux**.

2.2.2 Unix

The **UNIX operating system** was developed as a **non-proprietary** (ie not specific to one manufacturer) operating system. UNIX works equally well in a PC network environment or in a mainframe system. Particular areas where UNIX has demonstrated its capabilities are **communications**, where the ability to accommodate PC operating systems in the UNIX environment supports the use of electronic mail, and **engineering**, where UNIX's capabilities are suited to driving high-resolution graphics systems.

2.2.3 Linux

Linux is a freely-distributable operating system that runs on many hardware platforms, including networks, PCs and Macs. Linux has become a popular alternative to more traditional operating systems.

Question — Operating systems

List five tasks typically performed by an operating system.

Answer

The operating system performs the following tasks:

(a) Initial set-up of the computer once it has 'booted up'
(b) Checking that the hardware (including peripheral devices such as printers) is functioning properly
(c) Calling up of program files and data files into memory
(d) Opening and closing of files and folders
(e) Controlling input and output devices, including the interaction with the user
(f) Controlling system security (for example, monitoring the use of passwords)
(g) Handling of interruptions (for example, program abnormalities or machine failure)
(h) Managing multitasking

2.3 Applications software

FAST FORWARD

> Software which processes data for a particular purpose, or which is written for a particular data processing function, is known as **applications software**. An example is a payroll package.
>
> **General purpose software** allows data to be handled in a particular way, for example Windows Explorer, but its specific use in a particular situation is determined by the user.
>
> The term **integrated software** is generally used in two different situations. Accounts packages often consist of individual program **modules** that link together while some packages include programs that provide a **range of tools**, such as word processing, spreadsheets and a database.

Key term

> **Applications software** consists of programs which carry out a task for the user as opposed to programs which control the workings of a computer.

2.3.1 Application packages

An **application package** is a program or set of programs that will carry out a specific processing application or job – for example, a payroll package is used for payroll processing. Application packages may be either written from scratch or purchased off the shelf. **Off the shelf** application packages are available for a wide range of business applications and provide a tested and cheaper means of obtaining a program than would be the case writing the programs from scratch.

2.3.2 General purpose packages

A **general purpose package** is an off the shelf program that can be used for processing of a general type, but the computer user can apply the package to a variety of uses. Windows is a general purpose package.

2.3.3 Integrated software

Integrated software refers to programs, or packages of programs, that perform a variety of different processing operations, using **data which is compatible** with whatever operation is being carried out. The term is generally used in two different situations.

(a) **Accounts packages** often consist of individual program **modules** that link together into a complete accounting system. For example, there will be a receivables ledger module, a payables ledger module a general ledger module and so on. Output from one 'module' in an integrated system can be used as input to another, without the need for re-entry of data.

(b) Some software packages include programs that provide a **range of tools**, such as word processing, spreadsheets and a database. An example of an integrated software package is Microsoft Office (a collection of high specification programs including spreadsheet and word processing software).

> **Exam focus point**
>
> Past exam questions on computer software have been general questions and will not require detailed knowledge of any particular package.

Chapter Roundup

- A computer may be defined as a device which will accept **input** data, **process** it according to certain rules and stores or **outputs** data.

- Computers have traditionally been classified as supercomputers, mainframes, minicomputers and microcomputers (or **PCs**), but the distinctions are less distinct with modern systems.

- The **processor** is at the heart of any computer. It consists of an arithmetic and logic unit and a control unit. Important concepts are clock speed (MHz) and RAM.

- Data may be **input** manually via a **keyboard**. Alternatively, data may be input using some **automated system**. The ideal method of data input in a given application is one which minimises input time, cost and errors.

- **Output** is usually sent to either the **screen**, to a **printer**, or to another **computer file** – possibly for processing by another computer.

- The most common type of storage is hard disk drives (HDD).

- **Operating system software** manages computer resources and supervises the running of other programs. It provides a 'bridge' between software programs and the hardware.

- The most widely used operating system is **Microsoft Windows**, which is available in a range of versions for both PCs and networks. Other operating systems include the Mac OS system, Unix and Linux.

- Software which processes data for a particular purpose, or which is written for a particular data processing function, is known as **applications software**. An example is a payroll package.

- **General purpose software** allows data to be handled in a particular way, for example Windows Explorer, but its specific use in a particular situation is determined by the user.

- The term **integrated software** is generally used in two different situations. Accounts packages often consist of individual program **modules** that link together while some packages include programs that provide a **range of tools**, such as word processing, spreadsheets and a database.

PART B BUSINESS INFORMATION TECHNOLOGY

Quick Quiz

1. Which one of the following options describes the term 'hardware'?

    (a) A set of programs that tell the computer what to do
    (b) A system of linked PCs
    (c) The various physical components which comprise a computer system
    (d) A storage device

2. The most powerful computers are known as:

    (a) Special computers
    (b) Super computers
    (c) Mainframe computers
    (d) Personal computers

3. Which one of the following options is sometimes described as the brain of the computer?

    (a) The ROM
    (b) The file server
    (c) The central processing unit (CPU)
    (d) The RAM

4. Memory that is directly available to the processing unit is called?

    (a) RAM
    (b) ROM
    (c) REM
    (d) RUM

5. Which one of the following is an output device?

    (a) A keyboard
    (b) A scanner
    (c) A smart card
    (d) A printer

6. Two statements follow about the operating system:

    (1) An operating system is a program that provides the 'bridge' between applications software and the hardware.

    (2) An operating system controls input and output devices.

    Are the above statements true or false?

    (a) Both are false
    (b) Both are true
    (c) Statement (1) is false but statement (2) is true
    (d) Statement (1) is true but statement (2) is false

7. Which one of following options is not an operating system?

    (a) Unix
    (b) Linux
    (c) Word
    (d) MacOS

Answers to Quick Quiz

1. (c) Option (a) refers to software. Option (b) refers to a local area network.
2. (b) Option (a) is fictitious. Mainframe and PCs are not as powerful as supercomputers.
3. (c) The CPU is the collection of circuitry and registers that performs the processing in a computer.
4. (a) Random access memory (RAM) is memory that is directly available to the processing unit.
5. (d) A printer. The other options are input devices.
6. (b) Both statements are true.
7. (c) Word. The others are operating systems.

End of Chapter Question

Hospital (AIA May 14)

As the IT trainer within a large hospital, you are required to develop new training programmes aimed at various administrative and support staff groups. You are making the assumption for the introductory training that the participants have no previous IT experience.

Required

Prepare notes to describe the concepts of computer hardware, computer software and communications technology aimed at these newly recruited employees with no previous IT experience. **(10 marks)**

PART B BUSINESS INFORMATION TECHNOLOGY

Managing data and information

Topic list	Syllabus reference
1 Data collection and storage	6.11
2 Data and information sources	6.11
3 The data hierarchy	6.11
4 Databases and database systems	6.11
5 Data storage models	6.11
6 Data modelling and design	6.11
7 Database implementation	6.11
8 Big Data	6.11

Introduction

In this chapter we consider the role played by data and databases within an organisation.

Data feeds an organisation's information systems. There is no point investing heavily in high quality information systems unless the data that feeds them is of an equally high standard – accurate, appropriate and up to date.

Most systems utilise databases in some way. In this chapter we explain how data and databases are structured and how they should be managed.

1 Data collection and storage

FAST FORWARD

Organisations need to collect and store data for a number of reasons:

- To record transactions
- For planning purposes
- To facilitate control
- To enable performance to be measured
- To facilitate decision-making

Key terms

Data are the raw material for data processing. Data consists of numbers, letters and symbols and relates to facts, events, and transactions.

Information is data that have been processed in such a way as to be meaningful to the person who receives it.

1.1 Recording transactions

Data relating to each business transaction or event is required for a number of reasons. Documentation of transactions can be used as **evidence** in a case of dispute. There may be a **legal requirement** to record transactions, for example for accounting and audit purposes. Detailed information on production costs can be built up allowing a better **assessment of profitability**. Similarly, labour utilised in providing a particular service can be measured. Information systems **capture transactions data**.

1.2 Planning

Organisations make **decisions** on a day to day basis. Once decisions are made, it is necessary to plan how to implement the steps necessary to make them effective. Planning requires data and information relating to available resources, possible time-scales for implementation and the likely outcome under alternative scenarios. Data feeds information systems that provide **planning tools**.

1.3 Controlling

Once a plan is implemented, data is required to assess **whether it is proceeding as expected** or whether there is some unexpected deviation from the plan. It may consequently be necessary to take some form of corrective action. Data captured by information systems can be used to **monitor** and **control** the outcomes of plans.

1.4 Performance measurement

Just as individual operations need to be controlled, so overall performance must be measured in order to enable **comparisons against budget or plan** to be made. This may involve the collection of data relating to, for example, costs, revenues, volumes, time-scale and profitability. The **collection**, **analysis** and **presentation** of such data can be performed by information systems.

1.5 Decision making

Data and information is also required to make **informed decisions**. There are information systems available that **support** the decisions of an **organisation's senior management**.

2 Data and information sources

FAST FORWARD

Data and information captured and stored in an organisation's information systems comes from a variety of **internal** and **external** sources.

Data and information collected and then utilised by information systems comes from both inside and outside the organisation.

2.1 Internal information

This is data collected from **within the organisation**. Capturing such data involves the following:

(a) A **system** for collecting or measuring **transactions** data – for example sales, purchases, inventory turnover and so on. This sets out procedures for **what** data is **collected**, how frequently, by whom, and by what methods, and how it is **processed**, and **filed** or **communicated**.

(b) **Informal communication** of information between **managers and staff** (for example, by word of mouth or at meetings).

(c) **Communication between managers**.

The following are examples of internal information.

2.1.1 Accounting records

Accounts receivable ledgers, **accounts payable** ledgers, **general ledgers**, **cash books** and other accounting records hold information that may be of great value outside the accounts department, for example sales information for the marketing function.

To maintain the integrity of its accounting records, an organisation operates **controls** over transactions. These also give rise to valuable information. An inventory control system, for example, will include details of purchase orders, goods received notes, goods returned notes and so on, which can be analysed to **provide management information** about speed of delivery, say, or the quality of supplies.

2.1.2 Staff records

Information about **staff** (employees) will be held, possibly linked to the **payroll** system. Additional information may be obtained from this source if, say, a project is being costed and it is necessary to ascertain the availability and rate of pay of different levels of staff, or the need for and cost of recruiting staff from outside the organisation.

2.1.3 Production data

Much information will be produced by a **production** department about machine capacity, fuel consumption, movement of people, materials, work in progress, set up times, maintenance requirements and so on.

2.1.4 Timesheets

Many **service** businesses, notably accountants and solicitors, need to keep detailed records of the **time spent** on various activities, both to justify fees to clients and to assess the efficiency and profitability of operations.

2.2 External data and information

Organisations often need to collect information concerning environmental factors. The following table describes some of these factors using the popular PEST framework (Political, Economic, Social and Technological).

Factor	Comment
Political/legal	National or local politics may affect how an organisation operates. Changes in legislation may put new responsibilities or liabilities on an organisation.
Economic	Economic factors affect an organisation's finances such as the availability of loans or sales levels.
Social	Society's views may put pressure on how the organisation is run, for example pressure to reduce environmental pollution.
Technological	Technological advances may affect an organisation's production and/or management processes. Technology may also allow the development of new products and services which were not previously possible.

Other areas an organisation may require external data and information on include:

(a) **Competitors** – how successful are they, are they developing new products?

(b) **Customers** – what are their needs, how large is the potential market, are there any new market segments?

(c) **Suppliers** – what are their prices, what is the quality of their products like, are there any new potential suppliers in the market?

Capturing data from outside the organisation might be entrusted to particular individuals, or might be 'informal'.

Routine formal collection of data from outside sources includes the following:

(a) A company's **tax specialists** will be expected to gather information about changes in tax law and how this will affect the company.

(b) Obtaining information about any new legislation on health and safety at work, or employment regulations.

(c) **Research and development** (R & D) work often relies on information about other R & D work being done by another company or by government institutions.

(d) **Marketing managers** need to know about the opinions and buying attitudes of potential customers. To obtain this information, they might carry out market research exercises.

Informal gathering of information from the environment **goes on all the time, consciously or unconsciously,** because the employees of an organisation learn **what is going on in the world around** them – perhaps from newspapers, online articles, television reports, meetings with business associates or the trade press.

3 The data hierarchy

The way in which computer data is stored can be viewed as a **hierarchy** as follows: bit, byte, data field, field, record, file and database.

3.1 The data hierarchy

Computer data is made up of a hierarchy: bit, field, record, file and database (as explained below).

3.1.1 Bit

As we mentioned in Chapter 10, the smallest item of computer storage is referred to as a bit.

3.1.2 Byte (or character)

Eight bits create a byte of data that can represent a single character, for example a letter.

3.1.3 Data field

Several characters combine to form a data field, for example an account balance. Other names for a data field are 'attribute,' 'column,' or simply 'field.'

3.1.4 Record

At the fourth level, data fields combine to form a complete record. A database record stores all the information about one file entity, for example one employee in a payroll file.

Record structure

The data fields in each record are referred to collectively as the record structure. In many accounting applications, this structure is fixed, meaning that each record contains the same number, same type, and same-sized data fields as every other record on the file. This would probably be the case for payroll records.

In other applications, either the number of data fields in each record might vary, or the size of a given data field in each record might vary. For example, in a file of customer complaints, the memo field in each record might vary in length to accommodate different-sized descriptions of customer problems.

Primary key or key field

The primary key is the data field in each record that enables a database system to uniquely distinguish one record from another. In a payroll record, the primary key might be the employee's Social Security number. Other organisations may allocate each employee a unique employee number and use this as the key field. The primary key enables users and computer programs to find a specific record.

It is possible to search a database using data fields which are not unique across records, for example a payroll file could be searched by surname.

Data fields from a payroll record

Employee number (key field)	Surname	First name	Social security number	Start date	Dept	Hourly rated?	Rate
E01046	Walsh	Barry	NR123456 Z	01/01/20X0	M	Y	$22.50

3.1.5 File (or table)

At the fifth level of the data hierarchy, a set of common records forms a file, or using Microsoft Access terminology, a table. A file or table contains a set of related records, for example a set of employee or customer records.

Master files store relatively permanent or static information, for example, part number and part description for an individual inventory record. **Transaction files** typically store transient information, for example inventory purchases and issues for a specific time period.

3.1.6 Database

Finally, at the highest level, several tables or files create a database, for example a collection of files that contain all the information for an accounting application. In an inventory module, for example, this database might contain a part-number master table, a supplier table, a price table, an order transaction table, and so on.

4 Databases and database systems

FAST FORWARD

The term '**database system**' is used to describe a wide range of systems that utilise a **central pool of data**.

Key terms

A **database** is a collection of data organised to service many applications. The database provides convenient access to data for a wide variety of users and user needs.

A **data warehouse** can be used to store vast amounts of operational and historical data in accessible form. Analytical and query software can then be used so that reports can be produced at any level of summarisation, and incorporate any comparisons or relationships desired.

A **database management system (DBMS)** is the software that centralises data and manages access to the database. It is a system which allows numerous applications to extract the data they need without the need for separate files.

The term 'database system' is used to describe a wide range of systems that utilise a central pool of data.

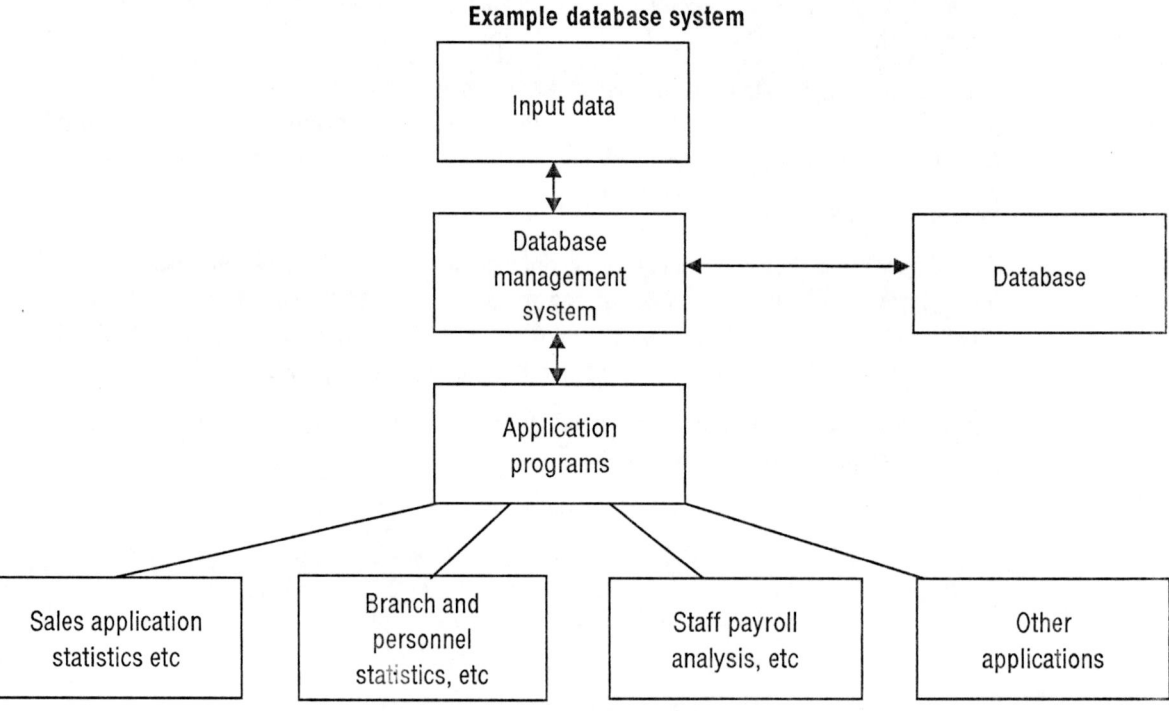

Example database system

Some of the more popular relational database management systems include:

- Microsoft Access
- DB2 from IBM
- Microsoft SQL Server
- MySQL – an open source DBMS
- Oracle RDBMS

4.1 The characteristics of a database system

The way in which data is held on a system affects the ease with which the data is able to be accessed and manipulated. A database system has the following characteristics:

(a) **Shared**. Different users are able to access the same data for their own processing applications. This removes the need to hold the same data in different files.

(b) **Controls** to preserve the **integrity** of the database.

(c) **Flexibility**. The database system should provide for the **needs of different users**, who each have their own processing requirements and data access methods. The database should be capable of **evolving** to meet **future** needs.

4.1.1 Database queries

A database can be interrogated by a **query language**. A query language is a formalised method of constructing queries in a database system. A query language provides the ways in which you ask a database for data. Some query languages can be used to change the contents of a database. SQL, short for **Structured Query Language**, is a popular language.

4.2 Advantages of database systems

The **advantages** of a database system include the following:

(a) Avoidance of **unnecessary duplication** of data (data redundancy).

(b) Data is looked upon as serving the **organisation as a whole**, not just for individual departments. The database concept encourages management to regard data as a resource that must be **properly managed**.

(c) The installation of a database system encourages management to **analyse data**, relationships between data items, and how data is used in different applications.

(d) **Consistency** – because data is only held once, the possibility of departments holding conflicting data on the same subject is reduced.

(e) Data on file is independent of the user programs that access the data. This allows **greater flexibility** in the ways that data can be used. New programs can be easily introduced to make use of existing data in a different way.

(f) Developing **new application programs** with a database system is easier because the programmer is not responsible for the file organisation.

4.3 Disadvantages of database systems

The **disadvantages** of database systems relate mainly to security and control:

(a) There are problems of **data security** and **data privacy**. There is potential for unauthorised access to data. Administrative procedures for data security must supplement software controls.

(b) Since there is only one set of data, it is essential that the data should be **accurate** and free from corruption.

(c) Since data is held once, but its use is widespread, the impact of **system failure** would be greater.

(d) If an organisation develops its own database system from scratch, **initial development costs** will be high.

5 Data storage models

FAST FORWARD

There are four main types of **database storage models** – hierarchical, network, relational and object-oriented.

5.1 The hierarchical model

The hierarchical model shows data in a tree-like format. Upper segments of the model are connected to lower segments in a parent-child relationship. A parent can have more than one child, but a child can have only set of parents. Such relationships can be expressed conveniently in a **hierarchy**. Each data item is related to only one item above it in the hierarchy, but to any number of data items below it.

In a customer database, for example, the hierarchical model might be used to show customers and customer orders. An extract from a **parts department database** might be structured as follows:

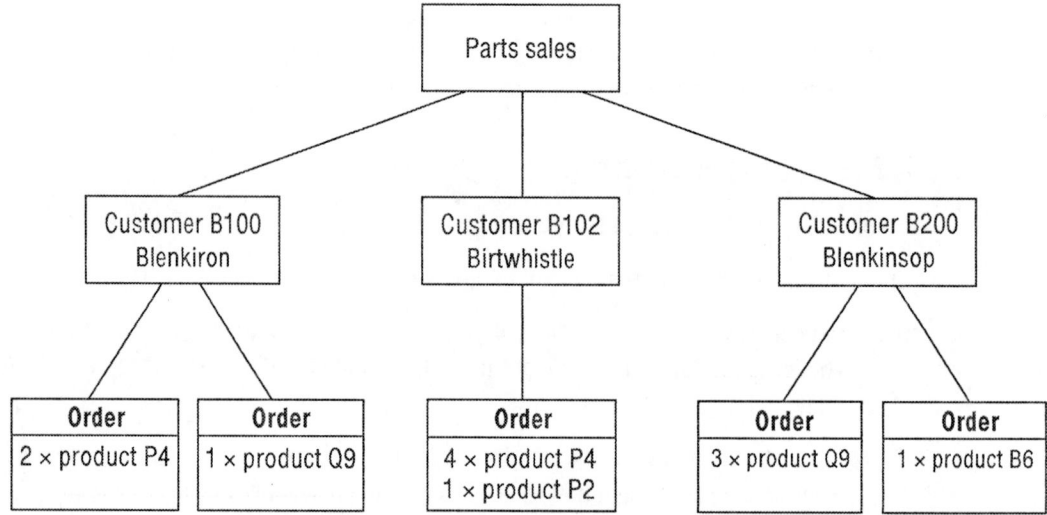

Hierarchical structures are appropriate when systems must handle large numbers of routine requests for information eg an airline reservation system. The hierarchical nature of the model makes it unsuitable for situations involving 'many-to-many' relationships.

5.2 The network model

The main advantage of a network database over the hierarchical model is that relationships can be established between the parent and child in both directions. This means that a child table can have multiple parents and a parent table can be linked to multiple child tables.

The network database model makes it much easier to build more complex databases, however, the user still must have a good understanding of the underlying structure to efficiently access and manage the data.

Returning to our part sales example, a network model is shown below:

```
   B100: Blenkiron          B102: Birtwhistle         B200: Blenkinsop
   /          \            /            \             /            \
B100: 2×P4  B100: 1×Q9  B102: 4×P4  B102: 1×P2   B200: 3×Q9   B200: 1×B6

   P2: Pin 2mm        P4: Pin 4mm        Q9: Quagga         B6: Bolt
```

5.3 The relational model

The relational database model is the most commonly used today. The model organises data elements in a series of **tables** consisting of rows and columns. A row represents a record (or entity). Each column is a field or attribute eg address, telephone number, part number.

Changes made in one portion of the database are propagated throughout the database through the usage of integrity constraints and relational links.

The **primary key** is used to identify a record. Data in one table can point to data in another table, as long as there is one data attribute that exists in both tables.

Customer table

B100	Blenkiron
B102	Birtwhistle
B200	Blenkinsop

Product table

B6	Bolt
P2	Pin 2mm
P4	Pin 4mm
Q9	Quagga

Order table

B100	P4	2
B100	Q9	1
B102	P4	4
B102	P2	1
B200	Q9	3
B200	B6	1

Data from these tables can be extracted and or linked provided that any two share a common data element. For example, the customer code could be used to link the Customer table with the Order table. Once the link has been established between two or more tables a query can permit any combination of the data from the tables to be viewed.

These views are obtained by using enquiry tools such as Structured Query Language (SQL). This permits an application to create a unique data set (record) from a common set of data (database) in a fashion that meets the application requirements. The two main benefits of a relational database are quick access to data and the easily implemented data integrity.

5.4 Object-oriented database

Object-oriented databases emerged in the mid-1980s, but relational databases remain the most popular.

The main difference with an object-oriented database is that database 'records' are treated as properties of an object rather than as a group of related fields. Links can be established between different objects and their associated properties and classes. Objects may hold other objects, allowing them to inherit properties.

The technical aspects of what exactly defines an object-orientated database and how such a database operates are relatively difficult to understand without a background in computer systems and object-orientated programming. These aspects are beyond the scope of this syllabus.

For our purposes, it is sufficient to know that object-orientated databases exist, and their main benefit is that modern programming languages are based around the use of objects and the ability of objects to automatically inherit properties from other objects.

Some computing observers recognise another type of database, the object-relational database. This combines aspects of the relational model with concepts from the object-oriented model. This model may eventually become the industry standard, but currently there are no recognised international standards.

As a result, databases built using this model are proprietary and may have compatibility issues with other implementations.

> **Exam focus point**
>
> Exam questions could test your knowledge and understanding of the different data storage models.

6 Data modelling and design

> **FAST FORWARD**
>
> An **Entity Relationship Model (ERM)** may be used to establish and model the logical data requirements of a system.

To ensure data is able to be used effectively, databases must be designed effectively and the data organised efficiently. There are several modelling techniques available to help plan and design a database.

6.1 A static structure model (Entity Relationship Model)

An **Entity Relationship Model** (ERM) (also known as an entity model or a logical data structure) provides an understanding of the logical data requirements of a system independently of the system's organisation and processes. An ERM is an example of a **static structure model**.

When talking about data and databases, an **entity** is an item (a person, a job, a business, an activity, a product, an inventory item and so on) about which information is stored. An **attribute** is a characteristic or property of an entity. For a customer, the main attributes include customer name and address, amounts owing, date of invoices sent and payments received, credit limit.

An ERM can show four relationships:

- One-to-one relationship (1:1)
- One-to-many relationship (1:M)
- Many-to-one relationship (M:1)
- Many-to-many relationship (M:M)

6.1.1 One-to-one relationship (1:1)

With a one-to-one relationship, an entity is related to only one of the other entity shown. For example, a one-to-one relationship exists between **company** and **finance director**. The model below shows one company which employs one finance director. These diagrams are sometimes called Bachmann diagrams.

Company — employs — Finance director

6.1.2 One-to-many relationship (1:M)

For example, the relationship **employs** also exists between **company** and **director**. The company employs more than one director.

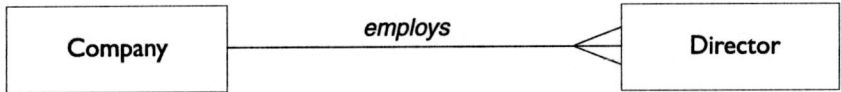

6.1.3 Many-to-one relationship (M:1)

This is really the same as the previous example, but **viewed from the opposite direction**. For example, many **sales managers** report to one **sales director**.

6.1.4 Many-to-many relationship (M:M)

The relationship between **product** and **part is many-to-many**. A product is composed of many parts, and a part might be used in many products.

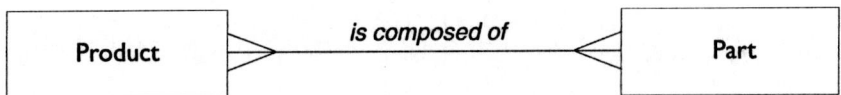

When analysing relationships the correct classification is important. If the one-to-many relationship customer order contains part numbers is incorrectly described as one-to-one, a system designed on the basis of this ERM might allow an order to be entered with one item and one item only.

Example: Building an ERM

A diagram modelling part of a warehousing and despatch system is shown below. This indicates that:

(a) A customer may make many orders.

(b) That an order form can contain several order lines.

(c) That each line on the order form can only detail one product, but that one product can appear on several lines of the order.

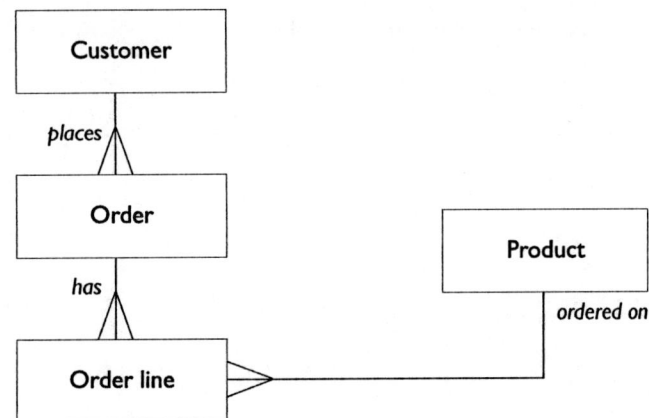

6.2 An event model (Entity Life History)

As we have seen, Entity Relationship Models take a static view of data. We will now look at a modelling tool that focuses on **data processes**.

An **Entity Life History** (ELH) shows the processes that happen to an entity. An ELH is a type of **event model**.

Data items do not always remain unchanged – they may come into existence by a specific operation and be destroyed by another. For example, a customer order forms part of a number of processes, and is affected by a number of different events. At its simplest, an entity life history displays the following structure.

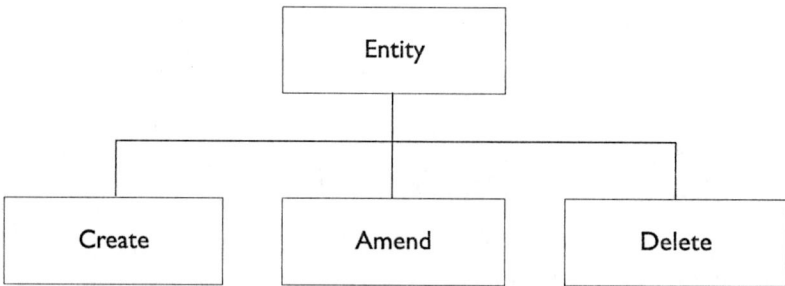

Entity life histories identify the various states in which an entity can legitimately be. It is really the functions and events which cause the state of the entity to change that are being analysed, rather than the entity itself.

The following notation rules are used for Entity life histories.

(a) Three symbols are used. The main one is a rectangular box. Within this may be placed an asterisk or a small circle, as explained below.

(b) At the top level the first box (the 'root node') shows the entity itself.

(c) At lower levels the boxes represent events that affect the life of the entity.

(d) The second level is most commonly some form of 'create, amend, delete', as explained earlier (or birth, life, death if you prefer). The boxes are read in **sequence** from top to bottom and left to right.

(e) If an event may affect an entity many times (**iteration**) this is shown by an **asterisk** in the top right hand corner of the box. A customer account, for example, will be updated many times.

(f) If events are alternatives (**selection**) – for example, accept large order or reject large order – a **small circle** is placed in the top right hand corner.

Note. There are three types of process logic referred to above:

- Sequence
- Iteration (or repetition)
- Selection

A simple example follows:

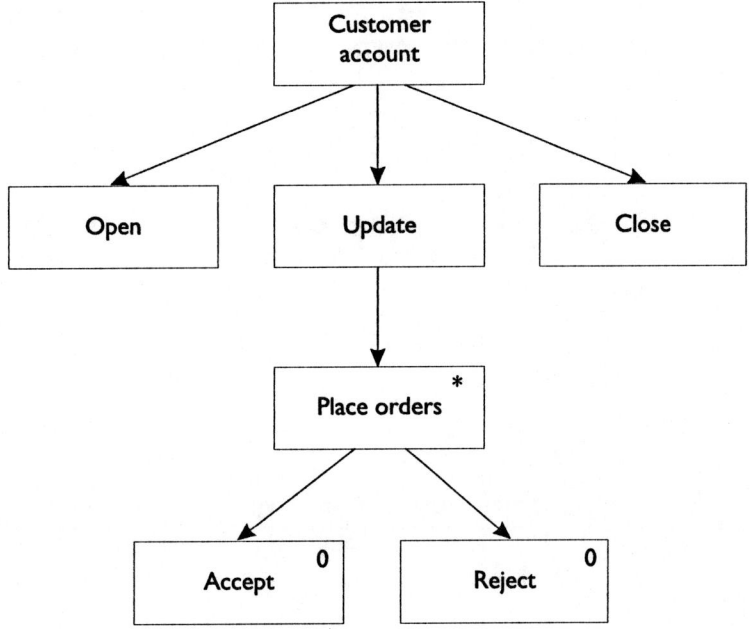

7 Database implementation

FAST FORWARD

Database **implementation** should be **formally planned** and **managed** to ensure the database is fit for purpose.

Implementing a database requires formal planning. Many of the steps involved are similar to other systems implementation projects.

Step 1: Define the scope of the project and the proposed database

- Identify the groups and functions within the organisation that will be served by the database.
- Identify the existing applications that will be converted to the database system.
- Prepare project proposal and obtain management approval.

Step 2: Organise the project

- Appoint a project manager and select the Database Administrator (DBA).
- Form a database design team.
- Establish regular meetings and periodic management reporting for design team.

Step 3: Select the Database Management System (DBMS)

- Document the database requirements in a formal request for tender document.
- Appraise the tenders.
- Select the DBMS vendor.

Step 4: Develop an implementation plan

- Identify data and files to be included.
- Estimate developer hours required to modify applications programs.
- Estimate support hours required to verify data using conversion.
- Develop implementation timetable.

Step 5: Design the database and the infrastructure

- Identify detailed data requirements.
- Determine data structure.
- Decide where in the organisation's IT infrastructure the database will be located.
- Identify hardware requirements.
- Decide security measures.
- Finalise and approve design specifications.

Step 6: Training

- Establish training requirements and the training schedule.
- Train programmers and the DBA.

Step 7: Generate a test database

- Programmers code database framework and DBMS.
- Code conversion programs for data to be transferred.
- Generate the database.
- Test and debug.
- Review and approve test results.

Step 8: Develop a detailed data conversion plan

- Plan programming assignments for each program to be modified and each data file to be converted.
- Schedule users to verify and correct file contents.
- Prepare conversion schedule and obtain approval from all involved.

Step 9: Incorporate existing applications and train database users

- If possible incorporate one application at a time into the new database.
- Ensure users are trained and are able to operate the database.
- Approve revised applications as they are converted.
- Begin using database for new applications.

Step 10: Fine-tune the database

- Speak to users and monitor DBMS data and modify database as required.
- Ensure database security is robust and working as intended.

Step 11: Periodically review database performance

- Ensure the database is operating as intended.
- Evaluate the database and the project.

Question — Quality

What is a database management system (DBMS)?

Answer

A database management system (DBMS) is the software that manages access to a database. The DBMS enables numerous applications to operate from the database without the need for separate files.

8 Big Data

FAST FORWARD

Big Data analytics is a term used to describe the extraction of meaning from vast quantities of data. Organisations are particularly interested in identifying trends and correlations in the data that they collect and store with the aim of putting this to commercial use.

Laney suggests that Big Data is comprised of 3 Vs (volume, velocity and variety).

Although the rise of Big Data analytics brings benefits, critics argue that it simply represents the latest buzzword and has not delivered the ground breaking discoveries initially thought possible.

8.1 What is Big Data?

Big Data is an emerging technology that has implications across all business departments. It involves the collection and analysis of large amounts of data to find trends, understand customer needs and help organisations to focus resources more effectively. The term 'Big Data' is used to describe the exponential growth and availability of data, both structured and unstructured. In a commercial setting 'Big Data' is being used to identify trends that may exist in vast quantities of data in the pursuit of value creation. Historically, organisations have been restricted as to the amount of data that they can process due to the storage limitations of existing computer systems. Due to the emergence of 'cloud based' data storage providers and improved computer technologies, these problems are gradually being overcome.

8.2 The 3 V's

Big Data has a role to play in information management. Laney suggests that 'Big Data' can be defined by considering the three V's: volume, velocity and variety.

	Comment
Volume	The volume of data generated is a key feature of 'Big Data'. The quantity of data now being produced is being driven by social media and transactional based data sets recorded by large organisations, for example data captured from in-store loyalty cards and till receipts.
	Data is also now being derived from the increasing use of 'sensors' in business and even outside of business (for example the use of data from traffic control systems to identify traffic jams).
Velocity	Velocity refers to the speed at which 'real time' data is being streamed into the organisation. To make data meaningful it needs to be processed in a reasonable time frame.
Variety	Modern data takes many different forms. Structured data may take the form of numerical data whereas unstructured data may be in the format of email or video. This presents a challenge for organisations as processing varied forms of data requires significant investment in people and IT infrastructure.

8.3 Effect of Big Data on decisions

The **key effects of Big Data on decisions** can be summarised as follows:

- Decisions can be made quickly.
- Businesses can respond earlier to environmental changes and be more flexible in their response.
- Decisions can be based on current situation but also have an element of taking potential future situations into account.
- Decisions are made on hard data evidence that can be quantified.
- Decisions can be made on a collaborative basis because data is easily shared and converted from one form into another.
- 'Outside the box' decisions are more likely because all factors are taken into account, not just the ones manager think of.

8.4 Benefits of 'Big Data' analytics

There are a number of potential benefits to organisations undertaking Big Data analytics.

Benefits	Comment
Examine vast quantities of data relatively quickly	Big Data analytics allows for large quantities of data to be examined to identify trends and correlations eg shopper buying habits
Improves organisational decision making	Better data analysis help management to take advantage of current social trends by introducing new products to meet customers needs
Greater focus on the individual customer	Organisations can target special offers or discounts directly to individual customers to entice repeat business
Cost reduction	Improved data about customers and internal operations may help to reduce costs.

8.5 Criticisms of 'Big Data'

Some doubt the ability of 'Big Data' to deliver the anticipated benefits.

Critics argue:

- 'Big Data' is simply a buzzword, a vague term that has turned into an obsession in large organisations and the media. Very few examples exist where analysing vast amounts of data have resulted in significant new discoveries.
- There is a focus on finding correlations between data sets and less of an emphasis on causation. Critics suggest that it is easier to identify correlations between two variables than to determine what is actually causing the correlation.

Chapter Roundup

- Organisations collect and store data for a number of reasons:
  - To record transactions.
  - For planning purposes.
  - To facilitate control.
  - To enable performance to be measured.
  - To facilitate decision-making.

- Data and information captured and stored in an organisation's information systems comes from a variety of **internal** and **external** sources.

- The way in which computer data is stored can be viewed as a **hierarchy** as follows: bit, field, record, file and database.

- The term **'database system'** is used to describe a wide range of systems that utilise a **central pool of data**.

- There are four main types of **database storage models**: hierarchical, network, relational and object-oriented.

- An **Entity Relationship Model (ERM)** may be used to establish and model the logical data requirements of a system.

- Database **implementation** should be **formally planned** and **managed** to ensure the database is fit for purpose.

- **Big Data analytics** is a term used to describe the extraction of meaning from vast quantities of data. Organisations are particularly interested in identifying trends and correlations in the data that they collect and store with the aim of putting this to commercial use.

- Laney suggests that Big Data is comprised of 3 Vs (volume, velocity and variety).

- Although the rise of Big Data analytics brings benefits, critics argue that it simply represents the latest buzzword and has not delivered the ground breaking discoveries initially thought possible.

PART B BUSINESS INFORMATION TECHNOLOGY

Quick Quiz

1 Which of the following are reasons an organisation would collect and store data and information.

   I   To help decision-making
   II   For planning purposes
   III To record transactions
   IV   To measure performance

   (a) All of the above
   (b) II and IV only
   (c) I and III only
   (d) I, III and IV only

2 Data and information captured and stored in an organisation's information systems comes from a variety of ………………….. and ………………….. sources.

   What two words are missing from the statement above?

3 A computer record would normally include more than one field.

   Is the statement above true or false?

4 What name is given to the software that extracts or selects items from within a database?

   (a) Record pointer
   (b) Query language
   (c) Data activity monitor
   (d) Data administrator

5 Which one of the following is **not** a database storage model?

   (a) Network
   (b) Hierarchical
   (c) SQL
   (d) Relational

6 What type of relationship is shown in the diagram below?

   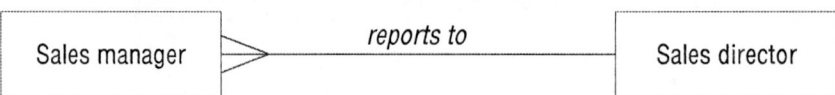

7 The implementation of a new database should not be constrained by formal planning – a flexible 'see how we go' approach is best.

   Is the statement above true or false?

Answers to Quick Quiz

1. (a) All four are reasons why an organisation may collect or store data and information.

2. Data and information captured and stored in an organisation's information systems comes from a variety of **internal** and **external** sources.

3. The statement is **True**. Computer data is made up of a hierarchy: bit, **field, record**, file and database.

4. (b) A query language Is used to **interrogate** a database, or in other words to select or extract data from a database.

5. (c) SQL is a **query language**.

6. The relationship shown is a many-to-one relationship (M:1), many sales managers reporting to one sales director.

7. The statement is **false**. Database implementation should be formally planned and managed to ensure the database is fit for purpose.

End of Chapter Question

Databases (AIA May 13)

A small local business produces and sells retro football shirts, which it supplies to a number of professional teams and specialist retailers. The business has expanded its operations and customer base substantially in the last five years. You have been awarded a contract to build a customer-order database for this small business, which currently uses only manual records, but have been persuaded by your advice as a consultant to automate their most recent customer records, given their recent investments in a suite of PCs, network facility and IT training for their employees. In starting this database development, you need to provide a briefing in which you:

Required

Describe the advantages and disadvantages of using a database system for an organisation of this size.

(10 marks)

PART B BUSINESS INFORMATION TECHNOLOGY

Telecommunications and networks

Topic list	Syllabus reference
1 Networks and communications	6.12
2 Communications	6.12

Introduction

Computers do not function in isolation. The power and usage of computers has increased dramatically because of their ability to communicate.

This chapter is divided into two. First, we look at telecommunications systems and networks. The second half looks at common communication applications.

PART B BUSINESS INFORMATION TECHNOLOGY

1 Networks and communications

FAST FORWARD

A **local area network** is a system of linked PCs and other devices such as printers. LANs can have a **server** computer holding files used by more than one computer, and providing storage capacity to the other computers in the network.

A **wide area network** is a network of computers which are dispersed on a wider geographical scale than LANs. They are connected over the public **telecommunications** network. A WAN will normally use a larger computer as a file server.

Computers used in organisations are usually part of a connected group of computers – known as a **network**. In this section we look at different types of computer networks.

A computer **network** is made up of a number of connected computers each with their own processor, for example a number of connected PCs. Networks are popular because they provide a number of users with access to **resources** (eg data files, printers, software). Therefore, a network allows computing resources to be used more efficiently between a group of users. There are two main types of network, a **local area network** (LAN) and a **wide area network** (WAN).

1.1 Local area networks (LANs)

Key term

A **local area network** (LAN) is a network of computers located in a single building or on a single site. The parts of the network are linked by computer cable rather than via telecommunications lines.

Network topology refers to the physical arrangement of items **(nodes)** in a network. A **node** is any device connected to a network: it can be a computer, or a peripheral device such as a printer.

There are several types of LAN system configuration. For example, in a **bus structure** (diagram follows), messages are sent out from one point along a single communication channel, and the messages are received by other connected machines.

Each device can **communicate with every other device** and communication is quick and reliable. Nodes can be **added or unplugged** very easily. Locating cable faults is also relatively simple.

Bus system

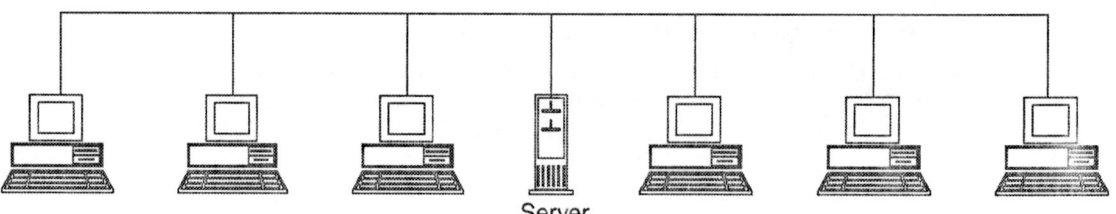

Server

Other types of LAN architectures are shown below. Which architecture is most appropriate depends upon a number of factors – such as which files are required to be accessed by many users. The number of printers to be shared and the relative power of the computers.

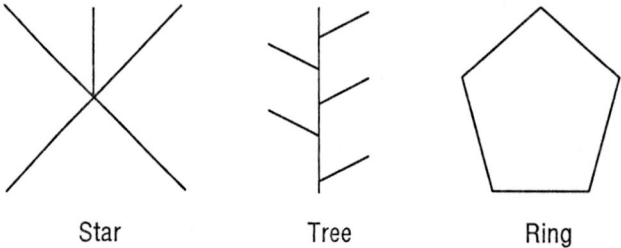

Star   Tree   Ring

Local area networks have been **successful** for a number of reasons. First of all, personal computers of sufficient power and related software were developed, so that network applications became possible. Some organisations which could not afford a mainframe or minicomputer with terminal links have been able to afford a LAN with personal computers.

Exam focus point

Past exams have asked for the features of basic Local Area Network topologies.

1.2 Wide area networks (WANs)

Key term

Wide area networks (WANs) are networks on a number of sites, perhaps on a wide geographical scale.

WANs often use mainframes as the 'pumps' that keep the data messages circulating, whereas shorter-distance LANs normally use PCs for this task.

A wide area network is similar to a local area network in concept, but the key differences are:

(a) The **geographical area** covered by the network is greater, not being limited to a single building or site.

(b) WANs will send data over **telecommunications links**.

(c) WANs will often use a **larger computer** as a file server.

(d) WANs will often be larger than LANs, with **more terminals or computers** linked to the network.

(e) A WAN can link two or more LANs.

1.3 Client-server computing

FAST FORWARD

Client-server computing is a configuration in which desktop PCs are regarded as 'clients' that request access to the services available on a more powerful server PC, such as access to a file, email, or printing facilities.

Key term

The term **client-server** is a way of describing the relationship between the devices in a network. With client-server computing, tasks are distributed among the machines on the network.

A **client** is a machine which requests a service, for example a PC running a spreadsheet application which the user wishes to print out.

A **server** is a machine which is dedicated to providing a particular function or service requested by a client. Servers include file servers (see below), print servers and email servers.

A client-server system allows **computer power** to be distributed to where it is most needed. The **client**, or user, will use a powerful personal workstation with local processing capability. The **server** provides services such as shared printers, communications links, special-purpose processing and database storage.

The file server may be a powerful PC or a midrange computer. As its name implies, it **serves** the rest of the network offering a generally-accessible hard disk. Clients on a network generally also have their **own hard disk** storage.

File servers must be powerful enough to handle **multiple user requests** and provide **adequate storage**. File servers are typically classified as 'low end' or 'high end':

(a) A **low end file server** might be used in a small office, running 'office' type software. A low end server is usually a highly specified standard PC.

(b) A **'mid range server'** might support a medium sized business.

(c) A **high end file server** might be used in a large department network of over 500 users. High end servers have now been joined by **superservers** and **'enterprise servers'** (effectively, mainframes). These are either departmental or organisation-wide, running sophisticated mission-critical systems and offering fault tolerance features.

1.3.1 The advantages of client-server computing

The advantages of a network that uses the client-server approach are as follows.

Advantage	Comment
Greater resilience	Processing is spread over several computers. If one server breaks down, other locations can carry on processing.
Scalability	They are highly scalable – hardware can be added as required.
Shared programs and data	Program and data files held on a file server can be shared by all the PCs in the network. Data duplication is avoided.
Shared work-loads	Each PC in a network can do the same work. If there were separate stand-alone PCs, A might do job 1, B might do job 2, C might do job 3 and so on. In a network, any PC, (A, B or C) could do any job (1, 2 or 3). This provides flexibility in sharing work-loads.
Shared peripherals	Peripheral equipment can be shared. For example, in a LAN, five PCs might share a single printer.
Communication	LANs can be linked up to the office communications network. Email, calendar and diary facilities can be used.
Compatibility	Client-server systems are more likely than centralised systems to have Windows interfaces, making it easier to move information between applications such as spreadsheets and accounting systems.
Ad hoc enquiries	Information may be moved to a separate server, allowing data to be manipulated without disrupting the main system.

1.3.2 The disadvantages of client-server computing

The client-server approach has two main drawbacks.

Disadvantage	Comment
Less powerful than large mainframes	Mainframes are more suited to dealing with very large volumes of transactions.
Control can be difficult	It is easier to control and maintain a system centrally. In particular it is easier to keep data secure.

1.4 Computer communications

Computers linked in a network need to be able to communicate with each other to allow the sharing of resources. Computers in one network may also require the ability to occasionally communicate with computers in a different network.

Communication may involve the transfer of data from one part of a system to another, for example transaction values may be posted from the receivables ledger module of an accounting system to the general ledger module, or could involve one-off messages, for example through the use of email or instant messaging.

1.4.1 Data links

When all data processing is done in the **same office**, the transmission of data between input and output devices and the central processor is usually provided for using **internal cables**.

When the input or output device is located away from the computer, so that it has to be transmitted along a **telecommunications** link (for example a telephone line) there are additional items of data transmission equipment which have to be used, and the way in which the data is to be transmitted has to be resolved.

A data link might typically connect the following.

(a) A **computer** and a **remote terminal** (keyboard and VDU). A computer may have a number of remote terminals linked to it by data transmission equipment.

(b) **Two computers** located some distance from each other (for example a mainframe and a PC, which would use the link to exchange data).

(c) Several **processors** in a **network**, with each computer in the network able to transmit data to any other.

1.5 Data transmission terminology

This section explains some common terms used in the context of data communications.

1.5.1 Modems and digital transmission

A modem converts the digital data from the computer into a continuous analogue wave form that the telephone system is designed to deal with (MODulation). The reason for this is that the telephone system was originally designed for the human voice ie continuous signals. The modem also converts the analogue signal from the telephone network back into digital data that the computer can understand. (DEModulation).

WiFi (Wireless Fidelity) modems – allow connection to WiFi networks (see Paragraph 1.5.7 below).

1.5.2 Bandwidth

The amount of data that can be sent down a telecommunications line is in part determined by the bandwidth. **Bandwidth** is the range of frequencies that the channel can carry. Frequencies are measured in cycles per second, or in **Hertz**. The wider the bandwidth, the greater the amount of data the channel can carry.

1.5.3 Broadband

Broadband means a relatively **high capacity internet connection**, and therefore a relatively **fast** communications link. DSL (Digital Subscriber Line) is an example of a broadband technology.

1.5.4 Network cards and connections

Computers and other devices on a network are connected to each other using computer cable (known as **coaxial cable**). This cable is plugged into all devices (eg computers, printers) on the network into a slot on the device (similar to a telephone connection slot). This connection connects the cable to a **network card** that holds the circuitry required for network communication.

1.5.5 Ports

A **port** is the **socket** on a computer into which you plug a peripheral device such as a printer. Ports can be serial, parallel or Universal Serial Bus (USB) as explained below. USB ports allow faster data transfer and are expected to eventually completely replace serial and parallel ports.

1.5.6 Interfaces

The term **interface** is frequently used in computer communications contexts, but it has at least three different meanings – as shown in the following table.

Interface – possible meanings	
What links two systems	The point at which two applications software systems are linked. For example, the **interface** between a computerised payables ledger and a general ledger will normally consist of an analysis file produced by the payables ledger being read by an **interface program** in the general ledger.
How you communicate with the computer	The point of interaction between the computer and the user, principally in terms of using a display screen for input and retrieval of information. The two principal forms of interface are often described as **Graphical User Interface** (GUI) or Character-based User Interface (CUI). GUIs (eg Windows) are now more favoured than CUIs (eg MS-DOS).
Electronic connections	The circuitry which connects two devices. Interfaces may be: **Serial**, in which case data is transmitted as a stream of individual bits through a single wire, or **Parallel**, where a number of wires each carry one bit so that eight wires, for example, will enable the eight bits comprising one byte to be transferred simultaneously, or **Universal Serial Bus (USB)** – a more recent type of port that supports data transfer at very fast rates. Most computer peripherals are now connected using USB.

1.5.7 Mobile communications

Digital networks for mobile telephone communications have been developed, which are better able to support data transmission than the older analogue networks. Digital networks offer **higher transmission speeds** and less likelihood of data corruption. Internet access through mobile phones is available, and combined handheld computer/cellular phones have been developed.

Examples of mobile IT devices include:

- Laptop and netbook computers
- Tablets (such as Apple iPads and the Samsung Galaxy range)
- Mobile phones and smartphones
- Global positioning system (GPS) devices
- Wireless debit/credit card payment terminals

Mobile devices can be enabled to use a variety of communications technologies such as:

(a) Wireless fidelity (WiFi) – a type of wireless local area network technology.

(b) Bluetooth – connects mobile devices wirelessly over short distances.

(c) Near field communication (NFC) – this is a form of contactless communication between devices like smartphones or tablets. NFC allows a user to send or receive information by waving their device over an NFC compatible device, or by tapping the device. There is no need to connect the devices together physically or to go through multiple steps such as those required to set up a connection in Bluetooth. NFC technology is used in the Apple Pay contactless payment facility (described in Chapter 10).

(d) 'Third generation' (3G), 'fourth generation' (4G), global system for mobile communications (GSM) and general packet radio service (GPRS) data services – data networking services for mobile phones.

(e) Virtual private networks – secure access to a private network. It is therefore possible to connect the mobile device to a home network or the internet while travelling.

Wireless-enabled devices can also be used to connect to the internet, office or email inbox using the wireless 'hot spots' that are often available in public places, eg wireless fidelity networks (WiFi).

WiFi is a technology that facilitates the mobile use of laptop computers and personal handheld devices away from the home or office. WiFi networks are created through an array of thousands of local 'hotspots' throughout metropolitan areas.

Initially, hotspots were rare but can now be found in most public buildings. Municipal WiFi is a newer application that is gaining popularity quickly. Some cities are partnering with Internet Service Providers (such as EarthLink) to build wireless networks that blanket every inch of their city. This new technology removes the need to be near a localised hotspot and provides wireless access to all residents and businesses within the city limits including open spaces such as parks and highways.

2 Communications

FAST FORWARD

> Advances in technology have led to increasingly advanced types of telecommunication applications. Applications including **voice messaging**, **video conferencing** and **email systems** have dramatically changed the way in which people communicate with each other.

In this section we discuss some other telecommunications applications.

2.1 Voice messaging systems

Voice messaging systems answer and route telephone calls. Typically, when a call is answered a recorded message tells the caller to dial the extension required, or to hold if they want to speak to the operator. Sometimes other options are offered, such as 'press 2 if you want to know about X service and 3 if you want to know about Y'.

Such systems work well if callers have similar needs that can be foreseen. They can be frustrating for callers with less routine enquiries. These can be effectively routed to an operator with the authority and knowledge to handle enquiries of the nature that might arise, complaints, supply problems and so forth.

2.2 Computer Telephony Integration (CTI)

Computer Telephony Integration (CTI) systems gather information about callers such as their telephone number and customer account number or demographic information (age, income, interests etc). This is stored on a customer database and can be called up and sent to the screen of the person dealing with the call, perhaps before the call has even been put through.

2.3 Video conferencing

Video conferencing is the use of computer and communications technology to conduct meetings with participants in different locations, by transmitting live video and audio between each participant.

Video conferencing is increasingly common as the internet and webcams have brought the service to desktop PCs at reasonable cost. Applications such as Skype are now commonly used.

More expensive systems feature a separate room with several video screens, which show the images of those participating in a meeting.

2.4 Web conferencing

A web conference (also referred to as a 'webinar') is similar to a video conference but focuses more on the collaborative sharing of files, documents, presentations and live screen captures of computer applications. However, as technology becomes more advanced, the terms video conferencing and web conferencing become more interchangeable as many services of this nature offer both video/audio transmission and collaborative sharing.

2.5 Electronic Data Interchange (EDI)

> **FAST FORWARD** — EDI is a method by which computers communicate with other.

EDI is a form of computer-to-computer data interchange. Instead of sending each other reams of paper in the form of invoices, statements and so on, details of inter-company transactions are sent via telecoms links, avoiding the need for output and paper at the sending end, and for re-keying of data at the receiving end.

2.6 Electronic Funds Transfer (EFT)

EFT describes a system whereby organisations are able to use their computer system to transfer funds – for example, make payments to a supplier, or pay salaries into employees' bank accounts.

2.7 Electronic mail (email)

Email is used for communication within organisations and between organisations. The term 'electronic mail', or email, is used to describe various systems of sending data or messages electronically using a computer.

In a typical email system, information is 'posted' by the sender to a central computer which allocates disk storage as a **mailbox** for each user. The information is subsequently collected by the receiver from the mailbox.

Email use is widespread both **within organisations** and **between** them – via the internet.

2.7.1 Disadvantages of email

Email has the following dangers:

- **Confidentiality** – passwords must be safeguarded
- Used to **replace** other communications that may be more appropriate (eg conversation)
- The key message of an email can be lost by turning the email into a long-threaded conversation
- Too many emails going to **people who don't need it** as it is so easy to send to many recipients
- Important emails might not go to **people who do need it**
- It can be difficult to send large file attachments by email

2.8 File storage services

The problem of sending large attachments by email can be addressed by using online file storage service. In Chapter 10 we looked at cloud storage. File storage services such as DropBox enable files to be transferred between users and devices by allowing multiple users to access files stored in a central server and accessed via the internet or the 'cloud'. This is a more efficient way of sharing files than sending files by email.

2.9 Bulletin boards

In the modern workplace, it is not uncommon for people to work together but be separated geographically. Email is often used as the primary method of communication in this situation. However because of the disadvantages of email described in section 2.7.1, this method might not be the most efficient.

This can be addressed by using alternative tools to share electronic messages such as a bulletin board (also referred to as a message board or a discussion board).

A bulletin board allows electronic messages to be shared in the form of a 'discussion' on a particular topic, on a webpage on the company's intranet. Users who have access to the board can post a message (ie send a message that is published on the board) on a particular topic, and can post responses in a discussion.

The main advantage of this method over email is that the discussion is contained in one area and not dispersed over multiple emails in several different email inboxes.

PART B   BUSINESS INFORMATION TECHNOLOGY

Chapter Roundup

- A **local area network** is a system of linked PCs and other devices such as printers. LANs can have a **server** computer holding files used by more than one computer, and providing storage capacity to the other computers in the network.

- A **wide area network** is a network of computers which are dispersed on a wider geographical scale than LANs. They are connected over the public **telecommunications** network. A WAN will normally use a larger computer as a file server.

- **Client-server** computing is a configuration in which desktop PCs are regarded as 'clients' that request access to the services available on a more powerful server PC, such as access to a file, email, or printing facilities.

- Advances in technology have led to increasingly advanced types of telecommunication applications. Applications including **voice messaging**, **video conferencing** and **email systems** have dramatically changed the way in which people communicate with each other.

- **EDI** is a method by which computers communicate with other.

Quick Quiz

1. What are the two forms of communication technology?

2. Define LAN and WAN.

3. Which of the following options refers to a network of computers which are connected over the public telecommunications network?

    (a) LAN
    (b) WAN
    (c) TAN
    (d) PAN

4. What is the fundamental difference between video conferencing and web conferencing?

5. Which one of the following is a possible disadvantage of email?

    (a) Economy
    (b) Speed
    (c) Delivery and read receipts
    (d) Large volumes of information

PART B BUSINESS INFORMATION TECHNOLOGY

Answers to Quick Quiz

1. Digital and analogue.

2. LAN = Local Area Network, usually in one building.
   WAN = Wide Area Network, usually covering larger geographical areas eg internet.

3. (b) Wide area network (WAN). These are dispersed on a wider geographical scale than LANs.

4. Video conferencing focuses on the transmission of video and audio between remote participants in a meeting whereas web conferencing focuses more on the collaborative sharing of files, documents, presentations and live screen captures of computer applications.

5. (d) The danger with email is that too much information will go to people who don't need it because it is so easy to send to many recipients.

End of Chapter Question

LAN
(AIA May 09 (amended))

At your department's Information Technology training day you are expected to lead the discussion. Accordingly prepare notes on the features of the three basic Local Area Network topologies. **(10 marks)**

Electronic commerce

Topic list	Syllabus reference
1 Web 2.0 and e-commerce	6.13

Introduction

Business information technology has had a profound impact on both consumers and businesses. Perhaps one of the most dramatic has been the rise and rise of electronic commerce. This final chapter looks at electronic commerce which is widely known as e-commerce.

PART B BUSINESS INFORMATION TECHNOLOGY

1 Web 2.0 and e-commerce

1.1 Web 2.0

FAST FORWARD

> **Web 2.0 applications** are 'second generation' internet-based services. These sites usually include tools that let people collaborate and share information online.

Examples of web 2.0 applications include **blogs** (short for web log), **RSS** feeds, **wikis** and **YouTube**. Social networking sites such as **Facebook, Twitter** and **Linkedin** are also part of the web 2.0 movement, and are increasingly being used by businesses (for example, to help them gain a better understanding of their customers).

Web applications present information through web browsers such in Internet Explorer, Mozilla Firefox and Google Chrome. Some companies use browsers and internet technology to present information internally to employees. For example employee handbooks, newsletters, telephone directories can be conveniently presented through a browser interface. These private networks are known as **intranets**.

Some organisations allow other organisations to access their networks. For example, a supermarket might allow a supplier to access its computer system so that it can monitor stock at the supermarket and anticipate when more stock has to be despatched. When one computer system accesses another's intranet in this way, the system is known as an **extranet**. Extranets provide mechanisms for sharing information online to selected third parties.

Many large organisations today operate **global information systems (GIS)** which enable the sharing of information around the world through the use of organisational networks and internet technologies. Many multinational organisations operate GIS in the form of enterprise resource planning (ERP) systems. ERP systems typically consist of a number of individual modules each of which is mapped to a given business function such as finance, purchasing, marketing and human resources. The system enables each function to share a central source of information to ensure that their activities are co-ordinated. The benefits of ERP systems are that they allow different users throughout the organisation to access the same information in real time which is relevant to their function and role.

1.1.1 E-commerce

E-commerce (the selling of goods or services over the internet) has developed alongside CRM (Customer Relationship Management) systems. E-commerce can take a number of forms. Two of the most common varieties are business-to-consumer (B2C) and business-to-business (B2B).

B2C (Business-to-Consumer) – involves businesses selling to the general public, typically through catalogues with **shopping cart software**.

B2B (Business-to-Business) – involves companies doing business with each other, as when manufacturers sell to distributors, and wholesalers sell to retailers.

A key part of e-commerce is aimed at providing the customer (whether that be the end consumer or another business) with a **unique shopping experience** that is tailored to their needs. The view and products presented to a customer is geared to their individual tastes, based on their profile and past behaviour on the site.

Most **organisations** have e-commerce capability on their website. Many have gone further, suggesting potential purchases for each customer when they log on. These suggestions are driven by the customer's previous orders and their history of viewing products.

Berens (2006) identified the following points to consider when building a website with e-commerce capability.

(a) Ensure transactions are **secure**, and tell customers they are. Customer trust is essential.
(b) **Comply** with all applicable consumer, privacy and data protection legislation.
(c) Have clear **terms of use** for the site.
(d) Don't require customers to provide **excessive amounts of information** as this may deter them.
(e) Maintain **ongoing communication** with willing customers, for example by email.

The term **e-business** refers to conducting business on the internet. It has a wider meaning than e-commerce, because it covers not only buying and selling but also servicing customers and collaborating with suppliers.

PART B   BUSINESS INFORMATION TECHNOLOGY

Chapter Roundup

- **Web 2.0 applications** are 'second generation' internet-based services. These sites usually include tools that let people collaborate and share information online.

Quick Quiz

1   What is e-commerce?
2   Which points should you consider when building a website with e-commerce capability?
3   What is e-business?

Answers to Quick Quiz

1. The selling of goods or services over the internet.
2. See paragraph 1.1.1.
3. General conducting of business on the internet.

End of Chapter Question

E-commerce (AIA Nov 08)

As someone who has been working in an electronic commerce environment for some time, you have been invited to address a business forum. Prepare some comments on the following:

(a) Discuss the significant reasons why a firm may be interested to become involved in e-commerce.
(16 marks)

(b) Give brief descriptions of a business which is suitable as an e-commerce application and another business which is not thought to be suitable.
(4 marks)

(Total = 20 marks)

PART B BUSINESS INFORMATION TECHNOLOGY

Answers to end of chapter questions

Chapter 2 – Primary data collection

> **Syllabus section 6.1 Statistical Sources**
>
> Candidates will be expected to describe methods of primary data collection.

(a) Methods of primary data collection:

- Observation – when responses from people are not required, examples are traffic survey, queues in a shop, work place situations etc.
- Questionnaire – series of questions sent via the post or email to a sample of people.
- Interview – data collected from individuals either at home or in a public place by an interviewer trained for the purpose.
- Telephone interview – data collected using telephone communication rather than face to face interview.

> **Syllabus section 6.1 Statistical Sources**
>
> Candidates will be expected to describe the types of questions used in questionnaire design, to identify points to consider when designing questionnaires.

(b) (i) **Classification of questions**:

- Dichotomous questions – where there are only two possible answers to choose from:

  eg Male/Female, Yes/No, Agree/Disagree

- Multiple choice questions – where a choice of a number of options is possible:

  eg Excellent/Good/OK/Poor/Very poor

- Open-ended questions – where respondents can respond as they feel appropriate:

  eg when any additional comments are requested.

(ii) **Designing questionnaires**:

- Purpose of the questionnaire should be stated at the beginning and perhaps some incentive for completion should be included
- At the end the respondent should be thanked and assured of anonymity
- The questionnaire should have a meaningful title, be as short as possible and be attractively presented
- The questions should be in a logical sequence
- The questions should be relatively simple, not too technical and not too personal or sensitive
- The questions should not be biased
- There should be adequate provision for additional comments

Chapter 3 – Presentation of data

> **Syllabus section 6.2 Presentation of Data**
>
> Candidates will be expected to plot a scatter diagram and to draw a cumulative frequency graph from a frequency distribution.

(a)

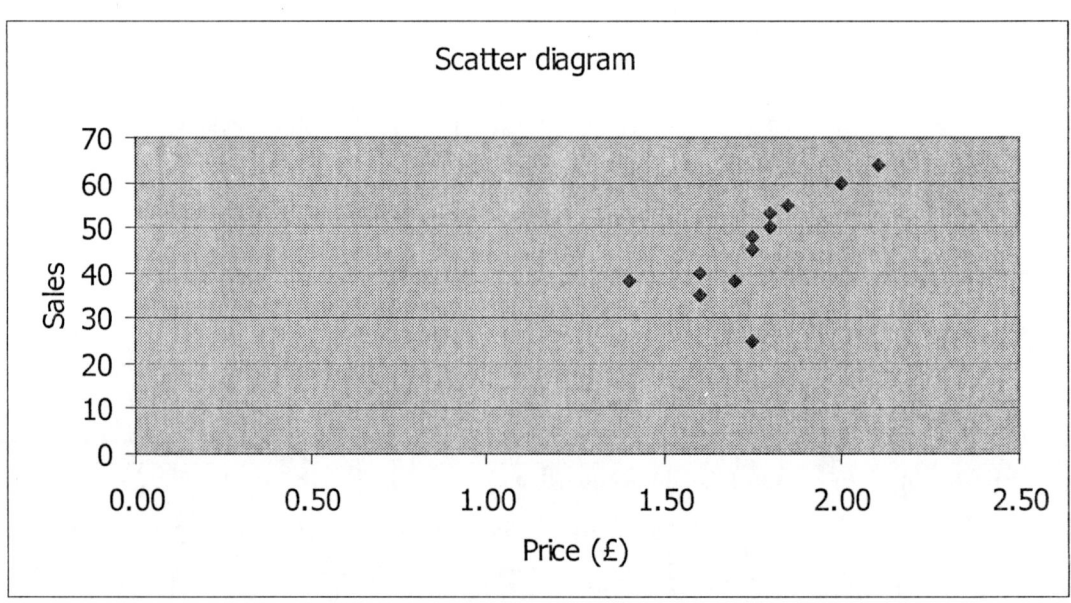

The scatter diagram indicates that there is a reasonably strong positive, increasing linear relationship between Sales and Price although there is one outlier.

(b) (i)

Age, ucl	Freq	Cum freq
20.5	5	5
25.5	20	25
30.5	24	49
35.5	30	79
40.5	27	106
45.5	22	128
50.5	18	146
55.5	12	158
60.5	8	166
65.5	3	169

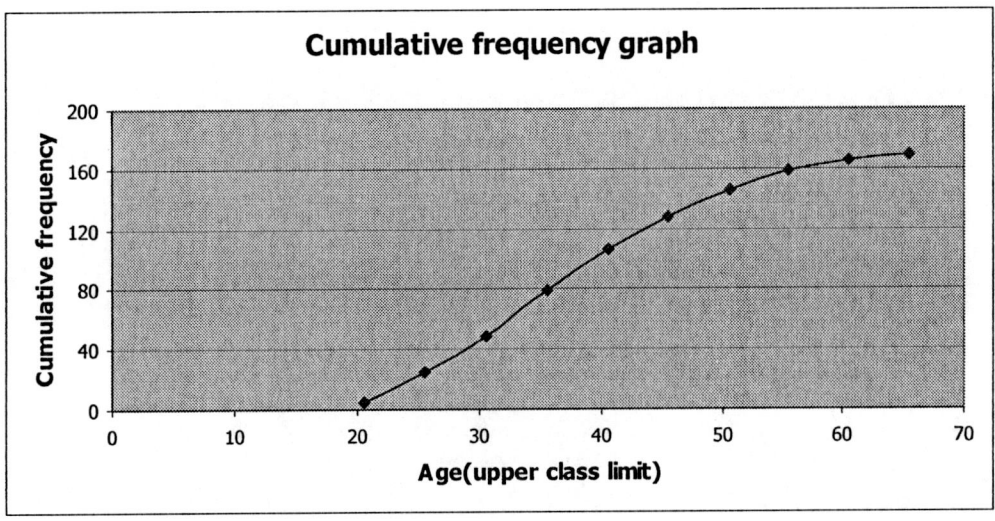

The cumulative frequency graph can be used to estimate summary measures such as the median or the inter quartile range as well as estimating frequencies less than or greater than certain values of the x variable.

Chapter 4a – Averages

> Syllabus sections 6.2 Presentation of Data and 6.3 Summary Statistics.
>
> Candidates will be expected to draw a cumulative frequency graph from a frequency distribution and to use the frequency distribution formulae to estimate the mean, mode and median values.

(a)

Age, ucl	Freq	Cum freq
20.5	5	5
25.5	20	25
30.5	24	49
35.5	30	79
40.5	27	106
45.5	22	128
50.5	18	146
55.5	12	158
60.5	8	166
65.5	3	169

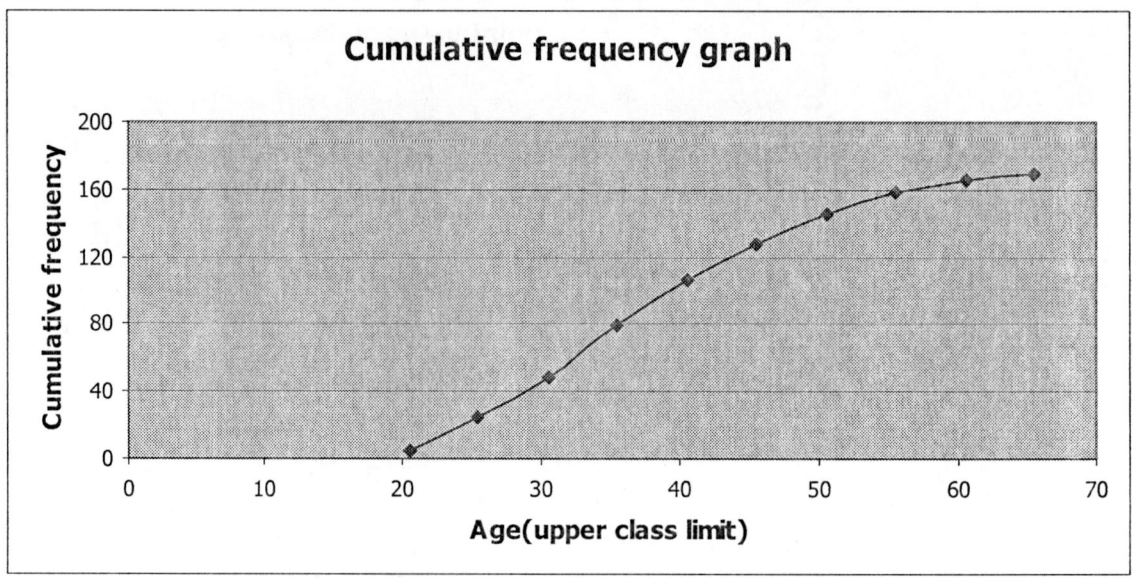

The cumulative frequency graph can be used to estimate summary measures such as the median or the inter quartile range as well as estimating frequencies less than or greater than certain values of the x variable.

(b)

lcl	ucl	x	f	fx	cum f
15.5	20.5	18	5	90	5
20.5	25.5	23	20	460	25
25.5	30.5	28	24	672	49
30.5	35.5	33	30	990	79
35.5	40.5	38	27	1,026	106
40.5	45.5	43	22	946	128
45.5	50.5	48	18	864	146
50.5	55.5	53	12	636	158
55.5	60.5	58	8	464	166
60.5	65.5	63	3	189	169
			169	6,337	

Mean $= \sum fx / \sum f$

$= 6{,}337/169$

$= 37.50$ years

Mode $= l_1 + \dfrac{(fm - fm_{-1})}{(fm - fm_{-1}) + (fm - fm_{+1})} \times \dfrac{(l_2 - l_1)}{1}$

$= 30.5 + (30 - 24)/((30 - 24) + (30 - 27)) \times 5$

$= 33.83$ years

Median $= l_1 + \dfrac{n/2 - Fm_{-1}}{fm} \times \dfrac{(l_2 - l_1)}{1}$

$= 35.5 + (84.5 - 79)/27 \times \times 5$

$= 36.52$ years

Chapter 4b – Dispersion

> Syllabus section 6.3 Summary Statistics.
>
> Candidates will be expected to calculate averages for raw data and to understand the difference between symmetrical and skewed data.

(a)

X
6
10
13
7
8
14
20
8
8
9
12
7

Mean = $\sum x/n$ = 122/12 = 10.167

Mode is most commonly occurring value = 8

Median is the value of the (n + 1)/2th item when sorted in order

X
6
7
7
8
8
8
9
10
12
13
14
20

Median = (8 + 9)/2 = 8.5

(b) Since mode<median<mean the data is said to be skewed rather than symmetrical.

The extreme value of 20 results in the distribution being positively skewed.

(c) When data is skewed the inter-quartile range is often selected as the best measure of variation to use rather than the standard deviation since the standard deviation will be distorted by any extreme values/outliers.

(d) When summary measures are computed for grouped frequency distributions then the mid points of the classes are used as the representative x values in the computations. Since the exact values of the variables are not known these x values are purely estimates and hence the summary measures are said to be approximate or estimated values.

ANSWERS TO END OF CHAPTER QUESTIONS

Chapter 5 – Applying probability to decision making

> **Syllabus section 6.4 Applying probability to decision making.**
>
> **Candidates will be expected to distinguish between different types of probability distribution, and to apply Binomial and Normal probabilities to practical problems.**

(a) The probability distribution of a discrete random variable is a list of all possible values of the variable together with their associated probabilities.

The probability distribution of a continuous random variable can be represented by a function where the total area under the curve is 1 and the probability of obtaining a value between two points is given by the area under the curve between those points.

(b) (i) Binomial probability with n = 7, P = 0.75 and Q = 0.25

$prob(x) = nCx \times P^x \times (1-P)^{n-x}$

Prob (6 or more) = Prob (6) + Prob (7)

Prob (7) = $_7C_7 \times 0.75^7 \times 0.25^0$ = 1 × 0.1335 × 1 = 0.1335

Prob (6) = $_7C_6 \times 0.75^6 \times 0.25^1$ = 7 × 0.177798 × 0.25 = 0.3115

Prob (6 or more) = 0.1335 + 0.3115 = 0.445

(ii) Prob (3 unsuccessful) = Prob (4)

Prob (4) = $_7C_4 \times 0.75^4 \times 0.25^3$ = 35 × 0.3164 × 0.0156 = 0.173

(c) Normal distribution with mean value of 20 and sd of 6

Using Normal variate $Z = \dfrac{x - \mu}{\sigma}$ to standardise values

(i) Prob(x > 30) = Prob(z > (30 – 20)/6)

= Prob(z > 1.67)

= 0.5 – 0.4525 using Normal tables

= 0.0475

(ii) Prob(18 < x < 23) = Prob((18 – 20)/6 < z < (23 – 20)/6) = Prob(–0.33 < z < 0.5)

= 0.1293 + 0.1915 using Normal Tables

= 0.3208

(iii) From Normal tables Prob(0 < z < 1.28) = 0.4

Prob(z < 1.28) = 0.9

Using $Z = \dfrac{x - \mu}{\sigma}$ then 1.28 = (x – 20)/6

x – 20 = 6 × 1.28 = 7.68

x = 27.68

Chapter 6 – Factory Manager

> Syllabus section 6.5 Measuring the relationship between two variables.
>
> Candidates will be expected to calculate and interpret values of the correlation coefficient, to determine a regression equation and discuss interpolation and extrapolation in forecasting.

(a)

Output, y	Experience, x	xy	x^2	y^2
80	36	2,880	1,296	6,400
65	25	1,625	625	4,225
78	34	2,652	1,156	6,084
67	38	2,546	1,444	4,489
90	43	3,870	,849	8,100
58	15	870	225	3,364
65	32	2,080	1,024	4,225
77	39	3,003	1,521	5,929
80	38	3,040	1,444	6,400
93	55	5,115	3,025	8,649
753	355	27,681	13,609	57,865

$$r = \frac{\frac{\Sigma xy}{n} - \bar{x}\bar{y}}{\sqrt{\left(\frac{\Sigma x^2}{n} - \bar{x}^2\right)\left(\frac{\Sigma y^2}{n} - \bar{y}^2\right)}}$$

= 94.95/108.24

= 0.8772

This value of r is closer to 1 than the value for the relationship between Output and Training (r = 0.724) so Experience is judged to be the better predictor of Output.

(b) Regression Coefficients

$$b = \frac{\Sigma xy - n\bar{x}\bar{y}}{\Sigma x^2 - n\bar{x}^2}; \quad a = \bar{y} - b\bar{x}$$

b = 949.5/1006.5 = 0.9434

a = 41.81

Estimated y = 41.81 + 0.9434x

(c) In forecasting if the value of the x variable used is within the range of the existing x values then the forecasting process is called interpolation and it is safe.

If the value of the x variable used lies outside the existing range of x values then the forecasting process is called extrapolation and it is said to be risky as the outcome is not predictable with any confidence.

Chapter 7 – Time series analysis

Syllabus section 6.6 Time Series Analysis.

Candidates will be expected to plot and comment on a time series, to calculate Trend by moving average and to estimate seasonal effects.

(a)

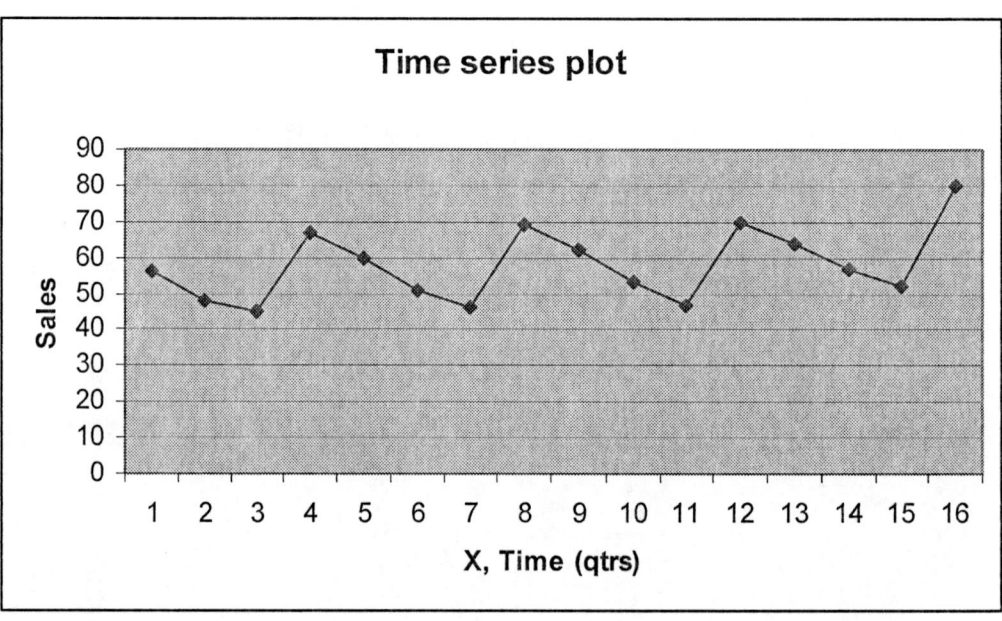

The time series plot of Sales over time shows an increasing trend with a repeating cycle every four quarters.

(b)

Year	Quarter	X, time (qtrs)	Sales	4 qtr MA	T, trend
20X4	1	1	56		
	2	2	48	54.00	
	3	3	45	55.00	54.500
	4	4	67	55.75	55.375
20X5	1	5	60	56.00	55.875
	2	6	51	56.50	56.250
	3	7	46	57.00	56.750
	4	8	69	57.50	57.250
20X6	1	9	62	57.75	57.625
	2	10	53	58.00	57.875
	3	11	47	58.50	58.250
	4	12	70	59.50	59.000
20X7	1	13	64	60.75	60.125
	2	14	57	63.25	62.000
	3	15	52		
	4	16	80		

(c) Since Y = T + S in an additive model, then the seasonal effect is found from S = Y − T

Year	Quarter	X, time (qtrs)	Sales	4 qtr MA	T, trend	S effect
20X4	1	1	56			
	2	2	48	54.00		
	3	3	45	55.00	54.500	−9.500
	4	4	67	55.75	55.375	11.625
20X5	1	5	60	56.00	55.875	4.125
	2	6	51	56.50	56.250	−5.250
	3	7	46	57.00	56.750	−10.750
	4	8	69	57.50	57.250	11.750
20X6	1	9	62	57.75	57.625	4.375
	2	10	53	58.00	57.875	−4.875
	3	11	47	58.50	58.250	−11.250
	4	12	70	59.50	59.000	11.000
20X7	1	13	64	60.75	60.125	3.875
	2	14	57	63.25	62.000	−5.000
	3	15	52			
	4	16	80			

The uncorrected S values are calculated as follows.

	Q1	Q2	Q3	Q4
			−9.500	11.625
	4.125	−5.250	−10.750	11.750
	4.375	−4.875	−11.250	11.000
	3.875	−5.000		
Ave S	**4.13**	**−5.04**	**−10.50**	**11.46**

ANSWERS TO END OF CHAPTER QUESTIONS

Chapter 8 – Index numbers

> Syllabus section 6.7 Index numbers.
>
> Candidates will be expected to calculate and comment on the Laspeyres and Paasche price index numbers and to discuss the Retail Price Index.

(a)

Po	Qo	Pn	Qn	PoQo	PnQo	PoQn	PnQn
17	25	19	30	425	475	510	570
13	15	18	18	195	270	234	324
5	20	6	26	100	120	130	156
12	14	16	15	168	224	180	240
22	19	24	17	418	456	374	408
				1,306	**1,545**	**1,428**	**1,698**

Laspeyres Price Index = $\sum P_n Q_0 / \sum P_0 Q_0$ = 1,545/1,306 × 100 = 118.3

Paasche Price Index = $\sum P_n Q_n / \sum P_0 Q_n$ = 1,698/1,428 × 100 = 118.9

(b) The Laspeyres Price Index is a weighted aggregated price index in which the weights used are the base year quantities purchased.

A disadvantage in using the base year quantities in the Laspeyres index is that it assumes that the consumption of the items is relatively constant and this may not be valid if there is a reasonable length of time between the base year and the current year.

The Paasche Price Index is a weighted aggregated price index in which the weights used are the current year quantities purchased.

A disadvantage of the current year weights in the Paasche Index is that it can be quite difficult to obtain the current year purchasing patterns.

(c) Retail Price Index:

RPI was compiled by the UK Government and published on a monthly basis.

It was a base weighted price index.

It was constructed from a basket of goods selected to reflect typical household expenditure.

The basket of goods was classified in groups such as food, housing, motoring, clothing, entertainment etc.

It showed how household expenditure changes over time.

The UK Government used it to identify inflation. Since 2013 the Consumer Price Index has become more widely used.

Chapter 9 – Systems Development Life Cycle

> **Syllabus section 6.8 Overview of Information Systems.**
>
> Candidates will be expected to describe the various stages in the systems development life cycle.

(i) Preliminary investigation and objective setting – proposal definition, terms of reference, initial feasibility study, clarification of users and general outcomes.

(ii) Detailed investigation – more detailed feasibility study involving technical and operational aspects.

(iii) Systems analysis – evaluation of existing system and the need for modifications or development of new system.

(iv) Systems design – development of processes and procedures including input and output formats.

(v) Development – conversion of design into programs by generating or purchasing software.

(vi) Systems testing – tests and trial runs to eliminate program and system errors and to ensure that the programs link together and perform to the specifications.

(vii) Implementation – further trials and parallel runs leading to the installation of the system, production of documentation including user guides and instructions for updating and training of users.

(viii) Systems maintenance – monitoring of the system in practice and modification of programs as necessary depending on feedback.

Chapter 10 – Hospital

> **Syllabus section 6.9 Computer hardware and 6.10 Computer software**
>
> Candidates will be expected to define the terms hardware, software and communications technology.

Definitions of computer hardware, computer software and communications technology.

Computer Hardware

A computer system has a range of physical components, including the monitor, keyboard, hard disk and cabling. Collectively, these represent the hardware.

Computer Software

The computer runs various programs as part of its operations, these represent computer software. These fall into two key categories, systems software and application software. Systems software exists to support the effective running of the computer. Application software are designed to allow the computer user to execute various activities, in the context of the hospital, specific to job role. These include word processor, spreadsheet, database and accounting programs.

Communications technology

Communication via computer is essential across the hospital and this is supported by various communications technologies. These comprise technology that supports such interaction, consisting of cables, wireless facilities and satellites and processors, examples including modems and multiplexers.

Chapter 11 – Databases

> **Syllabus section 6.11 Managing data and information**
>
> Candidates will be expected to explain the advantages and disadvantages of using databases.

For the small business owner, the advantages of the database system centre on the automation of its data records and sales history with the various professional teams and specialist retail outlets. By doing this, some sort of formalisation and consistency of data records can be achieved. In doing so, all of the staff within the small manufacturer can be encouraged to make use of the sales system, potential repetition of sales records can be eliminated and avoided in the future, analysis of sales data that may never have historically taken place can be encouraged and become part of team decision making.

The disadvantages of the system within such a small organisation are that data security and the integrity of customer relationships must be given formal importance. To achieve this, the small business must have its own systems beyond those relating to software controls. A small business may rely on one data set only, this needs accuracy in its maintenance and security safeguards against system failures and corruption. Cost and short-term disruption to the business will be inevitable, given the system is being built from new rather than being transformed from an existing automated provision.

Chapter 12 – LAN

> **Syllabus section 6.12 Telecommunications and Networks.**
>
> Candidates will be expected to identify the differences between various Local Area Network topologies.

(a) LAN features

Star Network:

- Consists of several nodes or computer devices connected to one central computer or host.
- All processing goes through the central computer first so that it monitors all communication.
- The central computer controls the operation, allocation of resources and workloads of all the other computer terminals in the LAN.
- There is no disruption if one computer breaks down.
- This simple configuration is suitable for branch offices with a central main office.

Ring Network:

- Consists of several computers connected to each other in a closed continuous loop.
- There is no central computer in this network.
- A message must travel around the ring to each computer in turn until the desired destination is reached.
- The ring may be unidirectional or bidirectional.
- If a computer breaks down special software may be needed to keep the ring working.

Bus Network:

- Each computer is connected to a single communication channel or cable using an interface.
- Every computer can communicate with every other computer in the network directly.
- Each computer has its own address for access purposes.
- Each computer can access a host computer with output facilities such as a printer directly.
- Ethernet uses a bus topology by interconnecting PCs via coaxial cable.

Chapter 13 – E-commerce

> **Syllabus section 6.13 Electronic commerce.**
>
> **Candidates will be expected to outline the reasons for a firm getting involved in e-commerce and to give examples of firms suited to and not suited to e-commerce.**

(a) Reasons for a firm being involved in e-commerce:

(i) Mainly to get involved in transactions and processes using the internet which support the buying and selling activities between businesses and with customers and suppliers.

(ii) Main aim is to increase profitability by decreasing costs and increasing revenue.

(iii) Keep up to date with new technology, research and development.

(iv) Increase publicity to possible customers by advertising on the internet and hence encourage business, and identify new suppliers and business partners.

(v) Communicate with specialised small markets worldwide using the internet which would be difficult and expensive otherwise.

(vi) Negotiate prices, discounts, delivery dates etc easily using internet facilities and make order taking and sales support more efficient.

(vii) Increase speed and accuracy with which businesses can exchange information and make decisions for the benefit of all parties.

(viii) Assist buyers with the variety of choices made readily available and the quality of detailed information provided instantly.

(b) Well suited to e-commerce:

A company involved in the selling of standard well known products or services, for example airline tickets, books, computer software.

Not suited to e-commerce:

A company using traditional commerce where customers prefer to see the products and where the company has experience of merchandising, for example a company involved in buying or selling high fashion articles or perishable foods.

ANSWERS TO END OF CHAPTER QUESTIONS

Exam question bank

SECTION A – Data Collection and Analysis

Question 1 (November 2014)   27 mins

A catering company provides packed lunches to a population of 50 customers, who are typically small professional businesses such as solicitors, accountants and health practitioners. For 20X3, the number of complaints registered by each customer is shown below:

Customer ID	Complaints	Customer ID	Complaints	Customer ID	Complaints	Customer ID	Complaints	Customer ID	Complaints
1	0	11	2	21	4	31	2	41	8
2	1	12	1	22	0	32	1	42	1
3	2	13	0	23	2	33	1	43	3
4	1	14	5	24	1	34	0	44	0
5	3	15	1	25	1	35	0	45	10
6	3	16	4	26	3	36	2	46	0
7	4	17	0	27	2	37	5	47	2
8	0	18	3	28	2	38	1	48	1
9	1	19	7	29	0	39	4	49	4
10	2	20	1	30	1	40	2	50	0

Required

(a) The data above are stored in Excel by the Operations Manager within the catering company. What source of data does this represent? **(1 mark)**

(b) The owner of the catering company wishes to analyse only a sample of customers, initially by means of statistical analysis. Describe why a simple random sample is an appropriate way to identify a group of customers to analyse and why such a sample of customers can easily be identified from the population data above. **(3 marks)**

(c) Using the following set of random numbers, starting with the first number in the table and using each row (reading left to right), provide a random sample of 15 customers presenting the data in a table of the form:

Random Number				
Sample Number	1	2	……	15
Complaints				

The random numbers are:

5	27	15	12	5	18	41	38	22	1
17	44	29	28	14	41	48	11	25	12
46	38	30	22	19	31	17	7	49	13

(3 marks)

(d) From the sample of 15 customers determined in part (c), calculate the modal, median and mean number of complaints. **(4 marks)**

(e) For this sample of customers, calculate the range and inter-quartile range for the number of complaints made. **(4 marks)**

(Total 15 marks)

EXAM QUESTION BANK

Question 2 (May 2015) 27 mins

A medium sized accounting company employs 50 staff across a range of job functions. For 20X4, the number of sick days registered by each employee is shown below:

Staff ID	Sick days	Staff ID	Sick days	Staff ID	Sick days	Staff ID	Sick days	Staff ID	Sick days
1	1	11	1	21	5	31	4	41	7
2	2	12	0	22	1	32	3	42	0
3	3	13	0	23	3	33	3	43	2
4	2	14	4	24	2	34	2	44	0
5	4	15	0	25	2	35	2	45	9
6	4	16	3	26	4	36	4	46	0
7	5	17	0	27	3	37	7	47	1
8	1	18	2	28	3	38	3	48	0
9	2	19	6	29	1	39	6	49	3
10	3	20	0	30	2	40	4	50	0

Required

(a) The data above are stored in Excel by the Human Resources Manager within the company. This secondary data source is arguably a better alternative than collecting primary data for the analysis of sickness absence. Explain what primary data is and why the data source above is more appropriate. **(2 marks)**

(b) The Human Resources Manager wishes to analyse only a sample of staff with respect to their sick days in 20X4. Describe why a simple random sample is an appropriate way to identify a group of employees to analyse and why such a sample of employees can easily be identified from the population data above. **(3 marks)**

(c) Using the following set of random numbers, starting with the first number in the table and using each row (reading left to right), provide a random sample of 15 employees presenting the data in a table of the form:

Random Number				
Sample Number	1	2	……	15
Sick days				

The random numbers are:

6	28	16	13	6	19	42	39	23	2
16	43	28	27	13	40	47	10	24	11
47	39	31	23	20	32	18	8	50	14

(3 marks)

(d) From the sample of 15 employees determined in part (c), present the data using an appropriate graphical display. **(3 marks)**

(e) From the sample of 15 employees determined in part (c), calculate the modal, median and mean number of sick days. **(4 marks)**

(Total 15 marks)

EXAM QUESTION BANK

Question 3 (November 2014)   27 mins

The Procurement Manager employed by a hotel chain has responsibility for dealing with suppliers specialising in electronic, electrical and telecommunications products. Her experience of such suppliers suggests that they have an 80% chance of successfully meeting standards relating to delivery, 90% for supply quality and a 50% chance on meeting standards pertaining to after sales service. For a supplier to be considered successful, they have to meet the hotel chain's standards on all three of these attributes. Suppliers meeting standards on either one or two of the areas are required to undertake improvements on their service provision and make bids for tender after a period of two years, whilst those failing on all three areas are recommended not to re-apply.

Required

(a) Represent the possible outcomes in the supplier problem described using a tree diagram.

(4 marks)

(b) From the tree diagram, calculate the following probabilities:

    (i) A company is successful.
    (ii) A company is unsuccessful but can re-apply after two years.
    (iii) A company is unsuccessful and is recommended not to re-apply.

(7 marks)

(c) If there are 150 applicants, what is the expected number of successful ones? **(1 mark)**

(d) If the time to process a tender is understood to be Normally distributed with a mean of 60 days and a standard deviation of 10 days, calculate the probability of this being processed within 45 days.

(3 marks)

(Total 15 marks)

Question 4 (May 2015)   27 mins

An Investment Manager employed by a medium sized accounting and financial planning firm has responsibility for making investments for a range of personal and corporate clients. One client has £10,000 to invest and wishes to put this into a new business start up. There are two alternatives put forward to her, which are shown below:

Alternative A				
Outcome	Poor	Fair	Good	Very Good
Probability	0.3	0.3	0.3	0.1
Income (£000s)	5.5	12.8	16.2	18.4
Alternative B				
Outcome	Poor	Fair	Good	Very Good
Probability	0.4	0.2	0.2	0.2
Income (£000s)	-4.8	15.0	17.9	30.6

Required

(a) Calculate the expected returns for each of the two alternatives A and B. **(6 marks)**

(b) Which of the two represents the better investment for the client? **(2 marks)**

(c) If the time for the Investment Manager to find a potential investment opportunity for the personal (rather than corporate) client is understood to be Normally distributed with a mean of 20 days and a standard deviation of 8 days, calculate the probability of this being processed within 24 days.

(3 marks)

(d) What would be the probability of finding such an investment taking between 16 and 28 days?

(4 marks)

(Total 15 marks)

Question 5 (November 2016)   27 mins

The Sales Director of a UK company specialising in classic sports cars would like her team of sales consultants to prioritise their sales activities by running sales and marketing events, believing these have a strong impact upon sales performance. A sample of 10 sales consultants were considered, with the number of events and unit sales achieved in 20X5 being presented below:

Sales Consultant	No. Events	No. Sales
A	12	35
B	16	40
C	8	20
D	14	33
E	25	50
F	20	43
G	6	15
H	10	30
I	14	24
J	9	34

Required

(a) Present the data above using an appropriate graphical display and comment on the overall shape of the data on the graph provided. **(3 marks)**

(b) The strength of the relationship between the number of events and the unit sales achieved in 20X5 has been measured using a correlation coefficient, giving a value of 0.868 (3dp). Suggest, with reasons, which measure of correlation should have been applied and describe what the value of the correlation coefficient indicates about the relationship between the two variables. **(3 marks)**

(c) Determine the relationship between unit sales and the numbers of events hosted using a simple linear regression model and provide a full interpretation of the coefficients calculated for this model. **(6 marks)**

(d) An additional sales representative is considered, who has run 18 events in 20X5. Using the regression model, forecast the number of sales likely to have been achieved and indicate how reliable such a forecast is likely to be. **(3 marks)**

(Total 15 marks)

Question 6 (May 2015)   27 mins

The manager of a sales team in a call centre specialising in household and motor insurance has concerns about the number of sick days taken by her sales staff. She believes this may be caused by the length of time the employees have been working in the call centre. To assess this, a random sample of 10 employees working within the sales team have been considered for the calendar year 20X4, their data are shown below:

Staff ID	Years service	Sick Days in 20X4
A	2	3
B	1	2
C	2	5
D	4	8
E	1	1
F	5	13
G	3	4
H	3	5
I	6	16
J	2	4

Required

(a) Present the relationship between the number of sick days and the number of years' service using an appropriate graphical display and comment on the shape of the graph. **(4 marks)**

(b) An appropriate correlation coefficient to assess the nature of this relationship is Pearson's product moment correlation coefficient. It has the value of 0.963 for this pair of variables. Suggest what this means for the relationship between the number of sick days and the number of years' service. **(2 marks)**

(c) Calculate a simple regression model to predict sick days from the number of years' service, providing an interpretation of the coefficients in the model. **(4 marks)**

(d) Two new members of staff assessed for absence, employee Y who has 3 years of service and employee Z who has 10 years of service. Estimate their expected levels of sick days and comment on the reliability of the forecasts made. **(5 marks)**

(Total 15 marks)

Question 7 (November 2014)   27 mins

A small travel retailer that deals in short European city-break holidays for couples has recorded the following unit sales of such holidays for each quarter in the years 20X0 to 20X3 inclusive:

	Quarterly unit sales			
Year	Q1	Q2	Q3	Q4
20X0	45	188	60	20
20X1	56	204	70	28
20X2	66	215	81	37
20X3	75	225	92	47

Required

(a) Present the data using a suitable graphical display. Indicate **precisely** the shape of the data presented. **(4 marks)**

(b) The trend line for the data is given by:

Trend T = 72.84 + 2.56t

Indicate **precisely** how this trend line would have been calculated for the data provided. Define and interpret the value of the coefficients in the relationship presented. **(6 marks)**

(c) The multiplicative and additive seasonal indices for the sales data are given by:

	Multiplicative Model	Additive Model
Q1	0.691	−30.60
Q2	2.218	115.94
Q3	0.787	−20.27
Q4	0.304	−65.06

Suggest which are the most appropriate indices for this sales data. **(1 mark)**

(d) Calculate forecasts of unit sales for the city-break holidays for the first two quarters of 20X4 using the most appropriate time series model. **(4 marks)**

(Total 15 marks)

Question 8 (May 2015)   27 mins

A City Council in Northern England has recorded the number of traffic violations for each quarter in the years 20X1 to 20X4 inclusive.

	Quarterly number of traffic violations			
Year	Q1	Q2	Q3	Q4
20X1	25	88	100	120
20X2	36	104	111	128
20X3	47	115	120	137
20X4	57	125	133	147

Required

(a) Present the data using a suitable graphical display. Indicate **precisely** the shape of the data presented. **(3 marks)**

(b) The trend line for the data is given by:

Trend T = 78.06 + 2.55t

Indicate **precisely** how this trend line would have been calculated for the data provided. Define and interpret the value of the coefficients in the relationship presented. **(5 marks)**

(c) The multiplicative and additive seasonal indices for the traffic violation data are given by:

	Multiplicative Model	Additive Model
Q1	0.456	−54.71
Q2	1.108	11.21
Q3	1.156	14.75
Q4	1.307	29.88

Suggest which are the most appropriate indices for this sales data and forecast the number of violations for the first quarter of **20X5**. **(3 marks)**

(d) The same City Council has permission to fine its residents for traffic violation, litter, incorrect use of the refuse collection service and late bills payments. The number of fines and the average fine for each of these offences for 20X0 and 20X4 are shown below. Calculate a Paasche Index to indicate the change in Council revenue between these two years.

	20X0		20X4	
	Number of fines	Average value of fine (£)	Number of fines	Average value of fine (£)
Traffic	1,235	60	967	90
Litter	2,550	25	2,100	30
Refuse	125	200	115	300
Late Bills	855	100	1,000	125

(4 marks)

(Total 15 marks)

SECTION B – Business Information Technology

Question 9 (May 2015) 18 mins

You are running a workshop for medium sized businesses investing in IT systems for the first time in their respective companies. An essential component of this workshop is the session dedicated to the systems development life cycle. Four important component parts of the systems development life cycle are systems investigation, systems analysis, systems design and systems implementation.

Required

Describe the role and importance of each of the four components listed above as part of the systems development life cycle. **(10 marks)**

Question 10 (November 2016) 18 mins

As a Project Manager in a medium-sized Information Technology (IT) Consultancy, you have won the contract to develop a new expert information system for an independent broker who deals in insurance and small consumer loans.

Required

(a) Define the term expert system. **(2 marks)**

(b) Describe the role of the expert system in dealing with small loan applications within the brokerage. **(4 marks)**

(c) Describe four essential conditions necessary for the implementation of an expert system. **(4 marks)**

(Total 10 marks)

Question 11 (May 2015) 18 mins

As Training Manager within a large manufacturing company, you have agreed your annual budget for the new financial year. You have decided to appoint two new staff to work as Administrators within the office that provides the administrative and financial support. They need to have an initial induction into the office and its process, including the use of Information Technology (IT).

Required

As part of the induction, provide bullet-point definitions for, and describe the roles and the users of, the following applications:

(a) General business computer software used in the office. **(4 marks)**
(b) Computer hardware found in the office. **(3 marks)**
(c) Specialist integrated financial software used in the office. **(3 marks)**

(Total 10 marks)

Question 12 (November 2014)   18 mins

You have recently been appointed as Director of Information Technology (IT) at a large online retail organisation that specialises in clothing for the 18–24 year-old markets. The organisation employs 250 people and has markets both in the UK and across Western Europe serving around 10,000 online customers.

Required

(a) Explain the application and essential characteristics of a database management system. **(5 marks)**

(b) Define the key challenges that an organisation may face with the implementation and application of a database management system. **(5 marks)**

(Total 10 marks)

Question 13 (May 2015)   18 mins

You have recently been appointed as Sales Director at a large mail-based retail organisation that specialises in classical music. The organisation employs 70 people and has markets both in the UK and across Western Europe serving around 5,000 customers whose details and purchasing records are on a manual system. The customer records need updating and you are employing a student on placement for a year from a UK University. A member of the IT team and two IT-trained administrators will support the student in the development of a database management system and data warehouse.

Required

Describe the essential requirements of the one-year role in the conversion of the current manual records system into a database management system that can be accessed, amended and queried by members of the sales team within the retail organisation. It is anticipated that the new system will be fully operational on the completion of the placement. **(10 marks)**

Question 14 (May 2017)   18 mins

As Director of Information Technology at a leading European University, you are proposing a significant investment in hardware within the University comprising certain types of computer.

Required

(a) Define the term supercomputer and identify where such computers may be used within the University. **(3 marks)**

(b) Define the term mainframe computer and indicate the benefits of the University making an investment in this type of hardware. **(4 marks)**

(c) Describe what is meant by a microcomputer and suggest where these are best deployed across the University. **(3 marks)**

(Total 10 marks)

Question 15 (May 2015) — 18 mins

You have just been appointed as a lecturer by a college that provides undergraduate degree programmes in Computing and Information Technology. The Head of Department has given you the opportunity to run a lecture programme for students in the second year of their degree programme and you have been given development time to produce some new lecture materials. To do this, prepare bullet-point notes on the following:

Required

Describe the necessary website development considerations for an individual wishing to engage in e-business. **(10 marks)**

Exam answer bank

SECTION A – Data Collection and Analysis

Question 1 (November 2014)

SUMMARY

Principles of Statistical Sources and Data Collection – Learning Outcomes 1, 4

Candidates will be expected to understand data sources, explain and implement an approach to sampling and in doing so, assessment criteria 1.1 and 1.4 will have been considered, covering syllabus area 6.1. Additionally, candidates will have calculated measures of average and dispersion, thus criteria 4.3 and 4.6 will have been considered, covering syllabus areas 6.1 and 6.3. See AIA Study Text, Chapters 2, 3, 4a, 4b.

(a) This is **secondary data**, given the source already exists internally within the organisation.

(b) In a simple random sample, every member of the population has an equal chance of being selected, therefore the approach is seen to be fair and unbiased. This is achievable here because all members of the population have been identified and all have been measured and data stored accordingly within which each population member has a unique ID attached. Random numbers can be used in conjunction with the latter to select the simple random sample.

(c) The random numbers used from the table ignoring any repeats are 5, 27, 15, 12, 18, 41, 38, 22, 1, 17, 44, 29, 28, 14 and 48.

The sample selected is:

Rand No.	5	27	15	12	18	41	38	22
Sample Member	1	2	3	4	5	6	7	8
Complaints	3	2	1	1	3	8	1	0
Rand No.	1	17	44	29	28	14	48	
Sample Member	9	10	11	12	13	14	15	
Complaints	0	0	0	0	2	5	1	

(d) Ordered array: 0 0 0 0 0 1 1 1 1 2 2 3 3 5 8
Mode = 0 complaints (occurs 5 times)
Median = ordered value $(n + 1)/2$ = ordered value number 8 = 1 complaint
Mean = $\Sigma x/n$ = 27/15 = 1.8 complaints

(e) Range = Max – Min = 8 – 0 = 8 complaints
IQR = Q3 – Q1
Q3 = ordered value $3(n + 1)/4$ = ordered value 12 = 3
Q1 = ordered value $(n + 1)/4$ = ordered value 4 = 0
IQR = 3 – 0 = 3 complaints

Question 2 (May 2015)

SUMMARY

Principles of Statistical Sources and Data Collection – Learning Outcomes 1, 4.

Candidates will be expected to understand data sources, explain and implement an approach to sampling and in doing so, assessment criteria 1.1 and 1.4 will have been considered, covering syllabus area 6.1. Additionally, candidates will have calculated measures of averages, thus criteria 4.3 will have been considered, covering syllabus area 6.3. Presenting data graphically will have covered syllabus area 6.2. See AIA Study Text, Chapters 2, 3, 4a, 4b.

(a) Primary data is new data specific to a particular project or business problem. It is up to date, accurate and relevant, but may be time consuming, difficult and costly to collect. This data presented is **secondary data**, is relatively new and fits the business problem being examined, so why invest more time and money collecting data that may be little better than this?

(b) In a simple random sample, every member of the population (ie all of the employees) has an equal chance of being selected. Therefore, the approach is seen to be fair and unbiased. This is achievable here because all employees have been identified and measured, their data stored accordingly within which each employee has a unique ID attached. Random numbers can be used in conjunction with the latter to select the simple random sample.

(c) The random numbers used from the table ignoring any repeats are 6, 28, 16, 13, 19, 42, 39, 23, 2, 43, 27, 40, 47, 10 and 24.

The sample selected is:

Rand No.	6	28	16	13	19	42	39	23
Sample Member	1	2	3	4	5	6	7	8
Sick days	4	3	3	0	6	0	6	3
Rand No.	2	43	27	40	47	10	24	
Sample Member	9	10	11	12	13	14	15	
Sick Days	2	2	3	4	1	3	2	

(d) The data are quantitative and discrete, so can be represented by a bar chart.

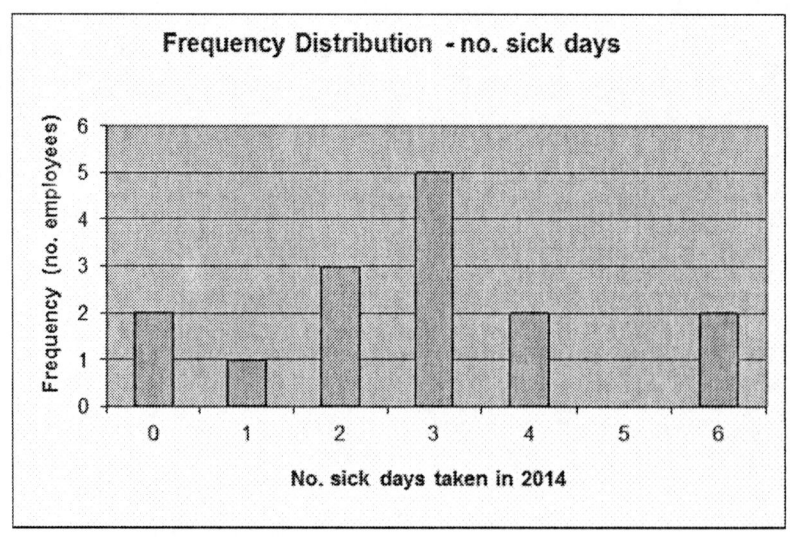

(e) Ordered array: 0 0 1 2 2 2 3 3 3 3 3 4 4 6 6
Mode = 3 sick days (occurs 5 times)
Median = ordered value (n + 1)/2 = ordered value number 8 = 3 sick days
Mean = $\Sigma x/n$ = 42/15 = 2.8 sick days

Question 3 (November 2014)

SUMMARY

Principles of Statistical Sources and Data Collection – Learning Outcome 3

Candidates will be expected to practically apply tree diagrams and the basic laws of probability, as well as the Normal statistical distributions to a business related scenario, and in doing so, explain one of the key statistical distributions in relation to decision making, thus considering assessment criteria 3.1, covering syllabus area 6.4. See AIA Study Text, Chapter 5.

(a) The tree diagram is shown below.

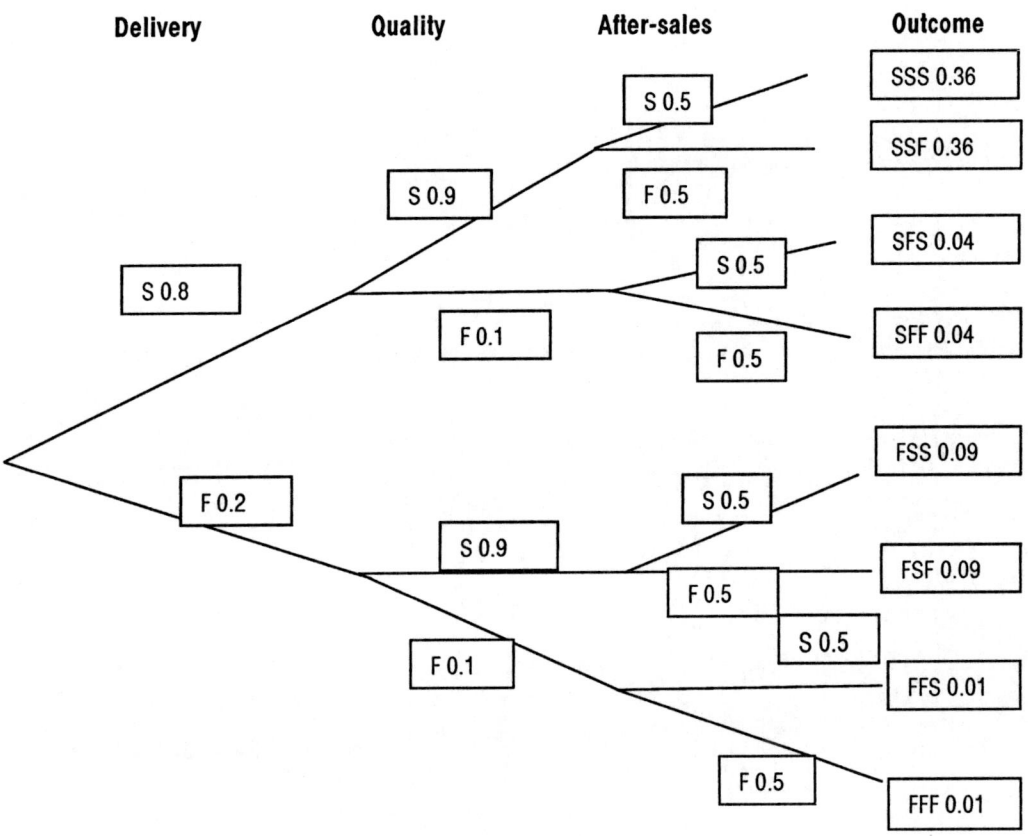

(b) The probabilities of the three outcomes are:

The company is successful = $0.8 \times 0.9 \times 0.5$ = **0.36**.

The company can come back in 2 years =
P(two successful areas) + P(one successful area) =
(SSF + SFS + FSS) + (SFF + FSF + FFS) =
(0.36 + 0.04 + 0.09) + (0.04 + 0.09 + 0.01) = 0.49 + 0.14 = **0.63**

The company is recommended not to re-apply = $0.2 \times 0.1 \times 0.5$ = **0.01**

(c) Expected number of successful applicants = np = 150×0.36 = **54 applicants**.

(d) $P(Z < z) = P(Z < (x - \mu)/\sigma) = P(Z < (45 - 60)/10) = P(Z < -1.5)$

Through symmetry, $P(Z < -1.5) = P(Z > 1.5) = 0.4332$ from statistical tables.
The probability of processing an application in less than 45 minutes is **43.32%**.

Question 4 (May 2015)

SUMMARY

Principles of Statistical Sources and Data Collection – Learning Outcome 3

Candidates will be expected to practically apply expected values to decision making, as well as the Normal statistical distributions to a business related scenario, and in doing so, explain one of the key statistical distributions in relation to decision making, thus considering assessment criteria 3.1, covering syllabus area 6.4. See AIA Study Text, Chapter 5.

(a) Alternative A: Expected value = $(0.3 \times 5.5) + (0.3 \times 12.8) + (0.3 \times 16.2) + (0.1 \times 18.4) - 10 = $ **2.19** (£000s)

Alternative B: Expected value = $(0.4 \times -4.8) + (0.2 \times 15.0) + (0.2 \times 17.9) + (0.2 \times 30.6) - 10 = $ **0.78 (£000s)**

(b) The better of the two alternatives is A with the highest expected value. The corresponding value of B is barely better than breakeven.

(c) $P(Z < z) = P(Z < (x - \mu)/\sigma) = P(Z < (24 - 20)/8) = P(Z < 0.5)$ $P(Z < 0.5) = 0.8085$ from statistical tables.

The probability of finding an investment within 24 days is **80.85%**.

(d) $P(z < Z < z) = P(Z < (x - \mu)/\sigma) - P(Z < (x - \mu)/\sigma$

$= P(Z < (28 - 20)/8) - P(Z < (16 - 20)/8) = P(Z < 1) - P(Z < -0.5)$
$= 0.6587 - 0.1915 = 0.4672$

The probability of finding an investment between 16 and 28 days is **46.72%**.

Question 5 (November 2016)

Principles of Statistical Sources and Data Collection – Learning Outcome 4

The analysis of relationships between variables using correlation and regression analysis addresses the assessment criteria 4.1 and syllabus section 6.5. See AIA Study Text, Chapter 3.

(a) The data provided should be presented on a scatter graph. The graph shows evidence of a strong, positive linear association, ie as number of events increases, so do the number of car sales made.

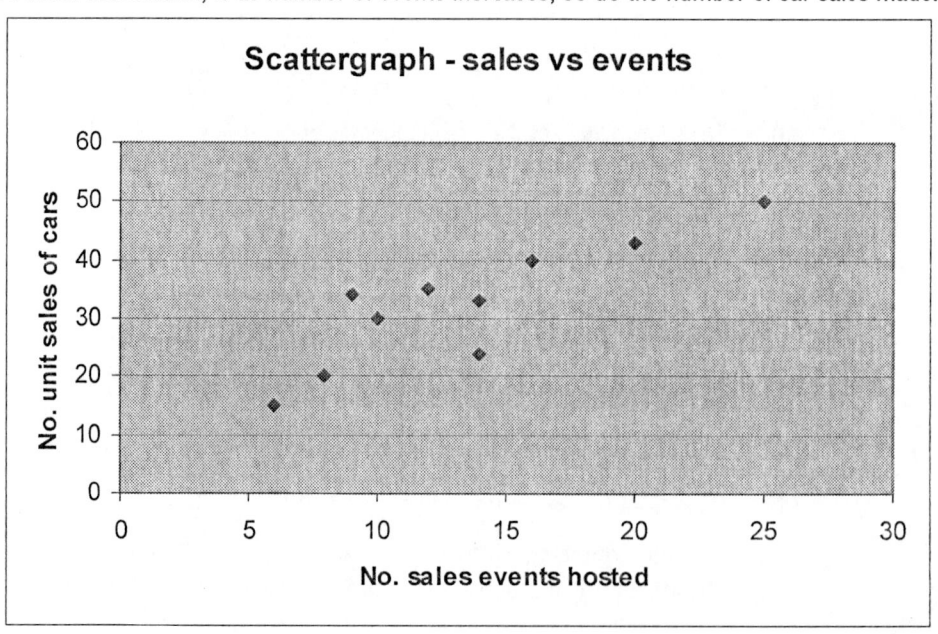

(b) To assess the strength of this association, use Pearson's correlation coefficient given that both measurements are quantitative data. The value of r is very close to +1, further supporting the comments above about the relationship being strong and positive.

(c) To develop the linear regression model, y = a + bx, x = number of events held, y = number of cars sold, the calculation is shown below.

	No. events (x)	No. Sales (y)	xy	x-squared
	12	35	420	144
	16	40	640	256
	8	20	160	64
	14	33	462	196
	25	50	1,250	625
	20	43	860	400
	6	15	90	36
	10	30	300	100
	14	24	336	196
	9	34	306	81
Total	134	324	4,824	2,098
Average	13.4	32.4		

The slope coefficient b =

$$b = \frac{n\Sigma xy - (\Sigma x)(\Sigma y)}{(n\Sigma x^2 - (\Sigma x)^2)}$$

b = (10 × 4,824 − 134 × 324)/(10 × 2,098 − 134^2)

b = 1.595 (3dp)

The value of b suggests for every extra sales event a consultant provides for the company, they are expected to make an extra 1.595 unit sales.

The intercept is given by a = Σy/n − bΣx/n = 32.4 − 1.595 × 13.4 = 11.024

The linear model is given by y = 11.024 + 1.595x

(d) For the new person who has run 18 events, y = 11.024 + 1.595x × 18 = 39.738 unit sales, ie 40 sales.

The value of r is high, the model fits the data well, with the forecast being an interpolation, given the value of x is inside the sample range (x range from 6 to 25 inclusive), hence the forecast is reliable.

Question 6 (May 2015)

SUMMARY

Principles of Statistical Sources and Data Collection – Learning Outcome 4

Candidates will be expected to summarise data graphically and calculate single regression model and provide interpretation and forecasts. In doing so, assessment criteria 4.1 and 4.2 are covered, covering syllabus areas 6.2 and 6.5. See AIA Study Text, Chapters 3 and 6.

(a) The scattergraph is the most appropriate presentation, as shown below.

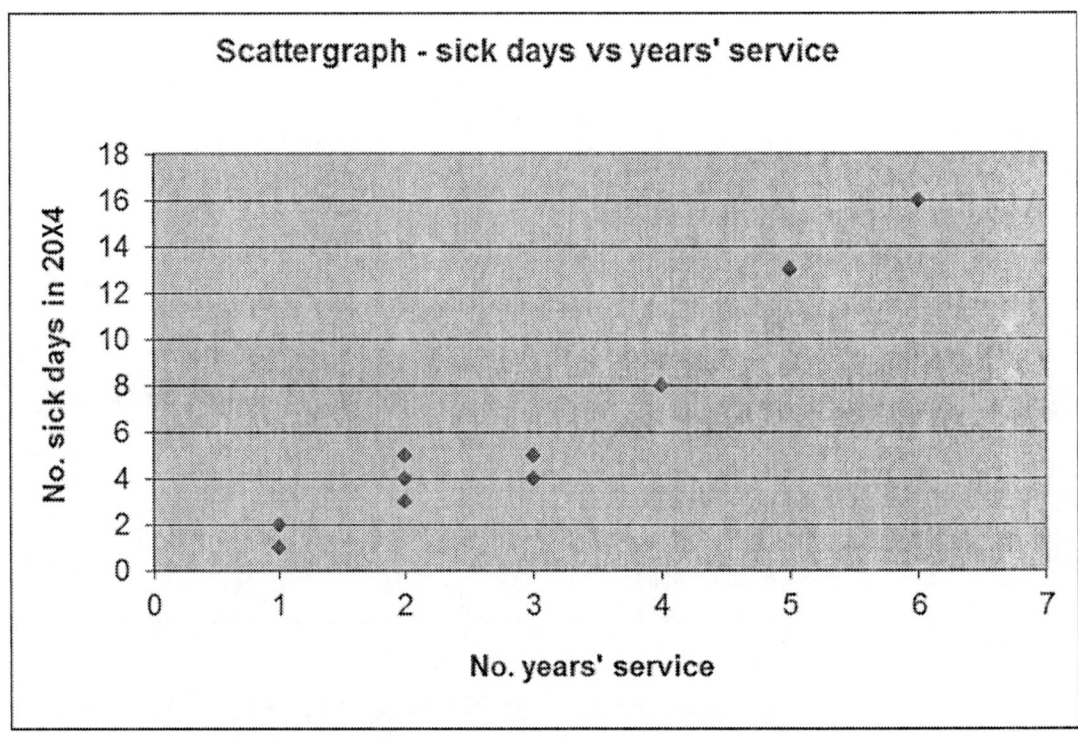

There is a very strong, positive and linear association apparent here, ie as length of service increases, so to do the number of sick days taken by the employees.

(b) The correlation coefficient presented has a value of 0.963, which is very close to +1, which supports the comments made in part a) about the strength and direction of the relationship presented.

(c) To develop the linear regression model, $y = a + bx$, x = number of years' service, y = number of sick days in 20X4, the calculation is shown below.

	x	y	xy	x-sqd
	2	3	6	4
	1	2	2	1
	2	5	10	4
	4	8	32	16
	1	1	1	1
	5	13	65	25
	3	4	12	9
	3	5	15	9
	6	16	96	36
	2	4	8	4
TOTAL	29	61	247	109
MEAN	2.9	6.1		

The slope coefficient b =

b = nΣxy − (Σx)(Σy)

(nΣx² − (Σx)²)

b = (10 × 247 − 29 × 61)/(10 × 109 − 29²)

b = 2.815 (3dp)

The value of b suggests for every extra years' service an employee provides to the company, they are expected to take an extra 2.815 sick days.

The intercept is given by a = Σy/n − bΣx/n = 6.1 − 2.815 × 2.9 = −2.064

The linear model is given by y = −2.064 + 2.815x

(d) For person Y with 3 years of service, y = −2.064 + 2.815 × 3 = 6.4 sick days. For person Z with 10 years of service, y = −2.064 + 2.815 × 10 = 26.1 sick days.

The value of r is high, the model fits the data well, but the second forecast is an extrapolation, given the value of x is outside the sample range, hence the forecast is less reliable.

Question 7 (November 2014)

SUMMARY

Principles of Statistical Sources and Data Collection − Learning Outcome 2

Candidates will be expected to use statistical techniques to identify time series models, apply a time series plot and choose appropriately between an additive and multiplicative model. After doing so, they will have analysed the time series to produce forecasts. In doing so, assessment criteria 2.1 and 2.2 will have been considered, covering syllabus area 6.6. See AIA Study Text, Chapter 7.

(a) The time series plot is given by the line graph below.

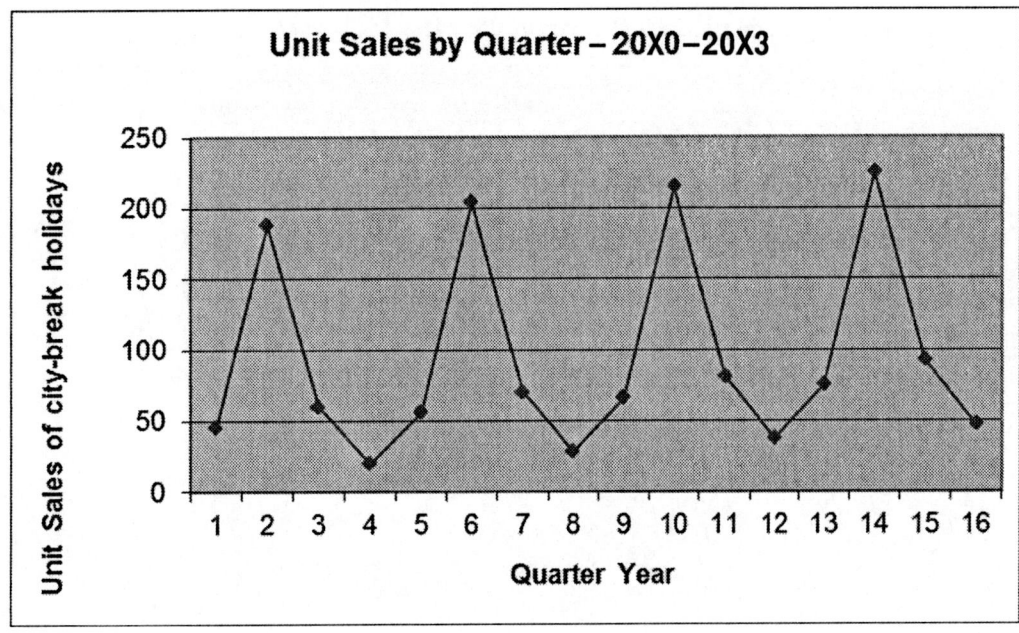

The graph shows the points are moving in an upward direction, hence there is a positive trend, ie sales are increasing over time. The sales have a seasonal pattern, with a peak in each year in Quarter 2, the lowest sales being in Quarter 4, the seasonal pattern is constant in size.

(b) The trend line is used to measure the true or underlying growth in sales. To calculate this, a 4 point moving average is calculated, 4 point because of the number of points (ie quarterly) in the repeating seasonal pattern. The first moving average calculation for time periods 1, 2, 3 and 4 is placed next to time period 3. The next calculated for time periods 2, 3, 4 and 5 is placed next to time period 4. Because of the even number of points in the pattern, a centred moving average is calculated, the first being the average of the two calculations above is then placed next to time period 3. This is repeated for the whole data set.

The trend line is calculated using a simple regression model, the y data being the centred moving average, the x data being time.

The trend line, $T = 72.84 + 2.56t$, tells us at the start of the time period the underlying value of sales was 72.84, with its seasonally adjusted growth being 2.56 units per quarter.

(c) The most appropriate indices are those relating to the additive model, given the constant size of the seasonal pattern shown on the time series plot.

(d) The forecast of sales for Q1 2014 = T + S = $(72.84 + 2.56 \times 17) - 30.60 = 85.68$ = **86 holidays**.

The forecast of sales for Q2 2014 = T + S = $(72.84 + 2.56 \times 18) + 115.94 = 234.77$ = **235 holidays**.

Question 8 (May 2015)

SUMMARY

Principles of Statistical Sources and Data Collection – Learning Outcome 2

Candidates will be expected to use statistical techniques to identify time series models, apply a time series plot and choose appropriately between an additive and multiplicative model. After doing so, they will have analysed the time series to produce forecasts. In doing so, assessment criteria 2.1 and 2.2 will have been considered, covering syllabus area 6.6. They will also have calculated a Paasche Index, covering assessment criteria 2.4 and syllabus area 6.7. See AIA Study Text, Chapters 7 and 8.

(a) The time series plot is given by the line graph below.

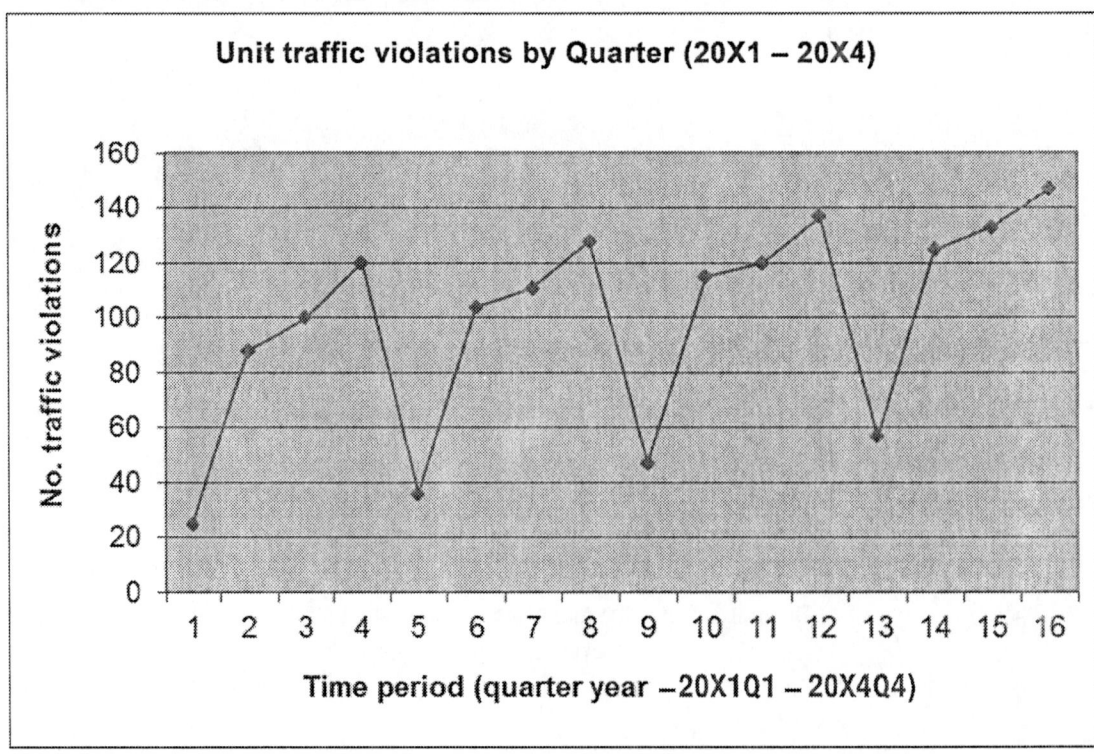

The graph shows the points are moving in an upward direction, hence there is a positive trend, ie traffic violations are increasing over time. The offences have a seasonal pattern, with a peak in each year in Quarters 2 to 4 (peaking in 4), the lowest number of violations being in Quarter 1, the seasonal pattern is constant in size.

(b) The trend line is used to measure the true or underlying growth in number of traffic violations. To calculate this, a 4 point moving average is calculated, 4 point because of the number of points (ie quarterly) in the repeating seasonal pattern. The first moving average calculation for time periods 1, 2, 3 and 4 is placed next to time period 3. The next calculated for time periods 2, 3, 4 and 5 is placed next to time period 4. Because of the even number of points in the pattern, a centred moving average is calculated, the first being the average of the two calculations above is then placed next to time period 3. This is repeated for the whole data set.

The trend line is calculated using a simple regression model, the y data being the centred moving average, the x data being time.

The trend line, $T = 78.06 + 2.55t$, tells us at the start of the time period the underlying value of traffic offences was 78.06, with its seasonally adjusted growth being 2.55 units per quarter.

(c) The most appropriate indices are those relating to the additive model, given the constant size of the seasonal pattern shown on the time series plot. The forecast is given by Q1 2014 = T + S = $(78.06 + 2.55 \times 17) - 54.71 = 66.7 =$ **67 traffic violations**.

(d) The Paasche Index is given by the formula $100 \times \Sigma P_n Q_n / \Sigma P_0 Q_n$

	Qn	P0	Pn	P0 × Qn	Pn × Qn
Traffic	967	60	90	58,020	87,030
Litter	2,100	25	30	52,500	63,000
Refuse	115	200	300	23,000	34,500
Late Bills	1,000	100	125	100,000	125,000
			TOTAL	233,520	309,530

The Index = $100 \times 309{,}530/233{,}520 = 132.55$. Between 20X0 and 20X4, council revenue through fines has increased by 32.55%.

EXAM ANSWER BANK

SECTION B – Business Information Processing

Question 9 (May 2015)

SUMMARY

Business Information Processing – Learning Outcome 1

Candidates will be expected to understand the role of four key stages in the systems development life cycle. In doing so, assessment criteria 1.3 will have been considered, covering syllabus area 6.8. See AIA Study Text, Chapter 9.

Systems Investigation – Assessment of the current systems in terms of how it performs well alongside its limitations. An evaluation of data types and volumes alongside the level of employee usage will also take place here to assess the potential requirements of the existing system in the future or the capacity and features of any alternative.

Systems Analysis – The documentation of the current system based on the issues highlighted during the investigation stage and an analysis of the systems' performance, against a range of organisation set key performance indicators (KPIs). The analysis will examine the rationale for the current system with a comparison of the alternatives to provide the same or improved solutions, together with an assessment of the KPIs relevant to the chosen alternative.

Systems Design – Inputs, outputs, programme and file design, alongside support and security are identified for current systems implementation, alongside new (alternative) processes to identify the most appropriate way forward leading to a comprehensive design of the new system with a specification that covers all of the areas listed above.

Systems Implementation – This covers the life of the new system to the point of being fully operational. This will cover software development or procurement, testing, conversion of existing files or data (from computer or manual sources), hardware development or procurement, then live implementation involving appropriate employees.

Question 10 (November 2016)

SUMMARY

Business Information Processing – Learning Outcome 1

Candidates will be expected to understand the key concept of an expert system, alongside its organisational role and potential scope of application. In doing so, assessment criteria 1.1 and 1.2 will have been considered, covering syllabus area 6.8. See AIA Study Text, Chapter 9.

(a) Expert systems are decision support systems that comprise a database housing specialist information and associated rules for interpretation and application.

(b) For the small loan application, the broker will seek various pieces of information from the loan applicant. This will comprise name, address, income, financial obligations including day-to-day expenditure and both current and historic loans. This data is entered into the expert system to be verified and to assess the credit worthiness of the applicant. As appropriate, relevant calculations can be undertaken to assess how easily the applicant can make loan repayments. Additional criteria, as relevant, such as loan security or purpose for borrowing can be considered. Based on this data processing, a decision on whether to grant the loan or reject the application can be made at point of request.

(c) For an expert system to be justified, it must be cost beneficial in terms of the time saved thereby allowing the broker to work on other activities that require greater intervention, time, judgement and personal decision making. The expert system is reserved for loan applications that are straightforward and well defined. Such applications can be judged based on a suite of set rules that are applicable to all consumers who are judged by the system.

Question 11 (May 2015)

SUMMARY

Business Information Processing – Learning Outcome 2

Candidates will be expected to assess the purpose of certain types of general and accounting-related application software. In doing so, assessment criteria 2.5 will have been considered, covering syllabus area 6.10. Candidates will also consider standard computer hardware covering assessment criteria 2.1 syllabus area 6.9. See AIA Study Text, Chapter 10.

(a) General business software is a user-oriented program in place to undertake various day-to-day tasks within the Administrative and Finance office. These are likely to be off the shelf applications, which are standard to business and its users. Examples are word processing, spreadsheet, database and presentation applications. The company are likely to have these as a matter of course, given the necessity to write formal correspondence (internal and external to the business) undertake various calculations including the development of templates, house specific records and be required to make formal presentations for events such as meetings. All members of the office will use this software.

(b) The computer hardware most prominent in this office environment is a number of personal computers configured to a network that supports the various general business and dedicated accounting software. Given the power and capability of such PCs and current networks, it is unlikely that mini or supercomputers will be in place. Other hardware to consider in the induction event are printing and fax facilities, again configured to the relevant networks. All members of the office will use this hardware.

(c) Integrated accounting software is built from a group of related accounting programs that perform a range of finance related activities that the company will expect to be provided from this office. The configuration of this software may comprise a number of distinct programmes which link together to provide a comprehensive accounting system. Compatibility of data is offered through this type of integration, allowing flow of data from one component to another, increasing speed and accuracy of work and avoiding repetition of data entry. This type of software is likely to be used by only a limited number of employees with specific skills and roles.

Question 12 (November 2014)

SUMMARY

Business Information Processing – Learning Outcome 3

Candidates will be expected to explain the role of database management systems, as well as identifying the challenges to an organisation of implementing data base systems. In doing so, assessment criteria 3.1 will have been considered, covering syllabus area 6.11. See AIA Study Text, Chapter 11.

(a) A database management system is one that provides a centralised source of data and supports appropriate employee access to it. Given the size of the retail operation being presented here in terms of potential customer enquiries and employees accessing relevant and up to date data, the necessity for a robust and unique data set that can respond to multiple, simultaneous access is essential. The system must be shared, it must be supported by controls that ensure the data is kept securely and not be subject to corruption or deletion and given the potential for customer variety and diversity, the system needs to permit employee flexibility in their requests and access to information in support.

(b) The challenges facing an organisation of this size given both the number of employees and registered clients is the development, testing and implementation costs, particularly if this represents the first computer-based system. Post-implementation, the retailer needs to protect against potential failures to the system, ensuring that adequate back-ups are taken of the system, should these occur. The application of a single, centralised source of data requires support in terms of being robust and free from corruption, whilst security, given customer information is being held is essential. The database should be run with the understanding of necessary regulation relating to data privacy, given its client content.

Question 13 (May 2015)

SUMMARY

Business Information Processing – Learning Outcome 3

Candidates will be expected to explain the role of database management systems, as well as identifying the challenges to an organisation of implementing data base systems. In doing so, assessment criteria 3.2 will have been considered, covering syllabus area 6.11. See AIA Study Text, Chapter 11.

Given the size of the organisation both in terms of the number of employees and registered clients, a clear priority is the development, testing and implementation time for the project, particularly if this represents the first computer-based system. The student must provide a timeline and cost breakdown for this project.

The application of a single, centralised source of data requires support in terms of being robust and free from corruption, whilst security, given customer information is being held is essential. All staff should be briefed on security; the IT support is fully trained on methods to combat any potential breakdowns or corruption. The student may support specific developments relating to both.

Given the potential for customer variety and diversity, the system needs to permit employee flexibility in their requests and access to information in support. They must be formally trained and developed by the student in writing database queries, handling and interpreting the system output.

The student must be able to support the concurrent running of the existing manual and new automated system in the first instance. Post-implementation, the student needs to ensure robust protection against potential failures to the system, ensuring that adequate back-ups are taken of the system, should these occur. Training of relevant IT support staff in these procedures is essential as indicated above.

The database should be run with the understanding of necessary regulation relating to data privacy, with across the company staff development and a training/regulation protocol being put in place to support this. The student can develop these protocols and training instruments.

Question 14 (May 2017)

SUMMARY

Business Information Processing – Learning Outcome 6

Candidates will be expected to assess the purpose of certain types of computer and therefore have considered alternatives in hardware. In doing so, assessment criteria 6.1 will have been considered, covering syllabus area 6.9. See AIA Study Text, Chapter 10.

(a) The supercomputer is the most powerful computer available to the University and as such, is the most expensive. If the University is engaged in significant and high-level scientific research involving highly complex data analysis, then it may be justifiable to make such an investment, particularly if the academic departments requiring this type of computer have funding to support its purchase.

(b) A mainframe computer is again relatively powerful and one or more of these could be purchased by the University to be used as the core or centre of a large computer system. This would be connected to various terminals around the University by means of appropriate telecommunications and affords its multiple users with significant processing power and data storage facilities. Depending upon the level of investment made, there may be a mainframe used as the central processing and storage point for academic systems and another for the various administrative support facilities. Back-up storage may also be part of the investment.

(c) The microcomputer is a general-purpose computer that is relatively inexpensive, so the investment could involve providing one each to every academic and administrative member of staff with various class-based and casual use facilities being provided for student use. The microcomputers will be networked as required to enable access to various University systems and the information sharing between users within similar roles.

Question 15 (May 2015)

SUMMARY

Business Information Processing – Learning Outcome 4

Candidates will be expected to define B2C applications of e-commerce and e-business. In doing so, assessment criteria 4.5 will have been considered, covering syllabus area 6.13. See AIA Study Text, Chapter 13.

Central to any successful business relationship is trust between the business and its customer base. In the environment of e-business, this trust has to be built upon secure IT systems and safe transactions particularly when money and customer details are involved. You must ensure such safety is in place and that the customers are fully aware of it.

You and your customers must be fully aware of the country's legal stance on e-business and fully comply with these regulations. From the company perspective, this involves full compliance with consumer legislation, as well as issues of privacy and data protection. From a consumer perspective, provide a clear code of conduct for using the website with rules for any potential violations.

Managed information to customers is essential particularly so that they trust you, do not come back for missing information and they are fully informed about the transactions and their rights. Ensure the information provided is not too significant; this may deter further business transaction.

In a managed, but not an excessive way, maintain contacts with your customers through email and the provision of future incentives (based on loyalty and frequency of transaction), with discounts etc.

Maintain the customer relationships further through activities such as servicing existing products or the offer of other business related activities beyond the buying and selling arrangements already described.

EXAM ANSWER BANK

Mock exam 1 questions and answers

MODULE B

FOUNDATION EXAMINATION

PAPER 6 – INFORMATION PROCESSING

WEDNESDAY 29th NOVEMBER 2017

Time allowed – 3 hours

SECTION A
Answer ALL questions

SECTION B
Answer ALL questions

Statistical tables and formulae are printed at the end of the question paper.

Graph Paper is provided

You are allowed an additional 15 minutes reading time before the exam begins, during which you should read the question paper and, if you wish, make notes on the question paper. You are **not** allowed to open the exam script booklet and start writing or use your calculator during the reading time.

Section A

Answer ALL questions

1   (a)   An Information Technology Diploma written for 16 to 18 year-olds who are working as Apprentice Technicians consists of three examinations. The Head of Training at a large retail consortium, who has set up a nationwide Technician Scheme employing 250 apprentices in her company, believes the pass rate for each of the three examinations is 80%. For each of the apprentice technicians entering these examinations, calculate the probability that:

   (i)   The candidate will be successful in none of the examinations.

   (ii) The candidate will be successful in either one or two of the examinations.

   (iii) The candidate will pass all three examinations.

   (iv) If a candidate fails all of the examinations, he/she will have to leave the apprenticeship, if one or two examinations are passed, they are offered one referral opportunity, whilst those passing all of the examinations are offered a permanent job contract. What is the expected number of apprentice technicians for each outcome in the retail consortium? **(9 marks)**

   (b)   After two years of post-diploma work experience, these Information Technology employees are permitted to sit an additional examination. The Chief Examiner has advised that in the most recent sitting, the examination marks are Normally distributed with a mean mark of 65% and a standard deviation of 30%.

   (i)   If the pass mark is 50%, determine the probability that an individual candidate has passed.

   (ii) Below what percentage mark do the lowest performing 10% of students lie on the distribution of examination marks presented above? **(6 marks)**

   (Total 15 marks)

2   A large Government department is located in a city about 300 miles from its country's capital. The department has been located here for 10 years as part of an initiative to generate employment in this smaller city. There is some belief that absence is a problem within the department, thereby deterring future job applicants. To assess this, a random sample of 55 employees have been assessed for their sick days' leave in 2016, the data are recorded in the table below.

1	1	3	2	0	1	7	9	0	4	3
1	1	6	3	1	0	1	2	2	2	2
4	5	0	1	2	1	1	1	7	1	1
1	1	1	3	5	1	8	0	1	0	0
4	2	2	4	1	1	0	2	10	0	2

Required

(a)   Tabulate the sickness data and display graphically, commenting upon the shape of the distribution. **(5 marks)**

(b)   From the data provided, calculate the most appropriate measure of central tendency. **(2 marks)**

(c)   From the data provided, calculate the most appropriate measure of dispersion. **(3 marks)**

(d)   With reference to the process of data collection, describe a likely data source, suggesting why this is most appropriate for the study. Also, comment on the necessity, or otherwise, for sampling with reference to this study. **(5 marks)**

(Total 15 marks)

3   An independent insurance broker has recorded the number of calls per working day (the working days being Monday to Friday) over a four-week period relating to the potential claims relating to property policies.

Week	Day				
	Mon	Tue	Wed	Thu	Fri
1	30	38	16	14	10
2	34	43	19	18	12
3	39	49	22	22	15
4	45	56	26	25	18

Required

(a) Present the data using a suitable graphical display. From this display, describe **precisely** the shape of the time series data. **(3 marks)**

(b) For the time series data shown below, describe how the trend line would be calculated for this data. Calculate this trend line, defining and interpreting the value of the coefficients in the relationship presented.

Week	Day	Time	Calls	5-pt MA
1	Mon	1	30	
	Tue	2	38	
	Wed	3	16	21.60
	Thu	4	14	22.40
	Fri	5	10	23.40
2	Mon	6	34	24.00
	Tue	7	43	24.80
	Wed	8	19	25.20
	Thu	9	18	26.20
	Fri	10	12	27.40
3	Mon	11	39	28.00
	Tue	12	49	28.80
	Wed	13	22	29.40
	Thu	14	22	30.60
	Fri	15	15	32.00
4	Mon	16	45	32.80
	Tue	17	56	33.40
	Wed	18	26	34.00
	Thu	19	25	
	Fri	20	18	

(7 marks)

(c) For the data set provided, choose the most appropriate seasonal indices for the time series presented.

	Adjusted Seasonal Indices	
Day	Additive	Multiplicative
Mon	10.880	1.402
Tue	20.147	1.714
Wed	−6.987	0.756
Thu	−8.587	0.681
Fri	−15.453	0.447

(1 mark)

(d) Using your calculations in part (b) and your choice as the most relevant information provided in part (c), forecast the number of calls received by the insurance broker for Monday and Tuesday of week 5. **(4 marks)**

(Total 15 marks)

4 The Sales Director of a telesales organisation in the UK has concerns that sales target achievement of her staff declines relative to time spent in the sales role. A sample of 10 sales consultants are considered, with the number of years in role and the sales level as a percentage of target for the last year being presented in the table below:

Employee	Years in Employment	Percentage of Target
A	3	110
B	2	95
C	5	85
D	10	80
E	1	105
F	4	90
G	8	85
H	5	88
I	7	90
J	8	75

Required

(a) Present the data above using an appropriate graphical display and comment on the overall shape of the data on the graph provided. **(4 marks)**

(b) Assess the strength and direction of the relationship between the number of years in role and the sales achieved as a percentage of target using an appropriate correlation coefficient. **(8 marks)**

(c) Describe what the value of the correlation coefficient indicates about the relationship between the two variables and what should be the course of action for the Sales Director. **(3 marks)**

(Total 15 marks)

Section B

Answer ALL questions

5   You have just been appointed as the Office Manager at a medium sized Accounting practice, which has 25 employees in total. Part of the responsibilities within your new role includes managing the information technology provision within the practice. The current Office Manager, as part of the handover of duties to you, has provided a set of notes that cover this provision.

Required

Provide bullet-point definitions for, and describe the roles of, the following applications:

(a)   Specific computer hardware such as the Personal Computers (PCs) and the mainframe computer used within the practice. **(4 marks)**

(b)   Both integrated and specialist computer software used across the practice in support of its internal work and its external accounting services. **(6 marks)**

(Total 10 marks)

6   You have recently been appointed as a Consultant by a medium sized company that provides advice to start-up companies about various business activities including the purchase and application of information technology. You are asked to advise one individual entrepreneur who has set up an online company, employing a total of five people, that sells music products (for example, CDs, records, taped recordings). She is about to start, with help from an external agent, the development and implementation of her company's first customer database.

Required

Provide bullet-point definitions for, and describe the roles of, the following parts of the database implementation process to provide a clear project road map for the entrepreneur:

(a)   Define and describe briefly the components of the planning stage of the project. **(3 marks)**

(b)   Define and describe briefly the components of the development stage of the project. **(3 marks)**

(c)   Define and describe briefly the components of the implementation stage of the project. **(4 marks)**

(Total 10 marks)

7   Employed as a systems analyst within a large teaching University, you are required to lead a project involved in the implementation of a new marks recording system.

Required

(a)   Describe the process of system investigation. **(3 marks)**
(b)   Describe the work undertaken as part of systems analysis and design. **(4 marks)**
(c)   Describe the activities that comprise system implementation. **(3 marks)**

(Total = 10 marks)

8   You have a successful business providing information technology (IT) advice to organisations in the developing world. One such organisation has won a five-year contract to provide a call centre service to a UK-based energy supplier whose customers are exclusively from their domestic market. The guidance you are required to provide covers both the implementation of particular IT applications together with aspects of responsible working relating to IT.

Required

(a)   Describe the advantages of investing in voice messaging systems, computer telephony integration and computer bulletin boards within the call centre. **(6 marks)**

(b)   There will be a significant amount of customer work involving email. Describe the advantages and challenges that email will offer to the employees of the call centre, which should be presented to staff as a guideline to its daily use. **(4 marks)**

(Total 10 marks)

MODEL ANSWERS

MODULE B

FOUNDATION EXAMINATION

PAPER 6 – INFORMATION PROCESSING

WEDNESDAY 29th NOVEMBER 2017

Section A

1 SUMMARY

Principles of Statistical Sources and Data Collection – Learning Outcomes 3

Candidates will be expected to apply the Binomial and Normal distributions to a business related scenario, as well as expected values, thus considering assessment criteria 3.1, covering syllabus area 6.4.

(a) The three questions below are based on the Binomial distribution, followed by calculations of expected values.

- P(0 successful examinations) = P(0)
  Here, $p = 0.8$, $q = 1 - p = 0.2$, $n = 3$
  $P(0) = 0.2^3 =$ **0.008** (3dp).

- P(1 or 2 successful examinations) = P(1) + P(2)
  Here, $p = 0.8$, $q = 1 - p = 0.2$, $n = 3$
  $P(1) + P(2) = 3*0.8^1*0.2^2 + 3*0.8^2*0.2^1 = 0.096 + 0.384 =$ **0.480** (3dp).

- P(3 successful examinations) = P(3)
  Here, $p = 0.8$, $q = 1 - p = 0.2$, $n = 3$
  $P(3) = 0.8^3 =$ **0.512** (3dp).

- The respective expected values for apprentice technicians losing their job, having to take extra apprentice time or being offered a full-time position are respectively $250*0.008 =$ **2**, $250*0.480 =$ **120**, and $250*0.512 =$ **128**.

(b) The two answers below are based on the Normal distribution.

- $P(X > 50) = P(z > (50 - 65)/30) = P(z > -0.5)$
  $P(Z > -0.5) = P(Z < 0.5)$ through symmetry
  $P(Z < 0.5) =$ **0.6915** (4dp).
  69.15% of candidates have passed the examination.

- Area under Normal curve is 0.1, in bottom left hand tail, $Z = -1.28$
  $X = Z\sigma + \mu = -1.28*30 + 65 =$ **26.6%** (1dp).

  The lowest performing 10% of candidates score 26.6% or lower in the examination.

2 SUMMARY

Principles of Statistical Sources and Data Collection – Learning Outcomes 1 and 4.

Candidates will be expected to understand data sources differentiating between primary and secondary sources, explain and implement an approach to sampling/census in the context of survey and in doing so, assessment criteria 1.1, 1.3 and 1.4 will have been considered, covering syllabus area 6.1. Candidates will be expected to summarise data graphically covering syllabus areas 6.2. They will have also calculated measures of averages and dispersion, covering syllabus area 6.3, these respectively covering assessment criteria 4.3, 4.5 and 4.6.

(a) For discrete, quantitative data, the bar chart is the most appropriate presentation, as shown below, alongside a table indicating the discrete values of number of sick days taken by the employees.

Days	Frequency
0	9
1	20
2	10
3	4
4	4
5	2
6	1
7	2
8	1
9	1
10	1
Total	55

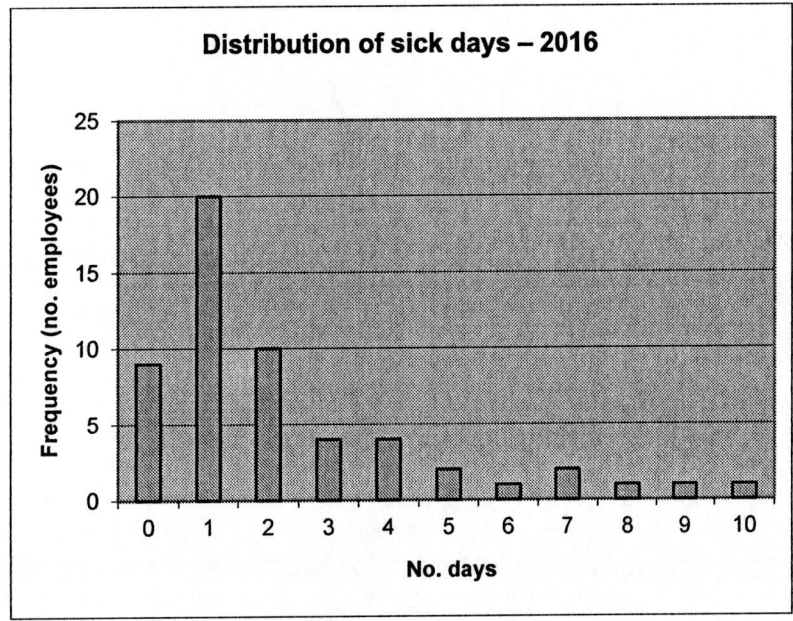

The data are shown to have a right or positively skewed distribution, peaking on the left hand side of the graph at 1 sick day per year.

(b) The most appropriate measure of central tendency is the median for a skewed data set.

The median is ordered value (n+1)/2 = ordered value 28, ie **the median is 1 sick day**.

(c) The most appropriate measure of central tendency is the inter-quartile range for a skewed data set.

Q1 is ordered value (n + 1)/4 = ordered value 14, ie Q1 is 1 sick day.
Q3 is ordered value 3(n + 1)/4 = ordered value 42, ie Q3 is 3 sick days.
IQR = Q3 − Q1 = 3 − 1 = 2 sick days.

(d) The Government department will be recording the number of sick days per employee probably electronically within the Human Resources (HR) function of the organisation. If the data are then used to assess the levels of employee absence as part of a subsequent study, like the one presented here, data can be retrieved from these existing HR sources, hence the data represents a **secondary source**. Given that the data are collected in this way for all employees as a single, central source, it is possible to consider data on a **census** basis to get a full department-wide assessment of absence than relying on a sample. Assessment of this much bigger data set is not appreciably more difficult given the availability of Excel or bespoke statistical software.

3. **SUMMARY**

Principles of Statistical Sources and Data Collection – Learning Outcomes 2

Candidates will be expected to use statistical techniques to identify time series models, apply a time series plot and choose appropriately between an additive and multiplicative model. After doing so, they will have analysed the time series to produce forecasts. In doing so, assessment criteria 2.1 and 2.2 will have been considered, covering syllabus area 6.6.

(a) The time series plot is given by the line graph below.

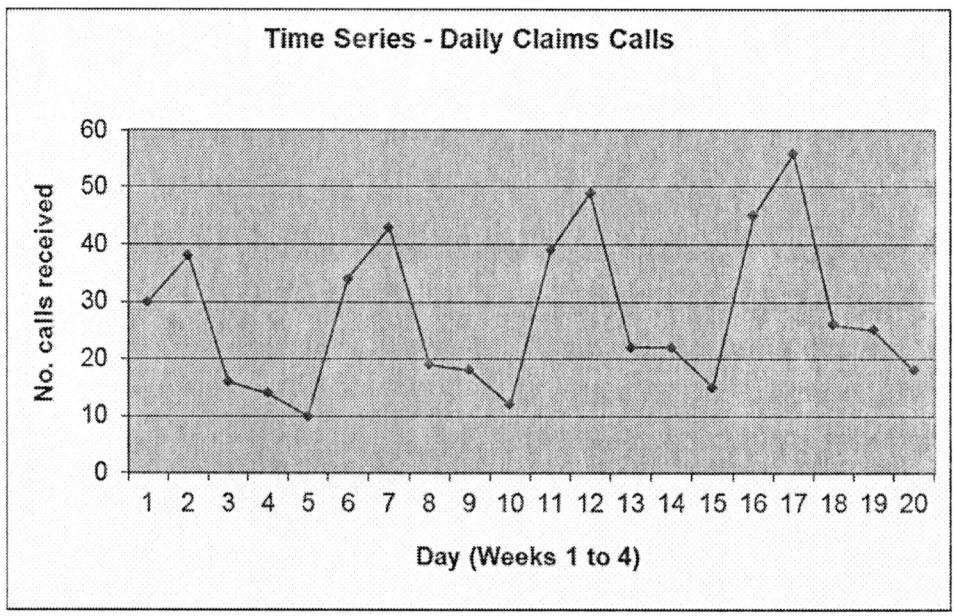

The graph shows the points are moving in an upward direction, hence there is a positive trend, ie calls received are increasing over time. The calls have a seasonal pattern, with a peak on each Tuesday, the lowest number of calls occur on Fridays, the seasonal pattern is increasing in size over time.

(b) The trend line is used to measure the true or underlying growth in number of calls. To calculate this, a 5 point moving average is calculated, 5 point because of the number of points (ie working days in each week when the office is open) in the repeating seasonal pattern. The first moving average calculation for time periods 1, 2, 3, 4 and 5 is placed next to time period 3. This is repeated for the whole data set.

The trend line is calculated using a simple regression model, the y data being the centred moving average, the x data being time.

Time (x)	T (y)	xy	x-sqd
3	21.6	64.8	9
4	22.4	89.6	16
5	23.4	117.0	25
6	24.0	144.0	36
7	24.8	173.6	49
8	25.2	201.6	64
9	26.2	235.8	81
10	27.4	274.0	100
11	28.0	308.0	121
12	28.8	345.6	144
13	29.4	382.2	169
14	30.6	428.4	196
15	32.0	480.0	225
16	32.8	524.8	256
17	33.4	567.8	289
18	34.0	612.0	324
Total 168	444	4,949.2	2,104
MEAN 10.5	27.75		

The slope coefficient b =

$$b = \frac{n\Sigma xy - (\Sigma x)(\Sigma y)}{n\Sigma x^2 - (\Sigma x)^2}$$

b = (16*4,949.2 − 168*444)/(16*2,104 − 168^2)]

b = 4,595.2/5,440.0 = **0.845 (3dp)**

a = Σy/n − bΣx/n = 27.75 − 0.845*10.5 = **18.841 (3dp)**

The trend line is given by T = 18.841 + 0.845t, suggesting the underlying level of calls is 18.841 at the start of the assessment, growing daily by 0.845 calls.

(c) The most appropriate indices are those relating to the multiplicative model, given the increasing size of the seasonal pattern shown on the time series plot.

(d) The forecasts are given by:

Monday week 5 = T × S = (18.841 + 0.845*21) * 1.402 = 51.3 = **51 calls**.
Tuesday week 5 = T × S = (18.841 + 0.845*22) * 1.714 = 64.2 = **64 calls**.

4 SUMMARY

Principles of Statistical Sources and Data Collection – Learning Outcomes 3

Candidates will be expected to practically apply scatter diagrams, thus applying appropriate graphical display and meeting syllabus section 6.5. The analysis of relationships between variables using correlation analysis addresses syllabus section 6.5 also.

(a) The most appropriate graphical display is a scatter plot, as shown below:

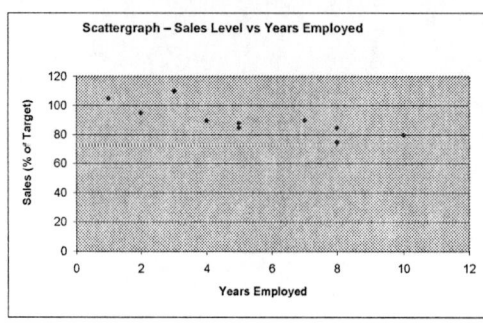

The graph presented shows a very strong, negative linear association, ie as the number of years' employed increases, then sales achieved as a percentage of target decreases.

(b) To assess the strength of this association, use Pearson's correlation coefficient given that both measurements are quantitative. The calculations are:

	Years (x)	% of Target (y)	xy	x-sqd	y-sqd
	3	110	330	9	12,100
	2	95	190	4	9,025
	5	85	425	25	7,225
	10	80	800	100	6,400
	1	105	105	1	11,025
	4	90	360	16	8,100
	8	85	680	64	7,225
	5	88	440	25	7,744
	7	90	630	49	8,100
	8	75	600	64	5,625
Total	53	903	4,560	357	82,569

The correlation coefficient r =

$$r = \frac{n\Sigma xy - (\Sigma x)(\Sigma y)}{\sqrt{[(n\Sigma y^2 - (\Sigma y)^2)(n\Sigma x^2 - (\Sigma x)^2)]}}$$

r = (10*4,560 − 53*903)/√[(10*82,569 − 903²)(10*357 − 53²)]

r = −2,259/√[10,281*761] = **−0.808 (3dp)**

The value of r being close to −1 in value suggests a very strong, negative linear relationship.

(c) The correlation analysis and the shape and direction of the points suggests a very strong, but negative association, ie as time in the sales role increases, sales performance as a percentage of target decreases. This could be caused by sales targets for more experienced staff being too high, therefore it may be possible to revise some of these downwards, it may be because after a period of time, these more experienced employees lose motivation in the sales role. A refresher course may offer some solution, as could moving to alternative duties.

Section B

5 SUMMARY

Business Information Processing – Learning Outcomes 2

Candidates will consider standard computer types covering assessment criteria 2.1 syllabus area 6.9. Candidates will also be expected to assess the purpose of certain integrated and accounting software. In doing so, assessment criteria 2.5 will have been considered, covering syllabus area 6.10.

(a) The single mainframe computer will act as the fileserver for the practice's computer system. It will be more powerful than the PCs deployed within the practice. This power is particularly useful given its central role within the computer network employed by the practice, since this crucial role at the heart of the practice network will require greater processing power to support the operating system shared by each user alongside various programmes common to each service user and relatively large data storage capability required for back-up to the individual PCs on the network.

The PCs will be used for both general purpose and Accounting-specific work. Each member of Accounting and office support staff will have their own PC, which is networked to the mainframe computer as well as to each of the other PCs that comprise the network. Data sharing and common facilities, operating system and bespoke software for example, will exist between all of these networked PCs.

(b) The integrated software that is likely to be employed across the Accounting practice is Microsoft Office. This collection of software affords numerous tools to support various different everyday business activities, including word-processing, a spreadsheet for common business calculations, database for specific records management, project management and data presentation facilities. All Accounting and support staff in the practice will use one or more of these facilities.

The accounting software may either be a single piece of software or one comprising a suite of linked programmes that form a complete system, used only by those staff offering the Accounting services within the practice. The various components of such a system are comprehensive in that they afford a full range of necessary accounting facilities to be provided and inter-compatible allowing transferability of data between the various components and potentially other general purpose business software.

6 SUMMARY

Business Information Processing – Learning Outcomes 3

Candidates will be expected to explain the role of database implementation in a start-up business or small organisation. In doing so, assessment criteria 3.2 will have been considered, covering syllabus area 6.11.

(a) The planning stage of the project will consist of the following:

Define the project scope and the database role

Identify likely users and business functions for the system, identify the current processes or activities that need to convert to this new system, define a project plan around these requirements, consult with the entrepreneur about the plan, timescale and budget.

Project organisation

Appoint a manager and team. Establish regular meetings with the entrepreneur, to be set out on a mutually agreeable timescale.

Select a specific database system

From a detailed database requirements list, create a tender for the system to be designed and implemented. For each tender, undertake a formal objective appraisal. From this tendering process, select an appropriate vendor.

(b) The design stage of the project will consist of the following:

Create a plan for implementation

Identification of all data and files (manual or computerised) to include in this system transfer. Determine the total work time to assess use of both database programme modification and creating support hours to achieve this. Convert these estimates into a project timetable.

Database and supporting infrastructure design

Identify the data structure requirements expected by the entrepreneur. Select a place on the IT network to locate this database. From this, assess the necessary hardware and network investment, create security measures to the new system.

Staff development

The staff chosen to work on this project need to be provided with development and an associated timeline to accompany this.

(c) The implementation stage of the project will consist of the following:

Create and apply a test database

Data developed by testers to assess both framework and management system by the team allowing subsequent database development, testing and debugging. Appraisal of the development based on test outcomes should follow.

Create a data conversion plan

Various programmes and data files (manual or computerised) will need to be converted for storage and application on the new system, after verification by those who interface with the old and new system, particularly the entrepreneur who is commissioning the project. Plan and implement the schedule for conversion subject to her final approval.

Transfer existing application and implement end-user training

Do this in the most beneficial way to the micro-business, perhaps one application at a time, with appropriate training and development for end users, particularly the owner-entrepreneur. Provide a systematic way of approving all changes and for effective handover to the new system. Make system available to new work, ie new customer information being added, accessed and applied.

Review and modify the database

Gain feedback from various users of the system, particularly the entrepreneur commissioning the project. Make necessary tweaks and ensure all security systems work appropriately given the now 'live' status of the database.

7. **Business Information Processing – Learning Outcomes 1**

Candidates will be expected to understand the key constraints necessary for successful systems development and implementation. In doing so, assessment criteria 1.3 will have been considered, covering syllabus area 6.8.

(a) Systems investigation will form the preliminary study for the project involving the new systems implementation, typically based on assessment of the existing systems provision. It will assess the strengths and limitations of the current systems, alongside the potential changes in the requirements of its various users. These changes will cover changes to data types, work volumes, user requests and the time taken to respond to various requests compared with the actual level of performance needed, in this case by the University.

(b) The first part of the actual development stage of the project involves a detailed analysis of the current system against end-user requirements. The analysis will assess current provision in terms of activities, capability, performance and features against alternatives that are affordable (relative to budget and timeframe set) with comparison made against these listed criteria. The alternatives are assessed to see whether or not improvements can be achieved, alongside the recalibration of associated performance criteria for the system to be introduced.

The design stage will consider input, outputs, processes, programme and file requirements, alongside system security. As it is designed, an associated system specification will be created to support its application, upkeep and future development once 'live'.

(c) System implementation moves the project from its design phase to being fully operational. To get to the stage of being a 'live' system, the implementation phase will comprise software procurement, testing, conversion of data or files from the outgoing system and interfacing with either existing or replacement computer hardware and networking.

8. SUMMARY

Business Information Processing – Learning Outcomes 4

Candidates will be expected to understand the key aspects of appropriate business behaviour that support business activity undertaken in a web-based arena. In doing so, assessment criteria 4.5 will have been considered, covering syllabus area 6.12.

(a) Many of the calls made by domestic purchasers of energy (electricity, gas, oil) will be routine, covering aspects such as bill payments, change of contracts, contract start-up or termination, service failure or complaint. As such, the voice messaging system can be used to answer the call and based on the nature of the enquiry, route the call accordingly using a pre-defined multi-option list. For non-routine enquiries, an additional option at the point of routing can be offered, thereby speeding up the response and limiting further complaint or negative perception of this service provider.

When an individual customer makes contact with a particular operator at the call centre, the computer telephony integration system will connect the telephone number used by the customer and link this with their historical stored account information which is automatically directed to the PC screen of the allocated operator. This is then ready on-screen as the call connection is made to the particular operator thereby reducing transaction time and cost for the customer.

The computer bulletin board is a shared central mailbox for message depositing and reading. This may be useful for call operatives working at the call-centre on different shifts and in a different time zone to the UK, thereby leaving messages on client correspondence that may have to be actioned by a particular person subject to context or be left given the complexity of the service request to be completed by someone else given shift changes or greater expertise becoming available at a later time within the call centre.

(b) Email offers advantage, particularly working in different time zones around speed of response to customer query, it is very inexpensive even with geographic distance, it offers efficiency if numerous clients are to receive the same correspondence and it can be made secure if financial or personal details have to be included, including the use of documents incorporated in attachment form. Acknowledgement of receipt and reading between either parties can form part of this type of correspondence and associated security.

Staff at the call centre has to be reminded of confidentiality issues regarding email, protocols around professionalism in the tone, language and style of correspondence, as well as the necessity to channel correspondence in terms of volume and to a focused audience depending upon the context. It should also not be used excessively to replace standard forms of communication internal to the workplace and be limited in its application internally outside the normal working hours of business thereby avoiding build up of work.

Mock exam 2 questions and answers

MODULE B

FOUNDATION EXAMINATION

PAPER 6 – INFORMATION PROCESSING

WEDNESDAY 23rd MAY 2018

Time allowed – 3 hours

SECTION A
Answer ALL questions

SECTION B
Answer ALL questions

Statistical tables and formulae are printed at the end of the question paper.

Graph Paper is provided

You are allowed an additional 15 minutes reading time before the exam begins, during which you should read the question paper and, if you wish, make notes on the question paper. You are **not** allowed to open the exam script booklet and start writing or use your calculator during the reading time.

Section A – Data Collection and Analysis

(Answer all four questions)

1. A call centre located in London sells savings and investment products to individual customers. The Human Resources Manager is interested in assessing the promotion record of its employees given that the organisation is working in a competitive environment where employee retention can be difficult. The promotion achievements at the call centre for a sample of employees is shown in the table below.

	No. of promotions				
Gender	0	1	2	3 or more	TOTAL
Female	45	30	25	10	110
Male	75	40	20	5	140
TOTAL	120	70	45	15	250

   Required

   (a) Calculate the probability that:

   (i) An employee selected at random has achieved at least one promotion.

   (ii) An employee selected at random is either Female or has achieved three or more promotions.

   (iii) An employee selected at random is Male and has achieved no promotions.

   (iv) An employee selected at random has achieved one or two promotions only.

   (8 marks)

   (b) For the employees with the company, the annual bonus in 2017 had a mean of £2,500 and a standard deviation of £450 and was assumed to be Normally distributed. Calculate the probability that:

   (i) An employee selected at random earned a bonus of less than £1,750.

   (ii) An employee selected at random earned a bonus between £2,750 and £3,500

   (7 marks)

   (Total 15 marks)

2. A City Council has 3,500 employees. Its Human Resources department has yet to computerise the records of its employees, but does store up-to-date manual records in paper files. The data, relating to 35 employees and recording the number of Council training courses each individual has attended, are presented in the table below.

0	1	2	1	0	3	8
0	2	2	1	1	2	2
1	3	4	2	2	7	6
2	2	2	1	4	0	2
1	1	2	2	3	1	4

   Required

   (a) Present the data in the form of an appropriate tabular and graphical display and comment upon the shape of the distribution. **(5 marks)**

   (b) From the data provided, calculate the most appropriate measure of central tendency. **(2 marks)**

   (c) From the data provided, calculate the most appropriate measure of dispersion. **(2 marks)**

   (d) With reference to the process of data collection, describe the type of data collected. **(2 marks)**

(e) If levels of employee training at the Council are to be assessed on a wider scale, suggest how this data may be collected from the Human Resource department's records to give a representative perspective across the organisation. **(4 marks)**

(Total 15 marks)

3   A Computer Science graduate has set up her own business servicing and repairing personal computers (PCs) in a small town in Western Europe. She has recorded the number of client calls received on a daily basis (her working days being Monday to Friday) over a four week period.

	Daily Calls				
Week	Mon	Tue	Wed	Thu	Fri
1	3	5	6	9	14
2	5	6	8	12	16
3	7	9	11	14	19
4	10	13	15	17	23

Required

(a) Describe the data using a suitable graphical display. Indicate **precisely** the shape of the data presented. **(3 marks)**

(b) For the time series data, calculate the trend line presenting your answer to three decimal places. Define and interpret the value of the coefficients in the relationship presented. **(7 marks)**

(c) For the data set provided indicate the most appropriate seasonal indices.

Day	Adjusted Additive Index	Day	Adjusted Multiplicative Index
Mon	−3.860	Mon	0.640
Tue	−2.393	Tue	0.772
Wed	−1.093	Wed	0.878
Thu	1.607	Thu	1.154
Fri	5.740	Fri	1.556
Average	0.000	**Average**	1.000

(1 mark)

(d) Using the most relevant information provided in part (c) and your calculations in part (b), forecast the number of calls received by the PC repair business for Monday and Tuesday of week 5 to zero decimal places. **(4 marks)**

(Total 15 marks)

4. The Training Manager at a large Accounting practice in the UK wishes to assess the effectiveness of two training options for its trainees pursuing professional Accounting qualifications; working on test papers and sending these to an external tutor for marking and feedback or attending a training seminar. For the Auditing examination, a sample of 10 trainees were considered, with the number of test papers attempted, number of seminars attended and their examination result (% mark) shown below:

Candidate	Test Papers	Seminars	Result
A	3	1	40
B	4	1	55
C	5	2	75
D	2	2	50
E	1	3	40
F	2	1	40
G	0	3	45
H	4	3	80
I	4	2	60
J	1	1	50

Required

(a) Determine the strength of the relationship between the number of test papers taken and examination result by calculating an appropriate statistical measure. **(6 marks)**

(b) Determine the strength of the relationship between the number of seminars attended and examination result by calculating an appropriate statistical measure. **(6 marks)**

(c) Which is the stronger of the two predictors of examination performance? Using this analysis, make recommendations to the Training Manager regarding future funding and training support for the Accounting trainees. **(3 marks)**

(Total 15 marks)

Section B – Business Information Technology

(Answer all four questions)

5   As Training Manager within a large University, you have agreed with the Human Resources Director to recruit ten Information Technology (IT) Apprentices, initially on a two-year training programme. They need to have an initial induction into the University and its IT systems and processes. It can be assumed that their recruitment is based on personal attributes and school-level qualifications rather than specific IT knowledge, skills and experience.

Required

As part of the induction programme for the Apprentices, provide bullet-point definitions for, and describe the roles and the users of, the following applications:

(a) General computer software used across the University by employees in management and administrative, rather than academic roles. **(4 marks)**

(b) Computer hardware used by the University across the University by employees in management and administrative, rather than academic roles. **(3 marks)**

(c) Specialist accounting and financial management software used by the University Finance and Procurement specialists. **(3 marks)**

(Total 10 marks)

6   You have recently been appointed as IT Manager at a medium-sized mail-based retail organisation that specialises in films and drama series in DVD medium. The organisation employs 45 people and has markets both in the UK and Ireland serving around 10,000 customers whose details and purchasing history are stored currently in manual form. These customer records need converting into electronic form and you are employing a systems specialist on a one-year fixed-term contract. A member of your IT team and an IT-trained administrator will support the systems specialist in the development of the database management system and associated data warehouse.

Required

(a) Describe the database characteristics of shared access, security, controls and flexibility from the perspective of the mail-based retailer. **(4 marks)**

(b) Describe three potential advantages the database system brings to the mail-based retailer. **(3 marks)**

(c) Describe three potential disadvantages the database system brings to the mail-based retailer. **(3 marks)**

(Total 10 marks)

7   As an IT Consultant working in the UK, you have won the contract awarded by a large medical practice to develop a new management information system. This management information system will be accessed by medical, management and administrative employees within the practice. At an initial briefing session, you are to meet a representative from each of these groups of employees to provide an overview of the management information system's role once it is fully implemented.

Required

(a) Define the term management information system. **(2 marks)**

(b) Describe the role of the management information system within this medical practice. **(4 marks)**

(c) Describe four limitations of a management information system from the perspective of the end users employed in different role sets within the medical practice. **(4 marks)**

(Total 10 marks)

8   You have just been appointed as a Lending Manager by a bank to specialise in small-business start ups. The bank particularly wishes to support new and recent graduates who plan to set up their own businesses. The bank has given you the opportunity to lead a seminar programme for a group of 20 graduates and you are required to produce the necessary presentation materials. To do this, you will prepare bullet-point notes covering the necessary website development considerations for an individual or small group planning to set up an e-business.

Required

Describe the key issues relating to the five areas of:

- Legal compliance.
- Systems security.
- Consumer rights.
- After sales service.
- Maintaining customer relationships and developing repeat business. **(5 × 2 marks)**

(Total 10 marks)

MODEL ANSWERS

MODULE B

FOUNDATION EXAMINATION

PAPER 6 – INFORMATION PROCESSING

WEDNESDAY 23rd MAY 2018

Section A – Data Collection and Analysis

1. **SUMMARY**

    Principles of Statistical Sources and Data Collection – Learning Outcomes 3

    Candidates will be expected to apply the rules of basic probability. They will also apply the Normal distribution to a business related scenario, thus considering assessment criteria 3.1, covering syllabus area 6.4.

    (a) The information provided can be used to assess the following probabilities:

    (i) P (employee has achieved at least one promotion) = 1 – P (no promotions) = 1 – 120/250 = 0.52.

    (ii) P (Female or has achieved three or more promotions) = (110 + 15 – 10)/250 = 115/250 = 0.46.

    (iii) P (Male and has achieved no promotions) = 75/250 = 0.30.

    (iv) P (employee has achieved 1 or 2 promotions only) = (75 + 45)/250 = 0.46.

    (b) The two questions below are based on the Normal distribution.

    (i) $P(x < 1{,}750) = P(Z < -1.67) = P(Z > 1.67)$ through symmetry = **0.0478** (4dp).

    (ii) $P(2{,}750 < x < 3{,}500) = P(x < 3{,}500) - P(x < 2{,}750) = P(Z < 2.22) - P(Z < 0.56)$, from tables = 0.9869 – 0.7107 = **0.2762** (4dp).

2. **SUMMARY**

    Principles of Statistical Sources and Data Collection – Learning Outcomes 1 and 4.

    Candidates will be expected to understand data sources, explain and implement an approach to sampling in the context of survey and in doing so, assessment criteria 1.1, 1.3 and 1.4 will have been considered, covering syllabus area 6.1. Candidates will be expected to summarise data graphically covering syllabus areas 6.2. They will have also calculated measures of averages and dispersion, covering syllabus area 6.3, these respectively covering assessment criteria 4.3, 4.5 and 4.6.

    (a) For discrete, quantitative data, the bar chart is the most appropriate presentation, as shown below, alongside a table indicating the discrete values of number of courses taken.

Courses	Frequency
0	4
1	9
2	13
3	3
4	3
5	0
6	1
7	1
8	1
Total	35

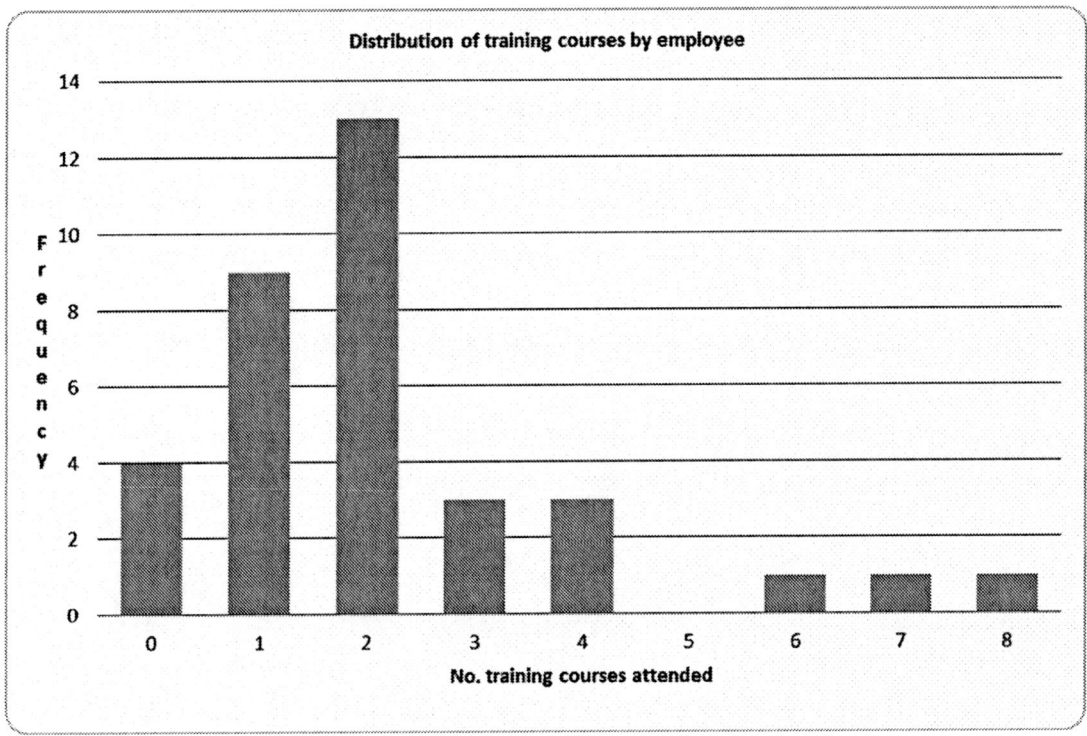

The data are shown to have a right or positively skewed distribution, peaking on the left hand side of the graph at 2 training courses.

(b) The most appropriate measure of central tendency is the median for a skewed data set.

The median is ordered value (n+1)/2 = ordered value 18, ie the median is 2 training courses.

(c) The most appropriate measure of central tendency is the inter-quartile range for a skewed data set.

Q1 is ordered value (n+1)/4 = ordered value 9, ie Q1 is 1 training course.
Q3 is ordered value 3(n+1)/4 = ordered value 27, ie Q1 is 3 training courses.
IQR = Q3 − Q1 = 3 − 1 = 2 training courses.

(d) The Council's Human Resources department keeps up-to-date records, so rather than ask individual employees, who may neither respond, will inaccurately report or cannot remember their complete training history, the data can be retrieved from the existing sources in Human Resources, hence the data represents a **secondary source**.

(e) 35,000 manual records are vast, so a census is not practical. To be representative across the organisation, this data collection has to involve a sample that represents the organisation by gender, age-band, length of service, role and level of seniority. A practical way of sampling in this way, especially given the manual rather than electronic status of the data, could be quota sampling based on the criteria listed. If this proves too difficult to implement and there is no recurring patterns in the alphabetic list of records, a systematic sample may be easier to collect.

3. **SUMMARY**

Principles of Statistical Sources and Data Collection – Learning Outcomes 2

Candidates will be expected to use statistical techniques to identify time series models, apply a time series plot and choose appropriately between an additive and multiplicative model. After doing so, they will have analysed the time series to produce forecasts. In doing so, assessment criteria 2.1 and 2.2 will have been considered, covering syllabus area 6.6.

(a) The time series plot is given by the line graph below.

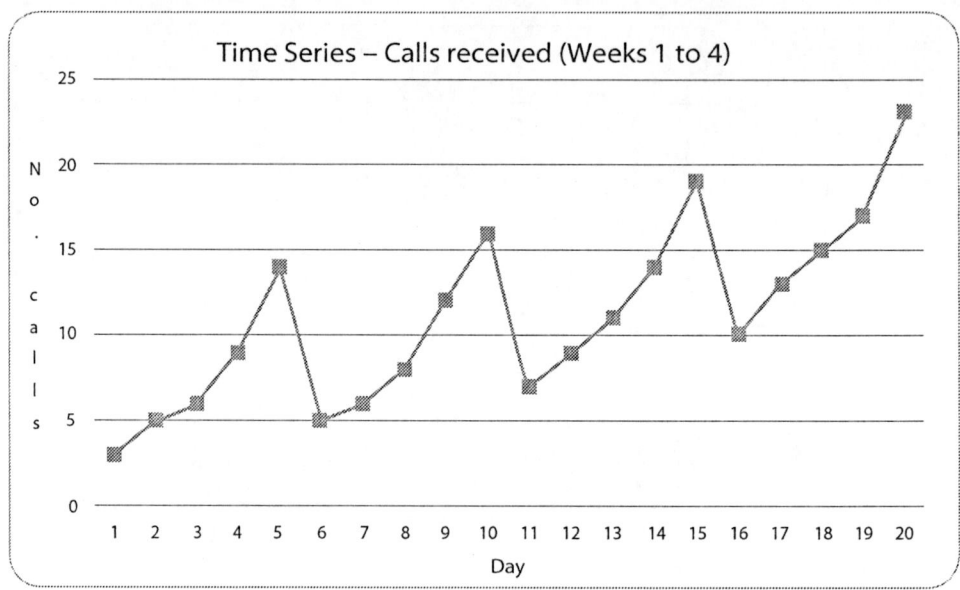

The graph shows the points are moving in an upward direction, hence there is a positive trend, ie calls are increasing over time. The calls have a seasonal pattern, with a peak on each Friday, with calls increasing over the week from a quiet day on Monday. The seasonal pattern is reasonably constant in size over time.

(b) The trend line is used to measure the true or underlying growth in number of calls to the business. To calculate this, a 5 point moving average is calculated, 5 point because of the number of points (ie working days in each week when the calls are taken and the business is open) in the repeating seasonal pattern. The first moving average calculation for time periods 1, 2, 3, 4 and 5 is placed next to time period 3. This is repeated for the whole data set.

The trend line is calculated using a simple regression model, the y data being the moving average, the x data being time.

	Time (x)	5-point MA (y)	x-sqd	xy
	3	7.4	9	22.2
	4	7.8	16	31.2
	5	8.0	25	40.0
	6	8.4	36	50.4
	7	9.0	49	63.0
	8	9.4	64	75.2
	9	9.8	81	88.2
	10	10.4	100	104.0
	11	11.0	121	121.0
	12	11.4	144	136.8
	13	12.0	169	156.0
	14	12.6	196	176.4
	15	13.4	225	201.0
	16	14.2	256	227.2
	17	14.8	289	251.6
	18	15.6	324	280.8
Total	168	175.2	2,104	2,025

The formula for the trend line is y = a + bx.

Slope coefficient $b = \dfrac{n\Sigma xy - (\Sigma x)(\Sigma y)}{(n\Sigma x^2 - (\Sigma x)^2)}$

Therefore, b = (16*2,025 − 168*175.2)/(16*2,014 − 168²) = 0.545

Constant coefficient a = (Σy/n) − b*(Σx/n) = 10.950 − 0.545*10.500 = 5.224

The trend line, T = 5.224 + 0.545t, tells us at the start of the time period the underlying value of client calls is 5.224 per day, with its seasonally adjusted growth being 0.545 units per working day.

(c) The most appropriate indices are those relating to the **additive model**, given the constant size of the seasonal pattern shown on the time series plot.

(d) The forecasts are given by:

Monday week 5 = T + S = (5.224 + 0.545*21) − 3.860 = **13 customer calls**.

Tuesday week 5 = T + S = (5.224 + 0.545*22) − 2.393 = **15 customer queries**.

4. **SUMMARY**

Principles of Statistical Sources and Data Collection – Learning Outcomes 4

The analysis of relationships between variables using correlation analysis addresses the assessment criteria 4.1 and syllabus section 6.5.

(a) To assess the strength of this association, use Pearson's correlation coefficient given that both measurements are quantitative. The calculations are:

	Paper (x)	Result (y)	xy	x-sqd	y-sqd
	3	40	120	9	1,600
	4	55	220	16	3,025
	5	75	375	25	5,625
	2	50	100	4	2,500
	1	40	40	1	1,600
	2	40	80	4	1,600
	0	45	0	0	2,025
	4	80	320	16	6,400
	4	60	240	16	3,600
	1	50	50	1	2,500
Total	26	535	1,545	92	30,475

The correlation coefficient r =

$r = \dfrac{n\Sigma xy - (\Sigma x)(\Sigma y)}{\sqrt{[(n\Sigma y^2 - (\Sigma y)^2)(n\Sigma x^2 - (\Sigma x)^2)]}}$

r = (10*1,545 − 26*535)/√[(10*30,475 − 535²)(10*92 − 26²)]

r = 1,540/√[18,525*244] = **0.724 (3dp)**

The value of r moving towards +1 in value suggests a strong, positive linear relationship.

(b) To assess the strength of this association, use Pearson's correlation coefficient given that both measurements are quantitative. The calculations are:

	Seminars (x)	Result (y)	xy	x-sqd	y-sqd
	1	40	40	1	1,600
	1	55	55	1	3,025
	2	75	150	4	5,625
	2	50	100	4	2,500
	3	40	120	9	1,600
	1	40	40	1	1,600
	3	45	135	9	2,025
	3	80	240	9	6,400
	2	60	120	4	3,600
	1	50	50	1	2,500
Total	19	535	1,050	43	30,475

The correlation coefficient r =

$$r = \frac{n\Sigma xy - (\Sigma x)(\Sigma y)}{\sqrt{[(n\Sigma y^2 - (\Sigma y)^2)(n\Sigma x^2 - (\Sigma x)^2)]}}$$

r = (10*1,050 − 19*535)/√[(10*30,475 − 535²)(10*43 − 19²)]

r = 335/√[18,525*69] = **0.296 (3dp)**

The value of r moving towards zero in value suggests a weak, positive linear relationship.

(c) The better predictor of examination performance is completion, marking and feedback of test papers rather than attending the seminars. The trainee Accountants should be encouraged to prepare for their professional examinations by their Training Manager through completion of these test papers. The option of the support seminars should be removed, it has limited impact on performance and it could save the organisation money.

Section B – Business Information Technology

5. **SUMMARY**

   Business Information Processing – Learning Outcomes 2

   Candidates will be expected to assess the purpose of certain types of general and accounting-related application software. In doing so, assessment criteria 2.5 will have been considered, covering syllabus area 6.10. Candidates will also consider standard computer hardware covering assessment criteria 2.1 syllabus area 6.9.

   (a) General software captures user-oriented programs used across the University to support numerous day-to-day tasks within the Administrative and Managerial functions. This software is likely to be off-the-shelf applications, which are standard to business and its users, the University being one of many types of organisation who utilise these applications. Software applications include word processing, spreadsheet, database and presentation applications. The University will have invested in these without need for additional or specialist budgets, given the necessity to write formal correspondence (internal and external to the University) undertake various calculations including the development of templates (eg Finance), house specific records (eg Human Resources for employees, plus student records) and be required to make formal presentations. All employees within the numerous Administrative and Managerial functions across the University will use some or all of this software.

   (b) The computer hardware most prominent in these University support functions are many personal computers configured to a network that supports the various general business and dedicated accounting software. Given the power and capability of these PCs and the network systems, it is unlikely that mini or supercomputers will be needed to aid these support roles. Other hardware to consider in the Apprentices' induction event is printing and fax facilities, again configured to the relevant networks. All members of the University's Administrative and Managerial teams will use some or all of this hardware.

   (c) Integrated accounting software is built from a group of related accounting programs that perform a range of finance related activities that the University and its specialist employees will expect to be supported. Various standalone accounting and finance related programmes will be configured into one, integrated finance system that will provide a comprehensive accounting facility. Data compatibility and transferability is afforded through this integration, allowing necessary information transfer one component of the integrated system to another. This increases both speed and accuracy of work by avoiding any data entry repetition. This type of software is likely to be used by only a limited number of University employees, for example those employed in the Finance and Procurement departments, who have specific skills, roles and work-related needs from the systems provided.

6. **SUMMARY**

   Business Information Processing – Learning Outcomes 3

   Candidates will be expected to explain the role of databases for the successful running of an organisation, alongside their advantages and disadvantages. In doing so, assessment criteria 3.1 will have been considered, covering syllabus area 6.11.

   (a) The system specialist will create a single database for the organisation, based on one data set, thereby eliminating multiple data files across the various business functions. Various individuals and user groups will be allowed data access, manipulation and updating, hence permitting changes to be made and increased data accuracy. Controls are required within the system to safeguard against data corruption. Passwords will ensure security by allowing only users with authorisation. The system will encompass various query facilities that allow data processing given the numerous work related requirements of different organisational users.

(b) The database will help reduce data duplication across the organisation, given the system represents the sole customer data source. Being the only version of the customer data, it will ensure consistency in content and form for its different organisational users. The related software and query facilities that accompany such a system will make data analysis easier for its end users.

(c) The system must be accompanied by clear and agreed procedures relating to data security to safeguard against potential issues of security and to make customer privacy paramount. The organisation is seeking to convert completely to a single data set, but currently has employees with limited day-to-day experience of using such a database, making the organisation vulnerable to system failure and data corruption. The systems development is starting from a position of a complete transfer from a manual records system, therefore the organisation may face in the short-term high development costs.

7 SUMMARY

Business Information Processing – Learning Outcomes 1

Candidates will be expected to understand the key concept of a management information system, alongside its organisational role and potential limitations. In doing so, assessment criteria 1.1 and 1.2 will have been considered, covering syllabus area 6.8.

(a) A management information system is a system deployed within the medical practice. It will provide various types of information to the different employee groups within the practice, ie medical, managerial and administrative. The information will take the form of standardised summary reports or exception reporting and will be based on data processing based on internal data sources.

(b) Within the medical practice, this management information system will process standard data for this type of user relating to patients (medical history, current details of illness and treatments, medication prescribed and taken, referrals) and organisational data (income, bank information, spending, bills payment), and medical investments (drugs, equipment, salaries etc.) and will convert these different information sources into reports that allow the senior medical practitioners and the Practice Manager to plan the work and resourcing of the medical practice, as well as placing levels of managerial control on each of these activity areas.

(c) Four potential limitations are: they provide highly structured output with limited flexibility, the focus is exclusively internal to the medical practice (with no source of external information – pricing for drugs, medical equipment and other medical resources), they report on existing practice work rather than planned activities (it may need to expand in response to population changes) and there is limited analytical capability built into these types of system.

8 SUMMARY

Business Information Processing – Learning Outcomes 4

Candidates will be expected to define B2C applications of e-commerce and e-business. In doing so, assessment criteria 4.5 will have been considered, covering syllabus area 6.13.

(a) The graduates as owners of the new businesses and their potential clients and customers need to be in full understanding of the country's legislation relating to e-business and this legislation must be fully complied with. From the business point of view, full compliance with consumer legislation and complying with privacy and data protection law is crucial. From the point of view of the client or customer, they should be provided with a clear code of conduct from the business for using the website with details of penalties rules for any violations.

(b) Business relationships that flourish in the e-business arena are highly dependent on trust. Trust is built on the foundations of secure IT systems and safe customer transactions particularly when bank and customer details form part of any transaction. The graduates need to ensure such safety is in place in their new e-business and they need to make potential customers aware of their security measures.

(c) In one single correspondence rather than meaning customers have to re-contact the e-business multiple times for information, the business starters must provide managed information relating to their transactions and their consumer rights. This information should be in manageable size; otherwise it may put off certain consumers from future transactions.

(d) The e-business owners should attempt to develop longstanding customer relationships through after-sales activities such as servicing existing products or offering other business related activities beyond the initial buying and selling transactions.

(e) Excessive contact may deter further business transactions, so in a managed way, the e-business owner should seek to maintain contacts with their customers through email, the provision of future incentives (based on loyalty and frequency of transaction) and information on new products and services based on their transaction preferences and history.

Formulae

FORMULAE

Note. These formulae are written in a widely used notation. Candidates are expected to have a sufficient knowledge to recognise the notation should they have used any other in their studies. Invigilators may not be consulted.

SAMPLE STATISTICS

Mean $\bar{x} = \dfrac{\Sigma x}{n}$ Variance $s^2 = \dfrac{\Sigma(x - \bar{x})^2}{n} = \dfrac{\Sigma x^2}{n} - \left(\dfrac{\Sigma x}{n}\right)^2$

$$s^2 = \dfrac{\Sigma(x - \bar{x})^2}{n-1} = \dfrac{n\Sigma x^2 - (\Sigma x)^2}{n(n-1)}$$

GROUPED DATA

$\bar{x} = A.A + \dfrac{\Sigma fd}{n} \times \dfrac{c}{1}$ $s^2 = c^2\left[\dfrac{\Sigma fd^2}{n} - \left(\dfrac{\Sigma fd}{n}\right)^2\right]$ or $\bar{x} = \dfrac{\Sigma fx}{\Sigma f}$ $s^2 = \dfrac{\Sigma fx^2}{\Sigma f} - \left(\dfrac{\Sigma fx}{\Sigma f}\right)^2$

Median $= 1_1 + \dfrac{n/2 - F_{m-1}}{f_m} \times \dfrac{(1_2 - 1_1)}{1}$

Mode $= 1_1 + \dfrac{(f_m - f_{m-1})}{(f_m - f_{m-1}) + (f_m - f_{m+1})} \times \dfrac{(1_2 - 1_1)}{1}$

Skewness $= \dfrac{\text{Mean} - \text{mode}}{\text{Standard deviation}}$ or $\dfrac{3(\text{Mean} - \text{Median})}{\text{Standard deviation}}$

Correlation Coefficients

Product moment (Pearson) $r = \dfrac{\Sigma(x - \bar{x})(y - \bar{y})}{\sqrt{(\Sigma x - \bar{x})^2 (\Sigma y - \bar{y})^2}}$

$$= \dfrac{\dfrac{\Sigma xy}{n} - \bar{x}\bar{y}}{\sqrt{\left(\dfrac{\Sigma x^2}{n} - \bar{x}^2\right)\left(\dfrac{\Sigma y^2}{n} - \bar{y}^2\right)}}$$

Rank (Spearman) $r = 1 - \dfrac{6\Sigma d^2}{n(n^2 - 1)}$

FORMULAE

REGRESSION EQUATION

$\hat{y} = a + bx$

$b = \dfrac{\Sigma xy - n\overline{xy}}{\Sigma x^2 - n\overline{x}^2}$; $a = \overline{y} - b\overline{x}$

normal equations
$\Sigma y = an + b\Sigma x$
$\Sigma xy = a\Sigma n + b\Sigma x^2$

PROBABILITY DISTRIBUTIONS

Normal deviate $\quad Z = \dfrac{x - \mu}{\sigma}$

Binominal distribution: $(Q + P)^n$ $\qquad$ *General term:* $\dfrac{n!}{x!\,(n-x)!} Q^{n-x} P^x$

Poisson distribution: $e^{-m}\left(1 + m + \dfrac{m^2}{2!} + \dfrac{m^3}{3!} \ldots \right)$ $\quad$ *General term:* $\dfrac{e^{-m} m^x}{x!}$

SIGNIFICANCE TESTS – LARGE INDEPENDENT SAMPLES

Means : $Z = \dfrac{x - \mu}{\dfrac{\sigma}{\sqrt{n}}}$

$x^2 = \Sigma \dfrac{(O - E)^2}{E}$

$Z = \dfrac{\overline{x}_1 - \overline{x}_2}{\sqrt{\dfrac{s1^2}{n1} + \dfrac{s2^2}{n2}}}$

Proportions $\quad Z = \dfrac{P - \pi}{\sqrt{\dfrac{\pi(100 - \pi)}{n}}}$: $\quad Z = \dfrac{P_1 - P_2}{\sqrt{\dfrac{P(100-P)}{n1} + \dfrac{P(100-P)}{n2}}}$ $\quad$ where $P = \dfrac{n1\,P_1 + n2\,P_2}{n1 + n2}$

CONFIDENCE INTERVALS

Means $\overline{x} \pm Z \dfrac{s}{\sqrt{n}}$ $\qquad\qquad$ *Proportions:* $P \pm Z \sqrt{\dfrac{P(100 - P)}{n}}$

FORMULAE

Table 1
NORMAL CURVE AREAS

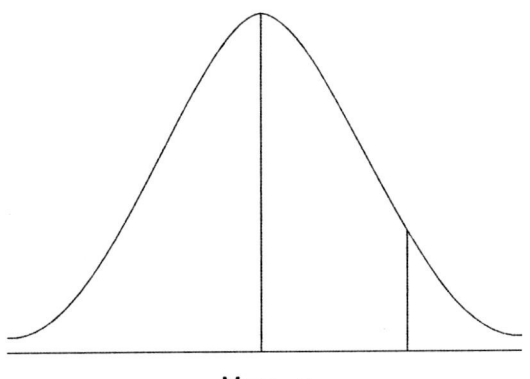

Mean   z

z is the distance the point lies from the mean measured in σ, ie

$$z = \frac{\text{Value} - \text{Mean}}{\sigma}$$

z	.00	.01	.02	.03	.04	.05	.06	.07	.08	.09
0.0	.0000	.0040	.0080	.0120	.0159	.0199	.0239	.0279	.0319	.0359
0.1	.0398	.0438	.0478	.0517	.0557	.0596	.0636	.0675	.0714	.0753
0.2	.0793	.0832	.0871	.0910	.0948	.0987	.1026	.1064	.1103	.1141
0.3	.1179	.1217	.1255	.1293	.1331	.1368	.1406	.1443	.1480	.1517
0.4	.1554	.1591	.1628	.1664	.1700	.1736	.1772	.1808	.1844	.1879
0.5	.1915	.1950	.1985	.2019	.2054	.2088	.2123	.2157	.2190	.2224
0.6	.2257	.2291	.2324	.2357	.2389	.2422	.2454	.2486	.2517	.2549
0.7	.2580	.2611	.2642	.2673	.2704	.2734	.2764	.2794	.2823	.2852
0.8	.2881	.2910	.2939	.2967	.2995	.3023	.3051	.3078	.3106	.3133
0.9	.3159	.3186	.3212	.3238	.3264	.3289	.3315	.3340	.3365	.3389
1.0	.3413	.3438	.3461	.3485	.3508	.3531	.3554	.3577	.3599	.3621
1.1	.3643	.3665	.3686	.3708	.3729	.3749	.3770	.3790	.3810	.3830
1.2	.3849	.3869	.3888	.3907	.3925	.3944	.3962	.3980	.3997	.4015
1.3	.4032	.4049	.4066	.4082	.4099	.4115	.4131	.4147	.4162	.4177
1.4	.4192	.4207	.4222	.4236	.4251	.4265	.4279	.4292	.4306	.4319
1.5	.4332	.4345	.4357	.4370	.4382	.4394	.4406	.4418	.4429	.4441
1.6	.4452	.4463	.4474	.4484	.4495	.4505	.4515	.4525	.4535	.4545
1.7	.4554	.4564	.4573	.4582	.4591	.4599	.4608	.4616	.4625	.4633
1.8	.4641	.4649	.4656	.4664	.4671	.4678	.4686	.4693	.4699	.4706
1.9	.4713	.4719	.4726	.4732	.4738	.4744	.4750	.4756	.4761	.4767
2.0	.4772	.4778	.4783	.4788	.4793	.4798	.4803	.4808	.4812	.4817
2.1	.4821	.4826	.4830	.4834	.4838	.4842	.4846	.4850	.4854	.4857
2.2	.4861	.4864	.4868	.4871	.4875	.4878	.4881	.4884	.4887	.4890
2.3	.4893	.4896	.4898	.4901	.4904	.4906	.4909	.4911	.4913	.4916
2.4	.4918	.4920	.4922	.4925	.4927	.4929	.4931	.4932	.4934	.4936
2.5	.4938	.4940	.4941	.4943	.4945	.4946	.4948	.4949	.4951	.4952
2.6	.4953	.4955	.4956	.4957	.4959	.4960	.4961	.4962	.4963	.4964
2.7	.4965	.4966	.4967	.4968	.4969	.4970	.4971	.4972	.4973	.4974
2.8	.4974	.4975	.4976	.4977	.4977	.4978	.4979	.4979	.4980	.4981
2.9	.4981	.4982	.4982	.4983	.4984	.4984	.4985	.4985	.4986	.4986
3.0	.4987	.4987	.4987	.4988	.4988	.4989	.4989	.4989	.4990	.4990

FORMULAE

Table 2

CHI-SQUARED DISTRIBUTION

Degrees of freedom	1	2	3	4	5	6	7	8	9	10
$\chi^2\ 0.05$	3.841	5.991	7.815	9.488	11.070	12.592	14.067	15.507	16.919	18.307
$\chi^2\ 0.01$	6.635	9.210	11.345	13.277	15.086	16.812	18.475	20.090	21.666	23.209

Table 3

TABLE FOR USE WITH THE POISSON DISTRIBUTION

x	0.4	0.6	0.8	1.0	1.5	2.0	2.5	3.0	3.5	4.0
e^{-x}	0.6703	0.5488	0.4493	0.3679	0.2231	0.1353	0.0821	0.0498	0.0302	0.0183

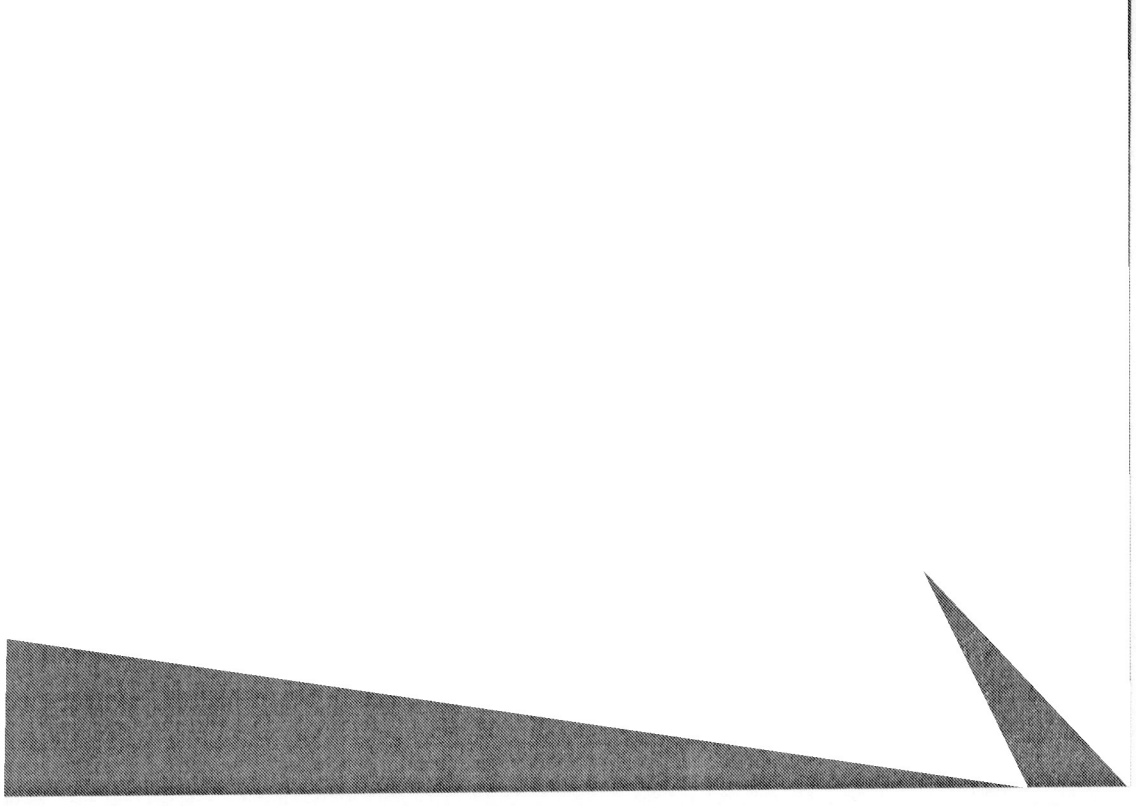

Index

INDEX

Note. **Key Terms** and their page references are given in **bold**.

Accounting records, 233, 269
Additive model, 190, 195, 197
AND law, 132
Apple, 251
Application packages, 261
Applications software, 259, **261**
Arithmetic mean of combined data, 100
Arithmetic mean of grouped data, 99
Arithmetic mean of ungrouped data, 98
Arithmetic mean, 98, 101
Array, 104
Automatic input devices, 254
Average relatives indices, 214

B2B (Business-to-Business), 300
B2C (Business-to-Consumer), 300
Bandwidth, 291
Banks, 54
Bar chart, 69
Bar coding, 255
Base period, 208
Base year, 208
BIOS, 253
Bits, 252, 271
Booting up, 253
Brackets, 10
Broadband, 291
Bubblejet printer, 256
Budget, 242
Bus, 252
Bus structure, 288
Business system, 230
Bytes, 252, 271

Cache, 253
Calculating z, 154, 161, 163
CD-ROM (Compact Disc – Read Only Memory), 257
Central Processing Unit (CPU), 251
Chain base method, 210
Characteristics of good information, 51
Charts, 69
Checkpoint, 243
Chip, 251
Client-server computing, 289
Client-server, 289
Clock speed, 252
Cluster sampling, 59
Coaxial cable, 291
Coefficient of determination, r^2, 177

Coefficient of rank correlation, 177, 178
Coefficient of variation, 120
Communications, 293
Complementary outcomes, 130
Component bar chart, 70
Component parts of a system, 230
Composite index numbers, 214
Compound bar chart, 72
Computer, 248
Computer communication, 290
Computer hardware, 248
Computer Telephony Integration (CTI), 293
Computer's memory, 252
Conditional events, 135
Conditional probability, 134, 135
Consumer Price Index (CPI), 220
Contingency tables, 135
Continuous data, 55
Control unit, 251, 252
Controlling, 233, 268
Correlation, 172
Correlation and causation, 177
Correlation coefficient, 174
CPU, 251
Cube root, 19, **20**
Cumulative frequency curve, 86
Cumulative frequency diagram, 86
Cumulative frequency distribution, 81
Cumulative frequency polygon, 86
Curve fitting, 89
Cycles, 251
Cyclical variations, 190

Data, 50, 200, **268**, 269
Data collection, 268
Data communications, 290
Data design, 276
Data hierarchy, 270, 271
Data links, 291
Data modelling, 276
Data sources, 269
Data storage models, 274
Data types, 53
Data warehouse, 272
Database, 272
Database implementation, 279
Database management system (DBMS), 272
Database queries, 273
Deciles, 114
Decimals, 4, 5, 6, 43
Decision making, 233, 268

Decision Support System (DSS), 236
Decision tree, 144, 165
Deflation, 213
Degrees of correlation, 173
Denominator, 5
Dependent events, 135
Dependent variable, 30
Deseasonalisation, 200
Discounts, 14
Discrete data, 55
Dispersion, 115
Document reading methods, 254
DOS, 260
Dot matrix printer, 256
Downward-sloping ogives, 87
DVD, 257

E-business, 301
E-commerce, 300
EFTPOS, 255
EIS, 235
Electronic Data Interchange (EDI), 294
Electronic Funds Transfer (EFT), 294
Electronic mail (email), 294
Electronic Point of Sale (EPOS), 255
Email dangers, 294
Enterprise servers, 248, 249
Entity Life History, 278
Entity relationship model (ERM), 276
Entity, 276, 277
Environment, 231
Environmental scanning, 234
EPOS, 255
Equation of a straight line, 180
Equations, 23, 25
Errors from rounding, 22
Errors, 22
ESS, 235
Event model (Entity Life History), 278
Event model, 278
Executive Information System (EIS), 235
Executive Support System (ESS), 235
Expectation and decision making, 140
Expected value, 137
Expert systems, 238
External data sources, 234
External data, 270
External information, 234, 270
Extranet, 240
Extrapolation, 183

Feasibility study, 241
Field, 271

File, 271
File servers, 250
Financial newspapers, 55
Fixed base method, 210
Floppy disk, 257
Forecasting, 201
Forecasting and scattergraphs, 181
Formulae, 23, 24
Fractions, 4, 5, 41
Frequency distributions, 78

General purpose package, 261
General rule of addition, 133
General rule of multiplication, 134
General systems theory, 230
Gigabytes, 252
GigaHertz (GHz), 252
Global information systems (GIS), 300
Governments, 54
Gradient, 32
Graphs, 31
Grouped data, 118, 119
Grouped frequency distributions, 78

Hard disk, 257
Hardware, 248
Hierarchical model, 274
High-end file server, 290
Highlight reports, 243
Histogram, 82

Independent events, 132
Independent variable, 30
Index, 208
Index numbers, 208
Index points, 208
Index relative, 208
Inequalities, 29
Information, 50, 268
Information systems (IS), 230, 235
Information technology (IT), 230
Information theory, 232
Inkjet printers, 256
Input, 230, 254
Input devices, 254
Instruction set, 251
Integer, 4, 43
Integrated circuit, 251
Integrated software, 262
Intel, 251
Intercept, 32
Intercept and the gradient, 33

Interface, 292
Internal data sources, 233
Internal information, 233, 269
Internal store, 252
Interpolation, 183
Inter-quartile range, 113
Intranet, 240
Iteration, 278

Key field, 271
Keyboard, 254
Kilobytes, 252
Knowledge Work Systems (KWS), 237
Knowledge Workers, 237

Laser printers, 256
Laspeyre indices, 217
Laspeyre price index, 217
Laspeyre quantity index, 219
Laws of probability, 129
Learning curve formula, 24
Least squares method of linear regression analysis, 181
Limitations of expected values, 143
Limitations of forecasting models, 203
Linear equation, 30
Linear regression analysis (the least squares method), 181
Linear regression analysis, 181
Lines of best fit, 179
Linux, 260, 261
Local area network (LAN), 288
Low end file server, 289
Lower quartile, 112

Mac OS, 260
Macs, 251
Macscomputers, 251
Magnetic ink character recognition (MICR), 254
Magnetic stripe cards, 255
Main store, 252
Mainframe computers, 248
Management Information Systems (MIS), 236
Many-to-many relationship, 277
Many-to-one relationship, 277
Master file, 271
Mean, 98
Mean deviation, 115
Measurement, 233
Median, 104, 112
Median from an ogive, 106
Median of a grouped frequency distribution, 105

Median of an ungrouped frequency distribution, 105
Megabytes, 252
Megahertz (MHz), 252
Memory, 252
Microcomputers, 248
Microsoft Windows, 259
Minicomputers, 248
Mobile communications, 292
Modal value, 102
Mode, 102
Mode from a histogram, 102
Mode of a grouped frequency distribution, 102
Modems, 291
Monitor, 254, 256
Motherboard, 251
Mouse, 254
Moving average, 191
Moving averages method, 191
Moving averages of an even number of results, 193
Moving averages of an odd number of results, 191
Multiple bar chart, 72
Multiplicative model, 190, 197
Multistage sampling, 58
Multitasking, 259
Mutually exclusive outcomes, 131

Negative correlation, 173
Negative numbers, 4
Negatively skewed distribution, 122
Network model, 274
Networks, 288
Non-linear equations, 36
Normal distribution tables, 151
Nth root, 19
Numerator, 5

OAS, 237
Object-oriented database, 275
Object-relational database, 276
OCR, 255
Office Automation System (OAS), 237
Off-the shelf-software, 261
Ogives, 85, 113
One-to-many relationship, 277
One-to-one relationship, 276
Operating system, 252, 258, **259**, 260, 261, 264
Optical Character Recognition (OCR), 255
Optical disks, 257
Optical Mark Reading (OMR), 254

Optical mouse, 254
OR law, 130
Order of operations, 10
Output, 231, 256
Output devices, 256

Paasche indices, 218
Paasche price index, 218
Paasche quantity index, 218
Parabolas, 38
Partial correlation, 173
Payoff table, 141, 142
PCs, 249
Percentage changes, 14
Percentage component bar chart, 71
Percentages, 11
Perfect correlation, 173
Performance measurement, 233, 268
Peripheral, 248
Personal Computers (PCs), 248, 249
Personnel records, 269
Pie chart, 74
Pixel, 256
Planning, 232, 268
Pocket computer, 250
Port, 291
Portables (or laptops), 250
Positive correlation, 173
Positively skewed distribution, 122
Powers, 19
Price index, 208
Price index number, 209
Price relative, 209, 215
Primary cache, 253
Primary data, 53
Primary external sources of information, 53
Primary field, 271
PRINCE2, 242
Printers, 256
Probability, 128, 129
Probability distribution, 149
Problems of identification, 241
Processes, 230
Processor, 251
Product moment correlation coefficient, 174
Production data, 269
Profit margins, 15
Profits, 15
Programs, 252
Project management, 241
Proportion, 17
Proportional model, 197

Quadratic equations, 37
Qualitative data, 51
Qualitative information, 51
Quality, 242
Quantitative data, 51
Quantitative information, 51
Quantity index, 208
Quantity index number, 208
Quantity indices, 208
Quantity relative, 209
Quartile deviation, 113
Quartiles, 112
Query languages, 273
Quota sampling, 59

RAM **(random access memory), 253**
Random sampling, 57
Range, 112
Rank correlation coefficient, 178
Ratios, 11, 17
Reciprocals, 5
Record, 271
Recording transactions, 233, 268
Relational model, 275
Residual, 203
Retail prices index (RPI), 220
Review and maintenance, 241
Ring, 288
Risk and uncertainty, 144
Risk, 144
Rollback analysis, 147
ROM (read-only memory), 253
Roots, 20
RPI, 221
Rules of probability, 129

Sampling, 57
Sampling methods, 57
Scanners, 255
Scanners and Optical Character Recognition, 255
Scatter diagrams, 88, 172
Scattergraph method, 180
Scientific calculator, 7
Seasonal variations, 189, 195
Seasonally-adjusted data (deseasonalised), 200
Secondary data, 53
Secondary external sources of information, 53
Selection, 278
Semi-interquartile range, 112, **113**
Sigma Σ, 99

Significant figures, 5, 6
Simple addition law, 130
Simple bar chart, 69
Simple linear regression, 180
Simple multiplication law, 132
Simple probability, 129
Simultaneous equations, 35
Single-item indices, 209
Skewed distributions, 122
Skewness, 122
Smart cards, 255
Socio-technical systems, 232
Software, 258, 259
Sound card, 251
Spearman's rank correlation coefficient, 177
Splicing a single index, 211
Splicing, 211
SQL, 273, 275
Square root, 19
Standard deviation, 117, 118, 119
Standard deviation (for grouped data), 118, 119
Standard deviation (for ungrouped data), 118, 119
Standard normal distribution, 150
Star, 288
Static structure model, 276
Storage devices, 257
Stratified random sampling, 58
Structured Query Language (SQL), 273, 275
Subsystems, 232
Supercomputers, 248, 249
Superservers, 290
Symmetrical frequency distributions, 122
System, 230
    component parts, 230
    environment, 231
System analysis, 241
System boundary, 231
System design, 241
System investigation, 241
Systematic sampling, 58
Systems development life cycle, 241

Table, 68, 271
Tabulation, 68
Tape storage, 258
Tape streamers, 258
Telecommunications, 291
Tied ranks, 178
Time series, 188
Time series analysis, 190
Time series deflation, 213
Time series of index relatives, 210
Timesheets, 269

Touch-sensitive screens, 250
Trade journals, 55
Transaction file, 271
Transaction Processing System (TPS), 238
Transactions, 233
Tree, 288
Trend, 188, 190
Trend line, 88
Types of memory, 253

Uncertainty, 144
Unequal class intervals, 82
Ungrouped data, 118, 119
Universal Serial Bus (USB), 291
Unix, 260
Upper quartile, 112
User friendly, 260

Variance, 117
Variance for grouped data, 118
Variance for ungrouped data, 117
Venn diagrams, 129
Video cards, 251
Videoconferencing, 293, 294
Visual display unit (VDU), 256
Voice messaging systems, 293
Voice recognition, 256
    volatile, 253

Waterfall model, 241
Web 2.0, 300
Weighted aggregate indices, 216
Weighted index numbers, 215
Wide area networks (WAN), 288, 289, 296
WIMP, 260
Windows, 254
Workstations, 251

Z score, 154, 160, 162, 166

INDEX